Religion and Secularity

Dynamics in the History of Religions

The titles published in this series are listed at brill.com/dhr

Religion and Secularity

Transformations and Transfers of Religious
Discourses in Europe and Asia

Edited by

Marion Eggert and Lucian Hölscher

BRILL

LEIDEN • BOSTON
2013

This publication has been typeset in the multilingual "Brill" typeface. With over 5,100 characters covering Latin, IPA, Greek, and Cyrillic, this typeface is especially suitable for use in the humanities. For more information, please see www.brill.com/brill-typeface.

ISSN 1878-8106
ISBN 978-90-04-25132-8 (hardback)
ISBN 978-90-04-25133-5 (e-book)

This book is printed on acid-free paper.

Printed by Printforce, the Netherlands

CONTENTS

LIST OF FIGURES

Secularization, Re-Enchantment, or Something in between? Methodical Considerations and Empirical Observations Concerning a Controversial Historical Idea by Volkhard Krech

Civic Piety: Visions of Secularity in Constitutional Iran by Nahid Mozaffari

The Historical Formation of the 'Religious-Secular' Dichotomy in Modern Korea by Jang Sukman

LIST OF UNCOMMON ABBREVIATIONS
(INCLUDING FOOTNOTES)

Bretfeld, Sven

MEP	Mahajana Eksath Peramuna
SLFP	Sri Lanka Freedom Party
JHU	Jātika Heḷa Urumaya
ITAK	Illankai Tamil Arasu Kachchi
TULF	Tamil United Liberation Front
LTTE	Liberation Tigers of Tamil Eelam
SSSL	Secular Society of Sri Lanka

Chen, Hsi-yüan

KJSN	*Kongjiao shinian dashiji*
KJHZZ	*Kongjiaohui zazhi*
CYPQJ	*Cai Yuanpei Quanji*

Krämer, Hans Martin

NKBT 68	Nihon koten bungaku taikei Vol. 68
NKBT 81	Nihon koten bungaku taikei Vol. 81

LIST OF CONTRIBUTORS

Dr. Marion Eggert
Professor, Director of the Department of Korean Studies
Faculty of East Asian Studies
Ruhr-University Bochum, Germany

Dr. Lucian Hölscher
Professor of Modern History and Theory of History
Institute of History (Faculty of Historical Science)
Ruhr-University Bochum, Germany

Dr. Sylvie Le Grand
Institute of German Studies
University of Paris Ouest—Nanterre, France

Dr. Volkhard Krech
Professor, Speaker of the Research Department CERES (Center for Religious Studies), Director of the Käte Hamburger Kolleg "Dynamics in the History of Religions"
Ruhr-University Bochum, Germany

Dr. Yochi Fischer
Acting director of the Advanced Studies unit
The Van Leer Jerusalem Institute, Israel

Dr. Anat Lapidot-Firilla
Academic director of the Mediterranean Neighbours unit
The Van Leer Jerusalem Institute, Israel

Dr. Nahid Mozaffari
Visiting Associate Professor at the Department of Middle Eastern and Islamic Studies
New York University, United States of America

Prof. Dr. Hans Martin Krämer
Professor for Japanese Studies
Heidelberg University, Germany

Prof. Dr. Heiner Roetz
Chair of the Department of Chinese History and Philosophy
Ruhr University, Bochum, Germany

Prof. Dr. Sven Bretfeld
Chair of Religious Studies, Department of Protestant Theology
Ruhr University, Bochum, Germany

Prof. Dr. Sukman Jang
Director of The Korea Institute for Religion and Culture
Seoul, South Korea

Prof. Dr. Hsi-yüan Chen
Associated Research Fellow
Academia Sinica, Taipeh, Taiwan

Prof. Dr. Jun'ichi Isomae
Visiting Professor
East Asian Department, University of Zurich, Switzerland
Center for Religious Studies CERES, Ruhr University Bochum, Germany

INTRODUCTION

Lucian Hölscher and Marion Eggert

The concept of 'secularization' was introduced at the turn of the nineteenth century—in the wake of many heated debates, some of which are described and discussed in this volume—into the general Western discourse on the relationship between religion, the state, and society at large. In the course of the twentieth century it became the most prominent paradigm not only for describing, but also for regulating the societal dynamics of religion (Krech): In many parts of the world the constitutional separation of state and church, of a secular and a religious sphere, has been recognised as one of the basic principles of liberal constitutionalism, even if the choices of whether and how to implement this separation have differed widely, depending on place and time. Concomitantly, the theory of secularization has long played the role of a master narrative about the converging modernities in an industrializing and globalizing world.

At the beginning of the twenty-first century, however, secularization is again surprisingly contested, both as a blueprint for political arrangements and, more importantly for our context, as a scholarly model of historical change. Whereas most scholars would now dispute the existence of a coherent process of secularization in today's world, a few highly acclaimed experts still defend the idea, and do so on the basis of an impressive amount of empirical data. Others try to clarify the concept by dissecting it so that it becomes more applicable to differing situations. Yet another approach is that of Charles Taylor who, on the basis of philosophically interpreted cultural history, argues against the inevitability and appropriateness of secularization, while in fact treating a deep-running process of erosion of religion as historical fact, albeit one that should be consciously countered.

This ongoing debate unquestionably provides the background to the present volume; however, our aim is not to enter this debate, but rather to furnish it with historical and semantic reference points. Rather than contributing to an overarching model of a universal historical process— or even progress—, we wish to excavate the historical and semantic particularities of the dynamic relationship between religion, politics and other societal spheres in different cultures throughout Eurasia. For as soon as the concept of secularization is extended to religions other than Christianity and to other parts of the world, the limits of any universalizing theory become obvious: In the case of religions without dogmas and defined membership, criteria for secularization as they apply to the Christian world are rather pointless. Answers to the questions whether the concept of secularization is a useful heuristic tool for detecting societal processes, what forms these processes take, and what significance they have necessarily differ, depending on the region of the world one has in mind. One expedient indicator of the relevance—if any—of the concept of secularization or related notions in a given society is whether a corresponding term exists, and how it is used. Thus, our approach is both *socio-historical* and *semantic*.

First, we ask about the country-specific structures and processes of secularization in the last two centuries. Studying examples that range from France and Germany, Turkey and Israel, Iran and India to the Far Eastern nations of China, Korea and Japan, the contributions present quite different national models of secularization, describing as they do the specific experiences of each country and their widely divergent ways of handling the problems of religious plurality, individual religious choices, and societal demands on uniformness and loyalty. Offering this spectrum of cases, we try to avoid both the idea of a coherent path of secularization all over the world, and any pre-mature assumption that the application of the concept is limited to Western Christianity. Indeed, secularization has been, and still is, a powerful force in many societies, outside Europe as much as within. But it means very different things in each cultural and societal framework.

Second, we start with the evidence given by the terms used in each linguistic community. Starting with philological questions such as what are the most important words used to translate the European notions 'religious' and 'secular', we go on to ask how contemporaries defined these notions and how the meaning of these notions changed over time, from discourse to discourse. However, in focussing on the usage and meaning of key words in each national culture, we are not interested in linguistic similarities and dissimilarities as such, but rather in the social, political and cultural realities indicated by these notions in the contemporary context of their usage. In other words, we view notions as concepts representing social structures. We are not looking for semantic equivalents for the term secularization in the various national languages, but rather are watching out for semantic differences and changes of meaning: Translations are not substitutions of equivalent expressions; rather they are acts of semantic transformation, with semantic extensions and connotations changing in step with the respective cultural and social frameworks.

Starting with the evidence of language also has the advantage of making it clear that we subscribe to neither an essentialist nor a functionalist theory of religion. We do not regard either religion or secularity as a given in the societies under our scrutiny; instead we take these concepts as hermeneutic tools for understanding the conceptual matrixes even of those societies that operate very little, if at all, with these terms. By looking for the way that these Western terms have been translated (which is the case for all the societies studied here), for the use that is made of these translated terms as well as for other terms or binaries that they have either replaced or alongside which they operate, we open windows into the discourses concerned with religion (or anything resembling it) and its respective place in a given society. Thus, our investigations are not confined to situations and developments which were defined by contemporaries as being religious or secular, but we feel free to describe situations in these terms according to our own historical and systematic interests.

In other words, the terms 'religion' and 'the secular', though derived from the object-language of certain historically defined religious discourses, are used here as meta-language to grasp and describe both these discourses and others that have employed different terminology. Though the terminological tension that we experience here poses a methodological problem, this problem is rooted in precisely the episode of history on which we are focussing, and shared, unavoidably, by all scholarship dealing with phenomena of globalization and modernity in a comparative way. 'Modernity' causes so much debate because of its two-fold dialectic complexity: It is both a Western export, forced upon civilizations world-wide in the wake of imperialism, *and* a result of entangled history in which the West was remodelled as much as other parts of the world; again, it is shaped both by the globalization of Western patterns *and* by their unique appropriation, re-configuration, and combination with indigenous patterns of multiple modernities. These dialectics inevitably inform our study of religious re-configurations as well: While we start by observing the concepts of 'religion' and 'the secular' as Western exports, we do not aim at mapping a history of uniform influences but at observing variations and particularities; and we assume that this terminology—and the conceptualization of the world that is expressed by it—is not of European ownership, but originated as a result of the European encounter with other, and especially with Asian, cultures in the course of its colonialist expansion.

This assumption is thrown into historical relief, and its plausibility demonstrated, in the first chapter of the book, which is devoted to the considerable influence exercised by the awareness of Eastern cultures, and especially of Confucianism as an ethico-political doctrine, on the Christian discourses of the seventeenth and eighteenth centuries (Roetz). Without these influences the religious discourse of authors such as Voltaire would never have taken such a hostile attitude to Christianity as in fact it did. But the influence went far beyond the group of inner-Christian opponents to Christian orthodoxies: It promoted the semantic extension of 'religion' from a highly normative concept for the only true worship of God to a more general concept for religious cults of equal value. This trend went along with the emergence of a concept of the 'secular', which identified a political and social sphere of religious coexistence and toleration. Some decades later the radicalized concepts of 'religion' and 'secularity' were exported from Europe to the East, in most cases by creating new autochthonous notions on the basis of older elements (Chen, Jang, Krämer, Isomae). Transported as much by Eastern travellers to Europe in the latter half of the nineteenth century as by Christian missionaries and merchants going to China, Korea and Japan, these concepts had considerable influence on East Asia's Westernization and modernization. Hence, the ideas of 'religion' and 'secularity' may be called the products of a transportation of ideas in both directions (Roetz).

Looking at the semantic history of secularization also teaches us not to forget the degree to which the West was transformed by the very same processes through which it became a transformative power, and how recent some of the formations are that we now regard as constitutive of Western modernity. Starting with the studies on the French and German concepts of secularity (*laicité, Weltlichkeit*), it becomes very clear that 'secularity' and 'secularization' are historically young concepts. While having been applied retrospectively to earlier periods of history, they were introduced to the religious-political discourse no earlier than the middle of the nineteenth century (Hölscher, LeGrand), the conceptual prehistory going back to the Enlightenment of the eighteenth century notwithstanding (Roetz). The linguistic evidence—overlooked by many studies on secularization—demonstrates that only from the mid-nineteenth century onwards were 'secularity' and 'secularization' used as conceptual means of arguing for or against the religious disenchantment of the modern world. It is only from then on that the concepts of 'secularism' and 'secularization' began to shape the understanding of the place of religion in society, the former bringing into focus belief systems outside and antagonist to religions, the latter the shrinking frame of reference for religion in the process of differentiation of social spheres.

Given that the religious/secular divide was such a recent and by no means uniform phenomenon in Western countries, that its implementation was still under way and its conceptualization contested, there is little wonder that the way it made its effects felt in the various regions and cultures that came under the sway of Western imperialism differed greatly from place to place. And it is not surprising that the notions formed and the uses made of the social realities behind these concepts had their own, often contradictory, trajectories in each of these places. Many of these differences can be related to the particular religious situation of the societies in question, as well as to their specific perception of the reasons for Western dominance. In the Islamic world, where the model of 'religion' represented by Christianity carried little surprise and the power of religion in society was very much a given, 'secularization' became the main issue of debate, appearing to some as a threat, but to many as the key to Western success and the most promising road to modernity and renewal of state power. In religiously pluralistic East Asia, on the contrary, where Christianity had been associated with a different form of civilization and (at least mercantile) intrusion since its (re-)introduction in the sixteenth century, what caught the imagination of intellectuals was the Christianity-derived concept of 'religion'. Especially after the Opium Wars in China, when missionary activities were often backed by Western powers, it was the interdependence of religion and the state rather than their separation that seemed to guarantee a nation's strength and progress. Freedom of religion and the religion-secularity divide were regarded as secondary ingredients in the mix of factors driving modernization. They appeared to some as relevant only to Europe with its pope and its religious wars. Adaptations of the new model of the state-religion relationship to this demand of Western constitutionalism could take rather awkward forms (Krämer). With 'science' becoming the new catch-word from the early twentieth century onwards, religion lost some of its appeal, but continued to appear to some as a panacea against the threat of loss of state sovereignty, which as a result perpetuated earlier movements to religionize Confucianism (Chen, Jang).

Even stronger was the influence of the Western concepts on countries and regions under direct European colonial rule, such as Iran and India. Just as they adopted the liberal constitutional separation of the 'religious' and the 'secular' sphere in the late nineteenth century, so they also echoed the European disputes about secularism und religious hegemony in the early twentieth century (Mozzafari, Bretfeld). But needless to say, here, too, the religious tradition of these countries shaped their adaptation of the European import: The example of Turkey and Israel demonstrate particularly well how the European concepts which were first adopted for nation building soon turned into semantic tools for establishing autochthonous models of secularity. In Turkey from the 1920s onwards the fundamental principle of *laicité* was observed only as far as the national and political interests were concerned (Lapidot). In Israel the old Jewish semantic tradition of *dat* (law) and *hiloni* ('stranger') began to undermine the imported European distinction of religion and secularity (Fischer).

The comparative, historical and semantic perspective on the concepts of 'religion', 'secularity' and 'secularization' that this volume attempts to achieve thus allows us to see that the concepts of 'secularity' and 'secularization' are far from being based on Christianity alone. While it is true that they first emerged in mid-nineteenth century Christian Europe, their evolvement is best seen as one of the developments produced by Europe's opening up, in the course of its expansion, to non-European and non-Christian influences, developments which then in turn soon gained significance for other parts of the world. Even more importantly, they are offshoots of modern societies, with only limited roots in the discourse of ancient and medieval Christianity. For in Christian discourse, up to the mid-nineteenth century the dichotomy 'religious' and 'secular' was still part of an inner-religious semantic structure which can be grasped equally well or better by the binary of the 'spiritual' and the 'temporal': The concepts stood for a kind of religious-political division between the eternal concerns of the church and the temporal concerns of state and society.

In the same vein, in non-European (esp. non-monotheistic) cultures the adaptation of the Western concept of differentiated religion, and of the notions of secularity that went with it, was part and parcel of an encompassing process of re-configuring society, often called modernization, in which the sources of legitimation of power as well as of social consensus had to be redefined. Taking up the concepts of (differentiated) 'religion' and 'secularization' was part of a larger epistemic restructuring that responded to the needs of a more complex and more interdependent age. To the degree to which these developments were triggered by encroaching Western power, they were usually understood as Westernization, and even today, any discourse on secularization tends to have implications concerning the cultural self-positioning vis-a-vis the West. Awareness of the plurality at the roots and the diversity of the development of this concept, as made possible by the synopsis of the articles in this volume, might help to remedy this situation.

By providing these insights, the volume presented here may be able to add three methodological aspects to the international debate on religion and secularization: First, the value of taking into account the wide range and historical variability of national and cultural models of secularity in an intercultural comparison; second, the necessity and potential of a conceptual history approach, which is able to clarify our own concepts as much as their fluctuating meanings in different historical and cultural contexts; and third, the importance of focussing on the transformations that concepts undergo during transport and exchange, on the trajectory of their own that they acquire by travelling from one part of the world to another, entering different political debates and epistemic horizons. Globalized secularization means nothing other than diversified secularization.

THE INFLUENCE OF FOREIGN KNOWLEDGE ON EIGHTEENTH CENTURY EUROPEAN SECULARISM

Heiner Roetz

Secularism in the title of this paper does not refer to the negative anti-religious ideology as which it is normally understood. Instead, I will use the term in its original meaning as a positive plea for a society free from the constraints of a religious doctrine. It had its roots in the epoch of the European Enlightenment with its peak in the eighteenth century but with a longer prehistory on which I will also focus.

By *foreign knowledge* I mean first of all knowledge about and from the world outside of the Judeo-Christian and Greek cultural sphere, which poured into Europe in the course of its colonial expansion from around 1500. But I will also mention earlier impacts from the Arab world inasmuch as they were of relevance to the topic that is at the centre of this volume: secular thought. My special focus will be on the role of China, which exerted a tremendous influence on Europe in this epoch. What happened in Europe was the product of a global encounter that represents the trans-cultural rather than the specifically European nature of the Enlightenment movement itself. It was the outcome of a confluence of ideas that for concrete historical reasons fell on fertile ground in this part of the world. But it took its ingredients and inspirations also from many other parts.

The European Enlightenment is as much a product of European history as it is an expression of an inter- and trans-cultural dynamics. This also applies to the secularist tendency of the age which is not a European invention only later to be exported to other cultures. I would like to emphasize this point in particular against Charles Taylor's voluminous analysis of the "Secular Age" which in all its learnedness is a formidable document of North-Atlantic parochialism. It dwells on the topic on nearly a thousand pages, without even once mentioning the influences of non-European cultures with partly much longer secular traditions, influences which are readily noticeable when one reads the relevant Western sources themselves.[1] But many of respective authors like Vossius, Bayle, Wolff

---

[1] For a critique of Taylor from a trans-cultural perspective cf. also Holenstein, "China—eine altsäkulare Zivilisation."

and others are absent from Taylor's book. Presumably, there is a strategy behind this neglect: To trump secular thought by making it part of the Christian culture itself.

Likewise, no mention is made of a nineteenth century English free-thinker who deserves a place in a history of European secular thought: George Holyoake (1817–1906), who to my knowledge coined the term *secularism*, which is not from the eighteenth century itself. Holyoake defines *secularism* as follows:

> Secularism relates to the present existence of man, and to action, the issues of which can be tested by the experience of this life. Its object is the development of the physical, moral, and intellectual nature of man to the highest perceivable point, as the immediate duty of society. Secularism accepts no authority but that of Nature, adopts no methods but those of science and philosophy, and respects in practice no rule but that of the conscience, illustrated by the common sense of mankind. It values the lessons of the past and looks to tradition as presenting a storehouse of materials for thought, and in many cases results of high wisdom for reverence; but it utterly disowns tradition as a ground of belief, whether miracles and supernaturalism be claimed or not claimed on its side. No sacred scripture can be made a basis of belief, for the obvious reason that its claim always needs to be proven. Individual members yield whatever respect their own good sense judges to be due to the opinions of great men, living or dead, spoken or written, as also to the practice of ancient communities, national or ecclesiastical. But they disown all appeal to such authorities as final tests of truth.[2]

From the beginning the freethinker Holyoake avoids a pitfall frequently encountered in the discussion of secularism: namely that secularism involves the disappearance of religion and the imposition of a secular ideology, and that, correspondingly, a secular society is unacceptable to religious believers. Although Holyoake was an atheist himself—he was actually the last Englishman to go to prison for denying the existence of God—his secularist project is not primarily a program of fighting religion, nor a program of fighting tradition. It is rather a struggle for a system of rights[3] that would allow the free expression of all, not only religious, but

---

[2] There are different versions of this programmatic description of secularism in publications by and on Holyoake. This one is taken from Fred Lee's thesis *Secularism from the Victorian age to the Twenty-first century: The History of the Leicester Secular Society*, as quoted on the homepage of the Leicester Secular Society, http://www.leicestersecular society.org.uk/holyoake.htm.

[3] Cf. Holyoake, *The Principles of Secularism*, 40: "Secularism, we have said, concerns itself with four rights: 1. The right to Think for one's self, which most Christians now admit, at least in theory. 2. The right to Differ, without which the right to think is nothing worth.

also non-religious opinions. Its institutional counterpart is nothing but a religiously neutral democracy built on a free and open public debate no longer substituting authority for argument—the only authority that it acknowledges being that of "nature," which in this context is just another word for common sense. A society is a secular society if it is institutionally based on this kind of decision finding rather than allowing unprovable contents of belief "belonging to the debatable ground of speculation"[4] determine its general orientation. Its members, this is at least Holyoake's hope, refrain from insisting on these beliefs as final instances of a truth for all. Religion is not dismissed from society, but it no longer determines the basic structure of the state.

What is remarkable within the context of my paper is that Holyoake defends his secularist project by referring to none other than the ancient Chinese philosopher Confucius and the latter's reluctance to speak about religious matters and his aversion to proclaim truths that everybody has to follow. As Holyoake says:

> For believing less where others believe more, for expressing decision of opinion which the reader may resent, I do but follow in the footsteps of Confucius, who, as stated by Allen Upward, 'declared that a principle of belief or even a rule of morality binding on himself need not bind a disciple whose own conscience did not enjoin it on him.' Confucius, says his expositor, thus 'reached a height to which mankind have hardly yet lifted their eyes, and announced a freedom compared with which ours is an empty name.'[5]

Allen Upward (1863–1926) was a British intellectual and poet who among other things published a selection of the Confucian *Analects* (*Lunyu*, Confucius' "Collected Sayings") based on James Legge's translation.[6] His description of Confucius quoted by Holyoake most probably refers to passages where Confucius encourages criticism of himself by his disciples and shows himself happy when others detect his mistakes.[7] Upward

---

3. The right to Assert difference of opinion, without which the right to differ is of no practical use. 4. The right to Debate all vital opinion, without which there is no intellectual equality—no defence against the errors of the state or the pulpit."

[4] Holyoake, *English Secularism*, 37.

[5] Holyoake, *Bygones*, 279.

[6] The edition available to me appeared in 1905 under the title *Sayings of K'ong the Master*. There was probably an earlier one quoted by Holyoake.

[7] In his selection, Upwards quotes Analects 11.4 ("Yan Hui gives me no help. There is nothing that I say in which he does not delight.") and 7.31 ("I am fortunate! If I have any errors people are sure to know them.") in *Sayings*, 23 and 41, after Legge, *Confucian Analects*.

attributes this decent attitude to Confucius' renunciation of taking recourse to a supernatural truth, and the corresponding accent on this life rather than on death, on this world rather than a realm beyond, as in the famous passage from the *Analects*:

> Ji Lu asked about serving the spirits. The Master said, 'While you are not able to serve men, how can you serve spirits?' Ji Lu added, 'I venture to ask about death.' He was answered, 'While you do not know life, how can you know about death?'[8]

Upward concludes:

> Is is on this plane that his morality is established. Making no claim to knowledge of the future life, it followed that he did not pretend to train men for it, but contented himself with the humbler task of teaching them how to live on earth. Mean and insufficient as such an aim may seem to those who have been vouchsafed a clear and certain revelation from the Beyond, it entitled the Master to a lofty rank among creatures of mortal birth.[9]

This assessment of Confucius understandably aroused Holyoake's sympathy. Confucius is today still a hero of the British Humanists, the successors of his secularist movement.[10] He is certainly not Holyoake's first source of inspiration, which is the freethought of the Enlightenment. But the Enlightenment thinkers whom Holyoake mentions among his predecessors, like Matthew Tindal and Voltaire, have themselves confessed their enthusiasm for Confucius. The secularist Holyoake's deep bow to the Chinese sage seems to be more than just than a casual compliment.

This takes us from the nineteenth to the eighteenth century and the time before that. Not only by his espousal of Confucian ideals, but by nearly all of his central topoi like the authority of nature, the emphasis on common sense, and his anti-ecclesiasticism Holyoake is a late child of the European Enlightenment.

The Enlightenment is not simply a late branch of the great tree of European cultural tradition that could be sufficiently explained by writing an internal history of the West. On the one hand, it was tantamount to a radical critique of this tradition, and on the other hand, it is characterized by a hitherto unknown interest in what has never been part of or come into close contact with it—the foreign. Both these aspects, calling

---

[8] Analects 11.12; Upward, *Sayings*, 19–20.
[9] Upward, *Sayings*, 8.
[10] Cf. for example the homepage of the British Humanist Association, http://www.humanism.org.uk/humanism, entrance "Confucius", and Knight, *Humanist Anthology*.

into question one's own heritage and opening one's eyes to the foreign, are two sides of the same coin. Genetically as well as systematically, the Enlightenment is best understood as an intercultural phenomenon.[11]

The Enlightenment is preceded by an unparalleled extension of the European horizon during the Renaissance, when in a transition "from the closed world to the infinite universe," as Alexandre Koyré put it in the title of his famous book,[12] the fixed hierarchies of the theocentric medieval ordo are caused to collapse. The Renaissance is the era in which all attributes of the medieval transcendent god—infinity, creativity, all, everything—are transferred to the creation itself which begins to "outglow"[13] the creator. It is the age of discovery and thus the disintegration of the geographic framework of the biblical landscape. It is the age of astronomy which likewise unbalances the centre of the hitherto known world. It is the age of the Reformation which opens the inner part of humans for an ardent search beyond known borders, often paired with cosmic speculation. It is the age of mystical pan-isms in the name of the *unomnia* (Patrizzi, 1519–97),[14] the all-in-one: pantheism (God in everything), panentheism (everything in God), panpsychism (holism of mind and matter), and pansophia (encyclopedic collection of all knowledge) or cosmosophia. The Renaissance is also the age of enhanced individuality, and both, the all-in-one and the specific, are integrated in the model of the dynamic monad. "The monads," says Giordano Bruno, "are, each in its own form, the divinity itself".[15] The smallest and the greatest part of the cosmos are related to each other, micro- and macrocosm are mutually mirroring, the study of the cosmic nature is the study of humans and vice versa. God and nature are one—*deus sive natura*.[16] "The face of the whole universe," says Spinoza, "however it varies in infinitely many modes, is always the same (*semper eadem*)."[17]

This prepares the mental ground to transcend the limits of the Christian world: positively via the new *unomnia*, which makes the world wider and nearer at the same time, and negatively through the weariness with

---

[11] Cf. for the following Roetz, *Mensch und Natur*, §1, Israel, *Radical Enlightenment*, and Israel, *Enlightenment contested*. Cf. also Lee Eun-jung, *Anti-Europa*.

[12] Koyré, *From the Closed World to the Infinite Universe*.

[13] Bloch, *Vorlesungen zur Philosophie der Renaissance*, 15 ("Die Schöpfung gilt mehr als der Schöpfer, sie überleuchtet den Schöpfer im Begriff.").

[14] Bloch, *Renaissance*, 17.

[15] Bruno, *Monas*.

[16] Spinoza, *Ethics*, 190, Part 4, Preface.

[17] Wolf, *Correspondence of Spinoza*, Letter 64, Spinoza to Schuller, 308.

ecclesiastical dogmatism that led to the "bloody barbarism" (Voltaire) of
the religious wars. Allies are found beyond the borders of the biblical-
Christian culture, first and foremost in the Stoic philosophy of pagan
European antiquity.

The Stoics, leaving behind the comparatively provincial thought of
Plato and Aristotle, had promulgated the notion of the *tou cosmou poli-
tai*, the Cosmopolitan. It was based on the ontological assumption of an
all-encompassing normative order overruling the differences between
cultures and representing a *nomos agraphos*, an unwritten law of nature
valid for everyone. The epistemological counterpart of this normative
ontology was the conviction that all human beings, because of the nature of
human thought, produce *koinai ennoiai*, in Latin translation *notiones com-
munes*—common ideas, later to become the common sense. These ensure
the *consensus gentium*, the unanimity of all human beings and peoples in
essential matters.

The Stoic line of thinking merges with another current that Bloch has
called "left Aristotelianism" and which influenced all heterodox movements of the late middle ages—the Arab cleansing of Aristotelian philosophy from Platonic detritus. This was the work, among others, of Ibn
Sina (Avicenna, 980–1037) and above all Ibn Roshd (Averroes, 1126–1198),
who abolished the Platonic separation of *morphe* and *hyle*, form und
stuff that had been the philosophical basis of the hierarchization of the
medieval world. In the following, the *natura naturata*, the created nature,
becomes the *natura naturans*, the creating nature itself. Bruno's notion of
the monad is deeply influenced by this tendency.

No less important was the Arab pioneering of tolerance connected
to these ontological, principally egalitarian shifts. It possibly influenced
Nikolaus Cusanus and certainly Jean Bodin.[18] In the religious wars of the
sixteenth century, Bodin (a contradictory figure also jointly responsible for
the witch craze) becomes the theoretician of a trans-confessional political
absolutism. In his *Colloquium Heptaplomeres* of 1593, which was later put
on the Index, he lets Coronaeus, a Catholic, Salomo, a Jew, Fridericus, a
Lutheran, Curtius, a Calvinist, Octavius, a Moslem, Senamus, a Sceptic,
and Toralba, a naturalist, debate about religion.[19] Toralba attacks the
positive religions: Dogmas, he says, are superfluous, and the Moslems and

[18] Cf. Griffel, "Toleranzkonzepte im Islam," Bobzin, "Islamkundliche Quellen in Jean
Bodins Heptaplomeres," and Forst, *Toleranz im Konflikt*, 116–120 (Averroes).
[19] Bodin, *Colloquium of the Seven*. Cf. Frost, *Toleranz im Konflikt*, 191–200.

Jews are closer to the true religion than the Christians. The true religion is the natural religion that God has implanted in every human being.

Natural religion, in the name of which the demand for tolerance was raised, becomes one of the central combat terms of the Enlightenment. *Natural* means based on general human reason rather than revelation, in accordance with the Stoic cosmology. A natural religion, therefore, must be found everywhere, outside the Christian realm as well. It was via this road that the decisive attacks against the claim for exclusiveness of Christianity were carried forward for more than a century, beginning with Edward Herbert of Cherbury (1581–1648).

Thus the theoretical framework was laid for a serious and systematic interest in the foreign, and it was filled with and corroborated by material from Asia, in particular from China.

The one hundred years before the French Revolution were a time of a rampant Sinophilia in many domains of European life—architecture, arts and crafts, literature and, last but not least, philosophy. Confucius in particular enjoyed extraordinary popularity. As Lionel Jensen writes,

> Confucius was a significant, and salient, artifact. The frequency with which his name and image appeared in letters, memoirs, treatises, travel literature, and histories suggests that he was moved like New World specie in an expanding market of new ideas joining Rome with Paris, London, Berlin, Prague and then, in turn, with the missionary outposts at Goa, Canton, Macao, and Beijing.[20]

The first engraving of an ideal portrait of Confucius was "plagiarized by countless works of the late seventeenth and the early eighteenth century".[21] The historical background of this Chinoiserie was not just the Christian missionary project but a global economic market where all kinds of commodities were traded all over the world, with China as one of its main hubs.

What was the interest which the European Enlightenment took in China, and what was the basis for it? The fascination emanating from China was first of all due to the impression that it was an "anti-Europe," as Leibniz says, in the sense of a "civilized world" that did not share some important characteristics with Europe, above all with regard to revealed religion, and had perhaps not brought forth so many sciences, but were on a level with Europe on the decisive questions of morality. This world at the

---

[20] Jensen, *Manufacturing Confucianism*, 9.
[21] Rule, *K'ung-tzu or Confucius*, 73.

other end of Eurasia, both alien and yet familiar at the same time, made possible "a *commercium* not only of commodities and manufactures, but also of light and wisdom".[22] China, which had been ruled by the Manchu dynasty since 1644, was regarded as the "wisest empire of the world"[23] and an exemplary case of an enlightened monarchy, the highest political ideal of most European intellectuals before the French Revolution. Unlike Europe, China appeared to be free from religious oppression. While Louis XIV had abolished the tolerance edict of Nantes in 1685, the Qing emperor Kangxi had afforded the Jesuit mission freedom to preach.

China had become known in the West above all through the reports of the Christian missionaries, mainly the Jesuits, and their translations of central Confucian writings that appeared from the end of the seventeenth century. The accommodative missionary practice of the Jesuits corresponded to the positive picture of China that they spread in Europe. Jesuit accommodation was justified by the argument that Confucianism, unlike Buddhism, was not a religion and thus did not collide with Christianity, and yet was sufficiently religiously tuned to enter into a liaison with it. The Dominicans and Franciscans, but also some Jesuits themselves, criticized this view and pleaded for a harder line. They spread the suspicion that what in fact was raging in China was atheism. The dispute finally ended in the 'rites controversy,' which resulted in the closure of the Jesuit mission.

It was this constellation that electrified critically minded European philosophers searching for alternatives beyond the religious fanaticism that was tearing Europe apart. One of the first was Pierre Bayle (1647–1706), who picked up the quarrel within the Christian mission in his *Dictionnaire historique et critique*. He refers to the opponents of the Jesuits and to the Jesuit minority opinion that "most of these scholars are simply denying the existence of God". The same Jesuit "bigots for faith," he says, report "that these scholars believe in nothing spiritual and think that the 'King on high'[24] which your Matteo Ricci has taken to be the true God is in reality nothing but the materialist heaven". "And Confucius," says Bayle, quoting Longobardi, Ricci's successor as head of the Jesuit mission in Beijing, "said some nice things with regard to morality and the art of rulership, but as far as the true God is concerned he was just as blind as all of the

---

[22] Leibniz, "Leibnizcus Denkschrift," 81.

[23] Voltaire, *Essai sur les mœurs* I, *Œuvres* 11, 180.

[24] Shang Di, the name of the high god of the Shang dynasty (17th–11th century B.C.), one of the candidates for the translation of *god* into Chinese.

others."[25] Bayle does not quote these voices in order to join the anti-Confucian camp but in order to strategically launch the conceivability of a society of atheists. If atheism became a realistic option, it was due to the backing that it received from the East.

Leibniz, in accordance with his monadology which assumes that in all parts of the universe the traces of the divine perfection must be found, is driven by an ecumenical interest similar to that of the religiously sceptical Enlightenment. But he seeks to win back China for religion and to prove the complete accord of Confucian philosophy with the principles not only of a natural religion but also of a natural theology, though without a full-fledged revelation.[26] This is one of the attempts to keep the new information from the East compatible with the biblical tradition, in order to forestall the denigration of the latter to a phenomenon of historical and local value only. For the same reason, the Jesuits Joachim Bouvet (1656–1730), with whom Leibniz corresponded, und Jacques Foucquet (1665–1741) invented a bizarre figurist hermeneutics which detected the enciphered figurations of revelation in Chinese characters and texts.[27]

Similarly, an answer was sought to the Chinese challenge to the mosaic chronology. In a fragment of his *Pensées* (ed. 1670) entitled "Histoire de la Chine," Blaise Pascal (1623–1662) asks: "Which is the more credible of the two, Moses or China?"[28] Pascal asks this question within the context of his polemic apology for Christianity. It is triggered by the shaking of the foundations of the biblical worldview due to the new accounts of Chinese history. The debate was advanced, among others, by the Dutch scholar Isaac Vossius (1618–1689), an influential China enthusiast about whom King Charles II of England reportedly said, "he believes everything except what is in the Bible."[29] It was a general assumption based on the book of *Genesis* and thus its presumed author Moses that the world had been created in about 4.000 B.C. or, to be more precise, that creation was completed on the twenty-third of October in the year 4.004 B.C. at 8 a.m. This was no longer tenable, if the Chinese dating for the periods of reign of their early emperors and cultural heroes was true. In fact, this dating was based on numerological speculations of later times.[30] In seventeenth

---

[25] Bayle, *Dictionnaire*, vol. 3, entrance "Maldonat," 296.
[26] See his *Novissima Sinica* and his *Discourse on the Natural Theology of the Chinese*.
[27] Cf. von Collani, *Die Figuristen*.
[28] Pascal, *Pensées*, Fragment 592.
[29] Weststeijn, "Spinoza sinicus," 541.
[30] Even the historicity of the respective rulers is uncertain—it cannot be proven because of the absence of writing.

century Europe, however, it sufficed to shatter an even more questionable chronology (although the hermeneutical means to alleviate the problem had been at hand since late antiquity), with far reaching consequences to the effect of historicizing the Bible. There is a premonition in Pascal's question that the debate on chronology was only the beginning, with China being the catalyser, of a development at the end of which Biblical-Christian teaching would not only lose control over the computation of time but also its monopoly of interpreting the world.

I cannot give a full account here of the arguments that the Enlightenment discussed with regard to the East. I will instead focus on four topics which, as I see it, were of special importance to fostering the secular tendencies of the time in terms of a gradual detachment from the Christian world-view and religious forms of legitimation. These are the topics of naturalism, rationalism, autonomy and secularity itself. There are many stakeholders in the debate, among them prominent figures like Pierre Bayle, François Quesnay, Voltaire and the historian Nicolas Fréret in France, Matthew Tindal and David Hume in England and Scotland, and Leibniz and Christian Wolff in Germany. One of the most dramatic events in the philosophical scene of the eighteenth century is closely connected to this debate—Wolff's expulsion from Prussia under threat of the death penalty after his provocative lecture of 1721 on the "practical philosophy of the Chinese," the *Oratio de Sinarum philosophia practica*, at the University of Halle.

1. *Naturalism.* Going beyond the distinctness of specific traditions, the Enlightenment thinkers assume a fundamental oneness of all mankind grounded in the oneness of nature. "All that differs between men," says Voltaire, possibly paraphrasing an almost identical statement by Confucius, "depends on habits," while "all what is based on human nature is similar to each other from the one end of the world to the other."[31] "The rule of habit," he adds, "refers to customs and practices, and it brings variation on to the stage of the world. But nature effects unity."[32]

Nature is the buzz word of the eighteenth century, alongside *cosmopolitan*, and both are internally connected to each other. In the philosophical discourse of the Enlightenment, which overlaps with the China discourse,

---

[31] Voltaire, *Essai sur les mœurs*, *Œuvres* 13, 182. Cf. Confucius in *Lunyu* 17.2: "[Human beings] by nature are close to each other. By daily practice (or: by custom) they diverge from one another."
[32] Voltaire, *Essai sur les mœurs*, *Œuvres* 13, 182.

nature is the all-encompassing normatively laden unity of macro- and microcosm where everything mirrors everything. This is the Stoic understanding of nature (as distinct from the developing outlook of the natural sciences) that the *lumières* rediscover in China. The Enlightenment sets nature against history, where, according to the Christian belief, the teleological process of salvation (*Heilsgeschichte*) takes place. With few exceptions, the philosophers cherish the beginning as the original and perfect, while history is the history of betrayal, above all by the priests. There is no truth in it; "it is," says Voltaire, "in the end nothing more than a tableau of crimes and misfortunes."[33] Progress in the understanding of the pre-revolutionary eighteenth century is the refinement of something already given, the unfolding of primordiality and the perfection of naturalness rather than a movement forward towards something completely novel. This made Chinese civilization, which according to its self-presentation had been preserved "without noticeable change"[34] for several thousand years and directly linked to its early origins, the foremost witness of the natural. "There is no other people," says Wolff, "that has preserved the natural power so entirely as the Chinese." They "only used their natural powers and did not receive anything by contacts with other peoples."[35] For François Quesnay (1694–1774), the intellectual leader of the physiocrats and according to Mirabeau "le Confucius de l'Europe," the "political and moral constitution of this great empire" is an authentic representation of the "natural law," the foundation of any positive law.[36] The extraordinary esteem for Confucius himself, too, must be seen in this context. The fact that Confucius called himself a "transmitter rather than an innovator"[37] does not make him a stolid traditionalist in the eyes of the eighteenth century, but the herald of a primordial truth unadulterated by time and thus an authority of the first rank. China, represented by the teachings of Confucius, illustrates "how capable nature is".[38]

2. *Rationalism. Nature* and *reason* are corresponding, if not identical terms for the Enlightenment. Reason is the *lumen naturale* standing above written law. And what is reasonable nature at large is natural reason within the human being. Again China delivers the paradigm case. "The

---

[33] Voltaire, *L'Ingénu*, 37: "En effet, l'histoire n'est que le tableau des crimes et des malheurs."
[34] Voltaire, *Œuvres* 11, 165.
[35] Wolff, *Rede*, 171 note 83.
[36] Quesnay, *Le Despotisme de la Chine*, 636.
[37] *Lunyu*, 7.1.
[38] Wolff, *Rede*, 171 note 83.

chief principle he seems to lay down for a foundation, and builds upon,"
the English statesman William Temple (1628–1699) says of Confucius,
"is that every man ought to study and endeavour the improving and perfection of his own natural reason to the greatest height he is capable, so
that he may never (or as seldom as he can) err and deviate from the law
of nature in the course and conduct of his life."[39] And Wolff writes:

> The Chinese have never ordered any human actions and never spoken of
> any exercise in the virtues and customs than what according to their insight
> corresponded with human reason. It comes as no surprise, therefore, that all
> of their undertakings went so well, since they did nothing than that which
> was seen as grounded in nature.[40]

Voltaire, again, praises Confucius in a poem put under an engraving with
a portrait of the Chinese sage:

> The salutary interpreter of the one and only reason,
> illuminating the minds without dazzling them,
> he only spoke as a sage and never as a prophet,
> and so they believed him even in his own country.[41]

Voltaire also lauds the reasonableness of the literature of the Chinese:

> The Chinese do not have any history prior to the history of their emperors.
> They have hardly any invented myths, not a single miracle and no inspired
> men who called themselves half gods like among the Egyptians and Greeks.
> Ever since this people began to write, it has written reasonably.[42]

3. *Autonomy.* The fact that the voice speaking through Confucius is the
voice of nature does not, in the eyes of his followers of the eighteenth
century, as distinct from Hegel's later view,[43] lead to an ethics adapted
to the given world and subsuming the individual under a greater whole.
It is just the opposite point that they make: The fact that the natural
human being is the moral human being endows man with an autonomous

---

[39] Quoted in Israel, *Enlightenment Contested*, 641f.

[40] Wolff, *Rede*, 103f.

[41] Voltaire, *Dictionnaire philosophique* II, *Œuvres* 18, 151. ("De la seule raison salutaire
interprète, Sans ébluir le monde éclairant les esprits, Il ne parlas qu'en sage, et jamais
en prophète: Cependant on le crut, et même en son pays.") The author of a letter published 1786 in *l'Année littéraire* commented: "What poison is contained in this inscription!"
(Voltaire, *Œuvres* 18, 151 note 1).

[42] Voltaire, *Essai sur les mœurs*, *Œuvres* 11, 61.

[43] Cf. Hegel, *Enzyklopädie* 397 (§ 502): "Self-determination is the opposite of the deter-
mination by nature." ("Selbstbestimmung ist das Gegenteil das Naturbestimmung").

maturity (*Mündigkeit*) beyond all external coercion. For the law of nature, as Wolff says, "is written into the human being so that he himself can see what is good".[44]

In a weaker form, this idea can be found in Voltaire. Countering Montesquieu's suspicion that the celebrated spirit of China, like that of Asia in general, is in reality the spirit of "slavery,"[45] Voltaire refers to the institution of critique that already existed in early China.[46] But it is above all Wolff who insists on a reading of the Confucian texts in terms of maturity. I have already quoted his sentence that "The Chinese have never ordered any human actions and never spoken of any exercise in the virtues and customs than what according to their insight corresponded exactly with human reason." The "foundation of the natural law," Wolff argues with China as example, is "that the free actions of man [...] should be determined by those general reasons to which the natural [actions] conform."[47] As he says,

> "The Chinese insisted on reason, because one must have a clear perception of good and evil if one wants to dedicate oneself to virtue without fear of one's superiors and without hope of being rewarded by them, but one will not achieve a perfect perception of good and evil unless one has examined exactly the nature and reasons of things."—"It is because he who is moved into certain actions by fear of a superior or by hope of a reward [...] does not do voluntarily what corresponds to reason, and the Chinese does not count it as a virtue."[48]

One does not need a guardian, then, in order to know the difference between good and evil, because one knows it by one's own nature.

Wolff's intellectual encounter with China culminating in his *Oratio* coincides with his work on *Deutsche Ethik* (*Ethics in German language*) which appeared in 1720, the year before the China lecture was held. Like all of Wolff's writings, it had a tremendous impact on the German Enlightenment. Wolff's description of the Chinese *philosophia practica* in terms of freedom and self-determination corresponds to the formulation of the principle of autonomy in paragraph 24 of *Deutsche Ethik*:

---

44 Wolff, *Rede*, 146f, note 71.
45 Montesquieu, *Spirit of the Laws* vol. 1, 269.
46 Voltaire, *Essai sur les mœurs*, *Œuvres* 11, 174, perhaps referring to *Dadai Liji* 48, 114.
47 Wolff, *Rede*, 175f, note 84.
48 Wolff, *Rede*, 211f and 237, note 142.

> Because we see by reason what the law of nature wants to have, therefore
> a reasonable man does not need any further law, but by his reason he is a
> law unto himself.[49]

Wolff insists that he has found his "invention," the formulation of the principle of autonomy on the basis of the unity of micro- and macrocosm "by
his own deliberation".[50] But he concedes to China not only the historical
priority in discovering this principle but also a decisive role in confirm-
ing it. This means that Confucius would also have indirectly influenced
Kant's secular ethics of autonomy, although Kant himself shared neither
the naturalistic approach of reasoning of the *Deutsche Ethik* nor Wolff's
enthusiasm for China which is based on this approach.

As a matter of fact, as I see it, Wolff has overemphasized the cosmological foundation of Confucius' ethics and deemphasized the religious
elements which still exist despite the secular tendencies.[51] Nevertheless,
Wolff does not follow a merely 'orientalist' image of China. The result of his
analysis can be defended despite problems in its derivation. He correctly
identifies in Confucian ethics inner sources of an autonomous morality
that later interpreters, allegedly much better informed, have overlooked
(see below).

4. *Secularism.* I have pointed out already that *secularism* as a term only
appears in the middle of the nineteenth century, coined by the English
freethinker Holyoake. But as far as its essence is concerned, the idea has
its forerunners in the much older history of materialism and particularly
in the Enlightenment philosophy to which Holyoake is indebted. The foremost Enlightenment protagonists of secularism are Spinoza and Bayle.

Spinoza confounds God with the order of nature and conceives of a
state in which human law as based on the law of nature should take priority over the divine law propagated by the positive religions. He was
excommunicated as a heretic by the Jewish community of Amsterdam in
1656. Thereafter, Spinozism is frequently attacked or defended as the paradigm of materialism and, interestingly, identified as such with "oriental
philosophy" where "all things are one"—*toutes choses sont un*, highlighted
as an *axiome chinois* by the Jesuits Nicolas Longobardi and Antoine de

---

[49] Wolff, *Vernünfftige Gedancken*, §24, 18f: "Ja weil wir durch die Vernunfft erkennen,
was das Gesetze der Natur haben will; so brauchet ein vernünfftiger Mensch kein weiteres
Gesetze, sondern vermittelst seiner Vernunfft ist er ihm selbst ein Gesetze."

[50] Wolff, *Rede*, 223f.

[51] For a critique, cf. Larrimore, "Orientalism and antivoluntarism," and Louden, "What
Does Heaven Say?," 73–93.

Sainte Marie.[52] In his *Entretien d'un Philosophe chrétien et d'un Philosophe chinois*, Nicolas Malebranche (1638–1715) presents the Chinese philosopher as a defender of Spinozism, and, in response to Jesuit criticism of his book, also directly identifies the Chinese with the "impious Spinoza".[53] In the entry "Japon" of his *Dictionnaire*, Bayle writes that what the Japanese teach is "very similar to the philosophy of Spinoza". "It is quite certain," he says, "that [Spinoza] has taught together with these Japanese preachers that the first principle of all things and all beings that constitute the universe is nothing but one and the same substance."[54]

These are just two examples of a standard comparison to be found in the European literature from the seventeenth century to Hegel.[55] Is the similarity only structural, or is there also a genetic dependency? Spinoza's sources are surely to be found in the Stoic philosophy of nature, and it comes as no surprise that the comparison between Stoics like Epiktet and Seneca on the one hand and Confucius on the other is also typical of the cosmos of thought of the Enlightenment.[56] However, is has been convincingly argued that there might also have been a direct stimulus on Spinoza from the East.[57] Spinoza not only belonged to an intellectual network that included the China fanatic Isaac Vossius,[58] whom I have already mentioned. There was also the publication of Bernhard Varen's *Descriptio regni Iaponiae* (1649) which, in an addendum on "Chinensum religio," reports that the Chinese

> [...] assert that the whole universe consists of one and the same substance and that its creator together with sky and earth, men and beasts, trees and plants, and finally the four elements[59] compose a single continuous body, of whose great body individual creatures are members. From the unity of this substance they teach [...] that we can arrive at similitude to god from the fact that he is one with him.[60]

If this did not directly influence Spinoza, the similarity with his philosophy is at least striking.

---

[52] Quoted in Leibniz, *Discours sur la théologie naturelle des Chinois*, §§ 21, 57 and 64.
[53] Malebranche, *Entretien*, 42.
[54] Bayle, *Dictionnaire*, vol. 2, 832, translation Weststeijn, "Spinoza sinicus," 537.
[55] Cf. Israel, *Enlightenment contested*, 454.
[56] Cf. Roetz, *Mensch und Natur*, 13f.
[57] Cf. already Maverick, "A Possible Chinese Source of Spinoza's Doctrine."
[58] Cf. Weststeijn, "Spinoza sinicus," 538.
[59] The correct number is five.
[60] Quoted after Maverick, "A Possible Chinese Source of Spinoza's Doctrine," 421.

Spinoza possibly also encouraged the translation of a twelfth century Arab story by Ibn Tufail (1110–1185) entitled *Hayy ibn Yaqzan*. It tells of a boy who grows up alone on an island, thus without religious instruction, and who yet achieves knowledge of himself and God.[61] The translator, Johannes Bouwmeester, states that he was "inspired by Eastern philosophy".[62]

As to Pierre Bayle, I have already mentioned his argument that China proves the possibility of an admirable social order without the guidance of religion, because the Chinese are atheists. Leibniz opposes this view, but it is confirmed again by Wolff. Unlike Leibniz, it is not Wolff's intention to defend Confucianism against the reproach of atheism, but to make use of this reproach and turn it against those who raised it. He stresses in the *Oratio* that the ancient Chinese "knew nothing of the creator of all things and had no natural service of God let alone traces of the divine revelation". And so they could use "no other forces than natural forces not based on any service of God in order to promote the exercise of virtue".[63] Wolff's naturalism and his alliance with China have an openly atheistic direction of assault, even if he later tactically modified some of his statements. The strategic goal is unmistakable: Wolff wants to replace the "external reasons" of religion which the Chinese "never have paid attention to" by the "internal reasons derived from the nature of human action itself," with China as the prime example "how far those internal reasons can take us."[64] This is the decisive move of Enlightenment secularism: There is no world beyond in which the human being would find his orientation. There is a direct line from here to the secular foundation of ethics in Kant. According to Charles Taylor, who neither mentions Wolff nor his possible Chinese inspirers, "the discovery of the intra-human sources of benevolence is one of the great achievements of our (!) civilization and the charter of modern unbelief," and, moreover, the decisive turning point to the 'secular age.'[65] Obviously, the Enlightenment cosmopolitans had a broader perspective on "our civilization" than the modern Canadian philosopher.

A more moderate critique of religion which, nevertheless, in the end likewise amounts to its subversion, was put forward by Deism. Deism pushes God out of the world to its very beginning where he initiates a

---

[61] For a modern translation, see Goldmann, *Ibn Tufayl's Hayy ibn Yaqzān*.
[62] Weststeijn, "Spinoza sinicus," 550.
[63] Wolff, *Rede*, 112ff.
[64] Wolff, *Rede*, 219f.
[65] Taylor, *A Secular Age*, 257.

process which then follows its natural rules without further divine intervention and mysteries and fully accessible to reason. Deism leaves the
belief in and even the veneration of a higher being intact, but in such
vagueness that any formation of a positive religion can only be a wrong
concretization of a 'religious normal truth' (religiöse Normalwahrheit).[66]
This conception not only corresponded to the new mechanistic world-
explanations, but also to the growing aversion to the intolerance and the
bloody quarrels among the confessions. Deism in the eighteenth century
was partly a private form of religiosity and partly a polite and socially
acceptable form of atheism, especially prominent in Britain, but also in
France. It drew its backing again from Confucian China.

"The only regular body of Deists in the universe," says David Hume,
with the later consent of Kant, are the Confucians.[67] There is not a single
one of the British Deists who would not pay tribute to Confucius. John
Toland reckons Confucius among the "Votaries of Truth" along with the
Greek philosophers,[68] Charles Blount uses Jesuit travelogues on China
to decry "particular religions" as well as the revealed religion. It cannot
be true, he says, because it is not known to all human beings.[69] Thomas
Gordon expresses his wish that "all fiery Catholicks and bigots everywhere
were converted into rational and sober Chinese".[70] And Matthew Tindal
(1656–1733) assures in his book Christianity as Old as the Creation (a typically Deist title): "I am so far from Thinking the Maxims of Confucius,
and Jesus Christ to differ; that I think the plain and simple Maxims of the
former, will help to illustrate the more obscure Ones of the latter; accom-
modated to the then Way of speaking."[71] Tindal also quotes the Spanish
self-critical missionary Navarrete, who says, agreeing with Leibniz, "It is
God's special Providence, that the Chinese did not know what is done in
Christendome, for if they did, there would be never a Man among them,
but wou'd spit in our face."[72]

The Deist Voltaire, as quoted above, praised the Chinese for not knowing miracles, which is a Deist topos. He lauded Confucius in his poem
as "the salutary interpreter of the one and only reason, illuminating the
minds without dazzling them". In a variant of this poem that according

---

[66] Troeltsch, "Der Deismus," 430.
[67] Hume, "Of superstition and enthusiasm," 71.
[68] Toland, Pantheisticon, 64.
[69] Cf. McDermott, Jonathan Edwards Confronts the Gods, 210.
[70] Quoted after Tarantino, "Le Symbole d'un Laïque," 426.
[71] Tindal, Christianity as Old as the Creation, 342.
[72] Tindal, Christianity as Old as the Creation, 405.

to Diderot adorned a portrait of Confucius at the entrance to his study in Fernay, Voltaire addresses Confucius as follows:

> The salutary interpreter of the simple virtue,
> who adores but one God and makes us love his law,
> who spoke as a sage and never as a prophet,
> and if there is a sage again he will think like you.[73]

These lines contain many of the critical motifs which characterize the Enlightenment attitude to religion as well as its interest in China: Confucius is not a prophet—he does not claim access to a revelation which he would then preach in the name of a transcendent personal god. Confucius is the sage who simply transmits a timeless, universally valid and 'simple,' neither secret- nor mystery-laden virtue or reason—both terms are interchangeable for the *lumières*—without adding any curious inventions.[74] He venerates the "one God" of the Deists, which is certainly directed against the Christian dogma of the Trinity. Chinese religion, Voltaire says, has never been adulterated by such "absurd innovations," and unlike the Christian religion, it is "free of all superstition and barbarism."[75] The teaching of Confucius "has never been disgraced by miracle tales nor been defiled by squabble and bloodshed".[76]

I have given an overview of the China discourse of the Enlightenment and its systematic interplay with the secularistic tendencies of the age. It cannot be doubted that the Sinophilia and the anti-religious or anti-ecclesiastical radicalism of the Enlightenment are closely interconnected, although certainly not in all authors. The European development towards secularism of the centuries in question can surely not be sufficiently explained by external influences like the ones mentioned. It is to a large extent the outcome of an internal dynamics of a gradual decline of the medieval *orbis christianus*, the separation of state and church beginning with the investiture controversy and continuing through the religious wars and their consequences, the rise of trans-confessional absolutism, and finally the French Revolution with its new understanding of a self-constituting citizenry, the culmination point and core of the secularization

---

[73] "De la simple vertu salutaire interprète, qui n'adoras qu'un Dieu, qui fis aimer sa loi, toi qui parlas en sage, et jamais en prophète, s'il est un sage encore, il pense comme toi." Quoted in von Grimm and Diderot, *Grimm's und Diderot's Correspondenz*, 251.

[74] Voltaire, *Essai sur les mœurs, Œuvres* 11, 57.

[75] Voltaire, *Essai sur les mœurs, Œuvres* 11, 57

[76] Voltaire, *Essai sur les mœurs, Œuvres* 11, 178.

project. However, that Europe found a solution to its centuries-long tur-moil at all was due to processes of learning, and what I have called 'foreign knowledge' played a role in these processes.

In view of this pace-making function of the 'foreign,' it seems astonish-ing how quickly modern Europe acquitted itself of this indebtedness after the Enlightenment. However, there is an explanation for China's image turning negative in the late eighteenth and early nineteenth century. It was due to the end of the Jesuit age in the aftermath of the rites contro-versy which threw a shadow on the positive picture of China. It was the end of the ancient regime and the French Revolution with a new concept of progress that no longer looked to an idealized past. And it was the end of the Stoic unity of nature and reason that had provided the backbone of the philosophical Chinoiserie. It was lastingly destroyed in Herder's cul-turalism and in Kant's criticism.[77] The principles of "natural theology and morality," says Kant, are in reality without "sufficient evidence".[78]

In what follows, rationality transcends nature, and nature becomes the object of an irrational feeling. Hegel has built his whole philosophical sys-tem on breaking up the "occidental philosophy" of Spinozism in the name of subjectivity, the new "principle of the modern world" which, as he says, is lacking in China.[79] China remains where the Enlightenment has put it: at the primordial beginning. However, it no longer bears witness to the unadulterated light of nature, but to an unenlightened backwardness. In later European philosophy, interest in China has mainly been linked to the anti-modern romantic rejection of so-called occidental reason, and the part that it played in paving the way for modernity is no longer in the collective consciousness of Western philosophy, as Taylor's A Secular Age shows.

There are only few notable exceptions. One of them is Albert Schweitzer who after the First World War did not share the fashionable romantic critique of "civilization". "Consciously and deliberately out of date,"[80] he joined hands with the eighteenth century again and undertook a new con-genial interpretation of Chinese philosophy on the basis of rationalism, hoping that China might bring Europe back to what it had lost: the ethical

---

[77] For Herder, cf. my article "Die chinesische Sprache und das chinesische Denken," 1of.
[78] Kant, Untersuchung über die Deutlichkeit der Grundsätze der natürlichen Theologie und Moral, 770 (A 96).
[79] Hegel, Vorlesungen über die Philosophie der Geschichte, 46 and 163, and Grundlinien der Philosophie des Rechts, §§ 273 and 124.
[80] Cassirer, "Albert Schweitzer," 245.

convictions of the age of Enlightenment. However, Schweitzer is careful
enough not to simply reinstall the problematic 'pre-critical' cosmological backing of ethics that had brought the Enlightenment on the side of
China. In a much more thorough and sophisticated reading of the early
Confucian texts, he recognizes that there is in reality only a weak link
between ethics and nature, yet still a necessary one without which ethics would be suspended in mid-air. Using one of his wonderful musical
metaphors, he writes:

> For the Chinese, the belief in an ethical world order (*sittliche Weltordnung*)
> stands in the background, but not in the sense that ethics would be depen-
> dent on it. The order of the world is a kind of basic harmony upon which
> the motifs of ethics freely develop.[81]

In the end, the "greatness" of Confucius, says Schweitzer, lies in "basing
ethics on nothing else but itself and on the fact that it is necessary and
true."[82] Whether or not there is an ethical order in the world is wholly
dependent on humankind. Schweitzer, the theologian, admires Confucius
for this "venture" of a secular ethics "out of its own power without any
support in a corresponding faith".[83]

However, are the secular and 'progressive' readings of Confucianism con-
vincing in the first place, regardless of how we evaluate their importance for
the development of the Enlightenment discourse? There are already sceptical voices in the eighteenth century. The religious vs. the secular nature of
Confucianism in particular has often been a topic of debate, with the pen-
dulum swinging towards the religious side in recent decades. For example, Tu Weiming, perhaps the most internationally renowned Confucian
thinker of the present day, defends the religious nature of Confucianism
and uses it as a weapon in his fight against what he calls the "secular
humanism" of the "enlightenment mentality".[84] According to this position,
the Enlightenment's resort to Confucius must have been based on a severe
misunderstanding. That the knowledge of China in the European seventeenth and eighteenth century was much too limited to produce more than
fantasy, myths, and 'images' has often been maintained. As a matter of fact,
the philosophers of the Enlightenment went too far in their idealization
and stereotyping of the Chinese empire. But it is not the case that more

---

[81] Schweitzer, *Geschichte des chinesischen Denkens*, 261.
[82] Schweitzer, *Geschichte des chinesischen Denkens*, 92.
[83] Schweitzer, *Geschichte des chinesischen Denkens*, 86.
[84] Cf. my article "Confucianism between Tradition and Modernity."

information would have rendered the secular reading of Confucianism implausible—it could even have corroborated the thesis that elements of a secular civilization were a reality in China long before latter-day Western philosophers strove for it.[85] The most important text in this respect, the *Book of Xunzi* from the third century B.C., was not even known in Europe. Xunzi 荀子 (Hsün-tzu, ca. 310–230 B.C.) is the most decidedly a-religious of all thinkers in ancient China. A rationalist par excellence, he regards institutions and morals as human inventions without religious or cosmological embedding and conceives of a state built on meritocracy and distributive justice rather than aristocratic descent[86]—something that would have been to the taste of the European eighteenth century, although the naturalistic foundation is largely lacking.[87]

Xunzi's materialism notwithstanding, there is a certain religious background to some prominent ethical tenets of classical Confucianism. Confucianism inherits the early Zhou religion which claims that Heaven (*tian* 天), a moral deity, confers a mandate (*ming* 命) of rule to the most virtuous. The Mandate of Heaven (*tian ming* 天命), an "external reason" of morality in the terminology of Wolff, is later turned into an internal reason by declaring it a part of human nature in Mengzi's (孟子 ca. 370–290 B.C.) line of Confucianism.[88] It now becomes the moral law within the human being, where it is a source of moral dignity (*liang gui* 良貴) surpassing the dignity given and taken away by the powerful.[89] This theory of "inner transcendence," as it is called in contemporary New Confucianism, together with its imaginable political consequences, comes very close to Wolff's interpretation of the Chinese *philosophia practica* in terms of "internal reason" and maturity grounded in human's natural reason. This shift from the veneration of a moral deity to a normatively charged

---

[85] Cf. for this point also Holenstein, "China—eine altsäkulare Zivilisation."

[86] Cf. my article "Xunzi's Vision of Society."

[87] Cf. Roetz, *Mensch und Natur im alten China*, §22. For a full translation of Xunzi's works, see Knoblock, *Xunzi*. For Xunzi's philosophy of nature see above all *Xunzi* Chapter 17, "On Heaven."

[88] In the *Book of Mengzi* and the *Zhongyong*. Cf. *Zhongyong* 1: "The mandate of Heaven means inborn nature. To follow inborn nature means the teaching." Quoted after Zhu Xi, *Sishu jizhu*. I deal with this turn in my article "Die Internalisierung des Himmelsmandats."

[89] Cf. *Mengzi* 6A17: "To desire dignity (*gui*, also 'high standing,' 'honor') is an aspiration all men have in common. But every single human being has a dignity within himself which he only does not think of. What men [normally] esteem as dignity is not the good dignity (*liang gui*). To whom [a potentate like] Zhao Meng can confer dignity, Zhao Meng can also degrade." Quoted after *Harvard Yenching Institute Sinological Index Series, A Concordance to Meng Tzu*.

anthropology can be viewed as a shift towards naturalizing and secularizing religion, although it does not completely abandon religious diction. The same applies to the European "discovery of the intra-human sources of benevolence," which it has obviously influenced and which, according to Taylor, marks the turning point towards the "secular age". China's specific role for the Enlightenment together with these actual changes in classical Confucianism are sufficient reasons to think of global processes of secularization not primarily in terms of modern Western influences on the non-Western world. They did not come about in modern Europe for the first time in world history.

But why did the internalisation of morality, which links early Confucianism to the Enlightenment project, not yield a result in China similar to that in Europe? Zhang Junmai (張君勱 Carsun Chang, 1886–1969), one of most prominent Chinese philosophers of the twentieth century, has tried to give an answer. He has argued that Confucianism and in particular Mengzi, with his ethics of respect for the human being as an *ens morale* by virtue of its very nature, has not only influenced Enlightenment philosophy but also the Declaration of Human Rights of the French Revolution. When the human rights idea, "the completion of the process of secularization,"[90] later became known in China, it returned there, as it were, like China's own grown-up child. The Chinese 'seeds' could sprout in the West under conditions more accommodative to them than were at hand in the East, above all because Confucianism itself with its hierarchical inclinations always stood in its own way. Zhang Junmai may have overstated his case, but there is a grain of truth in it. Regardless of what proportions, the development of Enlightenment secular thought, to which we owe our modern democratic institutions, was not simply the offspring of the cultural genes of the Occident. It was the outcome of a trans-cultural joint venture.

Bibliography

Bayle, Pierre. *Dictionnaire Historique et Critique*. Amsterdam, 1730.
Bloch, Ernst. *Vorlesungen zur Philosophie der Renaissance*. Frankfurt/M.: Suhrkamp, 1972.
Bobzin, Hartmut. "Islamkundliche Quellen in Jean Bodins Heptaplomeres." In *Jean Bodins Colloquium Heptaplomeres*, edited by G. G. Gawlick and F. Niewöhner, pp. 41–57. Wiesbaden: Harrassowitz, 1996.

---

[90] Bockenförde, *Der säkularisierte Staat*, 69. Bockenförde was judge of the German Federal Constitutional Court from 1983 to 1996.

Bockenförde, Ernst-Wolfgang. *Der säkularisierte Staat. Sein Charakter, seine Rechtfertigung und seine Probleme im 21. Jahrhundert.* München: Carl Friedrich von Siemens Stiftung, 2007.

Bodin, Jean. *Colloquium of the Seven About Secrets of the Sublime.* Translated by Marion Leathers Kuntz. Princeton: Princeton UP, 1975.

Bruno, Giordano. *Über die Monas, die Zahl und die Figur als Elemente einer sehr geheimen Physik, Mathematik und Metaphysik.* Edited by Elisabeth von Samsonow. Hamburg: Meiner, 1997.

Cassirer, Ernst. "Albert Schweitzer as Critic of Nineteenth-Century Ethics." In *The Albert Schweitzer Jubilee Book,* edited by A. A. Roback, pp. 241–257. Cambridge, MA: Sci-Art Publishers, 1946.

Collani, Claudia von. *Die Figuristen in der China-Mission.* Frankfurt/M.: P. Lang, 1981.

Forst, Rainer. *Toleranz im Konflikt.* Frankfurt/M.: Suhrkamp, 2003.

Gao Ming. *Dadai Liji jinzhu jinyi.* Taipei: Shangwu, 1975.

Griffel, Frank. "Toleranzkonzepte im Islam und ihr Einfluß auf Jean Bodins Colloquium Heptaplomeres." In *Bodinus Polymeres. Neue Studien zu Jean Bodins Spätwerk,* edited by Ralph Häfner, pp. 119–144. Wiesbaden: Harrassowitz, 1999.

Grimm, Friedrich Melchior von, and Denis Diderot. *Grimm's und Diderot's Correspondenz, von 1753 bis 1790, an einen regierenden Fürsten in Deutschland gerichtet.* Brandenburg: Wiesike, 1820.

Hegel, Georg Wilhelm Friedrich. "Grundlinien der Philosophie des Rechts." In *Hegel, Sämtliche Werke,* Vol. 7, edited by Hermann Glockner. Stuttgart: Frommann, 1940.

——. "Vorlesungen über die Philosophie der Geschichte." In *Hegel, Sämtliche Werke,* Vol. 11, edited by Hermann Glockner. Stuttgart: Frommann, 1940.

——. *Enzyklopädie der philosophischen Wissenschaften im Grundriss.* Hamburg: Meiner, 1991.

Holenstein, Elmar. "China—eine altsäkulare Zivilisation." In Holenstein, *China ist nicht ganz anders,* pp. 41–98. Zürich: Ammann, 2009.

Holyoake, George Jacob. *Bygones Worth Remembering.* Vol. II. London: T. Fisher Unwin, 1905.

——. *English Secularism. A Confession of Belief.* Chicago: Open Court, 1896.

——. *The Principles of Secularism.* 3rd ed. revised. London: Austin, 1870.

Hume, David. "Of superstition and enthusiasm." In Hume, *Essays and Treatises on Several Subjects in Two Volumes,* Vol. 1. Edinburgh: Bell and Bradfute, 1825.

Ibn Tufayl. *Ibn Tufayl's Hayy ibn Yaqzān: a philosophical tale.* Translated with introduction and notes by Lenn Evan Goodman. New York: Twayne, 1972.

Israel, Jonathan Irvine. *Enlightenment contested: philosophy, modernity, and the emancipation of man 1670–1752.* Oxford: Oxford UP, 2006.

——. *Radical Enlightenment: Philosophy and the Making of Modernity 1650–1750.* Oxford: Oxford UP, 2001.

Jensen, Lionel. *Manufacturing Confucianism.* Durham, N.C.: Duke UP, 1997.

Kant, Immanuel. "Untersuchung über die Deutlichkeit der Grundsätze der natürlichen Theologie und Moral." In *Kant, Werke in zehn Bänden,* Vol. 2, edited by W. Weischedel. Darmstadt: WBG, 1983.

Knight, Margaret. *Humanist Anthology: From Confucius to Attenborough.* New York: Prometheus Press in association with the Rationalist Press Association, 1995.

Knoblock, John. *Xunzi: A Translation and Study of the Complete Works.* 3 vols. Stanford: Stanford UP, 1988–1994.

Koyré, Alexandre. *From the Closed World to the Infinite Universe.* Baltimore: John Hopkins, 1957.

Larrimore, Mark. "Orientalism and antivoluntarism in the history of ethics. On Christian Wolff's Oratio de sinarum philosophia practica." *Journal of Religious Ethics* 28, no. 2 (2000): 189–219.

Lee, Eun-jeung. *Anti-Europa. Die Geschichte der Rezeption des Konfuzianismus und der konfuzianischen Gesellschaft seit der frühen Aufklärung.* Münster: LIT, 2002.

Legge, James. *Confucian Analects, The Great Learning, and The Doctrine of the Mean (The Chinese Classics*, vol. 1). Oxford: Clarendon Press, 1893.

Leibniz, Gottfried W. *Discours sur la théologie naturelle des Chinois, Lettre de M. G.G. de Leibniz sur la philosophie Chinoise à M. Rémond.* Edited by Li Wenchao. Frankfurt/M.: Klostermann, 2002.

——. "Leibnizcus Denkschrift in Bezug auf die Einrichtung einer Societas Scientiarum et Artium in Berlin vom 26. März 1700, bestimmt für den Kurfürsten." In *Geschichte der Königlich Preussischen Akademie der Wissenschaften zu Berlin,* im Auftrag der Akademie bearbeitet von Alfred Harnack, Zweiter Band. Berlin 1900.

——. *Discourse on the Natural Theology of the Chinese.* In, *Writings on China,* edited by Gottfried Wilhelm Leibniz, translated by Daniel J. Cook and Henry Rosemont. Chicago: Open Court, 1994. English translation of *Discours sur la théologie naturelle des Chinois, Lettre de M. G.G. de Leibniz sur la philosophie Chinoise à M. Rémond.*

Louden, Robert B. "What Does Heaven Say? Christian Wolff and Western Interpretations of Confucian Ethics." In *Confucius and the Analects. New Essays,* edited by Bryan W. van Norden, pp. 73–93. New York: Oxford UP, 2002.

Lunyu. Harvard-Yenching Sinological Index Series, *A Concordance to the Analects of Confucius.* Reprint Taipei: Ch'eng Wen, 1972.

Malebranche, Nicolas. "Entretien d'un Philosophe chrétien et d'un Philosophe chinois." In *Malebranche, Œuvres Complètes,* edited by Andre Robinet, Tome XV. Paris: Vrin, 1970.

Maverick, Lewis A. "A Possible Chinese Source of Spinoza's Doctrine." *Revue de littérature comparée* 19, no. 3 (1939): 417–428.

McDermott, Gerald R. *Jonathan Edwards Confronts the Gods: Christian Theology, Enlightenment, Religion and Non-Christian Faiths.* Oxford: Oxford UP, 2000.

Mengzi. Harvard Yenching Institute Sinological Index Series, *A Concordance to Meng Tzu.* Reprint Taipei: Ch'eng Wen, 1966.

Montesquieu. *The Spirit of the Laws.* Translated by Thomas Nugent. 2 vols. in one. New York: Hafner, 1949.

Pascal, Blaise. *Pascal's Pensées. Introduction by T. S. Eliot.* New York: Dutton, 1958.

Quesnay François. "Le Despotisme de la Chine." In Quesnay, *Œuvres économiques et philosophiques.* Aalen: Scientia, 1965.

Roetz, Heiner. "Confucianism between Tradition and Modernity, Religion, and Secularization: Questions to Tu Weiming." *Dao* 7, no. 4 (2008): 367–380.

——. "Die chinesische Sprache und das chinesische Denken. Positionen einer Debatte." *Bochumer Jahrbuch zur Ostasienforschung* 30 (2006): 9–37.

——. "Die Internalisierung des Himmelsmandats. Zum Verhältnis von Konfuzianismus und Religion." In *Philosophie und Religion,* edited by Hans Feger. Forthcoming.

——. "Xunzi's Vision of Society: Harmony by Justice." In *Governance for Harmony in Asia and Beyond,* edited by Julia Tao et al., pp. 315–328. London: Routledge, 2010.

——. *Mensch und Natur im alten China.* Frankfurt/M.: Lang, 1984

Rule, Paul A. *K'ung-tzu or Confucius? The Jesuit Interpretation of Confucianism.* Sydney: Allen and Unwin, 1986.

Schweitzer, Albert. *Geschichte des chinesischen Denkens. Werke aus dem Nachlaß,* München: Beck, 2002.

Spinoza, Benedict de. *Ethics.* Translated by R. H. M. Elwes. New York: Dover, 1951. English translation of *Ethica, ordine geometrico demonstrata.*

Tarantino, Giovanni, "Le Symbole d'un Laïque: il 'catechismo repubblicano' di Thomas Gordon", *Rivista Storica Italiana* CXII (2010) 2, 386–464.

Taylor, Charles. *A Secular Age.* Cambridge, MA: Harvard UP, 2007.

Tindal, Matthew. *Christianity as Old as the Creation.* London 1730.

Toland, John. *Pantheisticon: Or, the Form of Celebrating the Socratic Society.* London: Paterson, 1751.

Troeltsch, Ernst. "Der Deismus." In Troeltsch, *Gesammelte Schriften*, vol. 4. Tübingen: Mohr, 1925.

Upward, Allen. *The Sayings of K'ung the Master*. London: John Murray, 1905.

Voltaire. "Dictionnaire philosophique." In Voltaire, *Œuvres Complètes de Voltaire*, vols. 11–13. Paris: Garnier Frères, 1878.

———. "Essai sur les mœurs I." In Voltaire, *Œuvres Complètes de Voltaire*, vols. 11–13. Paris: Garnier Frères, 1878.

———. *L'Ingénu*. Paris: Éditions du Boucher, 2002.

Weststeijn, Thijs. "Spinoza sinicus: An Asian Paragraph in the History of the Radical Enlightenment." *Journal of the History of Ideas* 6, no. 4 (2007) 4: 537–561.

Wolf, A., transl. *The Correspondence of Spinoza*, London: Allen & Unwin, 1966.

Wolff, Christian. *Rede von der Sittenlehre der Sineser* (German translation of the Oratio de Sinarum philosophia practica, together with Wolff's commentaries). In *Wolff, Gesammlete kleine philosophische Schrifften*, vol. 6. Halle: Renger, 1740.

———. *Vernünfftige Gedancken von der Menschen Thun und Lassen: zu Beförderung ihrer Glückseeligkeit* (Deutsche Ethik). 5th edition. Frankfurt, 1736.

Zhu Xi. *Sishu jizhu*. Hong Kong: Taiping Shuju, 1986.

THE RELIGIOUS AND THE SECULAR: SEMANTIC RECONFIGURATIONS OF THE RELIGIOUS FIELD IN GERMANY FROM THE EIGHTEENTH TO THE TWENTIETH CENTURIES

Lucian Hölscher

The religious field has changed and is continuing to change in the modern world. What religion is, what secularity is, is under discussion and—especially when discussed in the framework of an intercultural comparison of many "religions"—is only clear as long as we do not try to define it. Religious studies usually try to deal with this awkward fact by giving definitions which are made to include as many 'religious' and 'secular' phenomena as possible. But this does not work, as we know from a long list of definitions given in the last half century.[1] And also, giving definitions of religion fails to ask what people mean by calling something 'religious' or 'secular' (disregarding our own opinion whether it should be called in that way).

Hence, it makes sense to deepen the question how and why these terms were used in the past: What kind of distinction did people want to establish by using terms such as 'religious' and 'secular', what kind of structural alternative did they want either to establish or promulgate?[2] Looking in that way at the employment of the terms 'religious', 'secular' and other related concepts in the historical sources, one may well come to a structural understanding of past discourses—and even more: of past mentalities, institutions, social groups etc. The analysis of religious discourses gives wide and privileged access to how past actors structured their own way of looking at the world. The method of conceptual analysis does not supersede the approach based on our own analytical concepts, but it gives historical analysis a pragmatic dimension.

Before I go into detail I would like to present the general idea of my argument: Today people are accustomed to thinking of the secular as opposed to the religious. 'Secularization' is a relational concept very often defining

---

[1] Cf. Volkhard Krech's article in this volume.

[2] For the concept of conceptional history cf. Koselleck, "Begriffsgeschichte und Sozialgeschichte"; Koselleck, "Sozialgeschichte und Begriffsgeschichte"; for the English reader cf. Hölscher, "The Concept of Conceptual History (Begriffsgeschichte) and 'Geschichtliche Grundbegriffe'".

the process of fading away of religion (but also the opposite: defining the realization of something divine). By using this concept many people try to distinguish a sphere of everyday life, of empirical perception, of material reality from a sphere of transcendence, which they may call "God" or "heaven". But this distinction is not very old. Looking back to the past, we find that the semantic dichotomy of 'the religious' and 'the secular', as it is used today in many discourses all over the world, is a relatively recent way of organizing the mental world.

Not until the middle of the nineteenth century was it established as a semantic pattern, and even then it was limited to a small part of the public discourse of religion, that is, the discourse of radicals on both sides of the religious spectrum: orthodox Christians on the one side, socialists and freethinkers on the other. In Germany it was only after World War One that the dichotomy of 'religious' and 'secular', i.e. the opportunity for institutions, people, mentalities to be either religious or secular, became popular with the wider public.

It is true that there was a period of preparation and transition, when from the late seventeenth century onwards agents of the radical Enlightenment began to collect arguments against religion. But they usually argued not for a world without religion, but rather for another kind of (enlightened) religion. Hence, what later turned out to be antagonism between religious and secular people was first seen as rivalry among various forms of religion.[3]

Why is all this important? First, 'secularity' is not only a concept alien to cultures and societies outside of Europe but it is also alien to premodern societies in Christian Europe. This is an important fact for construing the relationship between Christian and non-Christian, European and non-European cultures. It makes not Christianity as such the exceptional case, but European modernity.[4] Second, the modern antagonism between 'religious' and 'secular' grew out of a semantic field specific to Christian societies in early modern Europe. In describing these origins and semantic shifts throughout modern history I shall concentrate on German sources, occasionally indicating similar or contrasting developments in other European countries and languages.

But the semantic turn of the mid-nineteenth century was not the only one in the recent past: As I shall demonstrate in the last part of this article,

---

[3] A different view is offered in the article by Heiner Roetz in this volume.
[4] Cf. Jaeschke, "Säkularisierung", 9 f.

after World War Two the concepts 'religious' and 'secular' came together again, intermingling to form new blends of religious secularity and secular religion. A new age of secularity began to dawn, which only very recently may have come to a new crisis. Perhaps it is because of such a feeling of general uncertainty that a new discussion about the future of secularity has begun in recent times.

The Spiritual and the Temporal

For many centuries, from the late Middle Ages up to the nineteenth century, religious discourse and conflicts have been based on the semantic distinction of 'the spiritual' and 'the temporal': The German equivalents are *geistlich* and *weltlich*.[5] There were spiritual and temporal powers ("geistliche und weltliche Herrschaften"), symbolically embodied in the Pope and the Emperor respectively; spiritual and temporal laws, songs, books and so on. The whole world was divided into two realms, the spiritual and the temporal.

Neither the English term 'secular' nor the German *weltlich* clearly represents this basic structure of the pre-modern world. They both refer to the concept of temporality in the sense of "belonging to this world" in opposition to "the other world", "eternity". But they have been used in various meanings: beside "temporal" they might equally well be translated as "lay" or "mundane" (often with the negative tone of something sinful).[6] In the early modern debates about religion and secularity this was an important and much exploited ambiguity. It was a point of dispute, which side of the concept was stressed more: Some authors used it to discredit the influence of clerics or lay people; others used it for the allocation of things to "this" or "the other" world. And most often all these aspects of secularity were linked, as if they were two sides of the same coin. "Secular" things could be appreciated as being important for man's orientation in this world (as for instance science, laws, morals), but also discredited as being unimportant for orientation in the other world.

---

[5] The literal German translation of 'temporal' would be "zeitlich", which was also used in German sources. But *weltlich* was much more important in political and theological discourses, pointing to "this world" in contrast to the "other world".

[6] Cf. Johnson, *Dictionary of the English Language*, vol. 2, s.v. 'secular'; Sheridan, *A General Dictionary of the English Language*, s.v. 'secular'; *Oxford English Dictionary*, vol. 9 (1933), 1365 f.; Zedler, *Universal-Lexikon*, vol. 54 (1747), 1831.

But however this was handled, the concepts of 'the spiritual' and 'the temporal' complemented one another. Despite their rivalry in many political affairs the sphere of the spiritual and the sphere of the secular belonged together, they could not do without one another. For instance, when a craftsman had offended against the civil law, civil authorities would punish him as much as the church: the one by exclusion from the guild, the other by exclusion from the sacrament. And the same kind of cooperation worked when somebody had offended against the ecclesiastical law, for instance, by being constantly absent from Sunday services. Church and state, spiritual and temporal power formed an entity in the political and mental map of pre-modern observers.

This cooperation did not end with the Protestant Reformations of the sixteenth century, it was even intensified in Protestant countries. And even when at the end of the eighteenth and in the early nineteenth centuries church and state in many European countries began to be organized in separate constitutional bodies, they were not seen as antagonistic institutions, but rather as working together in a kind of division of labour: Both institutions were said to have their own sphere of relevance. But in doing their job they should cooperate with and not contradict each another.

It is true that this division of labour did not always work effectively. Especially in France at the end of the eighteenth century a growing part of the enlightened intelligentsia, people like Voltaire and his followers for instance, declared the Catholic Church to be irrational and authoritarian. Also, the Revolution dispossessed the Catholic Church of most of its estates, turning priests into civil servants and dissolving the Church as a public institution. But still the state was not declared to be "secular" in the modern sense of "non-religious", but rather to be the only relevant public power in temporal affairs, impartial towards the private religious cults. Sometimes republicanism was seen as the new civil religion, but this kind of religion (if it could be called a 'religion' at all) did not interfere with the eternal concerns of life beyond death.

Only in the second half of the nineteenth century, when secularism was proclaimed to be an alternative to religion, did the situation change. It was at this point that religious antagonisms of the past could be declared to have paved the way towards the modern secular society.[7] Only then,

---

[7] This perspective was first elaborated by the confessionalist neo-Lutheran orthodoxy of the early nineteenth century, but was later taken up by socialist authors such as Franz Mehring. Following the writings of Ernst Troeltsch the concept of secularization began to be a dominant interpretament of protestant history in Germany (cf. Schnabel, "Wege der

looking back on the development of modern science and philosophy, of public constitution and many spheres of social life, such as church activities in the late eighteenth century, secularists observed that for a long time "the secular" was no longer complementing, but rather disempowering religion, that rivalry had slowly turned into replacement. It was an observation ex post, which turned the Enlightenment into the beginning of a world without religion.

Looking back, the French Revolution now seemed to mark an early and most aggressive stage in the process of secularization. Evidence of this was found in many aspects of eighteenth and nineteenth centuries' life: The spiritual power had lost much of its former constitutional power, a growing number of citizens was turning away from participation in church activities, history and the natural sciences had proved the biblical account of creation to be wrong. In daily life also the authority of religious institutions vanished: In France, for instance, the biblical calendar of the world, which counted the years from creation in 4000 B.C.E., was replaced in 1792 by a new revolutionary calendar. In short: The religious influence on life diminished, a new secular age began to dawn. The French Revolution of 1789 was seen a watershed in world history.

But looking at the semantic evidence, we find that this is an ex-post narrative of secularization, established not before the second half of the nineteenth century. Contemporaries in the late eighteenth and early nineteenth centuries did not think in such antagonistic categories as 'religious' and 'secular', or to be more precise: They used these terms, but in a very different sense and semantic relation. When describing their religious constitution, they adhered to the old categories of 'spiritual' and 'temporal'. What we today call 'secular', in German *weltlich*, is different from what they meant in those days. This is less evident in the English language, where the term 'secular' was used throughout the centuries, though its meaning slowly changed from "temporal" to "non-religious".[8] The German term *weltlich* underwent the same semantic change, but was finally replaced by *säkular* in early twentieth century discourse. Hence, the German *säkular* clearly has the meaning of "non-religious", whereas the English 'secular' may also refer to the older meaning of "temporal", even today.

Verweltlichung," 279 ff.). In England Chadwick, *Secularization of the European Mind* paved the way for many modern historical interpretations.

   [8] Cf. *Oxford English Dictionary*, vol. 9 (1933), 365 f.

But what is most important in our context is the fact that the semantic change from "temporal" to "non-religious" did not happen in the age of the French Revolution but much later in the second half of the nineteenth century. There is a clear temporal gap between the timing of the established secularization narrative and the semantic evidence.

This can easily be demonstrated by looking at the German encyclopedias and dictionaries of the time. Still in the mid-eighteenth century encyclopedia of Johann Heinrich Zedler "Universal-Lexikon aller Wissenschaften und Künste" (1732–1750) the Latin term *saecularis* and the German term *weltlich* were used as semantic equivalents:[9] *Saecularis* also covered the ecclesiastic meaning of "laypersons" (*Weltliche* vs. *Geistliche*) and the negative sense of "worldly".[10] 'Secularization' (*Säkularisierung, Säkularisation*) was translated "making things or goods secular (*weltlich*), which had originally been spiritual (*geistlich*)."[11] But when the Latin term *saecularis* was incorporated into German as a loanword it was reduced to either the ecclesiastical meaning of laity ("Säkular-Geistlicher = Welt-Geistlicher") or to the temporal meaning of *saeculum*: A *Saekular-Feier* was a "centenary", a *Saekular-Ausgabe* an edition after one hundred years. The term was not adopted in the sense of "belonging to this world".

Instead of *säkular* the term *weltlich* was used when the opposite of church was at stake. It covered all aspects of secularity: Johann Christoph Adelung in his classical dictionary "Wörterbuch der Hochdeutschen Mundart" (1774–1786, second edition 1793–1801) distinguished three aspects: "1. belonging to the world, in opposition to the church; 2. in theology belonging to the present life, to external happiness; 3. in the narrow sense, earthly, carnal, fleshly."[12] From the negative connotation of the latter the term *Verweltlichung* (secularization) was often used when referring to a presumed sense for earthly and sensual affections,[13] whereas the term *Säkularisation* or *Säkularisierung* was limited to the expropriation of ecclesiastical goods by the state.[14]

---

[9] "saeculares causae: weltliche Rechts-Sachen", "saeculares imperii status: die weltlichen Reichs-Stände" etc. Cf. Zedler, *Universal-Lexikon*, vol. 36 (1747), 945 f.

[10] "saecularis: seculier, weltlich gesinnet; dem Weltwesen ergeben; desgleichen ein Laye, ein Welt-Mann, der in keinem geistlichen Amte oder Orden stehet." Ibid.

[11] Ibid.

[12] Adelung, *Grammatisch-kritisches Wörterbuch der Hochdeutschen Mundart*, second edition, vol. 4, 1483.

[13] Cf. Krug, *Allgemeines Handwörterbuch der philosophischen Wissenschaften*, second edition, vol. 4, 485.

[14] Lehmann, *Säkularisierung*, 36–56; Lübbe, *Säkularisierung*.

This did not change throughout the nineteenth century. It was only at the very end of the century when a new concept of *Weltlichkeit* (secularity), opposed to religion, emerged, that the German term *weltlich* (secular), and with it the term *säkular*, began to take on an anti-religious meaning.[15] The religious discourse had changed in the meantime: Where there had been cooperation of church and state, of spiritual and temporal worldviews there was now hostility—first only in the arguments of freethinkers and socialists, but later and gradually throughout the early twentieth century also of liberals and conservatives.

The Religious (religiös) and the Secular (säkular)

In the philosophical writings of German idealism we find how what today is called 'secularism' as a modern *Weltanschauung* was gradually excluded from theological and religious discourse in the first half of the nineteenth century. There is much evidence that secularism was not a counter-position to religion from the very beginning, but rather after a long period of rivalry about the true understanding of religion. Hence, in the following chapter I shall demonstrate how 'secularity' turned from being a heretic form of Christianity into a counter-position to religion as such:

1. In his famous "atheist" article of 1798 "Über den Grund unseres Glaubens an eine göttliche Weltregierung" (About the Reason why we Believe in a Divine Regiment) the German philosopher Johann Gottlieb Fichte argued that it was not the moral duty of man to believe in a moral world regiment or a God, but only to act *as if* he believed in such a regiment.[16] On the threshold of the nineteenth century, to deny the existence of God as an agent was sufficient reason for dismissing Fichte from his professorial chair at the University of Jena.

Today it is fair to take this affair as an early example of irreligiosity. However, looking at the semantic structure of his argument, one has to admit that Fichte did not leave the traditional semantic field of religious discourse. He simply defined religion in a way different from the orthodox understanding of theism, i. e. in terms of reason and morality. For him the world was not an assemblage of empirical data and natural laws but—taking up the theological description of God—an "*absolute being*":

---

[15] Cf. *Meyers Lexikon*, vol. 10, 866, s.v. säkular; Brockhaus, *Enzyklopädie*, vol. 19, 38, s.v. säkular.

[16] Fichte, "Über den Grund unseres Glaubens".

"The world is an entity which constitutes and justifies itself, a perfect and organized and therefore organizing whole...." To deny the idea of a personal God in favour of the identification of God with nature (Deus sive natura), qualified Fichte to be a follower of Spinoza's pantheism. But this does not mean that his philosophical system was not religious, at least in the eyes of those who embraced it.

At the time, to call Fichte's concept of God an "atheistic" concept was an orthodox, not undisputed strategy to narrow the concept of religion to the belief in God as a person separate from the world. And indeed, this is what happened in the following decades: All kinds of pantheism and even of deism, which were the dominating features of religiosity in the educated German middle classes of the late eighteenth century, were expelled from the Christian churches. The concept of 'religion' was limited to theological concepts based on the belief in a personal God.

2. Another supporter of Spinoza's pantheism, who was suspected by the theological orthodoxy of being an atheist, too, was the philosopher Georg Wilhelm Friedrich Hegel in Berlin. In his "Vorlesungen über die Philosophie der Religion" (Lectures on the Philosophy of Religion), held four times in the 1820s, he unfolded a dialectical process of the idea of religion. Here for the first time in German philosophy the semantic pattern of "geistlich/weltlich" (spiritual/temporal) was transformed into the new semantic paradigm of "religiös/weltlich" (religious/secular): Hegel argued that on a first level religion was inside the heart of man only, something different from and hostile to the world: "Secularity and religiosity have an external relation to one another, but they have to connect with one another." (Weltlichkeit und Religiosität bleiben einander äußerlich und sollen doch in Beziehung zueinander kommen)[17]

In Hegel's argument the term *Weltlichkeit* (secularity) referred to reality, *Religiosität* (religiosity) to irreality. Hegel saw religion as something not real because it is separated from reality, hence something that had to be reconciled with reality. On the other hand, secularity was not yet seen as a kind of counter-reality to religion, but rather as the crude expression of reality as long as it was not reconciled with religion in morality

---

[17] Hegel, *Vorlesungen über die Philosophie der Religion*, 331. The transformation was possible because in German the expression for spiritual ("geistlich") is very similar to 'spirit' ("Geist"), which is a key concept in Hegel's philosophy defining the absolute entity of God or the world.

(*Sittlichkeit*).[18] Hence, by the early nineteenth century the term *weltlich* could be used for something different from religion, but only in a religious perspective. Following Hegel's philosophical idea of the movement of the spirit the philosophical dialectic on God and the world produced a concept of *Verweltlichung* (secularization) in the following decades which could be read as a change for both better and worse.[19]

3. By the 1840s the Christian churches had already lost most of their former support by the enlightened middle classes. Disappointed by the churches' alliance with reactionary governments, many former liberals had turned away from orthodox Christianity. By the revolution of 1848 alternative religious systems such as the "Deutschkatholiken" (German Catholics) and the protestant "Lichtfreunde" (Friends of the Light) held a great appeal for opposing social groups, which later came together in the Liberal and the Social Democratic parties. Secular ideologies such as the Weltanschauung of Goethe and Schiller, Schopenhauer and Nietzsche or of the various branches of the life reform movement (vegetarians, naturists, dress reform movement etc.) were widespread among members of the middle classes.

As early as the 1830s, a growing number of radical left-wing intellectuals such as Karl Marx, Ludwig Büchner, Ernst Haeckel and others had denounced Christianity as immoral, irrational and outdated. 'Materialism' was the new keyword for many of them in search of an alternative. They were opposed to clericalism as much as to religiosity as such. But for all

---

[18] Cf. Jaeschke, "Säkularisierung," 10; Jaeschke, *Suche nach den eschatologischen Wurzeln*, 312 ff.

[19] To give but two examples, one for each of these changes: When in 1829 Johann Christian Heinroth, professor of psychotherapy in Leipzig, tried to explain the difference between "Weltgeschichte" (world history) and "Offenbarungsgeschichte" (history of revelation) he argued that in world history everything would become more and more secular: "Kurz, was der Mensch immer angreift und betastet, was immer er zu seinem Eigentum macht; er verweltlicht alles... sogar das in dieses Geschlecht der Menschen eintretende und sich ihm verwählende Göttliche (werde) gleichsam unter ihren Händen verweltlicht." (In brief: whatever man touches, whatever he makes his property, he secularizes everything... even the divine, which enters the family of man being united with it, is secularized almost without doing). (Heinroth, *Pisteodicee*, 204.)—Another example of this dialectic connection between God and the world was explained by the theologian Hermann F. W. Hinrichs in his work on Schiller in 1837: "Während die alte Kirche das Göttliche und das Weltliche einander streng entgegensetzt... hebt die neue Kirche diesen Gegensatz auf, das Göttliche im Weltlichen anerkennend... In dieser Verweltlichung des Göttlichen ist das Weltliche dem Göttlichen gemäß, und der Geist frei." (While the old church made the divine and the secular absolute opposites... the new church remedies this opposition acknowledging the divine in the secular... In this secularization the secular is in harmony with the divine, und the spirit free). (Hinrichs, *Schillers Dichtungen*, 209.)

of them the term *Weltlichkeit* (secularity) was not a relevant concept, because it was not used in the negative sense of the pietists but in the positive sense of Hegel. None of their writings dismissed or replaced the semantic structure of spiritual/temporal.

To make this more explicit it is useful to go deeper into the organization of these anti-clerical groups. There were two fractions of opposition to church-Christendom in Germany in the second half of the nineteenth century: One was the group of the "Freireligiöse" (the free-religious). David Friedrich Strauß, the famous author of "Das Leben Jesu" (1835/36) and one of the free-religious protagonists, may be taken as an example: In his book of 1872 "Der alte und der neue Glaube. Ein Bekenntnis" (The Old and the New Doctrine. A Confession) he contrasted the "alter Kirchenglaube" (old church doctrine) to the "new" or "modern Weltanschauung", based on historical and scientific knowledge.[20] The new doctrine, Strauss argued, would replace the old one, but Strauss defined it again as to be "religious", not as to be "secular".

The same is true of Ernst Haeckel's "Die Welträtsel" (The Enigmas of the world), a free-religious bestseller of 1899. There is no doubt that Haeckel was most serious about the hostility between Christianity and modern science. But nevertheless Haeckel did not use the term *weltlich* (secular) for this non-religious state of reason:

> Wirklicher Friede kann erst eintreten, wenn einer der beiden ringenden Kämpfer bewältigt am Boden liegt. Entweder siegt die 'allein selig machende Kirche', und dann hört 'freie Wissenschaft' und 'freie Lehre' überhaupt auf... Oder es siegt der moderne Vernunftstaat... (There can be no true and enduring peace until one of the combatants lies powerless on the ground. Either the Church wins, and then farewell to all 'free science and free teaching'... or else the modern rational State proves victorious...).[21]

The other fraction was the group of the freethinkers, who led by Ludwig Büchner had founded the German section of the "Internationale Freidenker-Verband" in 1881. Many social democrats were also members in this organization. Following the writings of Karl Marx and other members of the Hegelian school, they embraced a scientific worldview which was opposed to religion. But they, too, did not make use of the term *weltlich* (secular). August Bebel's bestseller of 1879 "Die Frau und der Sozialismus"

---

[20] Strauss, *Der alte und der neue Glaube*, 40 ff.
[21] Haeckel, *Die Welträtsel*, 427. Haeckel, *The Riddle of the Universe*, 335 f. Cf. also another key book of the materialistic philosophy: Büchner, *Kraft und Stoff*, which did not use the concept of 'secular'.

(Woman and Socialism) may be taken as a popular example: Being a private concern of man, Bebel argued, religion will fade away for enlightened people. "Permanent human progress and pure, unbiased knowledge will be their banner."[22] But even for socialists the term *weltlich* (secular) was not free to be used for their own ambitions. In expressing their "secularistic" position they did not make use of the term—up until 1890, when suddenly the situation changed.

The Case of the Secular School (weltliche Schule)

It is difficult to find a more radical concept of *Weltlichkeit* pointing to opposition to religion as such before the First World War. One of the most prominent fields for the development of such a concept was school reform. In this field one of the first and best known usages of the concept in the modern sense is the political program of the Social Democratic Party of 1891, the so-called "Erfurter Programm". In point seven the program demanded "Weltlichkeit der Schule, obligatorischen Besuch der öffentlichen Volksschulen, Unentgeltlichkeit des Unterrichts, der Lehrmittel und der Verpflegung..." (secularity of schools, compulsory public primary schools, teaching and meals free of charge).[23]

In order to understand the formula in the given context, it is necessary to consider the history of secular schools in Germany. The establishment of "weltliche Schulen" (secular schools) goes back to the reorganization of the educational system in Prussia in the 1760s.[24] In his "Methodenbuch für Väter und Mütter der Familien und Völker" of 1771[25] the Prussian educational reformer Johan Bernhard Basedow (1724–1790) designed the model of a "weltliche Schule", which was intended for students of all religious denominations. It established a form of religious teaching underlining only the common features of all religions and not their confessional peculiarities. Of course, such schools could only be run by the state, hence they were much opposed by the Christian churches, which by tradition were in charge of primary school education as much in Germany as in other European countries. At the time, the term *weltlich* still referred to the "temporal" power of the secular government (as opposed to the

---

[22] Bebel, Die *Frau und der Sozialismus*, 486.
[23] *Deutsche Parteiprogramme*, 352.
[24] Lachmann, Schröder, *Geschichte des evangelischen Religionsunterrichts.*
[25] Basedow, *Das Methodenbuch für Väter und Mütter.*

"spiritual" power of the clerics); it did not stand for an anti-religious school program.

After the reorganization of the German territories from the 1790s onwards, the idea of a primary school system organized by the state remained a favoured concept of the educational reform movement in the early nineteenth century, since Catholics and Protestants now had to live together in many states. However, these schools were not usually called "weltliche Schulen",[26] but "öffentliche Schulen" (public schools)— as far as pubic authority was involved, for instance in the "Allgemeine Landrecht für die Preussischen Staaten" of 1794.[27] Schools that provided education for students with different religious backgrounds were called "Simultanschulen" (simultaneous schools). Due to the mobility of the population in the course of the agrarian and industrial revolutions the need for such "Simultanschulen" grew in the following decades, but due to the increasing tension between Catholics and Protestants they were extremely controversial in public discussions. Hence they were only seldom installed, apart from in Silesia in 1801 only in Nassau in 1819.

In the 1820s the debate about the religious character of primary schools escalated when the reform bureaucracy of the Prussian ministry for education held onto the established system of "Simultanschulen", whereas the Christian church authorities called for "Konfessionsschulen" (confessional schools). Most radical clerics, such as pastor Friedrich A. Krummacher from Elberfeld, used to argue that public schools were on the way "zu verweltlichen" (to becoming secular) in the negative sense which this term still had in the Christian discourse of the time:[28] "Unsere Schulen verweltlichen und werden nur als Anstalten betrachtet, die Jugend zu irdischem Gewinn, Erwerb, Genuss abzurichten (Our schools are becoming secular and are seen only as institutions that train youth to gain and pleasure)." The main difference between "Simultanschulen" and "Konfessionsschulen" was that "Konfessionsschulen" were governed by clerical committees ("geistliche Schulaufsicht"), which ensured the employment of confessional teachers and adherence to confessional principals in all subjects of the school program, whereas the state bureaucracy still aimed to professionalize the training of teachers in state seminars. However, these teachers' seminars were dominated by liberal reformers

---

[26] The term *weltliche Schule* was seldom used in nineteenth century writings, usually referring to the public authority of the temporal power.

[27] Zwölfter Titel: Von niedern und höhern Schulen, § 9 ff.

[28] Krummacher, *Die christliche Volksschule*, 3.

who were mostly critical of the churches and many of whom had even been protagonists of the revolution in 1848.

That is why after the revolution the conservative Prussian ministry of education began to support the "Konfessionsschulen" albeit without giving up the claim for state authority: The Prussian constitution of 1850 declared primary school teachers to be civil servants, and clerics were said to govern primary schools only "on behalf" of the state. In fact, however, they were able to give these schools an orthodox confessional program.

In the following decades conservatives in Prussia were in a difficult position regarding the secular character of the primary school system: On the one hand, they wanted to maintain state authority without giving too much power to the churches; on the other hand, they wanted to ensure the basically religious nature of the primary schools. And fighting for such a religious education they were divided into two fractions: Many conservatives from a protestant background demanded a non-confessionalist, but protestant teaching, whereas others wanted confessionalist clerics to govern the schools. In their confessionalist understanding they were sympathetic towards the Catholic position, but of course they differed in supporting the idea of a basically protestant domination.[29]

After 1871 the National Liberals' position was similar: They wanted the school system to be liberated from church denomination (both Catholic and Protestant), but to remain religious: not religious in the sense of the confessionalists, who identified religion with the church doctrines of each Christian denomination, but religious in a general Christian sense, a kind of overarching Protestant civil religion. Between both, the national liberal and the conservative understanding of public education, the primary school system in Germany oscillated up to the end of World War One.

Against this ideological background the social democratic demand for a "weltliche Schule" (secular school) in the "Erfurter program" of 1891 reveals its specific profile. The program explicitly demanded that the attendance of public primary schools ("öffentliche Volksschulen") should be compulsory for all and that teaching, teaching materials and food should be financed from public funds. But, as Wilhelm Liebknecht made clear in his presentation of the program in Erfurt, the term *weltlich* also meant that the influence of church authorities should be excluded:[30]

---

[29] Cf. the parliamentary debate about the school reform of minister von Zedlitz in the Prussian Landtag in 1892.

[30] *Protokoll über die Verhandlungen*, 530.

"... In Verbindung mit diesem Passus fordern wir: 'Weltlichkeit der Schule'.
Das heißt, dass die Religion mit der Schule absolut nichts zu tun hat." (In
connection with this passage we demand 'secularity of the school', i.e. religion has absolutely nothing to do with the school).

The term *weltlich* signalized that now much more was at stake than
another equilibrium between the spiritual power of the churches and the
temporal power of the state: The intention was to exclude religion from
public school teaching and to replace religious worldviews by solid historical and scientific knowledge and practical abilities.

This was more than what the liberal reformers of the revolution of 1848
had asked for. When in the constitutional assembly of Frankfurt the fundamental laws of the future German constitution were discussed some
members demanded the separation of church and state, some even the
transformation of the churches into private associations.[31] But nobody at
all thought of excluding religion from school teaching.

Up to the revolution the exclusion of religion from school education
had not been on the agenda of any political group. In the pre-revolution
era even communists such as Wilhelm Weitling, the head of the working class "Bund der Kommunisten", in his sketch of a future communist
society in 1842, had not gone beyond the liberal demand for general, non-
confessional teaching:[32] "In der Schule sollte darum auch die Religion nur
so allgemein gelehrt werden, dass sie alle die verschiedenen religiösen
Parteien befriedigen; keine Religion darf ausschließlich hervorgehoben
warden." (In schools religion should be taught only in such general terms
that all religious parties are satisfied; no religion should be emphasized
exclusively).

But in the course of the revolution the position of the radical liberals
began to change. The "Deutscher Lehrerverein" (German teachers' association) for instance called for a "bekenntnisfreie" resp. a "religionsfreie
Schule" (a school free from confessional or religious influence).[33] Their
primary concern was to end the direct influence of the churches when,
for instance, teachers were accountable to the local pastor. But the more
"religion" was identified with "confession", i.e. an exclusive right of the
churches to define what religion is, the more their opponents were inclined
to demand the exclusion of religion from school education altogether.

---

[31] *Stenographische Berichte*, 1646 f.
[32] Weitling, *Garantien der Harmonie und Freiheit*, 243.
[33] Cf. Schulze, *Die 'Weltliche Schule'*, issue 4.

However, the term *weltliche Schule* was, as far as I can see, not used for this more radical demand.[34] The first document using the term which I have found so far, is a report on school reform in England, which was published twenty years later, in 1869.[35] The debate in England was very similar to the German discussion during and after the revolution: The commission installed by the House of Commons in 1864 had declared that parents wanted their children to be "religiös gebildet" (to have a religious education)—especially reading the Bible seemed to be important. But parents did not expect much from the "Confessionell-Dogmatischen" (of confessional-dogmatic aspects). The solution of this problem, as the German author of the article reported, would neither be found "in exklusiv-confessionellen Schulen" (exclusively confessional schools) nor in "rein weltlichen Schulen, die allen Religions-Unterricht ausschließen" (in purely secular schools, which exclude all religious teaching). Together with the "report of her Majesty's Commissioners" the author conceded that it was awkward to draw a line in practice between "was in der Schule weltlich und was religiös ist" (what at school is to be secular and what is to be religious).

The semantic antagonism between 'religious' and 'secular' in this document makes it clear that in the period after the revolution the semantic field had begun to change: School debates no longer centred exclusively on the question who would run the schools (the "secular" power of the state or the "spiritual" power of the church), but also how much religion should be included in school teaching at all. In the 1860s the demand for "weltliche Schulen" (secular schools) was still an extreme position in this debate, which only few people propagated, but at least it was in the debate.

A very similar discussion can be identified in France at the same time. As Sylvie Le Grand has demonstrated in her contribution to this volume,[36] the new concept of an *école laique* came up in the beginning of the Third

---

[34] According to Giese, *Quellen zur deutschen Schulgeschichte*, 29, the demand for a "weltliche Schule" was already expressed at the Arbeiterkongress of 1848, but this could not be proved so far. As an example of the traditional understanding of the term *weltliche Schule* in 1848 a passage from the debate of the Austrian diet in the province of Steiermark may be cited: "Auch in den weltlichen Schulen haben die kirchlichen Grundsätze Einfluß" (In secular schools also ecclesiastical principles have influence). Cf. *Verhandlungen des provisorischen Landtags der Herzogtums Steiermark am 8. Aug. 1848*, 71, § 76.

[35] Hollenberg, "Die Grundzüge der in England beabsichtigten Reform höherer Schulen."

[36] Cf. also the excellent article "laicization, laicisme, laicité" in *Catholicisme*, 1643–1666.

Republic providing a public education which was free from religion: In the legislation of 1879 and the following years not only clerics were excluded from public teaching and school government, but also religion was excluded from school programs.

The term *laique* as such is older. It can be found for example in the debates of the Second Chamber on the Loi Falloux in 1850, when the radical republican delegate Edgar Quinet asked on 19 July: "fonder l'école sur la principe qui se trouve au fond de tous nos lois...séculariser la legislation, séparer le pouvoir civil et le pouvoir écclesiastique, la société laique et l'Eglise."[37] (build the school on the principle underlying all our laws...secularize the legislation, separate the civil and the ecclesiastic power, the secular society and the Church).

However, Quinet did not argue against religious education at school as such but only against confessional teaching (*l'enseignement confessionel*). His book "L'Enseignement du peuple" (1850), often called "the bible of the republican party", had great impact on the founders of the école laique in the 1870s Ferdinand Buisson and Jules Ferry. As a Unitarian, Quinet's protestantism offered a kind of republican religion, a "religion laique" and "religion de l'avenir", as Jules Clamargeron had called it in the "Revue de Paris" in 1857.

In accordance with this new type of "religion laique", Ferdinand Buisson, who was very much responsible for the school laws of the years following 1879, asked for a new "foi laique". In his "Manifeste du christianisme liberal" (1869) Buisson had called for a Christianity without dogma open for theists, pantheists, positivists and materialists. They should all come together in a "union du christianisme liberal". So what he called "seculariser la religion" was still designated to form a new religion. Only gradually was the idea of *laicité* radicalized in the following decades, slowly abandoning the reference to some kind of new religion.

When the anti-religious radicals among the freethinking social democrats in Germany adopted the idea of a public education excluding religion in the Erfurter program of 1891, they fused it with the Marxist critique of religion, which aimed to get rid of religion altogether. Hence, compared to the French "école laique" the "weltliche Schule" of the Social Democrats in Germany was even more anti-religious, because here religion and morality, religion and science were seen as incompatible.

---

[37] Cit. Mayeur, *La question laique*, 30.

How new this concept of *Weltlichkeit* (secularity) was by that time in Germany may be deduced from the fact that within the next years almost nobody transferred it to another political agenda. Not until 1906 was a "Bund für weltliche Schule und Moralunterricht" founded on the initiative of some freethinkers.[38] The Bund was soon integrated into the "Weimarer Kartell", a broad coalition of all organizations opposed to the public influence of the established Christian churches. The liberal protestant encyclopedia "Die Religion in Geschichte und Gegenwart" summarized its aspirations in 1912:[39]

1. Freie Entwicklung des geistigen Lebens und Abwehr aller Unterdrückung (Free development of the spiritual life and defense against suppression),
2. Trennung von Schule und Kirche" (separation of school and church),
3. Vollständige Verweltlichung des Staates (total secularization of the state).

Expressed by many left-wing organizations even in the years before the war, the demand for a "religionslose weltliche Schule" (a secular school free from religion) became a prominent point on the political agenda of social democrats, who tried to put it into effect after the war in the constitution of the Weimar republic.[40] But despite some support in countries like Saxony they failed to establish the "weltliche Schule" as the normal school. Only as an exception established in response to the demand of a certain number of parents the "weltliche Schule" was accepted, but not very often realized. Up until the 1960s the normal type of school in the German primary education system was the *Konfessionsschule* (confessional school) run by church authorities.

At this point it is not necessary to follow the history of public schools in Germany any further. Important for my argument is the new idea of secularism behind such demands as "secular schools", "secular education" etc.: It was the idea of a society free from the public influence of religious organizations and the religious education offered by them in state schools. The idea that clerical influence should be reduced in a secular society had already been popular among critics of religion in many European

---

[38] Cf. Groschopp, *Dissidenten*, 76 ff.
[39] Lempp, "Weimarer Kartell," 1863 f.
[40] Cf. Giesecke, "Schulpolitik der Sozialdemokraten."

countries for a long time. But only in the second half of the nineteenth
century was a public order conceptionalized, which was based on a worldview alternative to religion.

The Rapprochement after World War Two

In the early twentieth century the idea of secularism had taken a different
shape in various Christian countries. The German case was different from
the French as much as from the American: Compared to France before
and after the First World War the constitutional system in Germany was
much more open to liberal religiosity, if religion did not imply ecclesiastical confessionalism. Only the pre-war social democrats and a handful of
extreme liberals argued for the radical elimination of religion from public
life, nobody else. And in the 1920s even social democrats began to accom-
modate themselves to their clerical opponents, in the common opposition
of the 1930s to National Socialism even forming a new platform for political cooperation with the churches. It is true that, compared to the United
States, German religious culture was more hostile to the public influence
of religious organizations. But on the other hand even after World War
One the political system gave the established churches more scope for
assuming public responsibility within the constitutional framework of a
Korporation des öffentlichen Rechts (public law corporation).

Nevertheless, summarizing developments on the level of semantic
structures the early twentieth century established an antagonistic system
of 'the religious' versus 'the secular'. Secularism was defined as the death
of religion, religion as the death of secularity. There was very little compromise and cooperation between both sides. Hence, in terms of religious
ideologies modern societies with a Christian cultural background were
divided into two parts: a secular and a religious group. They spoke different languages, the one avoiding religious vocabulary, religious symbols
and practices, the other using them.

A semantic indicator for that shift to aggressive secularism or antisecular-
ism can be seen in the use of the term *Säkularisierung* (secularization):[41]
It was first used by freethinkers who supported the idea that modern culture was characterized by the exclusion of church authorities from secular

---

[41] Cf. Lübbe, *Säkularisierung*; Zabel, *Verweltlichung/Säkularisierung*; Ruh, *Säkularisierung als Interpretationskategorie*; Strätz and Zabel, "Säkularisation, Säkularisierung";
Hölscher, "Säkularisierungsängste"; Barth, "Säkularisierung I"; Jaeschke, "Säkularisierung."

government, of religious dogmas and traditions from scientific explanation of the world, of religious morals from secular education. Influenced by the discussion about the dialectics of *Weltlichkeit* and *Religiosität* in the Hegelian tradition,[42] the term was accepted by Ernst Troeltsch, Max Weber and others signifying a positive direction in historical development also in Germany at the turn of the twentieth century.

But following the concept of Anglo-American missionaries after World War One the concept assumed a negative connotation, making 'secularization' equal to 'secularism' as a catchword for the dechristianization and moral decline of the modern world. Used by committed Christians, secularism and secularization were accused of being the cause of all the ills of modern society. In their hands the concepts turned out to be a major tool in fighting against the influences of the "secularists".

Even today two concepts, bound to the same word, are in conflict with one another. The secularists and their religious opponents do not agree in what they call 'religious' and what 'secular'. That is why the relation of religion and the secular can be described from two sides: From the perspective of a religious subject secularity is the field of action within this world, but truth can be found only with God. From the perspective of a secular subject truth is a thing of this world. Religion may be seen as one part of social organization and mental activities, but it is a social institution, nothing else.

However, after World War Two the situation began to change again:[43] In all modern Western societies Christians and secularists were forced to cooperate and to rely on one another. In Germany both, the Christian churches as much as the socialist secularists, had suffered from the ideological antagonism of the 1920s and the totalitarian religious policy of National Socialism after 1933. After the war they had to win back the credit that had been lost by approving the democratic constitution of the secular society. Expressed in semantic terms, the antagonism between the 'religious' and the 'secular' languages gradually relaxed: In the religious discourse of the churches the languages of both were bound together producing a kind of "secular religion" or "religious secularity", expressed by Catholic and Protestant theologians and church officials.

---

[42] See above note 18–20.
[43] For this last part cf. Hölscher, "Europe in the Age of Secularisation"; Hölscher, "Die Säkularisierung der Kirchen."

On the side of theology the input of two protestant theologians was most important for this new rapprochement between church and secular society: Dietrich Bonhoeffer and Friedrich Gogarten. Bonhoeffer, in his last period of imprisonment, had propagated a Christianity without religion.[44] Gogarten, a former friend and combatant of Karl Barth in the 1920s, in his widely read book "Verhängnis und Hoffnung der Neuzeit" of 1953 argued for a positive theological concept of 'secularization': According to him the highly stigmatized idea of a world being progressively corrupted by "secular" forces was to be replaced by the idea of God's incarnation in the world, leaving the idea of a world without God to those "secularists" who had no hope for a better future.

This positive concept of secularization was willingly adopted by many Catholics[45] and Protestants in the 1950s and 1960s who tried to break out of their growing isolation within secular society.

> To give but one example of this kind of diction: In the protestant journal "Zeitschrift für Evangelische Ethik" the director of the Protestant Academy in Wuppertal Oskar Hammelsbach argued in 1964 that the protestant church should, in solidarity with other religions and Christian denominations, engage "in der säkularisierten, in der mündigen Welt" (in the secularized, politically mature world); secularization would pave the way for cooperation with atheists and communists as much as with other churches; the "säkulare Vision" (secular vision) would rely on the belief "dass Gott in Christus die Welt mit sich selbst versöhnt hat (that God had reconciled the world with itself through Christ)".[46]

In the reform period of the 1960s the churches were open for the social and political agenda conceding that up to a certain point secular agenda had an "Eigengesetzlichkeit", their own logic and necessity. In order to break free from the chains of the established idiomatic formulas of religious discourse, church officials began to plead for a "secularization" of language, avoiding the "language of Canaan", as this artificial language of the nineteenth century was called in the ecclesiastical milieu. Instead they strived for a common, ordinary language to be spoken and, if for theological necessity religious terms had to be used, for these to be combined with secular concepts: Thus, 'world' and 'society', 'creation' and 'environment', 'charity' and 'solidarity' were taken to be interchangeable; obedience to

---

[44] Bonhoeffer, Widerstand und Ergebung.
[45] The catholic concept of *Weltlichkeit* had another theological background but came to a similar conclusion, cf. Metz, *Zur Theologie der Welt*.
[46] Hammelsbeck, "Säkularisation."

God was translated to social responsibility and so on. Again to give just one example, in 1960 the "Zeitschrift für Evangelische Ethik" declared:[47]

> Im vorliegenden Zusammenhang bedeutet 'Welt' die geschichtliche menschliche Gesellschaft... Gottes Liebe zur Welt (verbindet) Kirche und Welt miteinander" und ruft "die Kirchen zum Dienst an der Gesellschaft (In the given context 'world' means the historical human society... God's love to the world (connects) Church and world with one another (and calls) the churches to the service of society).

In doing so, the churches proclaimed a new political and social relevance of the Christian gospel for society as a whole. Secular religion was a message to all men, but called for the special engagement of Christians within all kinds of political and social institutions. Christians should not preach society what it had to do but rather they should stand at the forefront on all issues of this world.

Looking back to the last decades, we are aware that this type of secular religiosity had its climax in the 1960s and 1970s. In the 1980s, due to some disappointment about the failure of religious reform and religious revitalization in the past the concept of a secular religiosity seems to have declined, making room for a new turn to spirituality and concern for the inner life. Already in 1986 the Catholic theologian Eugen Biser considered secularization to have passed its climax, giving way to a post-secularist age—a diagnosis, which has become prominent by Jürgen Habermas in 2001.[48]

So again the religious discourse may today be on the point of producing a new semantic paradigm: In this paradigm secular religiosity may be linked with liberal political positions and opposed to fundamentalist religiosity. Unlike the antagonism between the religious and the secular, the new fracture cuts through religion itself. This is an indication that the pattern religious/secular (which in the last decades was most characteristic of all kinds of secularization theories) may today be exhausted.

What can we learn from all these changing semantic patterns?
1. Religion and secularity are relational terms. They unfold in changing semantic dichotomies: spiritual/temporal, religious/secular, fundamentalist/liberal and so on. There is no continuity in defining the identity of religion, but rather a transitory set of semantic patterns.

---

[47] "Aufgaben und Möglichkeiten kirchlichen Handelns," *Zeitschrift für Evangelische Ethik* 4 (1960): 257.
[48] Biser, *Die glaubensgeschichtliche Wende*; Habermas, *Glauben und Wissen*.

2. Secularity in its modern anti-religious meaning is a typical feature of twentieth century society, not only in Germany. In the age of secularity society defines religion as being opposed to secularity, and secularity as being opposed to religion. Today, at the end of this age, it is no longer important whether or not we are in the process of secularization, rather, we are faced with multiple secularities at different times and in different religious cultures.

3. Finally, this article should underline the importance of semantic patterns and the productivity of semantic analysis for describing changing religious life in modern societies. In a time when big institutions such as the Christian churches are becoming eroded, modern citizens in Germany and many other European countries no longer identify themselves primarily by their religious confession or their membership in religious institutions but rather by using certain languages, which may be identified by contemporaries or later observers as being religious or non-religious.

Bibliography

Adelung, Johann Christoph. *Grammatisch-kritisches Wörterbuch der Hochdeutschen Mundart*, second edition, 4 vols. Leipzig: Breitkopf & Sohn, 1808.

"Aufgaben und Möglichkeiten kirchlichen Handelns im raschen sozialen Umbruch. Ergebnis einer internationalen ökumenischen Studienkonferenz." *Zeitschrift für Evangelische Ethik* 4 (1960): 257.

Barth, Ulrich. "Säkularisierung I." In *Theologische Realenzyklopädie*, vol. 29, pp. 603–633. Berlin: De Gruyter, 1998.

Basedow, Johann Bernhard. *Das Methodenbuch für Väter und Mütter der Familien und Völker*, Facsimile. Vaduz: Topos, 1979.

Bebel, August. *Die Frau und der Sozialismus*, Berlin: Dietz-Verlag, 1974.

Biser, Eugen. *Die glaubensgeschichtliche Wende. Eine theologische Positionsbestimmung.* Graz: Styria, 1986.

Bonhoeffer, Dietrich. *Widerstand und Ergebung. Briefe und Aufzeichnungen aus der Haft*, edited by Christian Gremmels, Eberhard Bethge, and Renate Bethge. München: Gütersloher Verlagshaus, 2011.

Brockhaus Enzyklopädie. Studien: Limitierte Auflag, twentieth edition, 24 vols. Gütersloh: F. A. Brockhaus, 2001.

Büchner, Ludwig. *Kraft und Stoff. Empirisch-naturphilosophische Studien. In allgemein-verständlicher Darstellung.* Frankfurt am Main: Meidinger, 1855.

Catholicisme. Hier, aujourd'hui, demain, edited by G. Jacquemet, vol. 6. Paris: Letouzey et Ané, 1967.

Chadwick, Owen. *The Secularization of the European Mind in the Nineteenth Century.* Cambridge: Cambridge University Press, 1975.

Deutsche Parteiprogramme, edited by Wilhelm Mommsen, third edition. München: Isar-Verlag, 1960.

Fichte, Johann Gottlieb. "Über den Grund unseres Glaubens an eine göttliche Weltregierung." In *J. G. Fichtes Atheismus-Streit*, edited by Frank Böckelmann. München: Rogner und Bernhard, 1969.

——. "Über den Grund unseres Glaubens." In *Fichtes Werke*, edited by Immanuel H. Fichte, vol. 5, pp. 175–190. Berlin: De Gruyter, 1971.

Giese, Gerhardt. *Quellen zur deutschen Schulgeschichte seit 1800*. Göttingen: Musterschmidt, 1961.

Giesecke, Hermann. "Zur Schulpolitik der Sozialdemokraten in Preußen und im Reich." In *Vierteljahreshefte für Zeitgeschichte* 13 (1965): 162–177.

Groschopp, Horst. *Dissidenten. Freidenkerei und Kultur in Deutschland*. Berlin: Dietz-Verlag, 1997.

Habermas, Jürgen. *Glauben und Wissen—Friedenspreis des Deutschen Buchhandels 2001*. Frankfurt am Main: Börsenverein des Deutschen Buchhandels, 2001.

Haeckel, Ernst. *Die Welträtsel*. Reprint of the eleventh edition of 1919. Stuttgart: Kröner, 1984.

——. *The Riddle oft the Universe at the Close oft the Nineteenth Century*. Translated by Joseph McCabe. New York: Harper & Brothers Publishers, 1900.

Hammelsbeck, Oskar. "Säkularisation—Wegbereiterin für die Einheit der Kirchen?" *Zeitschrift für Evangelische Ethik* 8 (1964): 1–13.

Hegel, Georg Wilhelm Friedrich. *Vorlesungen über die Philosophie der Religion*. In *Werke in 20 Bänden*, edited by Eva Moldenhauer and Karl Markus Michel, vol. 17. Frankfurt am Main: Suhrkamp, 1969.

Heinroth, Johann Christian August. *Pisteodicee oder Resultate freier Forschung über Geschichte, Philosophie und Glauben*. Leipzig: Friedrich Christian Wilhelm Vogel, 1829.

Hinrichs, Hermann Friedrich Wilhelm. *Schillers Dichtungen nach ihren historischen Beziehungen und nach ihrem inneren Zusammenhange*, vol. 2. Leipzig: J. G. Hinrichschen Buchhandlung, 1837.

Hollenberg, W. "Die Grundzüge der in England beabsichtigten Reform höherer Schulen." *Zeitschrift für das Gymnasialwesen* 22 (1869): 257–272.

Hölscher, Lucian. "Die Säkularisierung der Kirchen. Sprachliche Transformationsprozesse in den langen 1960er Jahren." In *Soziale Strukturen und Semantiken des Religiösen im Wandel. Transformationen in der Bundesrepublik Deutschland 1949–1989*, edited by Wilhelm Damberg, pp. 203–214. Essen: Klartext-Verlag, 2011.

——. "Europe in the Age of Secularisation." In *Secularisation in the Christian World. Essays in Honour of Hugh McLeod*, edited by Callum Brown, Michael Snape, pp. 197–204. Surrey: Ashgate, 2010.

——. "The Concept of Conceptual History (Begriffsgeschichte) and the 'Geschichtliche Grundbegriffe'." *Concept and Communication* 1, no. 2 (2008): 179–198.

——. "Säkularisierungsängste in der neuzeitlichen Gesellschaft." *Nationalprotestantische Mentalitäten. Konturen, Entwicklungslinien und Umbrüche eines Weltbilds*, edited by M. Gailus, and H. Lehmann, pp. 133–147. Göttingen: Vandenhoeck & Ruprecht, 2005.

Huber, Ernst Rudolph. *Deutsche Verfassungsgeschichte*, vol. 4. Stuttgart: W. Kohlhammer, 1969.

Jaeschke, Walter. "Säkularisierung." In *Handbuch religionswissenschaftlicher Grundbegriffe*, edited by Hubert Cancik, Burkhard Gladigow, and Karl-Heinz Kohl, vol. 5, pp. 9–20. Stuttgart: W. Kohlhammer, 2001.

——. *Die Suche nach den eschatologischen Wurzeln der Geschichtsphilosophie. Eine historische Kritik der Säkularisierungsthese*. München: Kaiser, 1976.

Johnson, Samuel. *Dictionary of the English Language*, 2 vols. London: W. Strahan, 1832.

Koselleck, Reinhard. "Begriffsgeschichte und Sozialgeschichte." In *Vergangene Zukunft. Zur Semantik geschichtlicher Zeiten*, edited by Ibid., pp. 107–129. Frankfurt am Main: Suhrkamp Verlag, 1979.

——. "Sozialgeschichte und Begriffsgeschichte." In *Sozialgeschichte in Deutschland. Entwicklungen und Perspektiven im internationalen Zusammenhang*, edited by Wolfgang Schieder, and Volker Sellin, pp. 89–109. Göttingen: Vandenhoeck & Ruprecht 1986.

Krug, Wilhelm Traugott. *Allgemeines Handwörterbuch der philosophischen Wissenschaften*, second edition, 5 vols. Leipzig: F. Brockhaus, 1838.

Krummacher, Friedrich A. *Die christliche Volksschule im Bund mit der Kirche*. Essen: Bädecker Verlag, 1823.

Lachmann, Rainer, and Bernd Schröder, eds. *Geschichte des evangelischen Religionsunterrichts in Deutschland. Ein Studienbuch*. Neukirchen-Vluyn: Neukirchener Verlag, 2007.

Lehmann, Hartmut. *Säkularisierung. Der europäische Sonderweg in Sachen Religion*. Göttingen: Wallstein 2004.

Lempp, O. "Weimarer Kartell." In *Religion in Geschichte und Gegenwart*, edited by Friedrich Michael Schiele, and Leopold Zscharnack, first edition, vol. 5, p. 1863f. Tübingen: Mohr Siebeck Verlag, 1913.

Lübbe, Hermann. *Säkularisierung. Geschichte eines ideenpolitischen Begriffs*. Freiburg: Karl Alber, 1965.

Marx, Karl. "Einleitung zur Kritik der Hegelschen Rechtsphilosophie" In *Über Religion*, edited by Friedrich Engels, and Karl Marx. Berlin: Dietz-Verlag, 1958.

Mayeur, Jean-Marie. *La question laique, XIX–XXᵉ siècle*. Paris: Fayard, 1997.

Metz, Johann Baptist. *Zur Theologie der Welt*. Mainz: J. B. Metz, 1968.

Meyers Lexikon, seventh edition, 12 vols. Leipzig: Meyers Lexikonverlag, 1924–1930.

Oxford English Dictionary, vol. 9. Oxford: Oxford University Press, 1933.

Protokoll über die Verhandlungen des Parteitags der Sozialdemokratische Partei Deutschlands, abgehalten zu Erfurt vom 14. bis 20. Oktober 1891. Berlin: Th. Glocke Verlag, 1891.

Ruh, Ulrich. *Säkularisierung als Interpretationskategorie. Zur Bedeutung des christlichen Erbes in der modernen Geistesgeschichte*. Freiburg: Herder, 1981.

Schnabel, Franz. "Wege der Verweltlichung." In *Deutsche Geschichte im neunzehnten Jahrhundert, vol. 4. Die religiösen Kräfte*, edited by Franz Schnabel. Frankfurt am Main: Deutscher Taschenbuch Verlag, 1955.

Sheridan, Thomas. *A General Dictionary of the English Language*. London, 1780.

Stenographische Berichte über die Verhandlungen der deutschen konstituierenden Nationalversammlung zu Frankfurt am Main, edited by Franz Wigard, vol. 3. Leipzig, 1848.

Strätz, Wolfgang and Hermann Zabel. "Säkularisation, Säkularisierung." In *Geschichtliche Grundbegriffe. Historisches Lexikon zur politisch-sozialen Sprache in Deutschland*, edited by Otto Brunner, Werner Conze, Reinhart Koselleck, Vol. 5, pp. 789–830. Stuttgart: Klett-Cotta, 1984.

Strauss, David Friedrich. *Der alte und der neue Glaube. Ein Bekenntnis. Volksausgabe*. Stuttgart: Kröner, 1873.

Weitling, Wilhelm. *Garantien der Harmonie und Freiheit* [1842], edited by F. Mehring. Berlin: Hans Weber, 1908.

Zabel, Hermann. *Verweltlichung/Säkularisierung. Zur Geschichte einer Interpretationskategorie*. Münster: Dissertation, 1968.

Zedler, Johann Heinrich. *Grosses vollständiges Universal-Lexicon aller Wissenschaften und Künste*. 64 vols. and 4 supplements. Halle: Verlag Johann Heinrich Zedler, 1732–1754.

THE ORIGIN OF THE CONCEPT OF *LAÏCITÉ* IN NINETEENTH CENTURY FRANCE

Sylvie Le Grand

Laïcité is both a complex concept and reality in France: one can even say that it has become a key element of French republican identity; a founding value, even "part of the national heritage,"[1] according to the Debré report. It is no longer a divisive factor as it was during the "war of the two Frances";[2] its main foundations are the consensual bases of social life. Nonetheless the challenges or adaptations required as a result of new questions (the place of Islam, etc.) show that it continues to exert a strong pull in broad sections of society, regularly triggering passionate debates as few other topics are able to do in our country.

The current basis of this identity is first of all the constitutional enshrinement of the word *laïque* which has been part of the constitutional definition of the French Republic since the constitution of 1946,[3] and reaffirmed in 1958.[4]

---

[1] Debré, *La laïcité à l'école*, 11.

[2] This term expresses the antagonism and confrontation, not always of a uniquely symbolic nature, between the two camps of the "*catholiques*" and the "*laïcs*" in France during the course of the nineteenth and twentieth centuries. This conflict, which was very intense from the 1880s onwards, became less so after 1918. Cf. Poulat, *Liberté, laïcité*; Langlois, "Catholiques et laïcs".

[3] Constitution of 26 October 1946—Preamble: "...They [the French people] solemnly reaffirm the rights and freedoms of man and the citizen enshrined in the Declaration of Rights of 1789 and the fundamental principles acknowledged in the laws of the Republic.... No person may suffer prejudice in his work or employment by virtue of his origins, opinions or beliefs." The institutions of the Republic, Title 1: On Sovereignty. Source of the English translation: http://www.conseil-constitutionnel.fr/conseil-constitutionnel/root/bank_mm/anglais/cst3.pdf (accessed June 24, 2011). Art. 1: France shall be an indivisible, secular, democratic and social Republic. Source of the English translation: http://www.assemblee-nationale.fr/english/8ab.asp (accessed June 24, 2011).

[4] Constitution of 4 October 1958—Preamble: "The French people solemnly proclaim their attachment to the Rights of Man and the principles of national sovereignty as defined by the Declaration of 1789, confirmed and complemented by the Preamble to the Constitution of 1946..." Art. 1: "France shall be an indivisible, secular, democratic and social Republic. It shall ensure the equality of all citizens before the law, without distinction of origin, race or religion. It shall respect all beliefs..." http://www.assemblee-nationale.fr/english/8ab.asp (accessed June 24, 2011). The explicit references to the Declaration of the Rights of Man and of the Citizen of 1789 in the constitutions of 1946 and 1958 lead to this oddity: these constitutions are thus indirectly placed under the aegis of the Supreme Being cited in the aforementioned declaration ("As a result, the National Assembly recognises

Laïcité is therefore in some ways the fourth notion in the Republican motto![5]

As both a complex concept and reality, the word *laïcité* is not used in a univocal sense and is subject to multiple readings and perspectives: legal, ideological/philosophical, political and sociological. Let us focus on at least two of the principal levels of the meaning of the term: *laïcité* relates first of all to a legal system,[6] but it also makes reference to a symbolic universe. In these two areas at least, which do not exhaust its meaning, *laïcité* proves to be a plural and dynamic reality, hence the suggestion by some authors to talk of French "laïcités" in the plural.[7]

We must distinguish between the word and the thing. The two have not been studied equally. Whilst the genesis of the thing (the *laïque*[8] idea or notion of separation in particular) is now relatively well known and has been examined by a number of prominent French historians and sociologists,[9] the concept has not received sufficient attention. My thanks therefore go to Lucian Hölscher for having suggested this angle of "attack" for my contribution to the present volume.

More specifically, information on the concept of *laïcité* has been published in works not directly relating to the terminology of *laïcité*.[10] Another difficulty is linked to the *a posteriori* use of the term by the majority of

---

and declares, in the presence of and under the auspices of the Supreme Being, the following Rights of Man and of the Citizen," cf. Godechot, *Les constitutions de la France depuis 1789*, 33).

[5] This is what René Rémond suggests in the preface to the work by Bédouelle and Costa, *Laïcités à la française*, 3.

[6] The legal system of laïcité is itself defined by a heterogeneous body of texts of various kinds. Cf. *Traité de droit français des religions*. That's why one of the proposals by the Machelon committee on the relations between religious communities and public authorities in 2006 touched upon the creation of a code of laïcité. This idea is defended among others by the legal expert Francis Messner. Cf. La Croix, 21.3.2011, 17.

[7] Let us recall with regard to the legal side of things that the law on the Separation of the Churches and the State (1905) does not apply to the whole of French territory—Alsace-Moselle still being governed by the Concordat of 1801, whilst various overseas territories have their own specific systems. From another angle, some authors call for a distinction to be made between "laïcité réelle" (real laicity) and "laïcité rêvée" (dreamt laicity). There is indeed a wide gap in France between the reality of how religions are treated legally and the philosophical or ideological discourses on laicity. Cf. on all these points Bédouelle and Costa, *Laïcités à la française*.

[8] Let us cite the pioneer work: Weill, *Histoire de l'idée laïque*.

[9] Including Emile Poulat, Jean Baubérot, Jean-Paul Willaime, Jean-Marie Mayeur, Jacqueline Lalouette, and Patrick Cabanel in particular. Let us cite simply as examples: Lalouette, *La séparation des Eglises et de l'Etat*; Mayeur, *La question laïque*; Poulat, *Notre laïcité publique*; Poulat, *Scruter la loi de 1905*.

[10] See for instance Barbier, *La laïcité*, 6.

the authors (historians and sociologists). They apply the term 'laïcité' ret-rospectively to facts and debates which themselves had not yet used the term. Thus, the point in history always cited with regard to the emergence of modern laïcité is the French Revolution, followed by other milestones such as the Concordat of 1801, the Revolution of 1848, the school laws of 1881 and 1886, and finally the law on the Separation of the Churches and the State in 1905.[11] However, it is not until the 1870s, under the Third Republic, that the noun 'laïcité' appeared in a context linked to school education and the debate on the "laïcisation" of primary education. It makes sense therefore to study the significance and the reach of this his-torical coincidence.

Before examining the origin of the term in its historical context, which is the main purpose of my paper, let us return to the common idea widely spread in the discourse in the French media that laïcité is an "*exception française*", that is, a notion specific to France. It is difficult here to tell the difference between national narcissism and journalistic corner-cutting. At any rate we must put an end to this view that laïcité is a uniquely French idea. In fact, on the basis of the political and legal realities that it encompasses, one can largely "translate" the concept using one or several common denominators—namely the neutrality of the State, respect for freedom of conscience and religion, the separation of the political and religious spheres—which allow us to render it intelligible.[12] However, if there is a French singularity with regard to the relationship between reli-gion, the State and society, perhaps it lies precisely in this passion for the word and the subject of 'laïcité'. Hence, the interest in trying to under-stand how and via which detours it has been able to crystallise so many emotions and ideas.

After a brief review of the semantic origin of the word and its evolution, we will concentrate on the historical sequence, from the birth of the con-cept in 1871/73, and its development in the second half of the nineteenth century. This was the era of the struggle for the laicisation of education and the development of laic, republican morals. This will lead us to the founding fathers of the Third Republic: various republican currents such as the spiritualists, the positivists and the liberal Protestants, who will modify the concept in different ways. We will attempt to determine more

---

[11] Jean Baubérot groups these stages into two main "thresholds of laïcisation". Cf. Baubérot, *Histoire de la laïcité française*.

[12] This is the underlying procedure of Thierry Rambaud's thesis, *Le principe de séparation*.

precisely the influence of these movements and individuals on the evolution of the concept and to evaluate the importance of this period for the understanding of the current concept of 'laïcité'.

The Word and the Idea: Elements of Definition

Our objective is to carry out a two-fold review here, first by tracing the morphological and semantic evolution of the notion up until the appearance of the noun *laïcité* and, second, by analysing the principal constitutive elements of the '*laïcité* idea'. In French there are three parallel forms of adjectives *lai/laïc, laïque* (some of which also came to be used as nouns) and a noun *laïcité*. The only in-depth study known to this day and always cited by authors is by the lexicographer Pierre Fiala (1991).[13] Let us recall from his study that the appearance of the adjective precedes that of the noun; it is therefore the adjective which engendered the noun.

There is a pair of adjectives *lai/laïc* (scholarly/popular doublet) whose use becomes increasingly different over time. *Lai* (which comes from the Greek 'laos' = the people) becomes explicitly obsolete in the twentieth century and remains only in very rare expressions (*frère lai*—lay brother), whilst the forms *laïc/laïque* assert themselves as a noun and adjective as of 1798. These terms clearly belong to the religious field: they describe either people, or goods, not belonging to the clergy. They therefore refer to the opposition or separation between the cleric and secular. Let us note in passing that before 1762, the term *laïc* is still defined positively by its synonym "séculier" in the dictionary of the Academy, whilst later, it is negative definitions using antonyms or the idea of non-membership of an order which predominate.

The key point for us is as follows: in the middle of the nineteenth century we observe a semantic mutation and distortion in the use of the adjective. The difference in spelling is now accompanied by a semantic divergence. Whilst the noun *laïc* retains its meaning of "follower of a religion not belonging to his clergy" ("Dictionnaire de l'Académie" 1798), the form *laïque* (noun or adjective) defines itself as the non-membership of a positive, instituted religion. It "leaves its original semantic space" and "inaugurates a new semantic and terminological space" which prepares

---

[13] Fiala, "Les termes de la laïcité." Let us also note the comparative study by Toscer-Angot, "'Säkularisierung' und 'Laizität'," which takes up the conclusions by Fiala and also compares the usage, in particular the sociological usages, of the terms in the two languages.

the arrival of the noun "laïcité".[14] According to Pierre Ognier, this distortion probably occurs in the 1840s, due to the revolution of 1848 and the development of the bill on educational reform presented by Hippolyte Carnot (1891–1888), appointed minister of education in 1848. This new usage[15] is proved by Edgar Quinet in *L'enseignement du peuple* (1849, first ed.) where he speaks of "société laïque", "instituteur, enseignement laïques"—laic society, laic teachers and teaching. For Quinet, religious dogma has no place in the public education system.

As research stands today,[16] the first known usage of the noun *laïcité* is early November 1871. During a meeting of the Seine General Council on 8 November 1871, which was published in the newspaper *La patrie* on 11 November 1871, Vauthier and Cantagrel,[17] from the doctrinal movement of *la Morale indépendante*, are said to have presented a "proposition de *laïcité*" (proposal on *laicity*) during the discussion on primary school education and the exclusion of dogma in public education. The use of italics in the original text itself highlights that the word is not known.

What is striking is how quickly it is included in the dictionary: It enters the Grand Dictionnaire Larousse in 1873, and in 1877 the Littré supplement,[18] which leads one to think it should be possible to find other examples of uses of the term.[19] In 1873, one finds an occurrence in inverted commas in a text by Ferdinand Buisson.[20] The term is therefore a neologism, indicated as such in 1887 in a note in the "Dictionnaire de pédagogie et d'instruction

---

[14] Ognier, *Une école sans Dieu?*, 36–37.

[15] This meaning was, according to Fiala, present in embryonic form through Calvin who speaks of "juges laïcs" in *Institution chrétienne*. Later, Fiala says, we find a trace of it in l'Encyclopédie by Diderot and Alembert.

[16] The research in progress by Mayyada Kheir, who is preparing a thesis on "La laïcité de Guizot à Ferry" under the supervision of Philippe Boutry and Rita Hermon-Belot (EHESS, Paris), should allow headway to be made on this point.

[17] François, Jean Cantagrel (1810–1887). See his profile on the National Assemble website: http://www.assemblee-nationale.fr/sycamore/fiche.asp?num_dept=7912# biographie (accessed September 24, 2012).

[18] The definitions are succinct: "character of that which is laic, of a laic person" or "laic character". Fiala, "Les termes de la laïcité," 49.

[19] Pierre Ognier recommends studying in particular the minutes and official texts of the Commune or writings on the issue of schooling from the Masonic milieu, especially from the Parisian lodges of the Grand Orient de France at this time. cf. Ognier, *Une école sans Dieu?*, 36 (note 37).

[20] "We would get a very inexact idea of the different [international] legislation we have just stated as admitting the principle of "laïcité" in schools if we were to believe it to be inspired by a spirit of indifference or hostility towards Christianity". Buisson, *Rapport sur l'instruction primaire*, 145.

primaire" by Ferdinand Buisson, editor of the overall work (1882–1887), at that time director of primary education (1879–1896). It contains a long article on the noun *laïcité*,[21] ("it is the first systematic presentation of the notion").[22] The new abridged edition in 1911[23] even contains three mentions: the same article *in extenso* on the noun *laïcité*, another on the adjective *laïque*, and the term *laïcisation* which refers back to *laïcité*. There is on the other hand no article on "sécularisation" although the term is used fairly frequently by Buisson.

Etymological considerations regarding the adjective concentrate on the opposition between *clerc* and *laïque*, the latter being seen as what is popular and national, and, ultimately, between the clerical spirit of a chosen handful ("the claim by a minority to rule over the majority in the name of religion") and the "laïque" spirit ("all the aspirations of the people", "democratic and popular spirit").

The article on "laïcité" is instructive in many ways: the term is described as a "necessary neologism". The "laicisation" of the school system is presented as the final stage in a process of progressive differentiation between the areas or "functions of public life" previously merged (army, administrative, civil, justice functions). The analysis by Buisson heralds the classic thesis of institutional differentiation developed later by numerous sociologists. This process is described on two occasions as secularisation.

Laïcité is defined first as the end of the "confusion" or non-separation of powers, the end of their "subordination" to the authority of religion. Therefore, the idea underlying all of this here is the separation of areas and powers, the idea of the "profound delimitation between the temporal and the spiritual", specified by notions of neutrality ("the idea of the 'laïque' State, the State which is neutral towards all religions, independent of all the clergy, detached from all theological concepts"), of equality among citizens. If we except the notions of freedom of conscience, religious freedom, not precisely specified here, then we have here the principal

---

[21] *Dictionnaire de pédagogie et d'instruction primaire*, 1469–1474.

[22] Baubérot, *Laïcité 1905–2005*, 14.

[23] This edition from 1911 published under the title *Nouveau dictionnaire de pédagogie* has been fully digitised: http://www.inrp.fr/edition-electronique/lodel/dictionnaire-ferdinand-buisson/ (accessed September 24, 2012). Whilst the first edition (20,000 copies published) is marked by the context of the school laws of 1880–1882, the second (5,000 copies published) takes "stock of thirty years of actions and deals with the issue of the pedagogical methods after the reform of 1902" (cf. introduction to the digitised edition). Patrick Dubois quotes other figures in his thesis: 8,000 copies for the first edition, 5,500 for the second edition (cf. reference, note 36, 2).

constitutive elements of subsequent historical or sociological studies dedicated to *laïcité* as an idea, irrespective of the use of the word. There is also talk of the "system of laïcité" relating to primary school education which includes "laicity of teaching" and "laicity of teaching staff".

The articles in the Buisson dictionary confirm the close link at the time between the emergence of the concept of 'laïcité' and the struggle for the laicisation of education. What is surprising in this regard is the complete silence on the law on the Separation of the Churches and the State of 1905 which, it seems, receives no mention whatsoever in the second redrafted edition of 1911, and in any case not in the article on "laïcité". Buisson is both judge and judged in the process of laicisation, which is why the analysis of his position is at the intersection of the semantic and the historical study of it. He is one of the key players in the historical sequence that we will now study so as to shed more light on the conditions for the emergence of the concept of 'laïcité'. Reading his articles opens two or three perspectives of reflection, which can serve as a common thread in studying the historical sequence of events:

- Moral education (and, as a result, the need to establish laic moral education) is a key issue in laicised primary education.
- A form of continuity appears between the former confessional schools and the new laic schools. The teacher must be able to be a "master of morality", "he must continue to take charge of souls", and be responsible for "the education of the conscience" of each child.[24]
- From these two elements, a trend towards the sacralisation of laïcité emerges, which begins to take shape in Buisson's article on "laïcité".

Study of the Historical Sequence Which Gives Rise to the Concept:
The 1870s and Onwards

The birth of the Third Republic, proclaimed on 4 September 1870, occurs in the context of two traumatic experiences: first that of the French defeat by Prussia and its allies, definitively in January 1871, a few months after the proclamation; second that of the violent and bloodily repressed episode of the Paris Commune (March–May 1871). In the beginning the proclaimed

---

[24] But Buisson, aware of the danger incurred, quotes Jules Ferry saying during the discussion of the law of 1882 that one is establishing the "confessional neutrality" of schools, but not their "philosophical neutrality."

Republic is a reluctant Republic, which brings a monarchist majority to parliament planning the re-establishment of this regime. In spite of everything, an overhaul of public education is fashionable at the time. It appears as a condition for national recovery and the unification of the country. The conviction was widespread that it was the Prussian primary school teacher who won the war against Austria (1866), then France (1870/71)? There is therefore reformist fervour, which feeds off the international exhibitions of the time (Vienna 1873, Philadelphia 1876) and is used and spread by republicans in particular.

The "laïque" demands applied to primary education figure at the very top of the programmes and speeches of republicans. And so, in his famous Belleville manifesto, Léon Gambetta (1838–1882) calls in 1869 for "laïque", free and compulsory education. The free and obligatory nature is considered a precondition to laicisation.[25] Whilst the separation of the Churches and the State is still on the agenda in the Belleville manifesto, it soon will not be, as the Republicans realise that the Concordat does not necessarily imply a religious impregnation of the State and that it is useful for controlling the Catholic Church![26]

In his St. Quentin speech (16 November 1871), Gambetta states that morality must be taught "laïquement" (note the use of the adverb!), that "the education of the people" must be "imbued with the modern, civil spirit". The reference to the Pope's condemnation of "all the modern principles from which our civic and political laws are derived" in the syllabus of 1864 is important in this context. The author, for his part, claims to be part of the "society of 1789".

The question of *laic* education is not just a political manifesto, but above all a series of liberal measures (laws, circulars or decrees) discussed and then adopted once the Republicans are in power from the beginning of 1879. The two main laws are the Ferry Law of 28 March 1882 "on the obligatory nature of primary school education" for children from 6 to 13, which establishes the "laïcité" of educational syllabi and replaces the moral and religious education set forth in the Falloux Law (1850) with a course of moral and civic instruction, and the Goblet Law of October 1888, which laicises the teaching staff (whilst providing for a time-frame of five or more years for compliance in boys' schools and girls' schools

---

[25] Buisson also recalls this in the article "laïcité" in his *Dictionnaire de pédagogie*.
[26] Baubérot, *Laïcité 1905–2005*, 21.

respectively).[27] Outside of school, there is a series of "partial separations" in the field of administration, state services and private life: end to the ban (1814) on Sunday working in 1879; abolition of the confessional nature of cemeteries (1881) and the establishment of funerary liberty (1887), law on divorce (1884), abolition of public prayers in the Assemblies (1884), laicisation of Parisian hospitals as of 1879.[28]

The legislation on schooling is significantly shaped by Jules Ferry (1832–1893), member of the Republican Left (governmental left, moderate), appointed Minister of Education in February 1879, positivist, Freemason and atheist, but moderate and pragmatic in his political methods. It is interesting to compare him to Paul Bert (1833–1886), physiologist, member of the Republican Union (radical left) and chairman of the parliamentary committee, which draws up bills. The two republicans espouse slightly different points of view during the parliamentary debate. Paul Bert is a proponent of expedient methods and broad changes, whilst Jules Ferry is sensitive to shifts in opinion and careful not to snub the Catholic population in general and "universal suffrage Catholics" in particular. He thus criticises the decision by the prefect of Paris, who had had all religious symbols removed from the thirty-two schools in Paris without further ado, on 20 February 1881. He regards as a humiliation the ban finally imposed on the church minister on providing religious education on school premises during the day-off provided for by law and dedicated to the religious education of children.

This difference in political sensitivity between the two men is apparent in their vocabulary too: whilst Ferry prefers to speak of the neutrality of school, indeed of secularisation rather than "laïcité", Bert, on the

---

[27] Here is an outline of the measures taken at all levels of the education system: August 1879: obligation to the départements to establish a teacher training college (67 départements did not have one); February 1880: reform of the Conseil supérieur de l'Instruction publique excluding the ministers of the church; Law of March 1880: the award of university degrees is the preserve of the State; Law of December 1880: secondary schooling of girls will be carried out by women and requires the establishment of women's teacher training institutions; Law of 16 June 1881 on free education. (Cf. Mayeur, *Les débuts*, 111–119); Law of 16 June 1881 regarding the "titres de capacité"—teaching qualifications—required for primary school teaching: the "brevet de capacité" is obligatory for all teachers; the letter of obedience, that is the mission letter signed by the heads of the congregation, is no longer sufficient: http://mjp.univ-perp.fr/france/1881instituteur.htm (accessed June 24, 2011). Teacher training becomes laic: they no longer have to attend mass, courses on sacred chants and the catechism are abolished, biblical history disappears from the "brevet de capacité". The chaplain disappears from teacher training colleges (Decree of 9 January 1883). Cf. Condette, *Education, religion, laïcité*, 8.

[28] Mayeur, *Les débuts de la IIIè République*, 112; Lalouette, "Les lois laïques," 15–30.

other hand favours, like his political movement, the term *laïcité* (debate on 23 December 1880). Ferry wants to avoid the term *laïcité* in the texts of the laws on obligatory and free education; Bert, for his part, immediately links them: "La gratuité et la laïcité nous apparaissent, en effet, comme des conséquences forcées de l'obligation" (The free nature of education and laïcité seem to us, in fact, to be inevitable consequences of obligatory education).[29]

But let us press ahead in the analysis of the vocabulary by expanding the comparison and concentrating on the debate surrounding the "Law on obligatory primary education" (1882), studied by Mayyada Kheir.[30] Whilst the term *laïcité* is not part of either the title or the text of the law, it looms large in the discussions preceding the vote on the law. The author distinguishes four positions on the law (and the term *laïcité*): apart from those of Jules Ferry (moderate left) and Paul Bert (radical left) already mentioned, that of the right, and that, on the left, of some republican representatives of the spiritualist movement around Jules Simon.[31] The point in analysing this is to show that behind the disputes over the definition, the divisive issue hinges on the perception of French history. Whilst the moderate left represented by Ferry focuses on historical continuity and for this reason favours the term 'neutrality' rather than *laïcité*, the exact opposite happens at the heart of the radical left: They, through Paul Bert,[32] insist on a break with the past and make *laïcité* a positive ideology, in competition with clericalism. Whilst Ferry seeks to redefine the nation, unite it, unify it by constructing a non-confessional French identity, the radical left leads the fight against obscurantism and thus reactivates historical oppositions.

Consequently, in the discourse of the radical left, the term *laïcité* is disproportionately present, the noun occurring more frequently than the adjective. Meanwhile the right, as the mirror-image of the radical left, defends a confessional identity for France. Whilst initially it denounces the vagueness of the term, a smokescreen masking irreligion, there are attempts later to appropriate it for itself. Strangely enough, the left close to Jules Simon shares the pessimistic rhetoric of the right, denounces

---

[29] Baubérot, Gauthier, Legrand, and Ognier. *Histoire de la laïcité*, 84–85.

[30] Kheir, "D'une laïcité à l'autre."

[31] The author describes them as follows: "a small group, composed of former 48ers, some of whom are Catholic, but most of whom are spiritualists, does in fact oppose the law" (Kheir, "D'une laïcité à l'autre," 31).

[32] Mayyada Kheir underlines however that Paul Bert, himself, as the rapporteur of the law endeavours to be relatively moderate in what he says.

the attacks by atheism and the risks of moral education disconnected from religion. What the analysis by Mayyada Kheir shows is that the word *laïcité*, a term of controversy and compromise all at the same time, becomes indispensable during and by the end of this debate.

The decade 1879–1889 is therefore a decade of glory for the Republicans supporting the initiative for the laicisation of school. It is a period of creative effervescence and programme implementation. The actors of this laicisation are not only politicians or administrative staff; there are also important links and multipliers in favour of laicisation in society: directors of *Ecoles Normales* (which train primary school teachers), directors of the *Ecoles Normales Supérieures* of Fontenay and St Cloud (which train head teachers); teachers' magazines and associations such as the League of Teaching founded in 1866 by Jean Macé. In short, a whole network of very active people, a large number of whom are influenced by liberal Protestantism[33] or at least the (deist) spiritualist movement, in the majority at that time at university (Victor Cousin movement).[34]

Among them, a man whom we have already mentioned breaks away: Ferdinand Buisson (1841–1832), appointed director of primary education upon the arrival of Jules Ferry at the Ministry of Education in 1879 and who remains in this post until 1896. He then succeeds Henri Marion to the newly created Chair of Science and Education at the Sorbonne (1896–1902).[35] But what interests us here is his role as right-hand man of Jules Ferry and his influence because of his long service (seventeen years) in the post of Director of Primary Education and notably through the "Dictionnaire de Pédagogie", a real landmark, the "cathedral of primary school".[36] It may well be difficult to evaluate the real use made of this, but it does seem that the *Dictionnaire* allowed people of authority (directors of the teacher training universities, inspectors) to relay the

---

[33] Cabanel, *Le Dieu de la République.*

[34] Laurence Loeffel shows what "laïque" morality owes to the eclecticism of Victor Cousin as a "laïque" philosophy and his theory of impersonal reason. Loeffel, "La construction spiritualiste".

[35] In voluntary exile in Switzerland under the Second Empire, Buisson had returned to France after the proclamation of the Republic and was first of all appointed "inspector for the primary schools of the Seine", which meant him representing France at the international exhibitions of Vienna (1873) and Philadelphia (1876). His career does not stop at the Sorbonne (radical deputy of Paris in 1902; member of various associations: Human Rights League (1898), of which he is the co-founder; Chairman of the League of Teaching and of the Association of Free Thinkers; he even receives the Nobel Peace Prize in 1927). Cf. Loeffel, *Ferdinand Buisson.*

[36] Nora, *Les lieux de mémoire,* 353.

official discourse on the overhaul of education and from 1882 to work on the Republican socialisation of teachers and student-teachers.[37] So this dictionary contributed to spreading the concept of a religious *laïcité*—of which Buisson, along with others, was a disciple.

At the heart of the debates and reflections marking the first phase of the establishment of laicity in schools surrounding the 1882 law is the question of moral education. "Cette morale à usage scolaire représente l'enjeu le plus important de ce nouveau principe qui s'appelle la laïcité" (These morals for use in school are the most important issue in this new principle called "laicity").[38] This is already very clear, incidentally, when reading the *laïcité* article by Ferdinand Buisson in his "Dictionnaire de pédagogie". How can one teach morals without referring to religious dogma? Does one have to teach morals "laically" or teach "laic" morals? What is God's place in this education? How can this morality be founded? These are all questions that shook up the educational and republican microcosm of the time.

In Ferry's and Buisson's concept, it is not meant to be a matter of substituting one morality with another: apart from not wanting to divide the children, their religious education is considered something already acquired upon which moral education will build. Family, *laïque* schools and Churches are seen as partners in teaching children moral values.[39] Only instituted religion, and notably prayers and religious invocations at the beginning and end of the class were removed from school by law. Religious feeling and the belief in a God creator are included in the syllabus by the "Conseil supérieur de l'Instruction publique", as are the "duties towards God" excluded from the law (on the basis of the rejection by the Senate of the Simon amendment which wanted them included). They remain part of the syllabus until 1923, but empirical studies show that over the course of time they are taught less and less, if at all.[40] For a long time, they are part of the triad "duties towards oneself", "towards others",

---

[37] This is one of the hypotheses formulated by Dubois, *Le Dictionnaire de Ferdinand Buisson*, 224.

[38] Quote by Ognier, *Une école sans Dieu?*, 13. All the specialists of the period agree: the issue of "laïque" morality is "the cornerstone of the republican plan" (Loeffel, *Ferdinand Buisson*, 15), "the spearhead of republican laïcité" (Baubérot), "the sharp edge" of the debates surrounding laïcisation during the final decades of the nineteenth century (Loeffel, *Ferdinand Buisson*, 7).

[39] Ognier, *Une école sans Dieu?*, 150.

[40] Baubérot, *La morale laïque*; Cf. very instructive historical note on these duties towards God until 1941 by Poucet, "Education et religion," 73 (note 6).

"towards God" dear to Janet ("La morale," 1879) which thus influences the new school subject.

According to Buisson, moral education must not just make way for religious feeling, but develop and cultivate it through the conscience, its home. But this is a religious feeling both non-dogmatic and non-confessional. For Buisson, in fact it is in a de-confessionalized Christianity, in a religion without institution and in a faith without dogma that the foundation of morality lies. It is a religion of the Good, the Beautiful and the True whose essence is morality. Utilitarian morality is disqualified in this. Under the influence of Cousinism, it is a philosophy of interiority, of the internal transcendence expressed in that.[41]

The sources that this concept of a religious *laïcité* feeds on are neo-Kantism, spiritualism and above all, the liberal Protestantism or indeed ultraliberal Protestantism of the *Morale indépendante* movement. Furthermore, these neo-Kantian, spiritualist and liberal protestant networks will later play a role not just in "the process of the theoretical and doctrinal elaboration of the new morality", but also in its implementation and monitoring.[42]

Out in the field, the teaching of morality is not without its difficulties. During a survey of the state of disciplines taught at primary school (1889), the inspector Lichtenberger observes (and deplores) a tendency among teachers to present the "laïque" and religious as opposites in their classes. He sees in this an abdication from the initial project. The educational magazines of the time echo the specific problems encountered by teachers, who are ill-prepared for this new task: from being simple repeaters of the catechism, requiring no personal involvement from them, they have assumed the role of moral educators, invested with real moral authority. The Lichtenberger survey reveals that some teachers quite simply do not carry out the new teaching or teach a purely utilitarian morality without inspiration. Another obstacle is the absence of a sincere and deep-seated conviction amongst the majority of teachers. The near general consensus

---

[41] In doing so, God and religion are "internalised to the point of becoming part of human nature" as L. Loeffel underlines, who highlights "the dynamics of secularisation at work here". Loeffel, "La construction spiritualiste," 118.

[42] Ognier, *Une école sans Dieu?*, 14. There is a sort of division of roles, Ferdinand Buisson is the initiator, the general agent, Jules Steeg, is the journalist, the fighter, present at Parliament, Félix Pécaut is the Wiseman, preacher and mystic (Cabanel, *Le Dieu de la République*, 57). He works on the dissemination of the ideal of a "laïque" morality, whilst Henri Marion develops an official theory of the foundation of this morality which lies in the conscience, the source of duty (Loeffel, *Ferdinand Buisson*, 74, 77).

on religious *laïcité* is therefore short-lived according to Pierre Ognier, who from the end of 1893 onwards observes the emergence, even within the educational field itself, of a *laïcité* disassociated from the religious element, echoed again by educational magazines, in which some authors express the need for a new ideal to be defined, the idea of justice, for example.[43]

Other authors also underline a kind of swing towards another type of *laïcité*, more clearly anti-religious this time, in the decade following the introduction of *laïcité* in schools (1890s). What criteria do they propose for justifying this break with the old concept?

- The Masonic lodge, *Grand Orient de France*, starts campaigning against the duties towards God in 1894.[44] Since the 1860s, it has experienced regular growth, but also transforms into a militant Counter Church. In 1877, the mention of the "great architect of the Universe" disappears from its constitution. The search for truth means first rejecting religion.[45]
- 1896 sees the publication of *Solidarité* by Léon Bourgeois, former minister of education (1890; 1898), from the radical movement: his book becomes a new reference work on republican morality. Solidarism is both a legal-scientific concept and a moral value at the same time."[46]
- It is also the era of the triumph of positivism in sociology through the voice of Emile Durkheim (1858–1917).[47] He studies religion as a social fact. In his opinion, a higher level of morality can be achieved by understanding social facts. God is merely the "symbolic expression of society". He bases "laïque" morality on the development of sociology.

This swing seems to be accompanied by the development of moral and civic education in the field, increasingly marked by scientism. Around 1900, moral education is, according to Jean Grech, no longer only devoted to promoting the conscience, but is considered to be the effect of science. Using a three-fold model (mental treatment making use of the development of psychology, hypnosis; hygienism; the instructions of criminologists), the focus is now more on the development of the character and exercise of

---

[43] Ognier, *Une école sans Dieu?*, 156–176.
[44] Baubérot and others, *Histoire de la laïcité*, 118.
[45] Boutry, "Le triomphe de la liberté," 154.
[46] Baubérot and others, *Histoire de la laïcité*, 119.
[47] Ibid., 58 ff.; Cabanel, *Le Dieu de la République*, 241.

will. The figure of the doctor takes the role of philosopher or liberal pastor, as morality becomes a sort of medicine for social ills.[48]

This development is part of a context marked both by the transformation of political forces as of 1890 (electoral success of the radical republicans in 1893 and 1898), the Ralliement policy by the Holy See (and its relative failure with militant Catholics), and the Dreyfus affair. The fear of the Church and important Catholics, in the provinces in particular, regaining influence is firmly entrenched among the republicans who view the interventions by Rome with suspicion. They fear Christian socialism as much as they do clericalism.[49]

Concluding Elements

When viewed from abroad French *laïcité* is often associated with laicism and thus considered anti-religious. Our overview of the last third of the 19th century has allowed us to show that the historical reality is far more complex. In France itself the most recent works by a number of historians during the 1990s/2000s have shed light on a number of "blind spots" in this period and restored its intellectual or empirical nuances. Consequently, we have seen that within the republican movement itself, the driving force behind the initiative of *laïcisation* in education, there are at least three different schools of thought on *laïcité*—religious, areligious and anti-religious.

When the term first emerges, its terminology is still hesitant; there is no unanimity on the term or a reliably coherent use of it. But each camp, whether hostile or not to *laïcité*, seeks to define and even appropriate the term for itself, as Mayyada Kheir has shown. Here, we are dealing not only with interaction between semantics and politics—the semantic battle itself becomes a political issue. Now as then, a "battle surrounding the true meaning" (Fiala) of *laïcité* is still regularly revived.

Above and beyond the different movements identified, the common ground and the powerful driving force behind the actions of the pro-laïcité currents at the time is anticlericalism. This anticlericalism is not

---

[48] Grech, "Les premiers bilans."
[49] Mayeur, *Les débuts de la IIIè République*, 218–222. Following the elections of May 1898, the radicals, supported by the Masonic lodges, want to put an end to the "reactionary and clerical government" and fight "the Black International" Baubérot, *Histoire de la laïcité française*, 72.

"fantastical".[50] It is a response to the very real hold of Catholicism on society, a hold probably at its peak in the area of education especially. And the laws on schooling are also above all a retort, which the republicans regard as indispensable, to the successful campaign previously led by the Catholics for the freedom of education (laws of 1833, 1850, and 1875, establishing freedom in primary, secondary or higher education respectively).[51]

Thus we see that the philosophical logic underlying the phenomena studied, that is, the intrinsic link since the Revolution between the Republic and education also has an empirical, pragmatic dimension. From the philosophical point of view, the line which begins with Condorcet continues with Quinet and Hugo and ends in the "educating Republic". One of the greatest successes of this Third Republic is that many generations are brought up with republican ideals. The school system of this time has also become a myth in France, which persists in the idea of school as a sanctuary or temple of republican universalism.

Let me risk, finally, this concluding hypothesis: in line with the origin of the term, which draws a distinction inside the religious field, the term *laïcité* did not allow them to completely leave the field of the sacred, contrary to the intentions of emancipation and breaking with the past the founding fathers of the Third Republic harboured. With the emergence of *laïcité* as a term, a transfer of sacrality takes place, a new republican and *laïque* form of the sacred is established, a civic religion *à la française*. This explains both the passionate and emotional nature of the debates surrounding it and the fact that the history of *laïcité* in France is far from over: we are seeing a trend towards the "laïcisation de la laïcité".[52] No doubt that goes some way to explaining the appearance of qualifiers such as "laïcité apaisée" (Jean-Paul Willaime), "laïcité d'intelligence" (Régis Debray) and a better alignment of the discourse on *laïcité* with the complex legal reality.[53]

Translated from French by Kathrin Waldie

---

[50] Langlois, "La fin de l'alliance," 123.
[51] Langlois, "La fin de l'alliance," 116. The law of 1875 creates five Catholic institutes.
[52] Willaime, *Europe et religions*, 12, 242, 307.
[53] Public opinion thus seems, for instance, to be more aware that the legal absence of official recognition of particular cults does not mean their existence is denied or dialogue is absent in the political field.

Bibliography

Barbier, Maurice. *La laïcité*. Paris: L'Harmattan, 1995.

Baubérot, Jean. *Histoire de la laïcité française*. Paris: PUF, 2000.

——. *Laïcité 1905–2005. Entre passion et raison*. Paris: Seuil, 2004.

——. *La morale laïque contre l'ordre moral*. Paris: Seuil, 1997.

Baubérot, Jean, Guy Gauthier, Louis Legrand, and Pierre Ognier. *Histoire de la laïcité*. Besançon: CRDP de Franche-Comté, 1994.

Bédouelle, Guy and Jean-Paul Costa. *Les laïcités à la française*. Paris: PUF, 1998.

Boutry, Philippe. "Le triomphe de la liberté de conscience et la formation du parti laïc." In *Histoire de la France religieuse. Vol. 3 Du roi Très Chrétien à la laïcité républicaine XVIIIe siècle-XXe siècle*, edited by Jacques Le Goff, René Rémond. Paris: Points Seuil, 1991/2001.

Buisson, Ferdinand. *Rapport sur l'instruction primaire à l'exposition universelle de Vienne en 1873*. Paris: Imprimerie Nationale, 1875.

Cabanel, Patrick. *Le Dieu de la République. Aux sources protestantes de la laïcité (1860–1900)*. Rennes: Presses universitaires de Rennes, 2003.

Condette, Jean-François, ed. *Education, religion, laïcité (XVIe-XXe siècle). Continuités, tensions et ruptures dans la formation des élèves et des enseignants*. Villeneuve d'Ascq: IRHIS-CEGES, 2010.

Debré, Jean-Louis, ed. *La laïcité à l'école. Un principe républicain à réaffirmer*. Paris: Odile Jacob, 2004.

Dictionnaire de pédagogie et d'instruction primaire. Part 1, vol. 2. Published under the editorial supervision of Ferdinand Buisson. Paris: Hachette, 1887.

Dubois, Patrick. *Le Dictionnaire de Ferdinand Buisson. Aux fondations de l'école républicaine 1878–1911*. Bern: Peter Lang, 2002.

Fiala, Pierre. "Les termes de la laïcité. Différenciation morphologique et conflits sémantiques." *Mots. Les langages du politique*, no. 27 (1991): 41–57.

Grech, Jean. "Les premiers bilans de l'éducation morale laïque en France: 1882–1900." In *Ecole, morale laïque et citoyenneté aujourd'hui*, edited by Laurence Loeffel, pp. 27–35. Villeneuve d'Ascq: Presses universitaires du Septentrion, 2009.

Kheir, Mayyada "D'une laïcité à l'autre: Les débats sur le voile et la mémoire de la loi Ferry." *Historical Reflections* 34, no. 3 (2008): 21–36.

Lalouette, Jacqueline. *La séparation des Eglises et de l'Etat. Genèse et développement d'une idée 1789–1905*. Paris: Seuil, 2005.

——. "Les lois laïques des années 1879–1904, un long prélude à la séparation des Eglises et de l'Etat." In *1905: Séparation des Eglises et de l'Etat. La réception de la loi à Lyon, en France et en Europe*. Publication of the study day by Jean-Pierre Chantin, Musée Gadagne, 12.12.2005. Lyon: Rencontres de Gadagne, 2006.

Langlois, Claude. "Catholiques et laïcs." In *Les lieux de mémoire*, edited by Pierre Nora, vol. 2, pp. 2327–2358. Paris: Gallimard, 1997.

——. "La fin de l'alliance du trône et de l'autel (1789–1880). Politique et religion." In *Histoire de la France religieuse. Vol. 3 Du roi Très Chrétien à la laïcité républicaine XVIIIe siècle-XXe siècle*, edited by Jacques Le Goff, René Rémond. Paris: Points Seuil, 1991/2001.

Loeffel, Laurence. "La construction spiritualiste de la morale laïque." In *Les sources de la morale laïque. Héritages croisés*, edited by Anne-Claire Husser, Bruno Barthelmé, and Nicolas Piqué, pp. 103–121. Lyon: ENS éditions, 2009.

——. *Ferdinand Buisson, apôtre de l'école laïque*. Paris: Hachette, 1999.

Mayeur, Jean-Marie. *La question laïque XIXe-XXe siècles*. Paris: Fayard, 1997.

——. *Les débuts de la IIIe République 1871–1898*. Paris, Seuil, 1973.

Nora, Pierre. *Les lieux de mémoire*, vol. 1: "La République". Paris: Gallimard, 1984.

Ognier, Pierre. *Une école sans Dieu? 1880–1885, L'invention d'une morale laïque sous la IIIe République*. Toulouse: Presses Universitaires du Mirail, 2008.

Poucet, Bruno. "Education et religion." In *Une histoire de l'école. Anthologie de l'éducation et de l'enseignement en France XVIIIe–XXe siècle*, edited by François Jacquet-Francillon. Paris: Retz, 2010.

Poulat, Emile. *Liberté, laïcité. La guerre des deux France et le principe de la modernité*. Paris: Éditions Cujas, 1988.

——. *Notre laïcité publique: "La France est une République laïque" (Constitutions de 1946 et 1958)*. Paris: Berg International, 2003.

——. *Scruter la loi de 1905: La République française et la religion*. Paris: Fayard, 2010.

Rambaud, Thierry. *Le principe de séparation des cultes et de l'Etat en droit public comparé. Analyse comparative des régimes français et allemand*. Paris: LGDJ, 2004.

Toscer-Angot, Sylvie. "Zur Genealogie der Begriffe 'Säkularisierung' und 'Laizität'." In *Religionskontroversen in Frankreich und Deutschland*, edited by Matthias Koenig, and Jean-Paul Willaime, pp. 39–57. Hamburg: Hamburger Edition, 2008.

Traité de droit français des religions, edited by Francis Messner, Pierre-Henri Prélot, and Jean-Marie Woehrling. Paris: Litec, 2003.

Weill, Georges. *Histoire de l'idée laïque en France au XIXe siècle*. Réédition. Paris: Hachette, 2004 (1929).

Willaime, Jean-Paul. *Europe et religions: Les enjeux du XXe siècle*. Paris: Fayard, 2004.

SECULARIZATION, RE-ENCHANTMENT, OR SOMETHING IN BETWEEN? METHODICAL CONSIDERATIONS AND EMPIRICAL OBSERVATIONS CONCERNING A CONTROVERSIAL HISTORICAL IDEA

Volkhard Krech

Säkularisierung—ein moderner Mythos? (2003), this title of a book on the religious situation in Germany published by Detlef Pollack[1] describes in a nutshell the actual state of the ongoing and constantly re-emerging debate on secularization. Some scholars describe the theory of secularization as a 'myth'—despite the question whether the use of the term myth is adequate here—, with which modern society reflects on itself without regard to the 'facts'. Others—the abovementioned Detlef Pollack amongst them—do not share this sceptical view and try to strengthen the notion of secularization in various modifications. However, from the perspective of conceptual history there are no pure facts as such; rather, they are constructed and dealt with in order to describe and evaluate the world we live in.

In his book on the secular Talal Asad[2] presents a genealogy of the secular and of secularism rather than a history of social and societal processes which are generally thought of as 'modern'. He did not want to write a history of secularization, not even a history of it as an idea. Rather, his book intends to be "an exploration of epistemological assumptions of the secular that might help us to be a little clearer about what is involved in the anthropology of secularism".[3] While the secular is "an epistemic category", secularism is a "political doctrine".[4] Asad understands the secular as "a concept that brings together certain behaviours, forms of knowledge, and sensibilities in modern life,"[5] i.e. a notion which has a certain impact on the individual's conduct of life, perceptions and feelings—even on the body. Secularism is a derivate from the secular and is based on the

---

[1] Cf. Pollack, *Säkularisierung—ein moderner Mythos?*; Aubrey, *Secularism*; Comblin, "Säkularisierung."

[2] Cf. Asad, *Formation of the Secular.*

[3] Ibid., 25.

[4] Ibid., 1.

[5] Ibid., 25.

secularization thesis that "in its entirety has always been at once descriptive and normative".[6]

Following Asad's genealogy, one might assume that there is a more complex history of religious development than the secularization thesis suggests, and maybe even a preconception inherent in empirical research on secularization. The secular "is neither continuous with the religious that supposedly preceded it (that is, it is not the latest phase of sacred origin) nor a simple break from it (that is, it is not the opposite, an essence that excludes the sacred)."[7] From this perspective the ambiguity of the secular and of secularism arises—whether or not one accepts secularization as a given 'fact' or tries to substitute it by confronting ideas such as 're-sacralization' or 're-enchantment'[8] or the idea of a post-secular society.[9] These notions are still just negative affirmations of the idea of secularization.

On the one hand, the epistemic concept of the secular and the derived doctrine of secularism are contingent social constructions which—once they are in the world—have influence on our behaviour, feelings and cognitions. But on the other hand, there is no doubt that analytical notions of process are necessary within social sciences in general and religious studies in particular to grasp larger historical developments. If the socio-cultural reality were just to be recognized as a continuum, there would be no change and as such no history and *ergo* no historical consciousness. In consequence: If everything were just in flow, we could not perceive anything in its historic dimension. Notions and concepts—including the ideas of process—are necessary for perception and knowledge; this is a philosophical commonplace. A notion—if it is not to be understood as a scientific positivism—represents the condensation of a question at hand. Thus, concepts structure the empirical reality as well as research-programs provisionally and have to be modified or replaced, if different questions emerge. Even if they are basic ideas, fundamental terms, they represent a question which only arose in its historical setting. This historicity of questions urges us to recognize that "the history of phenomena is foremost a history of the controversial explanation of these phenomena".[10] This

---

[6] Ibid., 181.

[7] Ibid., 25.

[8] Ibid.; Berman, *Reenchantment of the world*; Isenberg, "Konsum als Religion?"

[9] Cf. Habermas, *Glauben und Wissen*; Eder, "Europäische Säkularisierung."

[10] Graf, "'Dechristianisierung'," 33.

statement is true of all phenomena, but especially so of religious ones and as such of the idea of secularization and the questions inherent in it.

Herrmann Lübbe presented in detail the politics of ideas concerning the notion of secularization,[11] while Herrmann Zabel and Ulrich Ruth described secularization as a "category of interpretation".[12] Numerous sociologists of religion, first among them Thomas Luckmann in the 1960s and many social scientists and historians with him, doubt the concept of secularization in part or generally—to name just a few: Sarah Williams, Stephen Yeo, Jeffrey Cox and Linda Woodhead. Other historians like Hugh McLeod[13] and sociologists like Bryan Wilson, Steve Bruce[14] and, in Germany, Detlef Pollack, for example, still think of secularization as a productive idea. In the French-speaking area the word *déchristianisation* (dechristianization) is used instead of secularization, and Hartmut Lehmann suggested analyzing the interactions between the ideas of processes of secularization, dechristianization and rechristianization.[15] The ideas of the de-institutionalization of religion and the processes of diffusion of religion would have to be added to Lehmann's advice.

The heuristical power of the secularization concept depends on what is to be understood by its idea. In its strongest version the concept of secularization suggests nothing less than the unilinear, irresistible and irreversible process of religion losing all of its significance—from marginalization to complete annihilation. Responsible for this is the universal and equally irresistible and irreversible process of rationalization, according to which everything is reduced to being just a question of (intentional) accountability. Or to phrase this in accordance with the history of semantics: The complex and historically speaking rather dynamic relation between divine forethought and individual trial has changed into matter-of-fact appreciation of risks. The most radical concept of secularization combines this idea with a strong optimism toward progress, according to which the rational world view means nothing less than total emancipation from religious dependency. Another notion in this radical concept is the idea of the deterioration of good morals and social cohesion due to

---

[11] Lübbe, *Säkularisierung*.
[12] Cf. Zabel, *Verweltlichung/Säkularisierung*; Ruh, *Säkularisierung als Interpretationskategorie*; As far as the philosophical view in general is concerned: cf. Jaeschke, *Wurzeln der Geschichtsphilosophie*; Jaeschke and Laeyendecker, "Säkularisierung/Säkularismus"; Jaeschke, "Säkularisierung."
[13] Cf. McLeod, "Comparing Secularisations: Germany and Britain."
[14] Cf. Bruce, *God is Dead*.
[15] Cf. Lehmann, *Säkularisierung, Dechristianisierung, Rechristianisierung*.

religion's loss of significance in modernity. In both assumptions modernity and religion are considered incompatible. Thus, religion functions as the negative blueprint for the concept of modernity.

Even if there is some empirical evidence of this characterization during the intellectual history of modern times, it still seems an exaggeration. If such a strong concept of secularization is purported dogmatically, it becomes mere ideology. Accordingly, this narrow concept has been softened in several modifications. The outcome of this modification process, however, is secularization describing the development of religion in modern times as (a) an ongoing process and not as seasonal fluctuations during the course of which (b) religion no longer has the importance which was formerly ascribed to it (not taking into account the question if religion really had more significance in earlier times).[16] José Casanova has presented perhaps the most severely analytical considerations on the secularization thesis.[17] He points to three elements in that thesis, all of which have been taken to be essential to the development of modernity: (1) increasing structural (functional) societal differentiation,[18] (2) the privatization of religion, and (3) the declining social significance of religious belief. Casanova holds that only the first and third elements are viable.

I do not plan to add another definition of secularization. Instead I would like to take up Asad's definition of the secular as an "epistemic concept" and in the same instant to present some empirical observations on the social and societal history of religions—being aware of Asad's examination of the role statistical representation has played in creating the world of modern power that social scientists inhabit.[19] On the one hand, I agree with Asad's methodology of genealogy: We have to sharpen the scientific understanding of the problem of handling the idea of secularization within scientific and public discourses. Thus, I will point out some dimensions that have to be distinguished when dealing with the question of secularization and present some considerations concerning the interaction between the history of religions, social history, and the history of semantics. On the other hand, just reflecting on the constructions and conducting discourse analysis might be insufficient. If epistemic

---

[16] With Lucian Hölscher one should rather assume that the European societies of the 18th century had an ideational affiliation with religion; cf. Hölscher, "Religion des Bürgers," 597.

[17] Cf. Casanova, *Public Religions.*

[18] According to David Martin the concept of social differentiation has been its "most useful element" (Martin, *On Secularization,* 20).

[19] Cf. Asad, "Ethnographic Representation."

concepts—and as such the secular—have impacts upon people's behavior—this is what Asad states—, we have to look for quantitative indicators in order to be able to measure them und thus evaluate their relevance. We certainly cannot take quantitative data as a simple copy of reality, since quantitative as well as qualitative data, such as texts, are much less complex than the social practice they represent. However, we need a heuristic epistemology of the "empirical reality" behind or followed by the epistemic concept of the secular. Therefore, in a second step I use the methodical considerations to generate some indicators for measuring secularization, which will then lead to some empirical observations. The data stem from the history of religious development in Germany—with some insight into the twentieth century as far as the empirical data permits such an endeavour.

The Interaction between the History of Religions, Social History, and the History of Semantics

In the beginning there was the history of religions. At least this is what the nineteenth century theory of pansacrality argues, according to which the entire societal and cultural development stems from religion. This theory is still in effect today but is becoming more and more problematic. Whatever one's position in regard to the question of the chronological origin of society and culture, one cannot deny that the history of religions can no longer be looked at from an inside perspective, as the phenomenology of religion has done for so long.[20] The idea that religion is based on culture and society goes back to ancient Greece. The social and political function of religion is referred to in the "Fragment des Kritias",[21] by Polybios in his *Historiae*,[22] by Cicero in *De natura deorum*[23] and by Livius in his *Ab Urbe Condita*.[24] All these texts were used in the seventeenth and eighteenth century as basis for a controversy which tried to establish philosophical atheism with just these abovementioned arguments.[25] Religion was understood and denoted as an element of oppression. The

---

[20] Cf. Lanczkowski, *Einführung in die Religionswissenschaft*, 77, who describes religion as a phenomenon resting in itself, sui generis.

[21] Diels, Kranz, *Fragmente der Vorsokratiker*, B25.

[22] Polybius, *Historiae* VI, 56.6–12.

[23] Cicero, *De natura deorum* I, 118.

[24] Livius, *Ab Urbe Condita* I, 19.4.

[25] Cf. Schröder, *Ursprünge des Atheismus*.

theory of religion as a fraud perpetuated by deceitful priests—which can be traced back to Herbert of Cherbury (1583–1648), the founder of the concept of 'natural religion'—belongs to this line of thinking. This normative discourse is to be distinguished from the scholarly research in the field of religious developments from the point of view of social history and sociology. Around 1900, scholars like Émile Durkheim, Max Weber, Ernst Troeltsch and Georg Simmel started placing the history of religions in the context of socio-historical developments. Nowadays the idea that religious thought is only self-reliant seems absurd.

The connection between history of religions and social history, however, is not a one-way street as historical materialism suggests. This concept has its followers in the social sciences even nowadays, although it lacks the political verve. Religion is sometimes still looked upon as an ideological superstructure, which is determined by the predominant political and economic motives and at the same time conceals them. All of the classical sociologists of religion had a different view. To paraphrase Georg Simmel, their idea was to build a floor just underneath historical materialism.[26] To measure up to the complexity of socio-cultural reality, one has to determine the interconnections between the history of religions and social history: "Without an understanding of religious change in modern society . . . there can be no reliable social history."[27] Max Weber determined the relationship between ideas and interests, whereby the ideas are the basis for successfully attending to ones interests while interests are the historically significant forces;[28] both can be dependent or independent variables in a research setting. In the same way the history of religions is connected with social history and vice versa.

---

[26] It is the intention of Georg Simmel's *Philosophie des Geldes*, "dem historischen Materialismus ein Stockwerk unterzubauen, derart, daß der Einbeziehung des wirtschaftlichen Lebens in die Ursachen der geistigen Kultur ihr Erklärungswert gewahrt wird, aber eben jene wirtschaftlichen Formen selbst als das Ergebnis tieferer Wertungen und Strömungen, psychologischer, ja, metaphysischer Voraussetzungen erkannt werden" (Frisby and Köhnke, *Simmel. Philosophie des Geldes*, 13).

[27] "Ohne das Verständnis des religiösen Wandels in der modernen Gesellschaft ist . . . eine verläßliche Sozialgeschichte nicht möglich." Schieder, "Religion in der Sozialgeschichte," 25.

[28] Cf. Weber, *Gesammelte Aufsätze zur Religionssoziologie*, 252: "Interessen (materielle und ideelle) nicht: Ideen, beherrschen unmittelbar das Handeln der Menschen. Aber: die 'Weltbilder', welche durch 'Ideen' geschaffen werden, haben sehr oft als Weichensteller die Bahnen bestimmt, in denen die Dynamik der Interessen das Handeln fortbewegte." (interests (material and ideal) not ideas rule men's acting? / actions? But the world views which are created by these ideas have very often led the way for the dynamics of interests which finally ruled men's acting? / actions?)

Beyond the relationship between the history of religions and social history there is the history of semantics with its inner- and outer-religious aspects. In historical research this dimension is pursued by approaches like history of ideas, notions, and concepts as well as by discourse analysis.[29] A possible complement to this arsenal of methods is Klaus Heinrich's concept of *Faszinationsgeschichte* (the history of fascinations). The history of semantics recognizes that religious ideas and concepts change, that the meaning of religious notions varies in different contexts and that even the concept of religion itself is constantly changing. Religion and related notions such as religiosity, piety, faith, asceticism, mysticism, and ritual are part of an ongoing process of reflection—both from outside the religious field and from an inside perspective.

Many parts of the societal self-description and reflection have been taken over by the social sciences during the course of modernity. Our world views have been shaped by them, and this has had an impact on the history of religions as well. But, as the connection between social history and the history of religions has shown, there is no linear or even one-way effect. Modern practice of reflection stems from and has been stimulated by the history of religions. Thus, in the relation between the history of semantics in general and the history of religions there are strong interactions (see fig. 1).

From the perspective of the social sciences all three dimensions can be described as a relation according to the sociology of knowledge: Religious semantics and processes of reflection on the one hand and socio-structural and societal developments on the other hand influence each other. In sociology the question of the temporal succession of semantic and socio-structural developments is being discussed.[30] This can be understood as a follow-up to the dispute concerning the alternative between idealistic and materialistic perspective. As I stated above, the idea of reciprocal influence shows that this dispute is nothing more than a proverbial catch-22 situation, comparable to the chicken or egg problem. As ever, only empirical research can help to answer the question of causation in its respective context. Furthermore, the relationship between two of the three dimensions can be mediated by the third, i.e. the relation between the history of religions and the history of semantics by social history and so on. As the diagram tries to show, this is a circuit which works in both directions.

---

[29] Cf. e.g. Bödeker, *Begriffsgeschichte, Diskursgeschichte, Metapherngeschichte.*
[30] Cf. Stäheli, "Die Nachträglichkeit der Semantik."

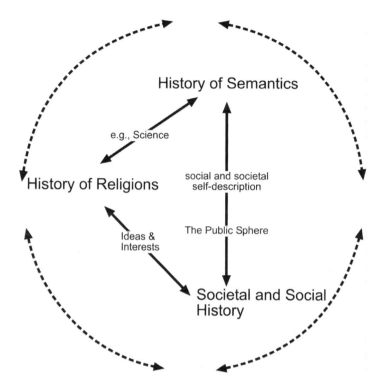

Fig. 1: The circle of history of religions, semantics, and societal processes.

I would now like to apply this model to the topic of secularization. I will not attempt to answer the question of secularization with one of the options I have outlined above, but rather approach the matter of secularization from the circle of reciprocal influence between the history of semantics, the history of religions and social history—and as such relate the discourse on secularization to socio-structural and societal developments.

Indicators for Measuring Secularization

In order to answer the question of the heuristic potency of the concept of secularization in its minimal version and its adequateness concerning socio-cultural reality, one has to establish which indicators are adequate for measuring secularization. If the concept of secularization has more than just a hermeneutical function for the self-description of modernity,

	religious history	social history	history of ideas and reflection
individual	human being as a divine medium or tool	privatization	personality, subjectivity
institution / organization	e.g., church as the body of Christ	religious organizations as bureaucratic entities	loss of relevance or intermediate entities?
society	world rejection or world domination	religion as an autonomous societal sphere with interferences to others	relation between religion and modernity

Fig. 2: Matrix of different levels of conceptualization.

then it should be possible to operationalize and thereby prove it.[31] Quite a few suggestions on how to operationalize the measurement of secularization have been made,[32] and I do not want to simply add another one. Rather, I would like to focus on different dimensions of secularization, which I will derive from the history of religions, social history and the history of semantics.

In order to operationalize secularization, I suggest not only to distinguish between the abovementioned methodical triad, but also between three social dimensions, namely the individual, institutional-organizational and the societal dimension (as known as the distinction between the micro, meso, and macro level). Together with the methodical dimensions, the following matrix results. For a better understanding I will restrict myself to some prominent examples mentioned in figure 2.

Actually, the matrix is more complex than this, because the methodical and the social dimensions are interdependent concerning the topic of secularization. The matrix should therefore be three-dimensional and in

---

[31] Cf. Dobbelaere, *Secularisation. A multi-dimensional Concept*; Dobbelaere, *Secularisation. An Analysis at three Levels*; Jagodzinski, "Säkularisierung und religiöser Glaube"; Pollack, *Säkularisierung*.

[32] Cf. e.g. Pollack, *Säkularisierung*.

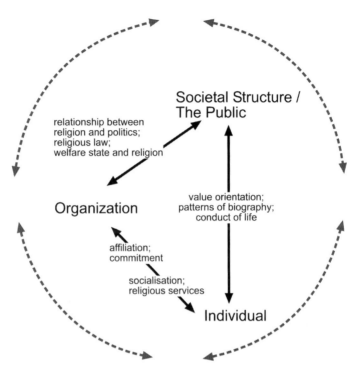

Fig. 3: The circle of the individual, organizational, and societal level.

its third dimension interdependent concerning the relation between the social and methodical dimensions. Not only is such a matrix difficult to depict, it would probably not serve to clarify things. I therefore restrict myself to giving some examples of interdependencies between individuals, institutions and the societal dimension. The methodical triad is always implied, as shown in figure 3.

Examples of the relationship between individuals and religious organizations are on the one hand types of affiliation and commitment. In accordance with these criteria Weber developed his contrast-typology between church and sect. Whereas the church as agency of salvation and grace relies on formal membership and not on emphatic affiliation or commitment, the sect on the other hand is dependent on these two. However, organizations also affect personal attitudes and actions via socialization. Furthermore, they provide services for people, for example worship and pastoral care.

The relationship between individual and society can be described by the terms value orientation, patterns of biography and conduct of life.

These can be imparted by organizations or institutions, but also exist relatively independent of organizations and more or less institutionally.

Examples of the relation between organizations and society are the relation of religion and politics, constellations of religious law, and the welfare state of Western democracies as a possible secular expression of religious ethics.

Just as the relationship between individual and society can be shaped institutionally or organizationally, the relation between institutions or organizations can be mediated by individuals, which is the case especially in times of societal change when institutions lose plausibility and stability and become obsolete, or during the history of religions in situations of religious change or new beginnings. Weber calls this the *"status nascendi"*, the state in which religious ideas start to work via charismatic persons. This, too, is a circuit with two directions.

The following indicators for measuring secularization can be deduced from this model:

- The religious attitudes, orientations or values of persons and types of religious conducts of life, including styles of religiosity and piety; social strata, movements and specific milieus are of special interest;
- the normative power and societal relevance of religious institutions (like religious rituals);
- the number of members, the degree of affiliation and the societal influence of religious organizations, movements and groups;
- the importance of religion for the structure of society, as well as the relevance of religion in other societal spheres and the public.

These indicators certainly do not represent a complete list of all possibilities for measuring secularization but are rather an assemblage of representative examples of three social dimensions and their interrelation. To use these indicators as a basis for measuring secularization would require an extensive research program. I will therefore only use a select few of this exemplary collection of indicators.

I will concentrate on *measurable* indicators and as such on the 'visible' religion—except when dealing with indicators for religion's societal significance in the last part of this paper. The 'invisible', individual types of religiosity can hardly be measured by a quantitative approach and are extremely difficult to grasp in a scientific setting. Therefore, individual religiosity cannot be used to show long-term effects of secularization or religious diversity. I will restrict myself to the religious situation in

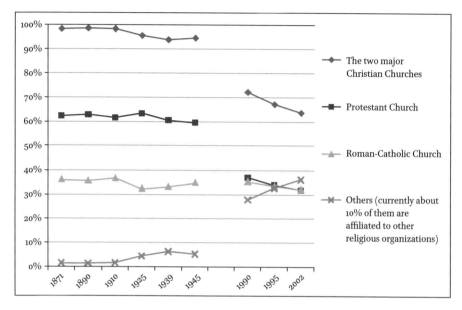

Fig. 4: Religious affiliation in the *"Kaiserreich"* (German Empire), the *"Weimarer Republik"* (Weimar Republic), the *"Dritte Reich"* (3rd Reich), and the Reunited Germany after 1990.

Germany during the twentieth century, as far as the empirical data is available.

Membership and Affiliation to the Church

First, I want to look at the general statistic of religion in the twentieth century, especially at the rough indicator of formal church membership (see fig. 4), namely the public interest in the *"Institut der christlichen Kirche"* (Institution of the Christian Church), as the theologian Karl Gottlieb Bretschneider defined *Kirchlichkeit* (church affiliation).[33]

The graphic shows religious affiliation to the Protestant and Roman Catholic Church during the *"Kaiserreich"* (German Empire), the *"Weimarer Republik"* (Weimar Republic), the *"Dritte Reich"* (3rd Reich), and in reunited Germany until 2002. The two major German churches together show no significant change in their number of members until 1910. From then on membership dropped until 1940. From 1910 until 1925 the Catholic Church

---

[33] Cf. Graf, " 'Dechristianisierung'," 47.

lost members, while the Protestant Church gained more members. This trend changes between 1925 and 1939. The biggest difference concerning membership in the two major German churches was seen between 1945 and 2002, which is hardly surprising. It is well known that Protestantism in the German Democratic Republic (GDR) lost many, if not most, of its members due to socialism and state-decreed atheism. The Roman Catholic Church was not as severely affected during this period. A comparison of religious affiliation in Eastern Germany at specific moments in time illustrates this quite clearly (see fig. 5):

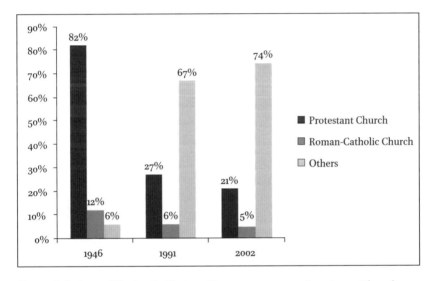

Fig. 5: Religious affiliation in Eastern Germany, a comparison in 1946/1991/2002.

While in 1946 members of the Protestant Church in the GDR still accounted for 81.6 per cent of the population, in 1991 they only represented twenty-seven per cent and in 2002 just 21.18 per cent of the East German population. The members of the Roman Catholic Church represented 12.2 per cent of the population in 1946, six per cent in 1991 and 5.08 per cent in 2002. The reason why religious politics in the GDR hit the Protestant Church so hard is simply that it was the major religious organization in Eastern Germany. While the Protestant Church lost seventy-four per cent of its members between 1946 and 2002, the Catholic Church lost fifty-eight per cent.

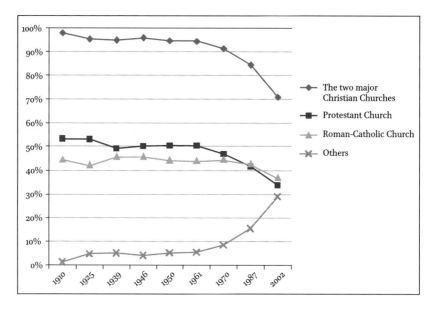

Fig. 6: Religious affiliation in West Germany between 1900 and 2002.

Thus, religious politics in the GDR had a strong influence on the statistics of church membership. However, this circumstance is not a
factor of secularization as a loss of religion's significance in the process of
a structural and thus unavoidable societal development. Religious politics
in the GDR are not part of structural development in modern society but a
cultural factor; religious politics are a *Weltanschauungskampf* (ideological
question), based on Marxist atheism. And as atheism can be understood
as a system of belief, religious politics in the GDR are part of the modern
history of religions. With regard to the topic of secularization it is necessary to isolate and analyze the factor of religious politics. I cannot do
so in this paper as the empirical material has not been prepared—if it
even exists. Important work has been done in this field by Kurt Nowack,
Jochen-Christoph Kaiser and Detlef Pollack. I will restrict myself to the
former Federal Republic of Germany (FRG) and the material available.

The statistics of church membership show that the two major churches
in the FRG experienced no significant change in membership from the end
of WW2 to the 1960s (see fig. 6).[34] When one church loses members, the

---

[34] Source of data: Kirchliche Jahrbücher (church statistics); Zentralstelle für Kirchliche
Statistik des Katholischen Deutschland; own analysis.

other one gains members. At the end of the 1960s the situation changed. At first only the Protestant Church loses a substantial number of members. At the beginning of the 1990s this likewise happens to the Roman Catholic Church. As this loss of members cannot be explained by religious politics in the GDR alone, I will take a closer look at a second indicator, namely movements encouraging people to leave the church (known as "Austrittsbewegungen").

Church Exit

In 1788 the "Wöllnersche Religionsedikt" (Edict on religion of 1788) allowed people in Germany to change their confession. Six years later in the "Allgemeine Preußische Landrecht" (General state laws for the Prussian states) freedom of conscience was acknowledged, and so the legal basis for church exit was laid. With the establishment of the register of births, marriages and deaths in 1874 in the whole of the Reich, church exit finally started to become evident. However, several edicts and decrees concerning fees, fiscal exoneration and suchlike stopped church exit abruptly. Not until the end of the nineteenth century did liberal religious law start to show effects.

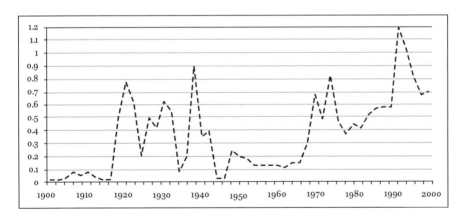

Fig. 7: Church exits from the Protestant Church in the *"Kaiserreich"* (German Empire), the *"Weimarer Republik"* (Weimar Republic), the *"Dritte Reich"* (Third Reich), and Reunited Germany, 1900–2000.[35]

---

[35] Source of data: Kirchliche Jahrbücher (church statistics).

Between 1884 and 1949, during the course of fifty-five years, approximately five million people in Germany left the Protestant Church (see fig. 7). This is equivalent to seventeen per cent of its members at the beginning of the period. The same number left the church between 1970 and 2000, during the course of just thirty years. These, too, represent seventeen per cent of its members at the beginning of the period. From 1906 just minor movement in the statistic of church exit is evident. From 1906 until 1914 organized church exit first took place.[36] This movement was essentially initiated by the Free Thinkers. As the church spoke out against social democrats and the workers' movement, these groups also started advocating church exit. In the words of Hans-Ulrich Wehler, people could get the impression that the church was turning towards the well affluent middle classes and the masters in their manor-houses rather than towards the peasant labourers and the exploited in the cities.[37] By leaving the church, one could express opposition towards the state in a relatively safe way. But even politically active Christians were disappointed with the church and joined movements advocating church exit. A prominent example is Paul Göhre, former vicar, factory labourer and friend of Max Weber.

Apart from ideological and political motives, financial reasons played an important role. The new law of 14 July 1905 on the financing of the churches in Prussia required more families, especially from the working class, to pay church taxes. As soon as the state was legally allowed to have insight into the actual income of the workers, many more workers had to pay taxes. Therefore, in 1908 the statistics on church exit show an increase of 118.9 per cent. This is clear evidence that not only ideological motives but also financial and other socio-historical conditions have to be considered in order to interpret the statistics.

At the end of the First World War the number of people leaving the church rose rapidly on an unprecedented scale. Parallel to this the Free Thinker Movement grew: In 1932 the Free Thinkers associations had about 800,000 members. They were primarily located in the centres of the workers movement, for example, in Saxony, Thuringia, the Rhineland and Westphalia.

---

[36] Cf. Göhre, *Die neueste Kirchenaustrittsbewegung*; Pfender, *Kirchenaustritt und Kirchenaustrittsbewegung*; Ermel, *Die Kirchenaustrittsbewegung*; Feige, *Kirchenaustritte*; Institut für Demoskopie Allensbach, *Kirchenaustritte*.

[37] Wehler, *Das Deutsche Kaiserreich*, 119.

When in 1933 the National Socialists came to power, the number of people leaving the church declined, and people started to join the churches again. To strengthen their position within the population the National Socialists had given the impression that they were in favour of church-friendly politics. They claimed "positive Christendom" and actually staged services—eventually in uniform.

After national-socialist church politics failed in 1934 and the "Reich" removed its foreign-political gloves after 1936, the number of people leaving the churches rose rapidly. The effect of this was even more noticeable than in the first years of the Weimar Republic. During the Second World War membership declined, as it did during the First World War. An all-time low was reached in 1945. After the end of the war the churches took over various important functions in the process of denazification and began and run social welfare organizations. As the churches were deemed to have been relatively 'innocent' and many people were looking for spiritual orientation after the war, the number of people (re-)joining churches grew. When in 1949 circumstances approached normalcy, the number of people leaving the churches rose again.

Between 1950 and 1967—a time of economical and societal consolidation which was coupled with restorative tendencies in many areas of society—the number of church exits remained low. A rapid rise of these numbers occurred at the end of the 1960s. In contrast to the years between 1906 and 1914 or after 1918 this development was attributable to deep structural change in society based on cultural developments and mental adjustments within the population of West Germany, which can accurately be described by the terms liberalization and individualization. Such a process set the potential free to criticize institutions—an occurrence which of course did not fail to target the churches as well.

The surge of people leaving the churches around 1970 is probably the only secularization movement of an organized religion that reflects structural change in society due to modernization independent of ideology or at least in addition to it. There is a strong correlation with a fundamental change in value orientation, which has been extensively covered in research. I want to give just one example, namely the decrease of acceptance of seemingly outdated values as an indicator for criticizing institutions.

Figure 8 shows a correlation between the receding level of church affiliation and the decreasing willingness to integrate oneself into a fixed order. The effects of the individualized conduct of life relate to an increasing

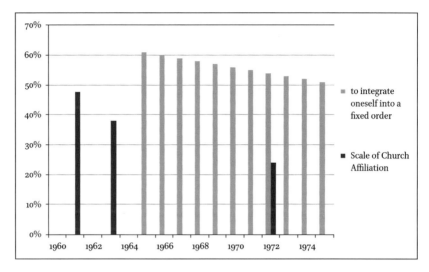

Fig. 8: Church affiliation and change in value orientation.[38]

distance to the church organization.[39] The sharpest rise in church exits can be seen in 1991. This is due to the so-called "Solidaritätszuschlag" (Solidarity Surcharge), a tax levied in the West of Germany to fund development in the East; it prompted people on a low income to save on church taxes.

The reasons for the church exits—with the exception of the developments at the end of the 1960s—can be summarized as social, political, economical, and cultural. The decreasing number of church members is therefore not necessarily part of a process of modernization but to a great extent just based on interest groups and therefore of a contingent nature.

Taking Part in Church Life

Theological church statistics of the 19th century already used participation in Sunday service and communion as the most important indicator for 'true religiosity'. I will now refer to communion statistics to exemplify participation in church life—not for theological reasons or consideration of church politics but rather for sociological reasons: As Lucian Hölscher

---

[38] Source of data: Allensbach Institute; Kaufmann, "Kirchlichkeit."
[39] This, however, says nothing about religiosity in general.

mentions in his "Datenatlas" (2003),[40] participation in communion is an indicator for *genuine religious* participation in church life in contrast to participation at baptisms or funerals, which may simply be motivated by conventional thinking. The communion statistics for the Protestant Church in Germany show the following results:[41]

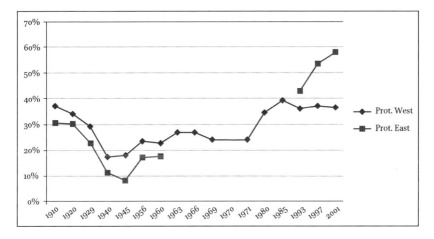

Fig. 9: Communion statistics for the Protestant Church in Germany, 1910–2001.

Between 1910 and 1945 attendance at communion declined rapidly (see fig. 9). In the 1960s it levelled out at about twenty-five per cent. In the 1980s attendance suddenly increased dramatically and levelled out until the present day. A possible reason for this increase is a strong interest in ritual performances in addition to rites of passage. Rituals are obviously not only to be celebrated traditionally but with a concentration on the religious dimension. The large numbers for Eastern Germany strengthen the hypothesis that the church in Eastern Germany is more dependent on its members' declaration of belief and religious interaction than the church in Western Germany. Secularization appears in a different light once qualitative aspects such as religious actions are taken into account in addition to statistics on church membership.

---

[40] Cf. Hölscher, *Datenatlas zur religiösen Geographie.*
[41] Source of data: Kirchliche Jahrbücher (church statistics); own analysis.

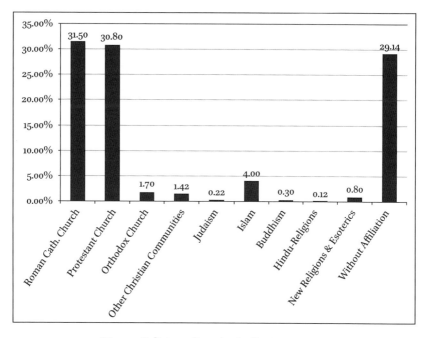

Fig. 10: Religious diversity in Germany, 2005.

Religious Pluralism versus Secularization?

The situation of religious pluralism in the USA inspired market- and rational-choice theoreticians to coin the idea that European secularization is a product of state churches, while the free religious market leads to increasing religiosity.[42] Independent of this assumption, the idea that declining numbers of church members do not necessarily reflect a decline in religiosity is certainly true. Therefore in the German situation the question arises concerning the identity of those I named 'others' in the graphic above.[43] The corresponding statistics are virtually impossible to create, as the statistical data over the years have used widely differing categories[44] and are furthermore rather rough and do not adequately meet the requirements for measuring religious diversity.

---

[42] For this dicussion cf. Young, *Rational Choice*.
[43] On religious pluralism in Germany cf. Wolf, "Religiöse Pluralisierung".
[44] On this problem cf. Ziegler, "Das Religionsverzeichnis".

Figure 10 shows religious statistics for Germany in 2005.[45] One can clearly see that religious diversity is increasing—at the moment there are at least 200 religious communities and systems of faith recorded in Germany.[46] However, the personal interest in religion—as far as membership or affiliation is concerned—is not rising. The number of non-denominationals is rising instead—not only in Eastern Germany. While the members of all religious groups without the two major Christian churches are just 7.3 per cent of the population, the number of non-denominationals is roughly twenty-eight per cent.

How does this help with the question of secularization? It is rather difficult—as mentioned above—to compare religious communities over time. One can, however, say that according to the internal statistics of the smaller religious communities, religion in its organizational form has declined quantitatively regardless of religious diversity. This can be the basis for some conclusions concerning the relation between religious organizations and individuals. The significance of organized religion in society cannot be deduced from this data.[47] Furthermore, it cannot be said that religiosity loses significance with the decline of organized religion. This takes us to the next indicator: religiosity in contrast to church affiliation.[48]

Religiosity versus Church Affiliation?

Since Thomas Luckmann coined the term 'invisible religion' in the 1960s—and from a theological point of view even as early as Friedrich Schleiermacher around 1900—the individual and deinstitutionalized forms of religiosity have come under scrutiny. Sociologists discuss the question whether the paradigm of individualization should replace the idea of

---

[45] This data is based on official statistics of the religious communities and on material accumulated by the *Religionswissenschaftlicher Medien- und Informationsdienst* in Marburg analysed by myself.

[46] My team and I recently conducted research on religious diversity in North Rhine-Westphalia, with North Rhine-Westphalia being the German federal state with the highest number of migrants and the Ruhr area within North Rhine-Westphalia being the largest metropolitan area in Europe. We have collected data on 228 religious communities and movements; for details cf.: www.religion-plural.org (accessed September 24, 2012).

[47] On the societal relevance of religious organizations cf. Geser, "Zwischen Anpassung, Selbstbehauptung und politischer Agitation."

[48] On operationalizing the dimensions religiosity and church affiliation cf. Höhmann, Krech, "Die vierte Kirchenmitgliedschaftsuntersuchung"; Höhmann, Krech, "Kirchenmitgliedschaft".

secularization.[49] So participation and affiliation as indicators for religiosity have to be complemented by other indicators. One of these can be the personal attitude towards questions or problems arising from religion.[50]

As a first indicator I want to refer to the question how many people deem themselves religious. A sociological survey from 2002[51] presents the following data:

		Valid per cent	
not religious		22,6%	
	−1−		
	−2−	8,6%	
	−3−	7,8%	
	−4−	4,0%	
	−5−	9,5%	
rather not religious			52,50%
	−6−	8,3%	
	−7−	11,1%	
	−8−	11,7%	
	−9−	6,9%	
religious −10−		9,5%	
rather religious			47,50%

Fig. 11: Degree of religiosity among the German Population in 2002.

According to these data 47.5 per cent of the German population think of themselves as rather religious, 52.5 per cent as rather not religious (see fig. 11). With regard to the studies on the change of value orientation conducted by Ronald Inglehart, this value has been a little higher in Western democracies over the last twenty years, namely fifty-five per cent.[52] However, the question arises what has been measured by such an indicator: Is this really the attitude towards religion or is it rather the expectations that are linked to orthopraxis? For this reason I will use the question of the importance of church and religion as a second indicator.

---

[49] Cf. Pollack and Pickel, "Individualisierung und religiöser Wandel"; Wohlrab-Sahr, Krüggeler, "Strukturelle Individualisierung"; Pollack, Pickel, "Religiöse Individualisierung statt Säkularisierung?"

[50] The problem is that the empirical material has only been available since the 1960s and 1970s.

[51] "Allgemeine Bevölkerungsumfrage in den Sozialwissenschaften" (ALLBUS).

[52] Inglehart, Minkenberg, "Transformation religiöser Werte", 136 ff.

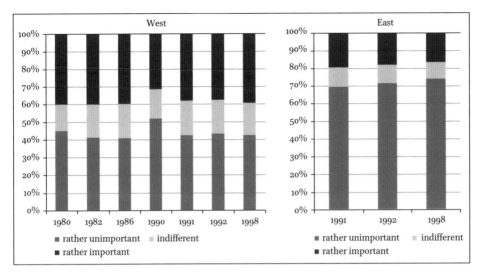

Fig. 12: Importance of Church and religion between 1980 and 2000.[53]

As was to be expected, there are large differences between the East and West German population. While fourty per cent of the people in the Western parts of Germany regard religion and church as important, only eighteen per cent of the East Germans think likewise. Processes of religious socialization have been largely abandoned here—for a long time now. What I want to focus on is the fact that the statistics and accordingly the attitude towards the church have been roughly the same for the last twenty years in Western Germany.

Though these numbers give a rather undisputed insight into the attitude towards religion and church, one has to ask what has been measured by the indicator named 'general religiosity'. While formal membership is probably too rough an indicator, measuring general religiosity is not specific enough. Therefore I would suggest taking concrete questions and statements of belief into account:

[53] Source of data: "Allgemeine Bevölkerungsumfrage in den Sozialwissenschaften" (ALLBUS).

	Valid per cent
Theistic belief	23
(Item: There is a personal god)	
General belief	31
(Item: There is a higher being or a higher spiritual power)	
Agnostics or undecided	15
(Item: I do not know what to believe)	
Atheism	31
(Item: I do not believe in a personal god, a higher being or a spiritual power.)	
Total	100

Fig. 13: Statements of belief among the German population in 2002.

According to the ALLBUS questionnaire of 2002, about twenty-three per cent share a theistic faith and thirty-one per cent believe in a general transcendent authority (see fig. 13); fifteen per cent are agnostic or undecided and some thirty per cent embrace atheism. There are good reasons to call atheism a system of faith. Atheists do not believe, but rather believe in the nonexistence of a transcendent authority. If we chose to ignore this, fifty-four per cent of the population can be classed as faithful and the other fourty-six per cent are agnostics, undecided or atheists. Unfortunately, we do not have such data for the first half of the twentieth century, and the data we have from the 1960s and 1970s are not comparable to the data shown above. There is, however, research done by Pippa Norris and Ronald Inglehart which provides ample evidence to assume that these data have been more or less constant between 1980 and today.[54] As such one cannot speak of secularization as the general loss of significance of religion during this period.

Societal Presence of Religion

In a further step I would like to deal with the sixth indicator, namely the societal presence of religion, beyond the personal and organizational dimension. When taking a closer look at societal public sphere, it becomes quite clear that secularization is born from modern society, beyond and maybe even independent of empirical evidence. Anyhow, the

[54] Cf. Norris and Inglehart, *Sacred and Secular.*

discussion concerning secularization itself—and that is the point I want to make—becomes an empirical fact. The history of the idea of secularization shows that—except for the legal term secularization—the notion of secularization stems from theology, from within the religious sphere. The 1928 world conference on mission in Stockholm dealt with the topic of "the fight against secularization". Parallel to church-building and the organization of mass religiosity Protestantism during the nineteenth century developed an idea of religious practice which is based on authenticity, faith and emphasis and in the light of which actual religious practice could only be seen as deficient. From within the religious field the idea of secularization was used as a societal stimulus for religion among the public and from thereon became an analytical term in the social sciences from the beginning of the 1950s on. This transfer from the religious sphere via the public to the social sciences led to a rapid increase in the production of books on the subject of secularization, as the statistics shown in figure 14 indicate:

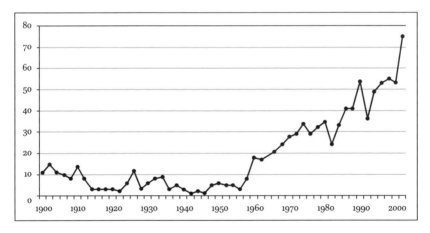

Fig. 14: German book titles containing *"säkular"*, *"Säkularisation"* or *"Säkularisierung"*, 1900–2003.[55]

---

55 Source of data: "Verbundkatalog GBV"; own analysis.

Even if one does not go deeper into the content of the books produced, the sheer number of books on secularization can be used as an indicator of secularization being in greater and greater demand during the course of the twentieth century. After a slow start at the beginning of the century, the curve rises rapidly from the early 1950s until today. The responsibility for this development lies both with the proponents and with the critics of the idea of secularization.

In a second step I want to compare the numbers of church exits with the course of the statistic on literature on the subject of secularization (see fig. 15):

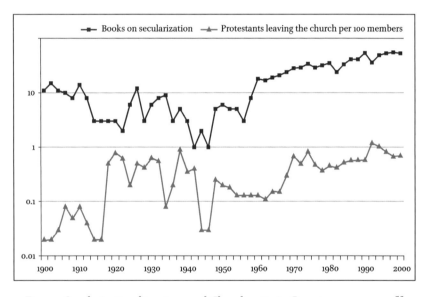

Fig. 15: Secularization literature and Church exits in Germany, 1900–2003.[56]

This comparison shows that literature on secularization booms just before waves of church exits. This is true of the situation at the beginning of the century, when secularization literature was in high demand, and the first large wave of church exits began in 1918. After the end of the Second World War secularization literature was being produced in ever-increasing numbers, from the beginning of the 1950s. The corresponding wave of

[56] Logarithmic scale, source of data: Verbundkatalog GBV and church statistics of the EKD; own analysis.

church exits started at the end of the 1960s. If taken with a grain of salt, one could suggest, that from then on secularization literature and church exits increase proportionally.

I do not want to construct a singular and thus simple causal relationship between these two indicators. But they do tend to inspire the idea that the history of the concept of secularization and its scholarly reflection stimulated church exits in addition to social and religious factors and vice versa. Apart from the literature on secularization, I have recorded the number of books on religious topics in comparison with overall book production (see fig. 16):

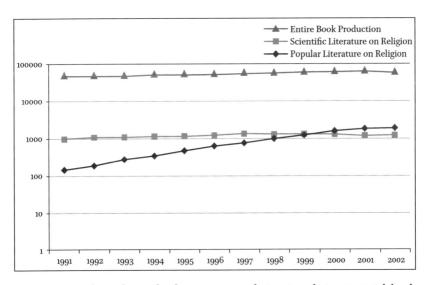

Fig. 16: Scientific and popular literature on religion in relation to total book production in Germany 1991–2002.[57]

The green upper curve shows overall book production in Germany. Below (in red) is the production of scholarly literature on religion and the blue curve which rises steeply shows the number of popular, non-scholarly literature on religion. While church membership has been in decline since the 1990s, the production of popular religious books has increased. The "Gesellschaft für Konsumforschung" (GfK Group) diagnosed a twenty per

---

[57] Logarithmic scale, source of data: Verbundkatalog GBV, Amazon, "Buch und Buchhandel in Zahlen"; own analysis.

cent growth rate for the esoteric book market, and in 1998 the volume of sales in this sector exceeded DM one hundred million. If one tries to interpret these facts as a growing interest in religious topics, one could easily argue that organized religion is evolving into vagrant religiosity—in accordance with Ernst Troeltsch and Thomas Nipperdey. Again, I do not want to state that there is a singular and direct connection between the abovementioned topics and facts but simply to point out the way in which indicators for societal virulence of religion can be constructed.

Summary

The indicators I have discussed as possible criteria for measuring secularization on different levels do not draw a clear image of what the notion of secularization might represent in regard to statistics. While church membership declines, the reasons for this decline are not based on the changing structure of society in terms of a process of modernization which is principally incompatible with religion. Although church membership is on the decline, there is good evidence for the fact that the interest in genuinely religious acts (here: communion) is rising. Religious diversity is more evident in Germany than ever before, but even this does not mean there is an expansion of religion in society—at least not on the level of organized religion. General religiosity and the acceptance of statements of faith can be ascribed to about fifty per cent of the population, an amount which has not been varied over the last twenty years. As the idea of secularization and the debate on it was in great demand before the respective waves of church exits, the secularization debate, amongst other sociohistoric factors, could possibly have stimulated those waves. And last but not least, a disproportionately large amount of religious books is being published on the subject of secularization beyond the scope of organized religion and affiliation to a religious organization.

The analytic model of functional differentiation might help to explain the rise of the secularization concept as the attempt to express the formation of religion as a functional system within society. From this perspective secularization describes the internal differentiation between diffuse and emphatic religiosity as well as the outer distinction between a religious and a non-religious description of the world. As such, secularization is part of religion's own positioning within a modern and functionally differentiated society. This perspective makes it quite clear that the religious and the secular are interdependent; one cannot exist without the other. To take this a step further, one could say that secularization is an ambivalent process with two directions: secularization, if looked at from the perspective of a modern—i.e. an emphatic—concept of religion, is interpreted as a process in which the importance and significance of religion in society diminishes. At the same time secularization reinforces and strengthens the position of religion within society as it refocuses religion on its specific function as a distinct societal sphere.

Even the non-religious self-description of society cannot avoid using the distinction (not the separation!) between the secular and the religious. Throughout modern times the question of secularization has been hotly debated again and again. As vehemently as secularization has been advocated it also has been denounced. This alone can be seen as a sign that modern society cannot exist without religion, even if it is just the negative blueprint of its self-description. Religion is a central part of the history of fascination to which society adheres. It is a mirror for modernity, the looking glass through which society may perceive itself. Even more than that, religion often serves as the projection surface for the most diverse demands. Religion can serve to represent the emphatic wish to denounce tradition and embrace progress. Or it can represent the deep yearning for the archaic—be it a utopian revision of it or the enlightened dissociation from the 'myths of modernity'. One might get the impression that religion and its place in modernity is becoming a figure of reflection on modernity itself, even more so as orthopractic religion appears to be on the decline.

Bibliography

Asad, Talal. "Ethnographic Representation, Statistics, and Modern Power." *Social Research* 61, no.1 (1994): 55–88.
——. *Formations of the Secular: Christianity, Islam, Modernity* (*Cultural Memory in the Present*). Palo Alto: Stanford University Press, 2003.
Aubrey, Edwin E. *Secularism: A Myth: An examination of the current attack on secularism.* New York: Harper & Brothers, 1954.
Berman, Morris. *The reenchantment of the world.* Ithaca: Cornell University Press, 1981.
Bödeker, Hans Erich. *Begriffsgeschichte, Diskursgeschichte, Metapherngeschichte.* Göttingen: Wallstein, 2002.
Bruce, Steve. *God is Dead: Secularization in the West.* Oxford: Blackwell, 2002.
Casanova, José. *Public Religions in the Modern World.* Chicago: University of Chicago Press, 1994.
Cicero, Marcus Tullius. *De natura deorum*, edited by Olof Gigon. Darmstadt: Wissenschaftliche Buchgesellschaft, Sammlung Tusculum, 1996.
Comblin, Joseph. "Säkularisierung: Mythen, Realitäten und Probleme." *Concilium* 5 (1969): 547–552.
Diels, Herman, and Walther Kranz, eds. *Die Fragmente der Vorsokratiker.* 3 vols. Hildesheim: Weidmann, 2004.

Dobbelaere, Karel. *Secularization. A multi-dimensional Concept.* London: Sage Publications, 1981.

———. *Secularization. An Analysis at three Levels.* Bruxelles: P.I.E. Peter Lang, 2002.

Eder, Klaus. "Europäische Säkularisierung—ein Sonderweg in die postsäkulare Gesellschaft?" *Berliner Journal für Soziologie* 3 (2002): 331–343.

Ermel, Horst D. *Die Kirchenaustrittsbewegung im Deutschen Reich 1906–1914.* Köln: Dissertation, 1971.

Feige, Andreas. *Kirchenaustritte. Eine soziologische Untersuchung von Ursachen und Bedingungen am Beispiel der Evangelischen Kirche von Berlin-Brandenburg,* second edition. Gelnhausen: Burckhardthaus-Verlag, 1977.

Frisby, David P., and Klaus Christian Köhnke, eds. *Georg Simmel. Philosophie des Geldes. Gesamtausgabe.* 24 vols. Frankfurt am Main: Suhrkamp, 1989, Vol. 6.

Geser, Hans. "Zwischen Anpassung, Selbstbehauptung und politischer Agitation. Zur aktuellen (und zukünftigen) Bedeutung religiöser Organisationen." In *Institution— Organisation—Bewegung. Sozialformen der Religion im Wandel,* edited by Michael Krüggeler, Karl Gabriel, and Winfried Gebhardt, pp. 39–69. Opladen: Leske + Budrich, 1999.

Göhre, Paul. *Die neueste Kirchenaustrittsbewegung aus den Landeskirchen in Deutschland.* Jena: Diederichs, 1909.

Graf, Friedrich Wilhelm. " 'Dechristianisierung'. Zur Problemgeschichte eines kulturpolitischen Topos." In *Säkularisierung, Dechristianisierung, Rechristianisierung im neuzeitlichen Europa. Bilanz und Perspektiven der Forschung,* edited by Hartmut Lehmann, pp. 32–66. Göttingen: Veröffentlichungen des Max-Planck-Instituts für Geschichte, vol. 130, 1997.

Habermas, Jürgen. *Glauben und Wissen.* Frankfurt am Main: Suhrkamp, 2001.

Hildebrandt, Mathias, Manfred Brocker, and Hartmut Behr, eds. *Säkularisierung und Resakralisierung in westlichen Gesellschaften.* Wiesbaden: Verlag für Sozialwissenschaften, 2001.

Höhmann, Peter, and Volkhard Krech. "Das weite Feld der Kirchenmitgliedschaft. Vermessungsversuche nach Typen, sozialstruktureller Verortung, alltäglicher Lebensführung und religiöser Indifferenz." In *Kirche in der Vielfalt der Lebensbezüge. Die vierte EKD-Erhebung über Kirchenmitgliedschaft,* edited by Wolfgang Huber, Johannes Friedrich, and Peter Steinacker, pp. 143–195. Gütersloh: Gütersloher Verlagshaus, 2006.

———. "Die vierte Kirchenmitgliedschaftsuntersuchung. Alles wie gehabt?" *Praktische Theologie* 1 (2004), 3–12.

Hölscher, Lucian. "Die Religion des Bürgers. Bürgerliche Frömmigkeit und protestantische Kirche im 19. Jahrhundert." *Historische Zeitschrift* 250 (1990): 595–627.

———. *Datenatlas zur religiösen Geographie im protestantischen Deutschland, Von der Mitte des 19. Jahrhunderts bis zum Zweiten Weltkrieg.* Berlin: Walter de Gruyter, 2001.

Inglehart, Ronald, and Michael Minkenberg. "Die Transformation religiöser Werte in entwickelten Industriegesellschaften." *Jahrbuch für Europa- und Nordamerika-Studien 2: Religion und Politik. Zwischen Universalismus und Partikularismus,* edited by Heinz-Dieter Meyer, Michael Minkenberg, an Ilona Ostner, pp. 125–138. Opladen: VS Verlag, 2000.

Institut für Demoskopie Allensbach. *Kirchenaustritte. Eine Untersuchung zur Entwicklung und zu den Motiven der Kirchenaustritte.* Allensbach: Institut für Demoskopie, 1992.

Isenberg, Wolfgang. *Konsum als Religion? Über die Wiederverzauberung der Welt.* Mönchengladbach: Kühlen, 2000.

Jaeschke, Walter. *Die Suche nach den eschatologischen Wurzeln der Geschichtsphilosophie. Eine historische Kritik der Säkularisierungsthese.* München: Chr. Kaiser, 1976.

———. "Säkularisierung." In *Handbuch religionswissenschaftlicher Grundbegriffe,* edited by Hubert Cancik, Burkhard Gladigow, and Karl-Heinz Kohl, vol. 4, pp. 9–20. Stuttgart: W. Kohlhammer, 2001.

Jaeschke, Walter, and Leo Laeyendecker. "Säkularisierung/Säkularismus." In *Evangelisches Kirchenlexikon. Internationale theologische Enzyklopädie*, edited by Erwin Fahlbusch, et al., pp. 37–40. Göttingen: Vandenhoeck & Ruprecht, 1994.

Jagodzinski, Wolfgang. "Säkularisierung und religiöser Glaube. Rückgang traditioneller Religiosität und religiöser Pluralismus in Westeuropa." In *Die deutsche Gesellschaft in vergleichender Perspektive. Festschrift für Erwin K. Scheuch*, edited by Karl-Heinz Reuband, Franz U. Pappi, and Heinrich Best, pp. 261–285. Opladen: Verlag für Sozialwissenschaften, 1995.

Kaufmann, Franz-Xaver. "Zur Bestimmung und Messung der Kirchlichkeit in der Bundesrepublik Deutschland." *Internationales Jahrbuch für Religionssoziologie*, vol. 4, pp. 63–100. Opladen: Westdeutscher Verlag, 1968.

Lanczkowski, Günter. *Einführung in die Religionswissenschaft*. Darmstadt: Wissenschaftliche Buchgesellschaft, 1980.

Lehmann, Hartmut, ed. *Säkularisierung, Dechristianisierung, Rechristianisierung im neuzeitlichen Europa. Bilanz und Perspektiven der Forschung*. Göttingen: Veröffentlichungen des Max-Planck-Instituts für Geschichte, vol. 130, 1997.

Livius, Titus. *Ab Urbe Condita. Liber I. Römische Geschichte. 1. Buch*. Translated by Robert Feger. Ditzingen: Reclam, 1986.

Lübbe, Hermann. *Säkularisierung. Geschichte eines ideenpolitischen Begriffs*. New second edition. Freiburg im Breisgau: Verlag Karl Alber, 2003.

Martin, David. *On Secularization: Toward a Revised General Theory*. Aldershot: Ashgate Publishing Company, 2005.

McLeod, Hugh. "Comparing Secularizations: Germany and Britain." In *Religionspolitik in Deutschland. Von der Frühen Neuzeit bis zur Gegenwart*, edited by Anselm Doering-Manteuffel, and Kurt Nowak, pp. 177–192. Stuttgart: W. Kohlhammer, 1999.

Norris, Pippa, and Ronald Inglehart, *Sacred and Secular. Religion and Politics Worldwide*. Cambridge: Cambridge University Press, 2004.

Pfender, Gottfried-Martin. *Kirchenaustritt und Kirchenaustrittsbewegung in Preußen*. Breslau: Mandel, 1930.

Pollack, Detlef. *Säkularisierung—ein moderner Mythos? Studien zum religiösen Wandel in Deutschland*. Tübingen: Mohr Siebeck, 2003.

Pollack Detlef, and Gert Pickel, "Individualisierung und religiöser Wandel in der Bundesrepublik Deutschland." *Zeitschrift für Soziologie* 28 (1999): 465–483.

———. "Religiöse Individualisierung statt Säkularisierung? Eine falsche Alternative: Antwort auf Monika Wohlrab-Sahr und Michael Krüggeler." *Zeitschrift für Soziologie* 29 (2000): 244–248.

Polybius. *Historiae*. Edition sterotypa, edited by Theodorus Buettner-Wobst, vol. 2. Stuttgart: Teubner, 1985.

Ruh, Ulrich. *Säkularisierung als Interpretationskategorie. Zur Bedeutung des christlichen Erbes in der modernen Geistesgeschichte*. Freiburg im Breisgau: Herder, 1981.

Schieder, Wolfgang. "Religion in der Sozialgeschichte," In *Sozialgeschichte in Deutschland. Entwicklungen und Perspektiven im internationalen Zusammenhang. Band III: Soziales Verhalten und soziale Aktionsformen in der Geschichte*, edited by Wolfgang Schieder, and Volker Sellin, pp. 9–31. Göttingen: 1987.

Schröder, Winfried. *Ursprünge des Atheismus. Untersuchungen zur Metaphysik- und Religionskritik des 17. und 18. Jahrhunderts*. Stuttgart-Bad Cannstatt: Frommann Holzboog, 1998.

Stäheli, Urs. "Die Nachträglichkeit der Semantik—Zum Verhältnis von Sozialstruktur und Semantik." *Soziale Systeme* 4, no. 2 (1998): 315–340.

Weber, Max. *Gesammelte Aufsätze zur Religionssoziologie*. Tübingen: Mohr Siebeck, 1920.

Wehler, Hans-Ulrich. *Das Deutsche Kaiserreich 1871–1918*, third edition. Göttingen: Kleine Vandenhoeck Reihe, 1977.

Wohlrab-Sahr, Monika, and Michael Krüggeler. "Strukturelle Individualisierung versus Autonome Personen. Wie individualisiert ist Religion? Antwort auf Detlef Pollack und Gert Pickel." *Zeitschrift für Soziologie* 29 (2000): 240–244.

Wolf, Christof. "Religiöse Pluralisierung in der Bundesrepublik Deutschland." *Kölner Zeitschrift für Soziologie und Sozialpsychologie. Soziale Integration. Sonderheft* 39 (1999): 320–349.

Young, Lawrence A. *Rational Choice Theory and Religion: Summary and Assessment.* New York: Routledge, 1997.

Zabel, Hermann. *Verweltlichung/Säkularisierung. Zur Geschichte einer Interpretationskategorie.* Münster: Dissertation, 1968.

Ziegler, Paul. "Das Religionsverzeichnis als Grundlage der Konfessionsstatistik." *Kirchliches Jahrbuch* 85 (1959): 422–436.

THE CONCEPTS OF 'RELIGION' AND 'SECULARISM' IN THE HEBREW LANGUAGE AND THEIR MANIFESTATIONS IN ISRAEL'S SOCIO-POLITICAL DYNAMICS

Yochi Fischer

The story most often heard in discussions of religion and secularity in Israel is the parable of the two wagons. It is taken from a famous debate between David Ben-Gurion, Israel's first prime minister, and Rabbi Avraham Yesha'ayahu Karelitz, popularly known as the Hazon Ish, a prominent religious leader at the time.

Ben-Gurion asked the rabbi for his views on the desired relations between church and state and between religious and nonreligious people in Israel. The rabbi answered that religious and secular Jews were like two wagoners trying to cross a narrow bridge from opposite directions. Who should cross first? The wagon that is less loaded and therefore lighter should move to the side and make way for the wagon with the heavier load, the rabbi argued. He explained the metaphor in the following way: There are two different cultural agendas in the State of Israel. One is the agenda of the secular Zionist Jews; the other is that of the religious Jews. The religious wagon should be allowed to cross first because it is much heavier, laden with tradition, values, commandments, and heritage.

Ben-Gurion adopted this metaphor and its implications, viewing the empty secular wagon as the one that had to make way for religious demands in the formation of church-state relations in the emerging state.

Some scholars claim that the story is an accurate portrayal of church-state relations in Israel to this day. They argue that although the majority of Israelis are secular Jews, the religious Jews in the country have excessive political influence. According to their line of argument, this is due to the historical error committed by the founders of the state and manifested, for example, in Ben-Gurion's actions and in those of other politicians who wanted the religious parties to join the government coalition at any price. The outcome of their actions is an ongoing conflict and a non-liberal system.

The linguistic correlation in Hebrew between the words *halal* (emptiness) and *hiloni* (secularist) encourages and reflects the Israeli political discourse on the issue. The "empty" part is allegedly lacking in fixed norms and values; that is, it is flexible and changeable, so it should adjust itself to religious seriousness and "fullness". However, the story of religion and secularization in Israel is much more complex and is built upon much more than clear-cut dichotomies, mutual misconceptions, and narrow political considerations.

The objective of this chapter is to analyze the complexities and dialectics of the concepts of religion and secularism in Israel and in the Hebrew language, as well as the manifestations of these complexities in Israel's socio-political dynamics. I examine some of the theological and practical aspects of religion and secularism in Israel, as well as the tensions and contradictions between religion and secularism and their various manifestations in contemporary processes.

The first part of the chapter analyzes the apparatus of Jewish-Israeli religion and secularism. This analysis focuses on parts of the linguistic and theological background of Israel's definition of religion, and on secularization processes and their impact on the formation of Israel's political identity. This contextualized analysis illustrates the complex nature of religion and secularism that is peculiar to Israel. The second part of the chapter addresses few manifestations of the religious and secular formations in various spheres of Israeli socio-political life. The chapter concludes by pointing to current changes in the formation of the religious and the secular in Israel, changes that may be labeled "post-secularism".

Religious-Secular (Dati-Hiloni*):*
Linguistic and Theological Settings

There is no Hebrew equivalent for the word 'religion' and its variants in Latin. Discussion of religion in its Christian sense usually focuses on the configuration of faith, institutions, theology, and practices. It is a category that stems from the peculiarities of Western Christian history. In late antiquity it developed within the broader context of Roman culture and the Church, to distinguish between the corpus of a person's civil pursuits and the worship of God. However, even in Christian tradition, this concept was not static throughout history. The term *religio* came into frequent use in its modern sense only in the fifteenth century. Prior to that, the discussion revolved around *fides* (faith) at all its levels and with all its mystical, theological, and practical meanings. *Religio* entered the discussion when it became necessary to offer a new formation of the religion in opposition to the state and the new science, as part of the adoption and consolidation of new religious identities. The modern 'religion' as a category is a relatively new concept, produced by the Enlightenment and built on the Protestant model, which stresses the importance of personal and voluntary confessions of faith.[1] The modern Christian notion of 'religion' also embodies the pre-modern distinctions between the spiritual and the secular, or the sacred and the temporal.

Translating the Christian notion of 'religion' into the Jewish-Hebrew semantic field is problematic, above all because, according to Jewish epistemology, religious existence and experience is all-inclusive and cannot distinguish between the spiritual and the temporal, or the sacred and the secular, as far as human activity is concerned. Judaism lacks a "secular" law and as such it does not recognize sacred as opposed to profane areas of occupation.[2] Jewish religion, in essence, contains secular, that is, worldly, elements. Its aims are precisely to sanctify the secular, not in the sense of making the secular mystical, but by giving religious meaning to every aspect of daily life. In trying to convert 'religion' into the sacred language of Judaism, namely, Hebrew, we thus have to perform semantic and theological transformative acts.

In modern Hebrew, the word for religion is *dat*. But *dat* originally meant something totally different. *Dat* appears in the Bible; it is derived from a Persian word and means "the law" (see, for example, the Book of Esther 1:13). The word *data* comes from the same origin: something that is given and cannot be changed. The '*dat*' of the king refers to the laws of the king.

Until the eighteenth century, the word *dat* had by and large no other meaning for Jews than religious law, and there was no other equivalent Hebrew word to signify Jewish religion as distinct from Jewish nationality or culture. In the eighteenth and nineteenth centuries, the influence of the Enlightenment and the movement to emancipate Jews forced European Jews to reshape their personal and collective identity, using Christian notions of secular civil society and the separate private realm of religion.

In 1806 Napoleon, who wished to emancipate the Jews in France and in the nations he had conquered, convened a Jewish Assembly of Notables to answer questions put to it by his emissaries, and then convened the Sanhedrin (the Jewish high court) to give religious sanction to those answers. The assembly's task was to discuss the relationship of French

---

[1] Baird, "Late Secularisms"; Peterson and Walhof, *Invention of Religion*.
[2] Dan, *On Sanctity*.

Jewry with the French nation-state. Napoleon wished to provide the Jews with rights, but these were conditional on the Jews' changing their self-perception as a people and as a separate political entity. By means of various tactics, Napoleon made participation in the secular state contingent on the Jews' choosing to be a religious group, rather than a nation.[3]

Later, the intellectual elite of Jews in Germany who wished to re-shape the Jewish collective identity based it on 'confession-religion' to make it structurally parallel to the German confessional system. This, they hoped, would help their integration in the German collective.[4] The question of the Jews was connected to the Oriental question. Could the Jews assimilate and become a civilized Western religion, or did they belong to the uncivilized Oriental world?[5] In that historical atmosphere of defining the borders of the various European nations and the civilized West, the Jews, who wanted to show their loyalty to their homeland nations, had to reformulate the notion of *dat* (Jewish religion) as a notion separate from Jewish peoplehood and nationhood and in fact as a Christian secular term alien to the essence of Jewishness. Thus, the Jewish 'religion' (*dat*), as opposed to the all-inclusive Jewish existence, which cannot separate the religious sphere from the secular, was born, not surprisingly, together with Jewish modern critical thinking and ways of behavior that can be labeled 'secular'.

The term commonly used to identify a nonreligious person in contemporary Israel is *hiloni*. This word has different meanings in different contexts, but it is usually understood as various degrees of not obeying Jewish injunctions.[6] Although the word *hiloni* appears in mishnaic Hebrew, until the nineteenth century it was not used in Jewish writings to describe individual cases of people who did not observe the Torah and its injunctions. Such individuals were denoted by other names, such as *kofer* or *apikores* (both meaning "apostate" or "unbeliever"), or by terms that described them as having cast off the yoke of the commandments, such as *freier* in Yiddish and *hofshi* in Hebrew (both meaning "free"). One of the most common Yiddish terms used to describe such people was *veltlech* (worldly), or in other words, the modern Christian 'secular'.

---

[3] Raz-Krakotzkin, "Religion and Nationality." Unpublished paper. I thank the author for his permission to use this insight.

[4] Volkov. "Inventing Tradition."

[5] Raz-Krakotzkin, "Religion and Nationality", "A National Colonial Theology."

[6] Liebman and Yadgar, "Secular Jewish Identity."

The root of the Hebrew word *hiloni* is the three-letter root *het lamed lamed*, which signifies the transformation of the sacred to the profane. The Hebrew terms for secularism (*hiloniut*) and secularization (*hilon*) both have two meanings: "secular" (*hol*) and "profane" (*halal*). The main differentiation is between the sacred and the secular or profane. The equivalent Christian differentiation would be between 'the spiritual' and 'the temporal'.[7]

The word *hiloni* entered the Hebrew language through the ancient language of Aramaic. The Talmudic word *zar* (stranger) is translated as *hiloni*. The *zar* in this context, however, is not merely someone who is not of local origin. Rather, the context is that of the laws of the *cohanim* (the priesthood). *Zar* or *hiloni* is anyone who is not a priest. Thus *hiloni* denotes a negative identity pertaining to anyone outside the circle of the priesthood. Just as the diverse layers of the Christian *saeculum* evolved within the religious realm, so the definition of the Jewish "secular" derives from the religious sphere of the sanctity of the priests. However, as mentioned above, until the nineteenth century, Hebrew sources did not use the term to describe individuals who failed to observe their religious obligations.

Manifestations of rebellion against religious conventions and of an agenda that was not necessarily dictated by a religious authority existed long before the nineteenth century. Individual cases of people who did not observe the Jewish laws and the injunctions always existed. The same is true with respect to heretic voices that criticized Jewish theology and practices. But until the end of the eighteenth century such manifestations were sporadic and usually had no theoretical or institutional backup. But in the nineteenth century, as an increasing number of Jews and Jewish institutions ceased to obey the injunctions and started questioning their philosophical and theological basis, new distinctions between the 'observant' and 'nonobservant' began to emerge.[8]

When therefore was the term *hiloni* (in the sense of "secularist") reintroduced into Hebrew? When did the phenomenon, which had always existed to a certain degree, come to be signified by a noun? It seems that we must distinguish between two stages: the first, when *hiloni* reappears in Hebrew at the end of the nineteenth century; the second, when the word enters everyday language and public discourse, in Israel of the 1950s

---

[7] Hölscher, "The Religious and the Secular: Semantic Reconfigurations of the Religious Field in Germany from the Eighteenth to the Twentieth Centuries" (in this volume).

[8] Feiner, *Origins of Jewish Secularization.*

and 1960s and with the emergence of the term "the *hiloni* (secular) public"
as opposed to "the *dati* (religious) public".

In the first stage, the term reemerged concurrently with the emergence
of Zionism. It was part of the construction of a new secular Jewish identity and the secularization of the Hebrew language. No less significant,
it emerged concurrently with the birth of the modern term *secularist* in
other languages, as part of Zionism's adaptation to Western culture and the
desire for Western normalization of religion and of religious institutions.

The first to use the term *hiloni* in the modern sense were Jewish writers in the nineteenth century and early twentieth century who began to
use Hebrew as a 'secular' language. The term appears, for example, in the
work of the famous national poet Chaim Nachman Bialik (1873–1934) in
his unfinished essay "Jewish Literature in Foreign Languages", in which he
refers to the history of literature in Hebrew:

> In that era, the era of religion, the language did not have the same national
> value that it has in our era, the era of *hiloni* culture.... In those days religion
> was the supreme form of life.... The importance of the language for the
> nation was felt especially in the religious form but also in the *hiloni* form....
> And even from the time of the Renaissance... all our *hiloni* writers who were
> well acquainted with their country's languages wrote in Hebrew.[9]

Bialik's use of the words *dati* (religious) and *hiloni* (secular) is typified
by the differentiation between two Jewish cultures: the religious and the
secular. Ours is an era of secular culture, Bialik tells his readers; although
secular elements existed in the religious past, they were manifested to a
lesser degree. Bialik sees the flourishing of secular elements in his time
as connected with the national awakening. He uses the old-new Hebrew
term *hiloni*, but his *hiloni* is much nearer to the sense of the Christian
'temporal' or 'this-worldliness' than to a comprehensive or all-inclusive
personal or communal secular identity. For Bialik's generation, a *hiloni* is
not essentially a nonreligious person, but rather one who is characterized
by materialism, which was considered a positive and necessary element
for the transformation of the old spiritual Jew into the "new" nationalist
Jew after generations of spirituality and other-worldliness.[10]

The second stage in the use of the term *hiloni* in modern times was
characterized by categorization. It evolved during the first decades of the

---

[9] Bialik, *Jewish Literature* (translation mine).
[10] Liebman and Yadgar, "Beyond the Religious-Secular Dichotomy", "Secular Jewish
Identity."

State of Israel, alongside the processes of defining the new state's norms, ethics, and laws regarding religion. The establishment of the state in 1948 intensified the division between what was to be portrayed as two conflicting communities, the religious (*dati*) and the secular (*hiloni*), engaged in polemical exchanges. Put differently, political autonomy created the sharp religious/secular distinction and introduced categorization.

As with other concepts that were invented for phenomena that already existed, such as 'homosexuality', from the moment the term *hiloni* (secularist) in the sense of non-observant came into use, it became a category for classification and segregation. Interesting evidence for the process by which the term *hiloni* came to be used as a classification category in Israeli public discourse can be found on the pages of the daily newspaper "Ha'aretz" from the mid-1960s.[11] The well-known linguist Moshe Goshen-Gottstein, who wrote a weekly linguistics column, devoted two columns in June 1965 to what he described as a relatively new dichotomy: *hiloni/dati* (secular/religious). He opened his first column with a quote, probably from the mass media, proclaiming that "a young *hiloni* dressed in long pants was removed from the place." Until ten years earlier (that is, the mid-1950s), Goshen-Gottstein noted, the meaning of the word *hiloni* had probably not been so clear to the public. He described the rise of the word *hiloni* as "one of the interesting developments in language and society in recent years". Until recently, he continued, the words that had been used to describe the non-observant were "nonreligious" or "free". These two words are disappearing, and *hiloni* is increasingly taking their place. However, Goshen-Gottstein argued, because of the old Aramaic origin of the word, meaning a (religious) stranger, this new use is inappropriate:

> The *hiloni* is related to reciprocal relations with the sacred. You can't have a *hiloni* who is not so in contradistinction to sanctity, though not to religion.... The *hiloni* is not a person who rejects the sacred realm; he is deprived of it.... One can speak about *hiloni* literature, *hiloni* values, *hiloni* professions—but not about a *hiloni* person. Or, if we would like to be helped by foreign languages: Wherever the profane or secular is intended, one may translate it as '*hiloni*' because it is the opposite of sacred, [but] not [the opposite] of religion and observance of the commandments.... These notions are on a par with words such as literature, profession, and so on, but a profane person is something totally different.[12]

---

[11] Cf. Liebman and Yadgar, "Secular Jewish Identity."
[12] Goshen-Gottstein, "Society, Culture, and Language." (Translation mine)

Goshen-Gottstein's columns provide a glimpse into the semantic hesi-
tancy and discontent regarding the new "contradictory" concepts of *dati/
hiloni* during the formative years of that dichotomy, when the concepts
became prevalent in the public discourse. However, the Israeli *hiloni* in
the sense of the 1950s and 1960s differed from Bialik's *hiloni* of the late
nineteenth and early twentieth centuries. In other words, the term *hiloni*
began to be attached to a specific community precisely when the characteristics of that community and its relations to religion changed. The
hiloni is not necessarily a heretic or someone free of observation of religious commandments, but rather someone who lives in a society that neither challenges nor denies tradition. Only when such a society existed was
a '*hiloni* community' created. The freethinker is still bound to religious law
but violates it, while the secularist, the *hiloni*, has much less knowledge of
religious law. What is interesting is that a word belonging to the theological discourse concerning the laws of sanctity and non-sanctity was revived
at a time when a social context emerged that was distinct from that earlier
world and was no longer engaged in an intensive dialogue with religion.

Examination of the linguistic sphere makes it clear that in the Jewish
context, as in other religious contexts, *hiloni* is a theological concept,
defined within the religious world. Although socio-linguistic reasoning does
not always take this theological background into account, 'the secular' is in
itself, like the term 'sanctity', a central category for understanding religion.

Moving from linguistic to theological contextualization, one of the differences underlying the disparity between Jewish (or Muslim) secularism,
on the one hand, and Christian secularism, on the other, is the attitude
toward religious rules and the connection between religion and nationality. Judaism, which is more law-oriented than faith-oriented, instructs its
followers how to act in every aspect of their lives and places less emphasis
on the formulation of systems of faith and paths to redemption. Therefore,
the background to Jewish secularization in its formative stages is the law
and its abandonment.

Jewish secularization can result in banishment from the community
or excommunication, but not in the revocation of nationality, which is
not separable in the Jewish case from the definition of religion. The *hiloni*
remains a Jew when he becomes secular; there is no neutral and universal
dimension to Jewishness. Whereas the various levels of historical Christian
secularism dealt intensively with the relations between the two realms
of the spiritual and the temporal, which underwent various changes but
never a total separation, Jewish secularism dealt not with the separate
realms but with the limits of the commandments—Halacha.

After Paul revoked the Old Testament Jewish rules, Christianity was preoccupied with the question of the sacred and the profane and struggled with the meaning of separation and the "two swords". In its desire to strengthen religion, the Reformation, for example, tried to overcome the separation and to erect various bridges between the sacred and the secular.[13] In contrast, the evolution of modern Jewish secularism had contrary implications: the attempt to extract the secular from the admixture of sacred and secular. In the Israeli context, this attempt was a priori doomed to failure, among other reasons because of the inseparability of religion and nationality in Judaism.

Jewish secularism, as it was imagined in the nineteenth century and at the beginning of the twentieth century, was an attempt to create secularism with a practical Jewish flavor. In a way, it tried to emulate Paul's revocation of the religious commandments[14] but at the same time to preserve the old alliance in some fashion and to avoid creating a new one. The outcome was a blend of the concept of Jewish secularism, as being unaffiliated with the priesthood but affiliated with God, with elements of the Christian concept of secularization, such as the separation of the sacred from the profane. If we add to this the fact that the Zionists accepted and maintained to a large degree the theology of religious salvation,[15] we can better understand why the outcome was unique and so complex.

Manifestations: Israel's Socio-Political Dynamics

The second part of this paper focuses on some of the manifestations of the cultural meanings of Jewish secularism (*hiloni*ut) and religion (*dat*) in the State of Israel. There is a well-known meta-narrative that describes the division between the religious and the secular in Israel in terms of a struggle over control of the public sphere. This narrative focuses on the alleged failure to structure a genuine secular state as dreamed of by the Zionist pioneers, a state based on shared secular civil values and practices.[16]

The place of (the Jewish) religion in the public sphere in Israel is indeed very dominant in comparison to that in other countries. However, such

---

[13] Casanova, "The Religious-Secular Binary Classification."
[14] Motzkin, "Secularization, Knowledge, and Authority."
[15] Raz-Krakotzkin, "There Is No God."
[16] Eilam, *End of Judaism*; Peres and Ben Rafael, *Cleavage in Israeli Society*; cf. Goodman and Yona, *Maelstrom of Identities*; Goodman and Yona, "Religion and Secularism."

dominance is not just the outcome of political compromises with religious politicians who have taken advantage of their political power. As revealed by the semantic and theological developments outlined above, Israel's "secular" nation-state relies in many respects on religious foundations.

The Zionist founders and the first-generation immigrants to Palestine selected nationalist elements from the religious tradition but tried to eliminate their transcendental religious meaning. The pioneers altered the religious elements by adding new values to them and presented their actions as a conversion of the false old tradition to a kind of 'civil religion'.[17] The complexity of constructing a solid, non-metaphysical system of ethics was a constitutive challenge for many Western secularization processes and was not unique to Zionism. In Zionism, however, even before the establishment of the state, an ambivalent relationship had been developing between Jewish secular nationalism and Jewish religion. On the one hand, the Jewish national movement attempted to detach itself from religion, but on the other hand, it was profoundly dependent on religious symbols and on a religion-based collective identity.[18]

One of the cultural arenas in which theology was incorporated in secularization efforts was the linguistic sphere. There is scholarly consensus that one of the great achievements of the Zionist movement is the revival of the Hebrew language. In the Diaspora, Jews developed other spoken languages, which were usually a combination of their native languages and some words from biblical Hebrew.

The task of reviving the language and of secularizing it so it could serve as an everyday, worldly language seemed unrealistic in the early days of Zionism. Religious leaders who perceived Hebrew as a sacred language even considered the secularization of Hebrew an act of profanity.

Hebrew revivalists changed, and are still changing, the meanings of Hebrew terms to fit the modern world. This has often entailed the semantic secularization of religious sacred terms. For example, the phrase *mishkán haknéset* (Israel's parliament building) stems from the biblical Hebrew *mish'kån*, which refers to the "Tabernacle of the Congregation" where Moses kept the Ark in the wilderness. The word *mishkán* is loaded with biblical holiness and evokes sanctity. Choosing to use the name of this

---

[17] Don-Yehia, *Civil Religion.*
[18] Ben-Porat, "State of Holiness."

sacred biblical building for the parliament upgrades the modern place, as if Israeli MKs were carrying out their duties in a sacred building.[19]

The Zionist project of "normalization" of Jewish existence, a project that included developing a common language, embraced a religious-sacred dimension that continues to influence the collective Israeli cultural identity. When an old religious word is taken out of its sacred context and introduced into everyday Hebrew, it is both a phenomenon of religious resurgence and of secularization.

Ben-Gurion, Israel's first prime minister, was aware of the sensitivities and contradictions regarding religious and nonreligious elements in Israeli society and he took them into consideration when formulating church-state relations in 1948. By that time he was also well aware of the extent of the Holocaust and of the destruction of the Jewish cultural and religious centers throughout Europe. In a way, he felt that this new state would now be responsible for maintaining the Jewish heritage. This explains, in part, why he consulted the Hazon Ish in the famous conversation with which this paper started, and why the old European version of Jewish observance known as Jewish Orthodoxy became hegemonic in defining Jewish religious observance in Israel.

Another dynamic that influenced the formation of Israel's religious and secular features was the massive immigration in the late 1940s and 1950s. This immigration caused a rapid and radical change in the demographic composition of the newly established state. The new immigrants brought with them different conceptions of Judaism and tradition. This was especially true of Jews who came from more traditional Jewish communities in Muslim countries.[20] These immigrants, together with Holocaust survivors from Eastern Europe, helped Ben-Gurion redefine some of the 'secular' dreams of the pioneers.

The shape that all this took, while the country's formal and informal agreements between the religious and the secular were being established, is manifested in the Israeli Declaration of Independence (May 1948). In the declaration, the secular Enlightenment ideas of freedom, justice, and peace are proclaimed alongside a religious and messianic message:

> The State of Israel will be open for Jewish immigration and for the ingathering of the Exiles; it will foster the development of the country for the benefit of all its inhabitants; *it will be based on freedom, justice and peace as*

---

[19] Zuckermann, "Do Israelis Understand the Hebrew Bible?"

[20] Goodman and Yona, *Maelstrom of Identities.*

envisaged by the prophets of Israel; it will ensure complete equality of social
and political rights to all its inhabitants irrespective of religion, race or sex;
it will guarantee freedom of religion, conscience, language, education and
culture...We appeal to the Jewish people throughout the Diaspora to rally
round the Jews of Eretz-Israel in the tasks of immigration and building up
and to stand by them *in the great struggle for the realization of the age-old
dream—the redemption of Israel...*

   Placing our trust in the Rock of Israel, we affix our signature to this proclamation at this session of the provisional Council of State, on the soil of the
homeland...Tel Aviv, on this Sabbath eve, the fifth day of Iyar, 5708 (14 May
1948). (Emphasis mine)

Reference to the prophets of Israel, the redemption of Israel, and trust in
the Rock of Israel (God), is a part of the newly born secular-religious state.
However, the declaration had no binding legal status and it certainly does
not amount to a formal constitution. The basic constituting agreement
outlining the place of Jewish religion in the public and private spheres of
this new state is embodied in a letter sent by Ben-Gurion to the largest
religious ultra-Orthodox group, Agudat Israel, and was meant to win its
support in the processes of state-building. The letter that is commonly
known as "the *status quo* letter" was intended to safeguard the basic religious arrangements that had prevailed earlier. It stipulated that the future
state would continue the previous arrangements that had been decided
on by the religious parties and by the "free", "general", "non-observant"
public, as the secular public was referred to before the 1950s.

   The *status quo* agreement includes establishing an independent religious education system, providing observance of Jewish dietary laws in
public and government institutions, recognizing the primacy of religious
courts in matters of personal status, making Saturday (the Sabbath) Israel's
official day of rest, and allowing a specific number of draft exemptions
for religious (*yeshiva*) students. The *status quo* arrangements have been
maintained by and large for the past sixty years and serve as the foundation for Israel's politics of accommodation.[21] Whatever was not resolved
by the *status quo* was left to the pragmatism of the politicians and to
grassroots cultural mechanisms and transformations. Decisive issues concerning the religious sphere are de-politicized by being transferred to the
local municipal or judicial level.[22]

---

[21] Don-Yehia, *Religion and Political Accommodation in Israel.*

[22] Don-Yehia, *Religion and Political Accommodation in Israel*; Cohen and Susser, "From
Accommodation to Decision"; Ben-Porat, "Multicultural Realities."

The *status quo* as the basis for political agreement on religion in Israel is a dynamic principle that allows for development and change. When a new government is formed or an agreement is struck between political parties, the *status quo* is usually mentioned as a principle that will continue to be upheld. In the first decades of the state, the words that were used to describe the opposing interests in such agreements were *dati* (religious) needs and *freedom of conscience regarding religious matters*. Although the word *hiloni*, or the phrase "*hiloni* public", as opposed to the "*dati* public", has been used in parliamentary discussions since the late 1950s, the dichotomy of *dati* and *hiloni*, which were understood as mutually exclusive categories, does not usually appear in the formal political coalition agreements until the 1990s.

One of the negative consequences of the *status quo* compromise was the granting to the Orthodox Jewish establishment control over some of the main features of civil life, from cradle to grave. State laws regarding religion do not grant equal status to other Jewish religious movements, such as the Reform movement. In the same vein, the Orthodox establishment with its European Ashkenazic background created a hegemonic order that marginalized the traditional Mizrahi (Oriental) Jews and their versions of Judaism for more than thirty years. This created a socio-political order that, simultaneously rejecting and employing religion in state policies and in political and cultural life in Israel, has also suppressed groups and individuals that do not fall within rigidly defined collective identities, either religious or secular.[23]

The exclusion of groups and collectives whose traditions do not conform to the Western religious-secular version was not, in the opinion of some critics, just an internal Jewish national act but rather part of a greater political process of colonization and marginalization of the non-Western elements, both Jewish and non-Jewish, in the new state.[24]

The ways in which the political *status quo* arrangements and other socio-cultural processes worked in shaping religious and secular formations in Israel will now be demonstrated with reference to three areas: public Sabbath observance, marital law, and education.

---

[23] Goodman and Yona, *Maelstrom of Identities.*
[24] Raz-Krakotzkin, "National Colonial Theology"; Shenhav, *Arab Jews.*

Public Sabbath Observance

One of the many examples of the intervention of religion in Israel's public sphere is the ruling regarding the Sabbath, the sacred day of rest. Basing itself directly on the *status quo* agreements, the state proclaimed the Sabbath a national day of rest and determined that there should be no violation of the Sabbath in the public sphere. The legal character of this day is an outcome of the Jewish religious laws pertaining to the Sabbath. Consequently, for example, by law there is no public transportation in Israel from Friday evening to Saturday night, virtually all the stores and many restaurants are closed, there are no flights of the Israeli air line El Al, hospitals work on reduced schedules, and there are nearly no official government activities. However, with respect to Sabbath observance, the *status quo* accommodations are only partly protected by law and there is a wide platform for negotiation and for struggles over the character of the public sphere on the Sabbath.

The Sabbath restrictions in the public sphere generate tensions and sometimes even harsh conflicts between ultra-Orthodox and secularist Jews. For example, private cars and taxis are allowed to operate on the Sabbath, but there are religious neighbourhoods, especially in Jerusalem, that are closed to cars on the Sabbath at the request of the inhabitants. Road traffic on the Sabbath may be prohibited at the municipal level or by the state. However, from time to time heated public disputes regarding road closures have led to the appointing of public committees to propose solutions. Nonreligious individuals usually chair these committees. The general public does not always accept their resolutions, as in the case of Bar-Ilan Street in Jerusalem. Here, violent demonstrations ensued, and the case was settled only after an intense battle in which religious and secular groups tried to close or open the street, respectively, using various tactics, including public protests and a petition to the High Court of Justice.[25]

Many nonobservant Israelis complain about the religious coercion in the public sphere on the Sabbath. However, interestingly enough, with hundreds of stores at malls violating Saturday closing laws and with Saturday becoming the biggest shopping day of the week, more and more nonobservant or "secular" Israelis have recently begun treating the Sabbath as a national treasure in need of preservation. They want to save the Sabbath from consumerism and insensitive capitalism and use the Jewish religious

---

[25] Don-Yehia, *Religion and Political Accommodation.*

laws to strengthen their claims. They then emphasize the social, humanistic, and egalitarian features of the Sabbath ideology, instead of its coercive elements.[26]

Marital Law

Another example of the socio-political processes in which the religious and the secular operate in Israel can be taken from the sphere of private life. Apart from being visible in the Israeli public sphere and on the institutional level, Orthodox-dominated religious laws and authorities also govern areas of private life. The most prominent of them are the laws regarding marriage and divorce.

Marital-status issues in Israel come under the exclusive jurisdiction of the religious court system. The only formal way for Jews to be married in Israel is by the religious-state Orthodox rabbis in a religious ceremony (The same is true in respect to other religious groups who are subjected to their own particular courts). The rabbinical courts have exclusive jurisdiction over the marriage and divorce of Jews. Nonreligious civil marriage and inter-religious marriage are not recognized. Other laws may prevent certain people from marrying. Those who are denied marriage licenses, or are opposed to what they feel as religious coercion, can marry abroad in a civil ceremony and then return to Israel and be recognized as a married couple. However, even a Jewish couple married in a civil ceremony abroad will have to turn to the rabbinical courts for a divorce.

The rationale underlying this arrangement was the perceived need to preserve Jewish national unity. Religious leaders claimed that two separate Jewish communities would develop if Jews in Israel were able to choose nonreligious marriage. Secular leaders, who were afraid to lose the religious-historical source of their legitimacy, took seriously the religious leaders' arguments that secular marriage would split the Jewish people. They were also afraid that the government coalitions, which were dependent on the support of the religious parties, would break up.

Of course, the law regarding marriage and divorce in Israel arouses antagonism and opposition. In recent years, however, more and more religious leaders have stressed the necessity of civil marriages, not just for the sake of liberalism and the individual's right to free choice, but also for religious reasons. They recognize that this law causes great harm, arouses

---

[26] Ben-Porat and Feniger, "Live and Let Buy"; Cohen and Susser, "From Accommodation to Decision."

antagonism, and increases the discourse that rejects religion. Indeed, today more and more couples are seeking a variety of alternatives to state-religious ceremonies.

Education

The last example of the ways in which the religious and secular operate in Israel today is taken from the education system. In 1953 the Knesset, Israel's parliament, established a unified public education system. The law stipulated two branches: public secular, which was not labelled *hiloni* but rather "state" or "general", and "state-religious". In addition, a system of "private" religious schools for every religion was established. These private schools enjoy state funding and autonomy. Until recently the state did not demand that they incorporate a core curriculum of nonreligious studies.

Religious studies in the general/secular Jewish public schools have undergone changes in recent decades. After recognizing in the late 1960s that after twenty years of state education the first-generation Israelis were by and large ignorant of their past and of Jewish tradition, efforts were made to root youngsters in the nation's past and to increase study of Jewish tradition. Secular schools were instructed to teach more about the religion. Although these studies were resented by secular parents who claimed that they were not about religion and tradition but rather were driven by a religious agenda, this trend continues.

Recently, new kinds of schools have been recognized by the state. These schools do not wish to classify themselves in accordance with the religious-secular dichotomy and argue that in the school system it has created mutual ignorance and segregation because it does not accept diversity. These new schools teach about religion and religious practice with a tolerant attitude and without forcing their students to observe the religious laws.

In addition, more and more Israelis have recently become interested in informal religious education and practices, in what is now called 'cultural Judaism,' as opposed to observant Judaism.[27] This kind of growing interest in religion is usually accompanied by tolerance of other religions, especially Islam. It is accompanied also by the affirmation of secularity and acknowledgment of the creativity that is integral to secularity. Secularity is thus understood not as a passionless state of being, but rather as a feature

---

[27] Malkin, *Secular Jewish Culture.*

of the religious aspect of morality and as a passionate state that can be very creative and that constantly renews itself.

Toward a 'Post-Secular Israel'?

The aim of part of the Zionist pioneers to build a sustainable new secular identity failed to produce a powerful, "pure" secular identity that would result in a collective secular Zionist identity. This failure is producing in contemporary Israel a shift to what can be labelled Israeli 'post-secularism'. Such a failure, coupled with the late recognition of the hybrid nature of the religious and secular in the national Jewish endeavour and the impact of global spiritual trends, is leading to the re-conceptualization of the fundamentals of Jewish culture and to new identity formations, which transcend the religious-secular dichotomy.[28]

Although religion was needed in the process of nation-building and identity-building, now that the concept and meaning of the Jewish nation-state are being challenged and these challenges are changing its character, the place of religion and the secular is also changing. Just as the political autonomy of the state created categorization and imposed restrictive and exclusive identities, the questions now confronting the Israeli political order and the impact of globalization are giving rise to what can be labelled post-secular formations.[29]

On the informal intellectual level, the change toward challenging the perceived dichotomy between religion and the secular is manifested in the emergence of a vast number of learning groups and private organizations devoted to learning Judaism in a pluralistic manner.[30] This cultural phenomenon is succeeding in introducing a growing number of secular people to some knowledge of (and intimacy with) religion, and in helping them to realize that religion does not belong only to the patriarchal Orthodoxy, to the religious nationalists, or to state officials.

The main aim of these Jewish renewal groups is to enable Israeli Jews to articulate their Jewish identity in pluralistic ways. One of the interesting manifestations of these cultural changes is taking place at the liturgical level with the growth of secular congregations who have established

---

[28] Goodman and Yona, *Maelstrom of Identities*; Sagi, "On Religious-Secular Tensions"; Peres, "Religious-Secular Cleavage"; Sheleg, *New Religious Jews*; Fischer, *Self-expression*; Liebman and Yadgar, "Secular Jewish Identity."

[29] Shenhav, "Invitation to a 'Post-Secular' Sociology"; Fischer, "Secularization in a Post-Secular Age."

[30] Werczberger, "Sacralization and Secularization."

prayer houses where they gather for prayers, holiday rituals, and life-cycle ritual celebrations.[31] One can see in this trend a kind of Israeli version of the Christian "belonging without believing". But in this case, as Judaism is orthopraxical by nature and is defined partly by the laws and their violation, the anomaly can be labelled as "belonging without practicing the religious law correctly". These cultural changes can be characterized concurrently as a process of sacralization and secularization. From the theological perspective, the Jewish praxis is secularized because it is cut off from its strict religious-law orientation. But in its identity-belonging aspect it is sacralized, because more and more emphasis is given to religion as a means of strengthening the personal and collective sense of belonging to the Jewish people.[32]

These new kinds of interest in religion are often also accompanied by affirmation of the epistemological state of secularity and as such can be seen as a new, non-defensive secular solution to the challenges posed by religious and national groups. While the first and second generations of Israelis were the first to collectively break one link of the "chain of memory" of Jewish tradition, to use Daniele Hervieu-Leger's terminology,[33] the third generation is trying to repair the chain by returning to the formative questions that were raised 150 years ago with the birth of Zionism.

However, in contrast to New Age spirituality manifested elsewhere, private meanings of sanctity are frequently intertwined in the Israeli-Jewish renewal movement with a strong sense of collective national Jewish belonging. The new pluralistic religious-secular constructions and the re-addressing of the fundamentals of Jewish culture are inclusive for Jewish society but still exclusive for non-Jews, especially the Arab population. The post-secular Israeli discourse is a project drawn along national borders. The Gordian knot that binds Jewish religion with nationality and Judaism with the State of Israel is setting the tone in these new pluralistic formations as it set the tone before. The reason lies not only in theological or ethnocentric infrastructures but also in the socio-political dynamics analyzed above.

In sum, Jewish-Israeli secularization has been an inconsistent process, darting between different approaches, needs, and practices. The feature common to almost all the stages has been the ongoing dependence on,

---

[31] Azulay and Tabory, "A House of Prayer for All Nations."
[32] Werczberger, "Sacralization and Secularization."
[33] Hervieu-Léger, *La Religion pour Mémoire*.

and connection with, various layers of religious existence. The Jewish religion was necessary for the processes of nation-building and state-building, for drawing the boundaries of identity, and for legitimizing claims over territory. Israeli society has incorporated traditional values in its evolution process, and a lot of power was granted to the religious parties in the process of state formation.

Many scholarly descriptions portray Israeli society as being divided between the religious and the secular. It is common to describe this division in terms of a struggle or *Kulturkampf* over control of the public sphere. The place of religion in the public sphere is indeed very dominant if one compares Israel to other 'secular' countries. However, one must transcend the secular/religious dichotomy in Israel in order to understand the complexities.

As in other cases of secularism, the Israeli desire to draw clear distinctions between secular and religious elements is artificial. The two are inextricably linked, and the ideologies and practices of both are of a hybrid nature.[34] The place of the Jewish religion and the meaning of secularism in Israel are constructed from various historical, cultural, and religious components. These components interact in a complex ongoing negotiation within Israeli society regarding their meaning and manifestations in many areas of life. What is considered religious practice or belief and what is considered nonreligious or secular is defined in each given context, and it changes through this continuing process of negotiation. Thus, Israel can be taken as an example of a particular secularity which, like any other secularity, may be metaphysical but is always built upon a particular religious and cultural foundation. As in any other culture, the meaning and definition of 'religious' is dependent, inter alia, on the ever-changing definition of 'the secular'.

Bibliography

Azulay, Na'ama, and Efraim Tabory. "A House of Prayer for All Nations: Unorthodox Prayer Houses for Nonreligious Israeli Jews." *Sociological Papers*, no. 13 (2008): 2–21.

Ben-Porat, Guy. "In a State of Holiness: Rethinking Israeli Secularism." *Alternatives* 25, no. 2 (2000): 223–246.

Ben-Porat, Guy and Yariv Feniger. "Live and Let Buy: Consumerism, Secularization and Liberalism." *Comparative Politics* 41, no. 3 (2009): 293–313.

---

[34] Goodman and Yona, *Maelstrom of Identities*.

Ben-Porat, Guy. "Multicultural Realities." *Israel Studies: An Anthology,* August 2009. http://www.jewishvirtuallibrary.org/jsource/isdf/text/benporat.html (accessed July, 2011)

Baird, Robert. "Late Secularisms." In *Secularisms,* edited by J. Jacobson, and A. Pellegrini, pp. 162–177. Durham, NC: Duke University Press, 2008.

Bialik, Chaim Nachman. Jewish Literature in Foreign Languages. *Knesset* 8 (1943). [Hebrew]

Casanova, Jose. "The Religious-Secular Binary Classification from the Comparative Perspective of the Axial Revolutions: Christian Western Secularization and Globalization." Paper presented at the conference: The Axial Age and its Consequences. Max Weber Centre, University of Erfurt, 3–5 July 2008.

Cohen, Asher and Bernard Susser. "From Accommodation to Decision: Transformations in Israel's Religio-Political Life." *Journal of Church and State* 38, no. 4 (1996): 817–839.

Dan, Joseph. *On Sanctity: Religion, Morality and Mysticism in Judaism and Other Religions.* Jerusalem: Magnes Press, 1998.

Don-Yehia, Eliezer. *Civil Religion in Israel: Traditional Judaism and Political Culture in the Jewish State.* Berkeley: University of California Press, 1983.

———. *Religion and Political Accommodation in Israel.* Jerusalem: The Floersheimer Institute for Policy Studies, 1996.

Eilam, Ygal. *The End of Judaism: Nation of Religion and the Kingdom.* Yediot Aharonoth: Tel Aviv, 2000. [Hebrew]

Feiner, Shmuel. *The Origins of Jewish Secularization in Eighteenth-Century Europe.* Jerusalem: The Zalman Shazar Centre for Jewish History, 2010. [Hebrew]

Fischer, Shlomo. *Self-expression and Democracy in Radical Religious Zionist Ideology.* Jerusalem: PhD dissertation, 2007.

Fischer, Yochi. "Secularization in a Post-Secular Age: Theoretical and Methodological Perspectives." In *Secularization and Secularism: Interdisciplinary Perspectives,* edited by Yochi Fischer. (Forthcoming) [Hebrew]

Goodman, Yehudah, and Yossi Yona. *Maelstrom of Identities: A Critical Look at Religion and Secularity in Israel.* Hakibbutz Hameuchad: Tel Aviv, 2004. [Hebrew]

———. "Religion and Secularism in Israel: The Inseparable Bond and its Transformations." In *Secularization and Secularism: Interdisciplinary Perspectives,* edited by Yochi Fischer. (Forthcoming) [Hebrew]

Goshen-Gottstein, Moshe. "Society, Culture, and Language: Secular and Religious." *Ha'aretz,* 11 June 1965, 18 June 1965. [Hebrew]

Hervieu-Léger, Danièle. *La Religion pour Mémoire.* Paris: Éditions du Cerf, 1993.

Hölscher, Lucian. "The Religious and the Secular: Semantic Reconfigurations of the Religious Field in Germany from the Eighteenth to the Twentieth Centuries" (in this volume)

Liebman, Charles S., and Yaacov Yadgar. "Beyond the Religious-Secular Dichotomy: Masortim in Israel." In *Religion or Ethnicity? Jewish Identities in Evolution,* edited by Zvi Gitelman, pp. 171–192. New Brunswick, NJ: Rutgers University Press, 2009.

Liebman, Charles S., and Yaacov Yadgar. "Secular Jewish Identity and the Condition of Secular Judaism in Israel." In *Religion or Ethnicity? Jewish Identities in Evolution,* edited by Zvi Gitelman, pp. 149–170. New Brunswick, NJ: Rutgers University Press, 2009.

Malkin, Yaakov, ed. *Secular Jewish Culture: New Jewish Thought in Israel.* Jerusalem: Keter, 2006. [Hebrew]

Motzkin, Gabriel. "Secularization, Knowledge, and Authority." In *Religion and Democracy in Contemporary Europe,* edited by Gabriel Motzkin, and Yochi Fischer, pp.35–53. London: Alliance, 2008.

Peres, Yochanan, and Eliezer Ben Rafael. *Cleavage in Israeli Society.* Tel Aviv: Am Oved, 2006. [Hebrew]

Peres, Yochanan. "The Religious-Secular Cleavage in Contemporary Israel." In *Jewry between Tradition and Secularism: Europe and Israel Compared,* edited by E. Ben Rafael, T. Gergely, and Y. Gorny, pp. 121–132. Leiden: Brill, 2006.

Peterson, Derek, and Darren Walhof, eds. *The Invention of Religion: Rethinking Belief in Politics and History.* New Brunswick, NJ: Rutgers University Press, 2002.

Raz-Krakotzkin, Amnon. "A National Colonial Theology: Religion, Orientalism, and the Construction of the Secular in Zionist Discourse." *Tel Aviver Jahrbuch für Deutsche Geschichte* 30 (2002): 304–317.

——. "There is No God But He Has Promised Us the Land." *Mita'am* 3 (2005): 71–76. [Hebrew]

——. *Religion and Nationality in the Jewish and Zionist Contexts,* Paper presented at the conference: Nationalism and Secularism. Van Leer Jerusalem Institute, 22–23 March 2009.

Sagi, Avi. "On Religious-Secular Tensions." In *Jewry between Tradition and Secularism: Europe and Israel Compared,* edited by E. Ben Rafael, T. Gergely, and Y. Gorny, pp. 105–120. Leiden: Brill, 2006.

Sheleg, Yair. *The New Religious Jews: Recent Developments among Observant Jews in Israel.* Jerusalem: Keter, 2000. [Hebrew].

Shenhav, Yehouda. *The Arab Jews.* Stanford: Stanford University Press, 2006.

——. "An Invitation to a 'Post-Secular' Sociology." *Israeli Sociology* 10, no. 1 (2008): 161–188. [Hebrew]

Volkov, Shulamit. "Inventing Tradition: On the Formation of Modern Jewish Culture." *Jewish Studies at the Central European University* 3 (2002–2003): 211–227.

Werczberger, Rachel. "Sacralization and Secularization, Identity and Belonging: The New Age and Jewish Renewal Movement in Israel." *In Secularization and Secularism: Interdisciplinary Perspectives,* edited by Yochi Fischer. (Forthcoming) [Hebrew]

Zuckermann, Ghil'ad. "Do Israelis Understand the Hebrew Bible?" *The Bible and Critical Theory* 6, no. 1 (March 2010): 1–6.

LAIKLIK AND ITS INTRODUCTION INTO
PUBLIC DISCOURSE IN TURKEY

Anat Lapidot-Firilla

In a lecture presented in Berlin in 2007, Erik Jan Zürcher, an eminent expert on Turkish history, described the character and development of Turkish secularism as a unique case. According to Zürcher "Turkish secularism is historically very specific, because it is indebted to two great but largely separate traditions, that of the six-hundred-year-old Ottoman Empire of which the republic is the direct heir and that of the French Enlightenment in its positivist guise."[1]

The content of Zürcher's lecture, which reflects the conventional approach to the study of modern Turkey, is of interest for the present discussion. But equally interesting is the context in which the lecture was delivered: a conference held in the center of Europe at the peak of an emotional public debate over the future of Turkey and the Turks as part of Europe—a political and social entity based on a Christian religious and secular heritage. The conference titled "The importance of being European: Turkey, the EU, and the Middle East" was held two years after Turkey's official acceptance as a candidate for membership in the European Union and almost five years after the coming to power of the post-Kemalist Justice and Development Party, which has defied the Turkish state's "sacred" principle of secularism. Whether this characterization of the new Turkish government is accurate, it is clear that the criticism of Turkish Kemalist policies and agents, especially those related to religion and to the state's authoritarian secularism, has become a dominant theme in Turkish-related studies and public debates. This was clearly reflected in Zürcher's talk.

The genealogy of secularism was described briefly at the conference and has been explored more extensively in many of the well-known books on the history of Turkey.[2] The relations between secularism and the positioning of Turkey in relation to Europe are closely connected and

---

[1] Zürcher, "Turkish secularism," 133–134.
[2] Lewis, *Emergence of Modern Turkey*; Berkes, *Türkiye'de Çağdaşlaşma*; Tunçay, *T.C.'nde Tek-Parti Yönetiminin Kurulması.*

are the core of my paper. My central argument is that the evolutional approach—which views the Kemalists' Turkish secularization project as an attempt to break with the religious past and move toward a Western conception of progress—is inaccurate. The established historiography has created an equation in which the Kemalist bureaucracy, leaning on positivism and anti-religious sentiments that were translated to harsh policies, is set against the ignorant masses that refused to see the light and become civilized through a process of secularization. This equation is not only inaccurate; it also precludes an understanding of Turkish secularism in its various forms and historical periods. Moreover, Turkish secularism is the product of a reform of religious laws, stemming from a perceived need to purify religious legal instruction by ridding it of popular mystical "faults" believed to be foreign to Islam. It was the purification of religious law, and not the rejection of religion, that brought about the secular age in Turkey.

Another argument that deserves attention relates to the inseparable connection between the discussion, both in Europe and in Turkey, of secularism and its various representations, on the one hand, and the nature of the relationship with Europe and "the Eastern question", on the other. By "the Eastern question" I refer not only to the representation of the East in the late Ottoman period but also to the fear of the East in general and to feelings regarding the Turkish quest to become part of Europe. Europe itself, from its commencement as a cultural unit, was defined by its borders with the East in its Persian, Mongol, and Ottoman incarnations.

Epistemology and the Theory of Secularism in Turkey

Zürcher's argument regarding the uniqueness of the Turkish experience of secularism is not unusual. The two basic assumptions of traditional Middle Eastern scholarship are: first, that Turkey and the Turkish people consist of a discrete cultural unit operating according to distinct laws and a unique internal logic; and, linked to the first, that there is a Turkish Islam, and that Sunni Hanafi Turkish Islam is by nature moderate and imbues its followers with conservative social family values. Therefore, dissemination of this moderate version of Islam, under controlled conditions, through state institutions (mosques, schools, cultural centres, and medical clinics) is likely to facilitate socio-political oversight and to reinforce the individual's loyalty to the state.

This perception, which views the Turks as people with natural resistance to radical Islam, is not new and is accepted by eminent Turkish scholars, including Lewis and Shaw, for whom the Turkish Republic is a distinct unit into which foreign influences from the East have not intruded.[3] Social scientists too, such as Daniel Lerner and the Huntingtons (Ellsworth and Samuel), have also tended to see Turkey as an exception in the Islamic world, not only because of the Kemalist reforms but also, chiefly, because of the existence of unique cultural-psychological attributes.[4] Niyazi Berkes (and later Lerner) suggests that these attributes stem from the Turkish quality of empathy, a form of cultural-emotional flexibility. The difference between the faltering Arab world and the prosperous Turkish world, immune to the processes of religious resurgence, Berkes argues, lies in "the personal attributes acquired over the course of generations and integrated because of geographical location and genetic qualities."[5] This perception takes many forms. Hakan Yavuz, one of the prominent contemporary scholars of Turkish society, in response to the question of whether there is a Turkish Islam, declares that:

> The main impacts of globalization have been the two contradictory processes of homogenization and fragmentation. At present, in most of the Arab and Muslim world, the fragmentation aspect is more dominant than homogenization or cooperation. Nonetheless, it would be legitimate to argue that globalization has created two competing visions of Islam. At the extreme end of the spectrum is the liberal and market friendly Islam, dominant in Turkey and Malaysia, and at the other is the 'ghetto Islam' of some parts of Pakistan and some Arab countries. Muslim reaction to these processes is very much shaped by idiosyncratic local histories and socio-political conditions.[6]

Like many others, Yavuz believes that Turkish Islam is moderate and friendly, largely owing to local Sufi traditions, which are voluntary (and have universal approaches that unify cultures), and because of the consistent rejection of "Arab" segregationist traditions.[7] Such a model of Islam allows the Turkish people to be simultaneously modern and traditional, loyal to religious instructions yet having no need for Sharia.

Without rejecting the uniqueness of each of the cultural and socio-political units in the Muslim world, be they Malaysian, Indonesian, Indian, Persian, or Turkish, and despite the importance Edward Said places on distinguishing between the various cultures, it is worth noting the price of such an approach. Mainly, it precludes an analytical examination of

---

[3] Stanford and Ezel Shaw, *History of the Ottoman Empire and Modern Turkey*.
[4] Lerner, *Passing of Traditional Society*.
[5] Berkes, *Türkiye'de Çağdaşlaşma*.
[6] Yavuz, "Is there a Turkish Islam?"
[7] Yavuz, "Is there a Turkish Islam?"

non-Western and non-Christian societies and the creation of a comparative analytical framework for that purpose. Furthermore, such an approach
prevents religion from entering into the discussion of secularism. Finally,
Turkish history is condemned for isolation and self-inclusion. This paper
is not comparative in nature, but there is a need to enrich the discussion
of Turkish history with some reflection on additional regional cases and
to place Turkey in a secular non-Christian matrix. Consequently, multiple
types of secularism may be developed as an analytical framework.

The academic literature on secularism in Turkey is rich. From the monumental book of Niyazi Berkes, *The Development of Secularism in Turkey*,
that was first published in 1964, to Davidson's book on the hermeneutics
of secularism,[8] they have all viewed secularism as part of the Ottoman
modernization in the nineteenth century, as an official ideology. This official ideology gained strength later as a major component in the republican
period. The literature reveals a recent demand to examine the ideology of
the state and its applications and reflections in various domains of social
life, as Sevgi Adak Turan did in his research about the Ramadans in the
early republican era.[9] Turan argues that secularization eliminates the
religious spheres of power in the political system. Therefore, secularization is a necessary condition for the achievement of national sovereignty.
That is why secularism was a crucial part of Kemalist ideology; Kemalists
attempted to establish a secular state right from the start. However, as
Turan points out, "rather than a solid project the application of which was
planned from the very beginning, Republican secularization followed a
'gradual' path, or an evolution towards a more authoritarian character."[10]

Most studies reflect the approach described above. They view secularism from a European point of view and ignore the obvious connection
between secularization and the colonization and de-colonization that
prevailed in the Asiatic and Middle Eastern spheres. Two exceptions
are Cemil Aydin's book, *Anti-Westernism in Asia*, in which the Ottoman
nineteenth century and the early republican intellectual debates are
situated in an Asian anti-colonial context, and Ahmet Davutoğlu's book,
on alternative paradigms.[11] Davutoğlu summarizes his understanding of
secularization in general and in reference to Turkey in particular in an

---

8 Berkes, *Türkiye'de Çağdaşlaşma*; Davidson, *Secularism and Revivalism*.
9 Turan, *Formation of Authoritarian Secularism*.
10 Turan, *Formation of Authoritarian Secularism*, 4–5.
11 Aydin, *Politics of Anti-Westernism*; Davutoğlu, "Dimensions of Secularisation";
Davutoğlu, *Alternative paradigms*.

article that argues that secularization was in fact a form of civilizational "conversion".[12]

From the inception of the Turkish Republic in 1923 to the present, the public and academic debate has revolved around this very issue in varying degrees. On the global axis, the discourse has focused on the spatial–cultural position of Turkey on the seam between the Muslim and the Western worlds. In other words, it has been closely related to the discourse on civilization and culture.

On the local level, the debate has concentrated on the tension between the centre and the periphery. Both of these axes, like other expressions of the secular paradigm, are characterized by a binary division, by a dichotomy between the dark Islamic past and 'the light', between good and evil, between the progressive and educated and the backward, thus ignoring the cultural and social complexity inherent in a country that was simultaneously conqueror and conquered. It was a colonial empire lasting 400 to 600 years that was culturally and politically overrun by foreign powers; prior to that, it was overrun by another canonical textual culture.[13]

It is important to explain the intellectual atmosphere, the political ideological background in which the secularist framework of the Turkish new elite evolved in the early days of the republic. Scholars like Aydin and Davutoğlu have already explained that the Kemalist reformers adopted the process of modernization in the belief that it was an inevitable universal phenomenon, with secularization as its rational essence. All the intellectuals, from Mustafa Fazil Pasha (the grandchild of Mehmet Ali Pasha, the governor of Egypt) to Ziya Gökalp, agreed that religious activity on the part of the state did not befit the modern state's structure. Thus, according to the intellectuals, the salvation of the state would originate in a secular (Western) conception of the state.[14]

Mustafa Kemal Atatürk emphasized the absolute necessity for modernization for the survival of the nation. In a speech commemorating the anniversary of the war of Independence he said:

> Surviving in the world of modern civilization depends upon changing ourselves. This is the sole law of any progress in the social, economic and scientific spheres of life. Changing the rules of life in accordance with the times is an absolute necessity.... There are now two roads for us to follow: to accept defeat and annihilation or to accept the same principles which have created

---

[12] Davutoğlu, "Dimensions of Secularisation."
[13] Deringil, "They Live in a State of Nomadism and Savagery."
[14] Saygin and Önal, " 'Secularism'," 27.

contemporary Western civilization. If we want to survive, we have to secu-larize our view of religion, morality, social relations and law.[15]

The same process of secular modernization, however, was seen by others, both Turks and foreigners, as a process of civilizational "conversion".[16]

If we follow the chronology of the late Ottoman approach to civiliza-tion, empire, secularization, and modernization, it is evident that until 1924, Islamic internationalism prevailed among Turkish intellectuals. The most prominent Turkish nationalist of the time, Ziya Gökalp, advo-cated a Muslim cultural internationalism, mediating as a supra-identity between the nation and the universal world order. Similarly, the socio-logist Mehmet Izzet, in his 1923 book, "Theories of Nationalism and National Life" (*Milliyet Nazariyeleri ve milli Hayat*), rejected the narrow vision of a nation-state.[17] However, upon the conclusion of the Treaty of Lausanne, which accorded Turkey sovereign status in the community of nations, leaders of the new republican elite saw Muslim internationalism that focused on the international influence of the Caliphate as a potential burden for the state. Transnational institutions were rejected. The abolish-ment of the Caliphate in 1924 contributed to the consolidation of nation-states as the organizational units of the postcolonial Islamic world.

After 1924, the Turkish government focused on its secular moderni-zation project of nation building. Even then, the leaders of the Turkish republic were happy to cooperate with like-minded Westernizing elites of independent Muslim states, such as Iran and Afghanistan.[18] Secular nationalists, such as Mustafa Kemal, and Turkish socialists inherited anti-Western critique mainly on issues related to imperialism. However, the republican elite adopted a radical Westernizing modernization project at home. As Aydin notes, this was possible because the elite made a mental separation between the universal West and the imperialist West: "Mustafa Kemal formulated this Westernism as the inevitability of mod-ern civilization."[19] Civilization, Kemal said, "has no pity on those who are ignorant or rebellious.... We cannot afford to hesitate any more. We have to move forward... Civilization is such a fire that it burns and destroys those who ignore it."[20]

---

15 Quoted by Davutoğlu, "Dimensions of Secularisation," 170–171.
16 Davutoğlu, "Dimensions of Secularisation," 171.
17 Aydin, "Between Occidentalism and the Global Left," 451.
18 Aydin, *Politics of Anti-Westernism.*
19 Aydin, *Politics of Anti-Westernism,* 452.
20 Quoted by Aydin, *Politics of Anti-Westernism,* 452.

Laiklik, a direct import from the French *laïcité*, entered this debate relatively late. No such concept existed in Turkish before the collapse of the empire. That is why this discussion directs us to the growing need for an examination of the discourse on secularization within the context of East-West relations and particularly within what may be described as cultural colonization.

Indeed, the view that secularism in Turkey was solely the result of an evolutionary process of estrangement from religion and the adoption of a rational vision of society and human nature is problematic. This view is expressed in Zürcher's explanation that the Kemalist elite juxtaposed knowledge and religion. The new Kemalist bureaucrats were entrusted with the task of guarding the boundaries between the public and the private, the secular and the religious, he explains. The republic that was established in 1923 became "fully secular," he argues.[21] "In the new order, Islam was under tight state control, but no influence of Islamic institutions on the administration, education or on the judiciary was allowed."[22] Furthermore, secularism was used as a defensive wall by the Westernized positivist elite against Islamic radicalism through the implementation of top-down policies forced on the masses. While such a view is not entirely wrong, there is a need to expose and to emphasize the complex relationship between the religious and the secular in Turkey.

Indeed, understanding the fear of peripheries is essential to an understanding of both secularism and republicanism. However, if building a wall between religion and the state was essential for overcoming their fears, it is hard to understand why the religious legal Sunni Hanafi heritage survived within the Kemalist establishment as a fundamental component and as a social marker. Moreover, if the Kemalist bureaucracy aimed at the elimination of religion on its own side of the wall, why did it establish the Directorate of Religious Affairs (*Diyanet İşleri Başkanlığı*) and thus contributed to the continuation of the religious mechanisms in the heart of the secular establishment? Does Turkish historiography represent accurately the ways in which secularism was introduced?

To answer this question one must examine secular genealogy; the historical context in which the notion was brought to the center of public debate. In other words, one must look at the quest for legal reforms in the nineteenth century and the crystallization of the anti-colonial position among

---

[21] Zürcher, "Turkish secularism," 135.
[22] Zürcher, "Turkish secularism," 135.

the Ottoman elite in that period. Such an approach reflects the existence of both colonization and de-colonization. As a Protestant Christian product, secularization reflects the invasion of Western concepts and thought into the Ottoman and Turkish spheres. At the same time, it was adopted as a last-ditch attempt to block Western forces and dominance. It was a way to protect Ottoman society from physical colonization. Thus the discussion of secularism in Turkey must be connected to the discussion of survival, civilizations, and colonialism. It must also offer new paradigms for the analysis of the relationship between secularism and Europe as an analytical category that is formed and that acts in various fields: administrative, legal, and cultural.

The following is not a chronological study of Turkish secularism, but rather an attempt to look at a few episodes that illuminate the above argument.

The Problem of Secularism as a Basic Paradigm of the Turkish Republic

Secularism is not a static concept. It is dynamic in nature and has acquired different meanings in different historic and ideological contexts. The principle of *laiklik* was introduced into the constitution in 1937, only a year before Atatürk's death. But on the basis of earlier discussions among the Ottoman elite, from the very establishment of the republic legal provisions and state-mandated regulations and instructions were geared toward the separation of religion from politics. It is therefore fair to argue that *laiklik* is a concept that better defines Kemalists in the post-Atatürk period.

Although the terms *laik* and *laiklik* were adopted from the French *laïcité*, with its distinct origin and experience, most scholars use the term 'secularism'. Turkish scholars, such as Mete Tunçay and Tarik Zafer Tunaya, refer to *laïcité* in their analysis, to suggest the authoritarian top-down policies of the Kemalist secular project.[23] Şerif Mardin uses "secularism".[24] In their famous works on the history of modern Turkey, Bernard Lewis, Feroz Ahmad, and Eric Zürcher tend to translate *laiklik* as "secularism".[25] Indeed, a discussion of the translation issue is imperative. Talal Asad has

---

[23] Tunçay, *T.C.'nde Tek-Parti Yönetiminin Kurulması*; Tunaya, "Atatürkçü Laiklik Politikası"; Tunaya, "Türkiye Büyük Millet Meclisi Hükümeti'nin Kuruluşu ve Siyasi Karakteri."

[24] Mardin, "Religion and Secularism in Turkey."

[25] Lewis, *Emergence of Modern Turkey*, 1968; Ahmad, *Making of Modern Turkey*; Zürcher, *Turkey*.

already noted in his discussion of the Egyptian response to the concept of secularism that Egyptian reactions, both positive and negative, were responses to connotations introduced in the process of translation.[26]

In the Turkish context, the eminent sociologist Ziya Gökalp was the first to introduce the concept of 'secularism' into the Ottoman language, using the term *la-dini*. But this translation, Lewis argues, "was often taken to mean 'irreligious' or even 'antireligious'," and these interpretations further increased the hostility with which the notion was received.[27] Perhaps that is why *la-dini* was soon replaced by the French *laïcité* and its Turkish version, *laiklik*. It is not entirely clear why there was no attempt to find a Turkish term that could have served as a cultural translation, as was the case in Hebrew or Arabic.

However, it is more important for this discussion to ask the following: If there was no attempt at a cultural translation, what made the creation of a laiklik approach possible and how was it shaped? If we set aside the popular understanding of 'secularism' and look at how the concept was used in the national republican language and instructions, it becomes clear that *laiklik* appeared mainly in the fields of law, administration, and education. As Asad points out, it is difficult to explain secularism and it is much easier to follow its shadow.[28] Indeed, 'secularism' is a combination of related concepts that in their relationships with one another create spaces in which they act.[29] Three such spaces to be examined are national symbolism, education, and citizenship.

De-Arabization of the Republic

In November 1932, during the holy month of Ramadan, Turkey's Kemalist bureaucrats tried to change the familiar character of the Adhan, the call to prayer sounded five times a day from the tops of minarets throughout the Muslim world. The bureaucrats established a committee of prominent academics, philologists, and clerics. After much discussion, the committee decided that there was no religious barrier to using the local language, instead of Arabic, to express and conduct the various aspects of religious life. Therefore, the use of the local language, Turkish, was permitted for the recital of religious texts. Instead of the Arabic call to prayer beginning with

---

[26] Asad, *Formations of the Secular*, 282.
[27] Lewis, *Political language*, 117.
[28] Asad, *Formations of the Secular*, 31.
[29] Asad, *Formations of the Secular*, 313.

Allahu akbar, which is used throughout the Muslim world, the Kemalists proposed replacing it with the Turkish call beginning with *Tanrı uludur*. But it soon became apparent that the Turkish public could not adapt to these new sounds.[30]

Shortly after the new regulation came into effect, the Kemalists had to admit their mistake, and a year and a half after the regulation was introduced but rarely implemented, it was ignored. It was formally revoked in 1951, two weeks after the election as prime minister of Adnan Menderes, who claimed that he represented the will of the people in opposing the repressive institutions of the state. To a great extent, the attempt to change the call to prayer denoted the limits of the secularization effort and the attempt to de-Arabize the public sphere in Kemalist Turkey. It marked the boundaries of legitimate discourse and the boundaries of the Turkish civilization project, but primarily the beginning of the long and successful struggle of the Turkish periphery against the culturally alienated and brutal worldview of the Kemalist bureaucracy.

The attempt to change the Adhan led to the popular view that the Kemalist revolution was secularist in the extreme and that it was trying to achieve an absolute separation of church and state, similar to that of the Jacobin *laïcité*. Whereas supporters of secularism often advocated such measures, its opponents, such as Kadir Misiroğlu, saw in Kemalist ideology and reform a form of *Jahiliyyah*—which refers to the Islamic concept of the Days of Ignorance in the pre-Islamic period. However, this view is unjustified. In fact, the abortive attempt to change the Adhan was characteristic of the Kemalist process of *laiklik*, because instead of trying to abolish the religion completely, it tried to Turkify it. The focus of the elitist Turkish civilization project was an attempt at de-Arabization (in this case, of Allah).

Moreover, Turkish nationalism, from its very beginnings at the end of the Ottoman period, incorporated clearly religious elements. This was true both at the administrative level and at the popular level, that is, the way in which the population perceived the function of religion. In fact, at the same time that the Kemalist bureaucracy adopted an aggressive secular rhetoric, it used religion as a category of social classification, that is, as a tool for identifying those who would be classified as Turks. Even more important, Islamic values continued to be included in narratives and thus also to shape the Turks' worldview and the way in which they told, heard,

---

[30] Turan, *Formation of Authoritarian Secularism*.

and argued their narrative.[31] Mustafa Kemal succeeded in changing the focus of Turkish identity from Ottoman-religious to Turkish-nationalist. But this did not prevent the Ottoman Islamic past from remaining a dominant component of Turkish identity.

The Kemalist photo album, from its inception, included images that definitively linked the Turkish people to Islamic history, both Ottoman and pan-Turkish. The imperial past, the great conquests, and the far-flung lands over which the magnificent empire ruled—none of these was left out. The struggle of the Kemalist bureaucracy focused on two central aspects of the Ottoman-Islamic past: core Islamic texts and their representatives, the *ulema* (clerics), on the one hand, and the clear regulation of the relations between religion and politics, on the other. The *laiklik* project dealt primarily with ordering those relations in a clear hierarchy of politics over religion.[32]

The battle against the core religious texts—the collections of the Hadith, the canonical fatwas, and the associated religious literature—was intense and determined. Kemal's view of the Islamic literature resulted from his modern Western education. For him, religious literature was foreign to Turkishness and even a threat to the survival of the Turkish people. However, in order to fight these canonical Islamic texts, which he considered Arab in nature, he chose to adopt and highlight popular elements in them that could be linked to the emerging Turkish nation. In contrast to the collections of the Hadith and the fatwas that linked the Turkish world to the Islamic and Arab worlds, both through their language and their religious content, Kemal defined as legitimately Turkish those religious elements that were understood as rituals, and therefore also characteristic of authentic Turkish (that is, local and Anatolian) rural and tribal life.[33]

One of the outstanding examples of the Kemalists' contempt for the written religious heritage is the fact that after coming to power, the bureaucrats disposed of the fatwas and royal decrees as garbage and as paper for recycling, which peddlers and grocers used to wrap their goods. This expression of deep contempt for the ancient Islamic culture was accompanied by punishment, both formal and informal, of anyone who violated the spirit and the regulations of the new civilizational project.

---

[31] Mardin, "Cultural Change and the Intellectual," 243–259.
[32] Turan, *Formation of Authoritarian Secularism in Turkey.*
[33] Mardin, "Cultural Change and the Intellectual."

Instituting codes of public behaviour that accorded with presenting a
fresh, modern, and Western face in the public spaces of the republic made
possible, perhaps even encouraged, local initiatives that met the needs
in places where the judicial system dared not go too far. For example,
soldiers forcibly removed the veils covering women's faces in the main
streets of Ankara and Istanbul. Meticulously presenting a modern urban
visual image is characteristic of the Kemalist vision, which focused on
changing the "street theater" and all its colors and symbols.

Folk tales from Anatolia were collected by ethnographers who were
sent to gather the remains of authentic Turkish culture, which had been
shunted aside, so the Kemalists claimed, by a process of intentional
Arabization that had begun in the sixteenth century and continued until
the end of the nineteenth. The establishment of the Ethnographic Museum
by a November 1925 government order—on the site of an ancient Muslim
cemetery on Namazgâh Hill, in the new capital, Ankara—symbolized the
burial of the old, religious, Islamic-Ottoman world by the collectors of
knowledge, the modernists, the scholars of the social sciences and the
humanities, who painstakingly classified and catalogued Turkish culture
in museums and introduced cultural initiatives to define the authentic, Anatolian Turk. The agents of preservation of the unifying, defining
images—the mosques, like the churches before them—were also turned
into museums, the temples of modern man. This process preserved them
as part of a patronizing framework: cages whose contents were gazed at
by modern man.

Whereas the process of de-Arabization and de-Ottomanization met
with little resistance, most Turks viewed the cultural revolution's de-
Islamization with mixed feelings. In various communities it was seen as
heresy and as a disaster comparable to what the Crusaders had brought
upon them in the Middle Ages. Many considered the process as alienating
and as requiring the abandonment of a system of values and behaviours
they had inherited from their forefathers. The closure of the Sufi orders by
government decree was seen as an attack not only on a religious institution but also on a social institution. After all, the Sufi orders were no less a
social organization than a religious one, and for many Turks they operated
as a broad social network touching on all aspects of life.

The reforms instituted by the republican regime did not totally eliminate religion as a matter of faith and certainly could not cope with the
social institutions in far-flung places. The way in which the government
persecuted the Sufi orders forced them to find new modes of action. They
did not disappear altogether, but rather went into exile or underground.

Ironically, while they were being persecuted in the name of the Westernization project, Sufi orders operated undisturbed in the West—in the United States and the European countries.[34] Those that remained in Anatolia found a sympathetic ear among the many in Turkey who saw themselves as victims of the new cultural dictatorship. Thus the Kemalists created, or at least caused the creation of, a double and parallel system.

But religious values were preserved not only among the diaspora communities or in the Turkish underground. Even the Kemalists' dominant target population maintained its religious views, especially when these could be disguised as, or when they conformed to, the local patriarchal, tribal, or cultural practices. Thus, and in other ways, both subversive and overt, religious elements were preserved in cultural mothballs in the core of the Kemalist knowledge about the past and the essence of being a Turk. These elements rose up in the very heart of Turkey at various junctures in republican history and forced the Kemalists to struggle throughout the century with the Trojan horse that was part of their vision.

One of the constant fears of the Ottoman elite from the sixteenth century onward was the spread of the periphery and the destruction of the center of sovereignty in Istanbul. This fear was well grounded in history. From the end of the sixteenth century, the Ottoman elite was occupied with trying to understand the reasons for the decline of the empire's power. Historians differ in their views on the reasons for this long process, which continued until the twentieth century. They also differ on whether, after the empire's high point in the sixteenth century, its decline was a steady process. In either case, from the nineteenth century onward, the bureaucracy of the Ottoman Empire was occupied with questions related to institutional collapse and loss of territory. Among the reasons for this loss were financial and economic processes connected to the discovery of America, the difficulty of managing large territories, and perhaps the too-great expansion on three continents, institutional changes in the system of inheritance, and the method of conscription.[35] All these brought about a shift in the balance of power with Europe. Finally, military defeats were the factor that accelerated the process of imperial reforms, known collectively as *Tanzimat*.[36]

---

[34] Ultanir, "Contribution of alleged secularists."
[35] See: Lewis, *The Emergence of Modern Turkey*.
[36] Shaw, *History of Ottoman Empire*.

These reforms included many changes in education and in the army. But most important was the aspect that may have been their motivation: the bureaucracy's need to find an effective solution to the empire's great loss of territory, which from the eighteenth century had included lands inhabited by Muslims—in the Balkans, Vlachia, Bessarabia and the Caucuses. This loss, which was known in Europe as "the Eastern problem", created two sets of pressures on the Ottoman center. The new reforms, the Tanzimat that began officially in 1839 after the defeat in Nusaybin, were the result of pressure from Europe and pressure within the Ottoman bureaucracy. The European powers debated how to prevent intra-European competition that could touch off a continental war and wanted to take advantage of the weakness of the "sick man of the Bosporus" to obtain concessions for Europeans living within the territories of the empire and their native dependents.

These aims coincided with the desire of the people within the Ottoman system to pressure the sultan into giving up some of his authority and creating a functional and effective system of registration and ownership of land. They hoped that this would restore the empire's ability to rule its territories and survive the struggles with the countries of the West. After all, survival of the political system in the face of Western imperialism was the main topic of discussion during the nineteenth and early twentieth centuries. The fear that the periphery would overrun the centre was always closely related to the question of survival and the political options that would ensure that survival.

Cemil Aydin presents the ideological options that were available to the Ottoman elite.[37] In opposition to them was the secular nationalist-territorial option, which gave up the imperial dreams and which triumphed at a relatively late stage. All the options considered at the end of the Ottoman period are preserved in the album of Turkish political memory and have surfaced at various times in response to international circumstances. An interesting point is the link between the strength of the intra-Turkish system and the ideological arguments within it, on the one hand, and Turkey's place in the international arena and the ambitions connected with that place, on the other. A good example of this is the defining memory of the capitulation agreements during the Ottoman period, or the humiliating 1920 Treaty of Sèvres, which had a traumatic effect, lasting to this day, on Turkey's view of security and foreign affairs.[38]

---

[37] Aydin, *Politics of Anti-Westernism.*
[38] Guida, "Sèvres Syndrome and 'Komplo' Theories."

The binary Kemalist version that became authoritative as a result of extensive academic research throughout the world, including Turkey, offered a clear but somewhat misleading picture. The Kemalist project had not left out religion, and Turkish nationalism was not created in opposition to religion. It was created as an option and strategy for survival. For Mustafa Kemal, the new Turk would survive the natural selection of global struggles. The discourse regarding the new Turk was accompanied by a belief derived from the temple of modernity that it was possible to create a "New Man", cut off from the past, history, and community. This man must have Western education and be aligned with Western civilization. But that man would remain culturally Turkish. To that end, it was important to carry out the de-Arabization and de-Ottomanization of the public and political spaces, and this included the removal of some Islamic elements.

The language reform is perhaps the most striking aspect in this context. The reform included linguistic purification, cleansing the language of foreign—especially Arabic and Persian—influences. Also, in the 1920s, the government conducted a national campaign calling upon the population to speak Turkish. This campaign was aimed at eliminating the differences between the various religious and ethnic groups.[39] This was in contrast to the policy of the Ottoman Empire, which had allowed and even encouraged the separateness of various groups, based on the logic of divide and rule. The Kemalist policy was also based on the belief that Arabic was not suited to the teaching of Western sciences and that it contained images and sounds that were linked to the Middle Ages and religion.

Of all the Kemalists' reforms, it seems that the one focusing on de-Ottomanization, which included not only abolishing the sultanate and creating the republic but also defaming the imperial family and its institutions, was the most successful of all, or as Geoffrey Lewis termed it, "catastrophically successful".[40] This process was relatively easy to implement because of the imperial family's unpopularity, which stemmed partly from the sultan's willingness to sign the humiliating Treaty of Sèvres and partly from the fact that the sultans were of non-Turkish extraction. These were also the reasons that, in contrast to other countries that underwent a revolution and banished the monarch, no movement arose in Turkey to restore the sultanate. The idea that the people needed to be sovereign became an unshakable principle.

---

[39] Lewis, *Turkish Language Reform.*
[40] Lewis, *Turkish Language Reform.*

The Trojan-Horse Construction of Turkish Republicanism

Another reason for the country's inability to remove Islam from the discourse on the politics of identity was the important role of religion in the establishment of the republic. The official Kemalist version presented the birth of the first republic as a natural step for the homogeneous Turkish population in Anatolia and Thrace. But in fact, after World War I, Anatolia became heterogeneous. During the war of independence, Islam served the nationalist forces as a melting pot in the war against the Greek occupation forces. The synergy between nationalism and religion created a rebellious Islamic identity.

The symbiotic relations between Islam and Turkish nationalism cemented the place of religion in Turkish identity. The rebellious element in this identity caused Kemal and his successors to institutionalize hierarchical relations with religion within the state's institutions. In practice, however, few in the periphery adopted this hierarchical order in their lives and in their worldview. The Sharia system became a parallel system with which the state had to contend repeatedly.

The Trojan introduction of religion into the national structure found powerful symbolic expression. A good example is the national anthem ("*Istiklâl Marşı*", The Independence March), which was written by the poet Mehmet Âkif Ersoy and adopted as early as 1921:

> Do not fear! The crimson flag that proudly ripples in this glorious dawn, shall not fade,
> Before the last fiery hearth that is ablaze within my nation is extinguished.
> That is the star of my nation, and it will forever shine;
> It is mine; and solely belongs to my valiant nation.
> Don't frown! I beseech you, oh thou coy crescent,
> But smile upon my heroic race! Why the anger, why the rage?
> This blood of ours which we shed for you shall not be blessed otherwise;
> For Freedom is the absolute right of my God-worshiping nation.
> I have been free since the beginning and forever shall be so.
> What madman shall put me in chains! I defy the very idea!
> I'm like the roaring flood; powerful and independent,
> I'll tear apart mountains, exceed the heavens and still gush out!
> The lands of the West may be armoured with walls of steel,
> But I have borders guarded by the mighty chest of a believer.
> Recognize your innate strength, my friend! And think: how can this fiery faith ever be killed,
> By that battered, single-fanged monster you call "civilization"?
> My friend! Leave not my homeland to the hands of villainous men!
> Render your chest as armor and your body as trench! Stop this disgraceful rush!.....

What man would not die for this heavenly piece of land?
Martyrs would gush out should one simply squeeze the soil! Martyrs!
May God take my life, all my loved ones and possessions from me if He
     will,
But may He not deprive me of my one true homeland for the world.
Oh glorious God, the sole wish of my pain-stricken heart is that,
No heathen's hand should ever touch the bosom of my sacred Temples.
These adhans, whose shahadahs are the foundations of my religion,
May their noble sound last loud and wide over my eternal homeland.
For only then, shall my fatigued tombstone, if there is one, prostrate a thou-
     sand times in ecstasy,
Neither you nor my race shall ever be extinguished!
For freedom is the absolute right of my ever-free flag;
For independence is the absolute right of my God-worshiping nation!

It was not only the anthem that wove together religious and nationalist
themes. The Turkish identity card, in which religion is listed and which
citizens were required to carry at all times, served as a tool for categorizing the population, overtly and covertly, by religious affiliation. Overtly, it
distinguished between Muslims and others; and covertly, it distinguished
between Kurds, most of whom were Alevis or Shafi'i Muslims, and Sunni
Hanafi Muslim Turks. The need in practice to identify Turkish Kurds,
despite the rhetoric that did not allow such distinctions in public, made
the religious-judicial affiliation a categorizing tool and a social marker.

The Trojan-horse nature of building religion into the national structure
found clear legal and administrative expression several times in Turkish
history. A famous example that has been much discussed in the literature
on Turkey is the population-exchange agreement with Greece, which was
signed by Kemal and Eleftherios Venizelos. This agreement provided for
the transfer from Greece to Turkey of hundreds of thousands of Muslims
of various ethnic backgrounds, and of hundreds of thousands of Christians
from Turkey to Greece.

According to this agreement, all the Muslim residents of Greece were
forcibly moved to Turkey, even if they were Greeks who had become
Muslims, and all the Greek-speaking Orthodox Christians were forcibly
moved from Turkey to Greece.[41] This traumatic forced population
exchange would perhaps prevent much political friction later on, but
its grave social, human, and cultural effects are in evidence to this day.
Hundreds of thousands of Orthodox Christians were cut off from their

---

[41] On the Population exchanges see: Pentzopoulos, *Balkan exchange of minorities*,
23–51.

roots and their sources of income and were transferred to Greece, where they were received as refugees, and more than a million Muslims suffered a similar fate in being transferred by force to Turkey. The outcome of this population exchange was that religion remained a central element in the national identity of both sides, despite their nationalist declarations. The few non-Muslims who remained in Turkey after the Armenian genocide, the Greek pogroms, and the population exchange became strangers in their homeland.

Another example of the way that religion was built into Turkish nationalism and the way that the Kemalist elite understood what it meant to be a Turk can be seen in the legislation and implementation of the "immigration and settlement" laws of the 1930s, which defined who was allowed to immigrate to Turkey and the places where immigrants were allowed to settle.[42] The first immigration laws were promulgated as early as the 1920s. Clause two of the Absorption and Settlement Law, passed on 31 May 1926, deals, for example, with the definition of populations and individuals that would not be allowed to immigrate to Turkey as part of the mass absorption in the first decade of the republic. The clause states that "people who are not part of the Turkish culture; people who are infected by syphilis; people who suffer from leprosy, and their families; people who have been imprisoned for murder, except for those who committed murder for political or military reasons; anarchists; spies; Gypsies; and those who have been expelled from Turkey—all these may not be absorbed in Turkey."[43]

The law may be considered the first attempt in the region to establish the right of return to a national homeland. It does not go into detail about who is included in the category of those who are part of Turkish culture, but the practice implemented by the state's bureaucracy shows how this category was understood. The immigration and settlement policy concerning immigrants within Anatolia aimed particularly at achieving the national goal of rebuilding the province that had been depopulated by World War I. Between 1923 and 1934, the young state absorbed some 800,000 immigrants who were seen as being part of Turkish culture. However, few of them were Turks and only some spoke Turkish. But all were Muslims,

---

[42] On population policies see: Karpat, "The Ethnicity Problem"; Karpat, "Ottoman Ethnic and Confessional Legacy."

[43] Aybay, *Vatandaşlık Hukuku.*

mainly from the Balkan countries, from the same areas that the republic's bureaucracy considered an integral part of the Ottoman Turkish space.

The immigration and settlement policy sought to put the non-Turkish Muslim immigrants in the Kurdish areas of Anatolia, in order to change the demographic balance there. Thus, the "imported" Muslims became agents of the Turkification of the Kurds.[44]

On 14 June 1934, Law No. 2510 went into effect. It stated that Turkish-speaking Muslims and other "white" Muslims from the Balkans, Central Asia, and the Caucasus were allowed to immigrate to Turkey. These included the Pomaks, the Tatars, the Bosnians, the Cherkessians, and Muslims from the area of Georgia (including Abkhazians), who were all allowed to immigrate even though they were not Turks and though Turkish was not their language. In this context, these white Muslims became Turks by adopting the language after their immigration.

The fate of the Jews of Thrace was also determined by their lack of a Sunni Islamic component in their identity. In 1934, this population, which was considered loyal throughout the Ottoman period and which had given up its minority rights in 1927 (the very rights that were guaranteed by the 1923 Treaty of Lausanne) to express its absolute loyalty to the republic, discovered the limits of integration. Thousands of Jews who had lived in the ancient cities of Edirne, Cenkale, and Babasaki, descendants of ancient communities, were evicted from their homes because the area was designated a top-security zone. The expulsion from cities that were close to the eastern borders was accompanied by unusually powerful expressions of anti-Semitism that made it clear that religion, that is, Islam, was necessary for inclusion in the new Turkishness. It was necessary but not sufficient, as Arab Muslims and Kurds discovered. Despite the increasing strength of the ethno-nationalist discourse, Ottoman views based on community logic and the memory of the ethno-religious millets shaped the civil logic of the republican government and of citizenship. The transition from the millet (religious affiliation) to the milli (national affiliation) was natural.

A third example, no less painful and especially revealing, is the imposition of a draconian property tax, the *Varlik Vergisi*, in November 1942, on all the country's citizens. The tax was intended to help the national treasury finance the arming of the defence forces at the height of World

---

[44] Cagaptay, *Islam*, chapter 5.

War II.[45] Although Turkey maintained its neutrality and did not enter the war until it had been won, the Turkish government prepared the army for possible involvement. The high cost required the levy of a special tax. However, there were other reasons for the tax, mainly the desire to expropriate from the non-Muslim minorities in Turkey control of many financial assets. Despite the tax imposed on all inhabitants, it was calculated differently for non-Muslims and for those who had adopted Islam (Dönmeh); these paid a much higher tax than did Muslims. The tax was so high that many could not pay it and thus became impoverished. More than 2,000 people who were unable to pay the tax within thirty days were sent to forced labour camps in eastern Turkey. In 1944, following great public pressure and international criticism, the tax was abolished. Within two years, however, the government had succeeded in transferring to Muslim hands nearly ninety-five percent of the real estate assets of non-Muslims.[46]

World War II provides one more opportunity for studying the differences between the treatment of Muslims and non-Muslims. Before the property tax there was another embarrassing incident connected to the call-up of members of the religious minorities for reserve duty. Unlike young Muslim men, Jews and Christians were called up to serve in units that were not armed and were not trained for a military encounter. They were sent to civilian settlements where they were required to haul away garbage and engage in maintenance, which was considered humiliating. This discrimination and the rough categorization by religion—Muslims and non-Muslims—was for many Jewish and Christian inhabitants an additional sign of the temporary nature of their status in the eyes of the government. The incident showed that citizenship was not egalitarian. Although ethnic differences are the real threat to Turkish sovereignty, this incident showed that the secular state saw religion as the differentiating factor between one citizen and another, between Turks and other inhabitants. Whereas the nationalist state adopted an inclusive policy with regard to various ethnic groups and refused to recognize ethnic differences, the religious differences were preserved and used as a clear criterion for national exclusion and inclusion. This was the case in the time of Kemal and throughout the history of the republic.

---

[45] Levi, *Türkiye Cumhuriyeti'nde Yahudiler*; Also see: Shaw, *Jews of the Ottoman Empire*; Weiker, *Ottomans, Turks and the Jewish Polity*.
[46] Levy, *Jews, Turks, and Ottoman*.

Whereas the Kurds were considered mountain Turks, the Alevis, Jews, Armenians, and, of course, the Dönmeh were pushed to the margins of the nation. The fact that the father of Turkish nationalist theory, Ziya Gökalp, was a Kurd was not surprising in his day. The fact that the Dönmeh, the descendants of the followers of Shabbetai Tsvi who converted to Islam collectively in the seventeenth century, were included among those who paid the higher tax is clear evidence that they were not considered true Turks. Only the Sunni Hannafis were so considered.

The Turkish identity card reveals the nature of secular Turkish categorization in the hands of the Kemalist bureaucracy. Until the 1950s, by indicating the religious-judicial affiliation of the bearer, the card included the ethno-religious identity by which the millets had been defined in the Ottoman past. In other words, the distinction between the Sunni Hanafi Turks and the Shafii Turks marked the ethno-religious distinction between Turks and Kurds, and between Sunni Turks, on the one hand, and Alevi Turks and Kurds, on the other.[47]

The case of Turkey shows that the cultural and judicial-administrative aspects of the republic had a built-in amorphousness that made it impossible to separate the processes of nation-building from religious ideas, language, and other social practices. In other words, religion and religious messages lived on within the nationalist structures. Religion was moved from the religious-judicial realm to the social-administrative realm and continued to exist in the album of images and memories, in the inventory of the Turkish imagination. The fact that the defining images from the Turkish past—the conquest of Constantinople and the Siege of Vienna—were linked to the Turkish relationship with European history and were also the defining images of Turkish pre-nationalist society is evidence mainly that Islam, as understood by the Ottomans, was also structured by means of the Turkish components. The conquests of Mehmet Fatih, as a defining image, were more important than those of the Prophet Muhammad. *Laiklik* was mainly shaped by the Ottoman and Turkish encounter with Europe and perhaps it should be examined in this context.

---

[47] **Please provide footnote text.**

Bibliography

Ahmad, Feroz. *The Making of Modern Turkey*. London: Routledge, 1993.

Akarlı, Engin Deniz. *Belgelerle Tanzimat: Osmanlı Sadrazamlarından Âli ve Fuad Paşaların Vasiyyetnâmeleri*. Istanbul: Boğaziçi Üniversitesi Yayınları, 1978.

Aydin, Cemil. *The Politics of Anti-Westernism in Asia: Visions of World Order in Pan-Islamic and Pan-Asian Thought. Columbia Studies in International and Global History*. New York: Columbia University Press, 2007.

Cemil Aydin. *"Between Occidentalism and the Global Left: Islamist Critiques of the West in Turkey,"* Comparative Studies of South Asia, Africa and the Middle East 26, no. 3 (2006): 446–461.

Belge, Murat. "Mustafa Kemal ve Kemalizm." In *Modern Türkiye'de Siyasi Düşünce Cilt 2: Kemalizm*, edited by Ahmet İnsel, pp. 29–43. Istanbul: İletişim, 2001.

Berkes, Niyazi. *Türkiye'de Çağdaşlaşma*. Istanbul: Bilgi Yayınevi, 1973.

Cagaptay, Soner. *Islam, Secularism, and Nationalism in Modern Turkey. Who Is a Turk?* London: Routledge, 2006.

Cündioğlu, Dücane. *Türkçe Kuran ve Cumhuriyet İdeolojisi*. Istanbul: Kitabevi, 1998.

———. *Bir Siyasi Proje Olarak Türkçe İbadet I: Türkçe Namaz (1923–1950)*. Istanbul: Kitabevi, 1999.

Davison, Andrew. *Türkiye'de Sekülarizm ve Modernlik*. Istanbul: İletişim, 2002.

Davutoğlu, Ahmet. "Philosophical and Institutional Dimensions of Secularisation: A Comparative Analysis." In *Islam and Secularism in the Middle East*, edited by Azzam Tamimi, and J. Esposito, pp. 170–208. London: Hurst & Company, 2002.

———. *Alternative paradigms: the impact of Islamic and Western Weltanschauungs on political theory*. Lanham: University Press of America, 1994.

Demirel, Ahmet. *Birinci Meclis'te Muhalefet*. Instanbul: İletişim, 1994.

Deringil, Selim. *İktidarın Sembolleri ve İdeoloji: II. Abdülhamit Dönemi (1876–1909)*. İstanbul: YKY, 2002.

Fortna, Benjamin. *Imperial Classroom: Islam, The State and Education in The Late Ottoman Empire*. Oxford: Oxford University Press, 2002.

Gellner, Ernest. "The Turkish Option in Comparative Perspective." In *Rethinking Modernity and National Identity in Turkey*, edited by Reşat Kasaba, and Sibel Bozdoğan, pp. 233–244. Seattle: University of Washington Press, 1997.

Göle, Nilüfer. "Authoritarian secularism and Islamist Politics: The Case of Turkey." In *Civil Society in the Middle East*, edited by Augustus Richard Norton, vol. 2, pp. 17–43. Leiden: E.J. Brill, 1996.

Guida, Michaelangelo. "The Sèvres Syndrome and 'Komplo' Theories in the Islamist and Secular Press." *Turkish Studies* (March 2008): 37–52.

Kara, İsmail. "Bir Tür Laiklik: Diyanet İşleri Başkanlığı Örneği." In *75 Yılda Düşünceler Tartışmalar, Türkiye Ekonomik ve Toplumsal Tarih Vakfı*, edited by Mete Tunçay, pp. 197–206. Istanbul: Türkiye Ekonomik ve Toplumsal Tarih Vakfı, 1999.

Karpat, Kemal H. "Millets and Nationality: The Roots of Incongruity of Nation and State in the Post-Ottoman Era." In *Christians and Jews in the Ottoman Empire: The Functioning of a Plural Society*, edited by Benjamin Braude, and Bernard Lewis. New York: Holmes & Meier, 1982.

———. *Ottoman Population, 1830–1914: Demographic and Social Characteristics*. Madison, Wisconsin: The University of Wisconsin Press, 1985.

———. "The Ethnicity Problem in a Multi-Ethnic Anational Islamic State: Continuity and Recasting of Ethnic Identity in the Ottoman Empire." In *Ethnic Groups and the State*, edited by Paul Brass, pp. 95–114. Totowa, N.J.: Barnes and Noble, 1985.

———. "The Ottoman Ethnic and Confessional Legacy in the Middle East." In *Ethnicity, Pluralism, and the State in the Middle East*, edited by M. J. Esman, and I. Rabinovich, pp. 35–54. Ithaca: Cornell University Press, 1988.

——. *The Politicization of Islam: Reconstructing Identity, State, Faith, and Community in the Late Ottoman Empire*. London: Oxford University Press, 2001.

Lerner, Daniel. *The Passing of Traditional Society: Modernizing the Middle East*. New York: The Free Press of Glencoe, 1958.

Lewis, Bernard. *The Emergence of Modern Turkey*. London: Oxford University Press, 1968.

——. *The Political Language of Islam*. Chicago: University of Chicago Press, 1988.

Lewis, Geoffrey. *The Turkish Language Reform: A Catastrophic Success*. Oxford: Oxford University Press, 2002.

Mardin, Şerif. *The Genesis of Young Ottoman Thought: A Study in the Modernization of Turkish Political Ideas*. Princeton: Princeton University Press, 1962.

——. *Din ve İdeoloji*. İstanbul: İletişim, 1992 (1969).

——. "Religion and Secularism in Turkey." In *Atatürk: Founder of a Nation State*, edited by Ali Kazancıgil & Ergun Özbudun, pp. 191–219. Hamden: CT: Archon, 1981.

——. "Kollektif Bellek ve Meşruiyetlerin Çatışması." In *Avrupa'da Etik, Din ve Laiklik, Metis*, edited by Oliver Abel, Mohammed Arkoun, and Şerif Mardin, pp. 7–14. İstanbul: İletişim, 1995.

——. "Yeni Osmanlı Düşüncesi." In *Modern Türkiye'de Siyasi Düşünce Cilt 1: Tanzimat ve Meşrutiyet'in Birikimi*, edited by Mehmet Ö. Alkan, pp. 42–53. İstanbul: İletişim, 2001.

Mert, Nuray. "Cumhuriyet Türkiye'sinde Laiklik ve Karşı Laikliğin Düşünsel Boyutu." In *Modern Türkiye'de Siyasî Düşünce, Cilt II: Kemalizm*, edited by Ahmet İnsel, pp. 197–209. Istanbul: İletişim, 2001.

——. *Laiklik Tartışmasına Kavramsal Bir Bakış: Cumhuriyet Kurulurken Laik Düşünce*. İstanbul: Bağlam Yayıncılık, 1994.

Parla, Taha. *Türkiye'de Siyasal Kültürün Resmi Kaynaklar Cilt 3: Kemalist Tek-Parti İdeolojisi ve Altı Ok'u*. İstanbul: İletişim, 1995.

Saygin, Tuncay & Mehmet Önal. " 'Secularism' From the Last Years of the Ottoman Empire to the Early Turkish Republic," *Journal for the Study of Religions and Ideologies* 7, no. 20 (Summer 2008): 26–48.

Shaw, Stanford J., and Ezel Kural-Shaw. *History of Ottoman Empire and Modern Turkey II*. Cambridge: Cambridge University Press, 1997.

Shaw, Stanford. *The Jews of the Ottoman Empire and the Turkish Republic*. New York: New York University Press, 1991.

Somel, Selçuk Akşin. *The Modernization of Public Education in The Ottoman Empire 1839–1908: Islamization, Autocracy and Discipline*. Leiden: Brill, 2001.

——. "Osmanlı Refom Çağında Osmanlıcılık Düşüncesi (1839–1913)." In *Modern Türkiye'de Siyasi Düşünce Cilt 1: Tanzimat ve Meşrutiyet'in Birikimi*, edited by Mehmet Ö. Alkan, pp. 88–116. İstanbul: İletişim, 2001.

Tanör, Bülent. "Laikleş(tir)me, Kemalistler ve Din." In *75 Yılda Düşünceler Tartışmalar, Türkiye Ekonomik ve Toplumsal Tarih Vakfı*, edited by Mete Tunçay, pp. 183–196. İstanbul: Türkiye Ekonomik ve Toplumsal Tarih Vakfı, 1999.

Tunaya, Tarık Zafer. "Atatürkçü Laiklik Politikası." In *Devrim Hareketleri İçinde Atatürk ve Atatürkçülük*, edited by Tarık Zafer Tunaya, pp. 323–342. Istanbul: İstanbul Bilgi Üniversitesi Yayınları, 2002.

Tunçay, Mete. *T.C.'nde Tek-Parti Yönetiminin Kurulması (1923–1931)*. İstanbul: Cem, 1992.

Turan, Sevgi Adak. *Formation of Authoritarian Secularism in Turkey: Ramadans in the Early Republican Era (1923–1938)*. Submitted to the Graduate School of Arts and Social Sciences in partial fulfillment of the requirements for the degree of Master of Arts. İstanbul: Sabancı University, Spring 2004.

Ultanir, Y. Gurcan. "The contribution of alleged secularists in Turkey to United States and Germany's Islamic organizations." *Educational Research* 1, no. 9 (October 2010): 345–355.

Yavuz, Hakan. "Is there a Turkish Islam?" *Journal of Muslim Minority Affairs* 24, no. 2 (2004): 213–232.

Yıldız, Ahmet. *"Ne Mutlu Türküm Diyebilene": Türk Ulusal Kimliğinin Etno-Seküler Sınırları (1919–1938).* İstanbul: İletişim, 2001.

Zürcher, Eric Jan. *Turkey: A Modern History.* London: I.B. Tauris, 1993 (Reprint 1997).

——. "Kemalist Düşüncenin Osmanlı Kaynakları." In *Modern Türkiye'de Siyasi Düşünce Cilt 2: Kemalism,* edited by Ahmet İnsel, pp. 44–55. İstanbul: İletişim, 2001.

——. "Turkish secularism in a European context." In: *The importance of being European: Turkey, the EU, and the Middle East,* edited by Nimrod Goren, and Amikam Nachmani, pp. 131–140. Jerusalem: European Forum at the Hebrew University, 2007.

CIVIC PIETY:
VISIONS OF SECULARITY IN CONSTITUTIONAL IRAN

Nahid Mozaffari

> In just regimes like constitutional and republican regimes, legitimacy is based on piety—not religious piety, but civic piety (*taqva-ye madani*).[1]

Introduction

The Iranian historical experience reveals the co-existence of complex discursive mélanges regarding religion and secularity.[2] In the nineteenth and twentieth centuries, the division between the discourse of the Enlightenment and the discourse of Islam and the separation of the realm of the state from the realm of religion was proposed alternately by dissident intellectuals, reforming bureaucrats, and the autocratic state, as a condition of modernity. Clashes between these discourses occurred intermittently, especially during the Constitutional Revolution of 1906–1911, but also in reaction to the reforms from above known as the White Revolution of 1963 and during the popular revolution of 1979, which overthrew the monarchy and resulted in an Islamic Republic.

However, except for a few historical instances, the lines between secularity and religion have remained blurred. For example, in the 1960s, both secular and religious intellectuals (such as Ali Shariati, Jalal Al-Ahmad), who were concerned with the formulation of a mobilizing ideology against the process of autocratic modernization without democratization, used an Islamic discourse towards the construction of an anti-materialist, anti-imperialist authenticity. Even Marxists such as Khosrow Golsorkhi used the martyrdom of Hussein, the third Shi'a Imam and the Karbala

---

[1] Cf. Dehkhoda's scrapbook.

[2] I would like to thank Ervand Abrahamian, Mangol Bayat, Lucian Hölscher, Sylvie Le Grand, Mohamad Tavakoli Targhi, Arash Naraghi, Fahimeh Gooran, Mahshad Mohit, and Sara Khalili whose ideas and discussions helped me formulate these preliminary thoughts on the history of secularity in Iran.

paradigm[3] to arouse the indignation and protest of people towards the injustices of the secular dictatorship.[4]

The blurring of the lines between the secular and the religious and the use of the religious discourse to address social inequities has continued to the present day. This is demonstrated by the fact that even in the first decade of the twenty-first century, there is no consensus on one Persian word for 'secularity', 'secularism' or 'the secular'.[5] The words *fara-dini* (beyond religion), *orfi* (based on custom as opposed to religion) *donyavi* (of this world), *qeir-e maz-habi* (other-than-religious), and derogatory or insulting terms such as *la maz-hab* or *bi-deen* (both meaning without religion and denoting immorality) are all used. In fact, today, when discussions about secularity and the separation of state and religion occupy an important place in the discourse of dissent in Iran, the words that are most often used in journals and at conferences are *sekular* or *sekularism* from the English, and *laique* and *laicite* from the French.

The clash between the discourse of the Enlightenment and the discourse of Islam first occurred among the reformists of the nineteenth century, but most openly and publicly in the discussions between the social democrat intellectuals and activists writing in the constitutionalist press and the anti-constitutionalist Muslim clerics (*ulama*). In this paper, I would like to focus on this particular clash, primarily because it was the first public discussion of the issue in the public space provided by the newly established newspapers; and secondly, because the discussion involved indigenous and European concepts, as they were understood at the time, with a focus on the use of words and their contextual meanings. The constitutional period (1906–11) is very important in Iranian history because it marks the beginning of a struggle for cultural modernism that has lasted to the present time; many of the issues that were raised then, including the boundaries between the secular and the religious, remain unresolved today.

---

[3] In the year 680, Imam Hussein fought against the forces of the Ummayid Caliph Yazid and was killed along with members of his family and supporters. For Shi'a Muslims, this tragic battle has come to represent principle and courage in the stand against violence and injustice.

[4] See his defense in court before his execution for armed resistance in 1974. See on youtube: "Khosro Golsorkhi" http://www.youtube.com/watch?v=buTlBLGdUfo (accessed November, 2010).

[5] See Talal Asad's distinctions between these words in Asad, *Formations of the Secular: Christianity.*

Historical Contexts

The Iranian Constitutional Revolution (1906–11) was characterized by a precarious alliance between secular liberal reformers from the aristocracy and state bureaucracy, middle-class secular intellectuals, and mostly religious merchants, clerics, and guildsmen from the traditional middle class.[6] These groups who supported a constitutional monarchy and an elected parliament united against the absolutist courtiers, aristocrats, landowners, Russian advisors and conservative *ulama* (Muslim clerics). With the death of Mozaffareddin Shah, who had given in to public demands and signed the royal proclamation to establish a constitution in 1906, his absolutist son Mohammad Ali Shah came to power in 1907 and led the anti-constitutionalist camp.

Within the alliance of constitutionalists, the presence of secular social democrats and religious dissidents was remarkable due to the radical nature of their influence within the *Majlis* (parliament) and their sizable/presence in the cultural realm through newspapers and public orators.[7] These "secular activists" were mainly from the middle class and had been exposed to both traditional and modern education and knowledge of Europe in some way. Others were clerics; all espoused a program of radical reform informed by the European Enlightenment and Russian Social Democracy. They knowingly solicited the aid of some clerical leaders who wished to set limits on the abuse of power, strengthen Muslim Iran against foreign intervention and, in particular, to protect Iranian merchants against foreign advantages. The complex combination of forces and motivations was further complicated by personal intrigues and rivalries within the ruling Qajar family as well as by the intricacies of the imperialist rivalry of Britain and Russia in Iran.

This general picture is more or less accepted by most historians of the constitutional period in Iran. What is addressed less frequently is the question: what precisely do we mean by 'secular' when we refer to the secular activists? Accepting Mohammad Tavakoli-Targhi's premise of the creation—since the late nineteenth century—of a "discursive mélange", an "inter-textualization of pre-Islamic, Islamic, and contemporary European histories and ideals"[8] to provide alternative social and political scenarios for

---

[6] By 'secular' I mean those who desired the constitutional separation of religion and state.

[7] See Nabavi, "Readership, the Press, and the Public Sphere."

[8] Tavakoli-Targhi, *Refashioning Iran*, 1–4.

change, I shall attempt to answer this question through a close reading of certain texts from the constitutional press. This is part of a larger study on the essays of Ali Akbar Dehkhoda that appeared in the press between 1907 and 1911 in an effort to map and explore the precise trajectory of ideas—their "creative relocation"—from different sources into a discursive mélange of the particular historical context of constitutional Iran.

Who Was Dehkhoda?

Born in 1879 in Tehran, Ali Akbar Dehkhoda was descended from a family of minor landowners. He received his early education in the traditional religious system which meant that he learned Arabic and the "formal sciences"—grammar, the interpretation of religious texts, ethics, and philosophy under the tutelage of a cleric. Dehkhoda continued his education at the School of Political Science in Tehran, where he studied the 'modern' sciences of world history, geography, international law, political science, and French language. After completing his studies, Dehkhoda was employed by the Iranian Ministry of Foreign Affairs and sent to the Balkans as a junior diplomat serving Ambassador Mo'aven Dowleh Ghaffari. Based in Bucharest and Vienna, he continued to study the European sciences and the French language.

When he returned to Iran in 1905, he was briefly employed by a modernist merchant, Haji Hossein Aqa Amin Zarb to act as translator to the Belgian engineer who was charged with building the Khorasan roadway. By this time, the constitutional movement was well under way. Dehkhoda thus found access to the network of dissident intellectuals who had organized secret societies and were actively recruiting supporters and organizing protests. He was invited to join the Revolutionary Committee as a young recruit. Shortly after the success of the revolution in 1906, Dehkhoda joined Mirza Jahangir Khan, a social democrat and a prominent constitutionalist, and Mirza Qasem Khan, a constitutionalist merchant from Tabriz, to publish *Sur Esrafil*, one of the most vocal, radical, and popular newspapers of the constitutional period. Each issue of *Sur Esrafil* carried an article on a current political or social issue written by Dehkhoda, several articles on current news and analysis written by Mirza Jahangir Khan and others, and finally, the popular satirical column written by Dehkhoda entitled *"Charand Parand"* (gibberish, poppycock).

In the first constitutional period—from May 1907 when the first issue of *Sur Esrafil* came out—to the absolutist coup on June 23, 1908, Dehkhoda focused on explaining the social democratic project to the people—to the educated by writing political and philosophical essays, and to the less educated population through the satirical "*Charand Parand*" column. The main brunt of his attacks at this time, the main objects of his critique were the absolutists and the conservative clerics or ulama—a group he referred to as "*kohneh-parastan*" (reactionaries).[9]

As editor and one of the main writers of the influential paper *Sur Esrafil* and later *Soroush* published in Istanbul, Dehkhoda set out to contribute to what he considered a primary task of the educated intellectual of the time, namely, the elaboration of the meaning of constitutionalism (*takmil-e ma'ni-ye mashrutiyat*). Aware that constitutionalism and other political concepts such as liberty, freedom, and the social contract were Western concepts not grounded in the historical experience of Iran, Dehkhoda and his colleagues believed that their precise meaning had to be constructed through discussion and dialogue, and had to be adapted to Iranian conditions and contexts. As such, he combined the unfamiliar new constructs with the more familiar ways of thinking in order to communicate with large audiences.

In his political essays, he was a fiery and passionate advocate of parliamentary democracy, socio-economic justice, and the modernization/rationalization of culture that coalesced into a movement in Iran after the constitutional revolution. To promote parliamentary democracy, he focused on crafting the definition of constitutionalism in its Iranian context and on defending the newly founded parliament (*Majlis*) against its religious and secular foes. To promote economic and social justice, he proposed a program of land and tax reform, and the reorganization of all institutions according to rational principles.[10]

The modernization of culture (secularization, rationalization, democratization) was the most complex and difficult agenda, and in retrospect, the one in which Dehkhoda made the most important and lasting contribution to Persian culture, particularly through his compilation of the voluminous "*Loghatnameh* or Lexicon of the Persian Language" later in his

---

[9] The Persian words used throughout the article are Dehkhoda's own; the translations are mine.

[10] The discussion in this paper is focused more on the relationship between French Enlightenment thought and Dehkhoda's political ideas. The elements of Russian social democratic thought that inspired Dehkhoda most can be seen in his programs for economic and agricultural change. See forthcoming Mozaffari, *Crafting Constitutionalism*.

life.[11] To define and promote this task, he launched a critique of religion as it was interpreted and practiced, advocated a modern secular education and justice system, and called for the direct participation of the people, particularly the disadvantaged, in determining the agenda and setting the priorities of state and society. His particular utilization of language to expose the ills of society, and to give a voice to the people, was one of his greatest achievements.

It is important to note that during this period, Dehkhoda was a revolutionary whose aim was not only to educate, but also to mobilize. This made him acutely aware of the different groups which made up his audience in *Sur Esrafil*. Street poetry, anecdote, satire, and complex essay genres and forms were all used to appeal to different audiences.

What the Secular Meant to Dehkhoda: The Discourse of the Enlightenment

The clue to understanding the meaning of 'secular' is the binary that he set up to differentiate reactionary backwardness from what he and other like-minded intellectuals framed as an Iranian modernity. Dehkhoda's critique addressed the different elements of "a culture of servility" (*farhang-e ta'abod*), which he considered to be the greatest obstacle to the establishment of "a modern culture" (*farhang-e jadid*). The culture of servility was sustained and nurtured by the alliance of reactionaries or *kohneh-parastan*—an ignorant self-serving despot, a corrupt court, oppressive governors and leaders in collusion with the reactionary *ulama* (*ulama-ye sou'*), promoting a backward-looking religion. Let us focus for a moment on Dehkhoda's critique of religion in the context of his epidemiology of culture.

Dehkhoda's understanding of religion and its role in Iranian society was extremely complex and seemingly contradictory. At times, he attacked and ridiculed it relentlessly; in other instances, he quoted the Quran and *hadiths* (traditions) at length, used the logic of religious arguments to legitimate his own positions, and pleaded for the support of the clerics or ulama against the monarchy. On occasion, we witness an uncomfortable dance

---

[11] After the failure of the Constitutional Revolution and the outbreak of the First World War when he was disillusioned with politics, Dehkhoda conceived the *Loghat-Nameh* (Lexicon/Encyclopedia) Project. He devoted the rest of this life to the compilation of this extraordinary encyclopedia of Persian words and foreign words used in Persian.

between secular content and religious form—secular projects framed in religious terms.[12] In many of his essays Dehkhoda appears to use religion to make new ideas either comprehensible or acceptable. However, careful consideration of his position indicates that he was most assuredly a secular thinker.[13] His vision of society, its problems and solutions, was a humanist one. He had the 'modern' penchant to relegate to religion a useful function in the rational organization of society—that of providing a moral and spiritual bond among its members.

In a series of essays on monotheism and superstition which he wrote as a response to the religious anti-constitutionalist discourse, Dehkhoda disclosed his definition of religion:

> Religion (*deen*) is the guardian of laws and the fulfilment of the morals of all the nations in the world. All the past prophets and great men of wisdom and intelligent men of religion know the benefit of religious belief to be this....[14]

Thus, religion became internalized as our conscience or "internal secret police", as Dehkhoda called it, and it assured our good behaviour and good deeds. Holy texts, such as the Quran, were to be regarded as constitutions for morality, just as constitutions for states proscribe and describe the powers of government and protection for the people.

Of course, this sociological view of religion has a great deal in common with Montesquieu's views on religion in *The Spirit of the Laws*. Though Montesquieu paid lip service to the "Christian religion as the first good"[15] he went to great lengths to establish that differences in "climate, laws, mores and manners" gave rise to different kinds of religions; that therefore, each religion was compatible with the physical and cultural characteristics of the areas in which it originated or was practiced.[16] Montesquieu also differentiated between the aims and functions of human laws and those of religion, and on this Dehkhoda definitely agreed. His view of the ideal society was one in which the affairs of men and women were governed by rational laws and their conscience by religious law.

---

[12] See for example, the references to *mozare'e* and *mozare-be* in his economic discussions in *Sur Esrafil*, issue 17–19.

[13] Secular is defined in this context as those who desired the constitutional separation of religion and state.

[14] *Sur Esrafil* editorial entitled "Moslemeen va sherk," issue 16, 1.

[15] Montesquieu, *The Spirit of the Laws*, 459.

[16] Montesquieu, *The Spirit of the Laws*, 476, 493.

> A rational Muslim is asked, "what is the divine purpose behind the sending of prophets and holy books, or, what benefit or harm does the Almighty derive from the faith or denial of people?" His answer of that rational Muslim was: "Only *our* need for the existence of an inner conscience within our hearts has led the Source of all Wisdom to send books and prophets such that we would come to recognize His Unique Essence.[17]

In this rational world where elected representatives would govern political and economic affairs through rational laws, and religion would be relegated to the role of the guardian of morality, Dehkhoda's predilection for the word *adam-parasti* or "humanism" becomes clearer. Linguistically, in Persian, *adam-parasti* (human-worship) was a word that was created as the translation of "humanism" (from the French); but it was modelled after the word *khoda-parasti* (God worship), which distinguished monotheism from *bot-parasti*, or idol worship. In effect and meaning, *adam-parasti* is an apparently deliberate creation of a contradistinction to *khoda-parasti*, putting the human being, as it does, at the center of concern.

The first openly and systematically critical article about the contemporary practice of religion to appear in *Sur Esrafil* was the editorial entitled "*Zohur-e Jadid*", which was published in *Sur Esrafil* dated 20 June 1907. This essay touched such a sensitive chord in the religious establishment that it led to Dehkhoda's denunciation by the Society of Religious Students as 'an unbeliever' and the closing of *Sur Esrafil*. With characteristic wit, Dehkhoda wrote:

> If you say to an Iranian Muslim, "O Man of Faith, clean your nose, O Holy One, clean your ears, O Enemy of Muawwiya, pull your socks up, such simple tasks prove to be too burdensome and difficult for the poor bloke. But if you say, O Seyyed, Become a Prophet! O Sheikh, Make claims to be an Imam! O Hojjat-ul Eslam, Be the Shadow of the Imam on Earth, in a flash, our noble man fixes his stunned eyes on a distant object and assumes a forlorn countenance. He begins to mumble softly. He sticks out his chest as a shield of protection against the nefarious arrow of hidden enemies, hypocrites and violators. In other words, every atom in the man's being becomes ready to receive revelation and inspiration. At first, he just hears noises—the movement of ants or the buzz of bees—but after a few days, in his mind's eye, he sees the angel Gabriel at the height of his majesty....
>
> These false prophets, fake *imams* and phony leaders have ignored the rest of the world, and have descended their holy selves right in this small piece of land which is the centre of the true religion of Islam. None of these useless good-for-nothings appear in any of the mountains of Farangistan

---

[17] *Sur Esrafil*, issue 16, 1. The emphasis is mine.

(Europe) or any of the villages in America, because of the rule of law and widespread education. And [there] even if Gabriel tries to anoint [someone] to prophethood and issue a direct command a thousand times, they will not hear of it. But *mashallah*, the bountiful soil of Iran produces a fresh prophet, a new Imam, even, Allah help us, a new God every hour. And stranger still is that their efforts take root and their movements spread. What is the reason for this?…

Whatever the stimuli for the imagination of the pretenders, the reasons for the acceptance of the people and receptivity of the Iranian populace are no more than two: One is ignorance, and the other, the habit of servility (*'adat be ta'abod*).

Dehkhoda blamed the *ulama* for not knowing and not imparting the "truth" of Islam. The body of religious knowledge which they studied and taught was convoluted and mixed with superstition, and they were more interested in power than truth and morality. As a consequence, the community of believers was in its entirety ignorant and susceptible to fear and superstition. The power of the *ulama* could only be maintained and perpetuated through the habit of servility that they encouraged amongst the believers. This was a general critique against the institution of organized religion and its members.

In Dehkhoda's writing, other elements of the culture of servility included illiteracy, ignorance, the lack of enlightened education leading to poverty and superstition, and the oppression of women and minorities. The people, *mellat*, were often portrayed as ignorant and unmotivated (symbolized by the image of the opium addict, the *tariyaki*). The stark division between rich and poor, the powerful and the powerless, led to the perpetuation of injustice. The culture of servility could not tolerate the freedom of expression or criticism; therefore, intellectuals could not freely function in it.[18] In contradistinction, modern culture was characterized by the rule of law, where the interests of the *mellat* (people) were fairly represented in an elected parliament; where modern education produced bright, energetic, honest and competent men and women. The gap between rich and poor became narrower. The pursuit of modern culture meant the recognition of women as productive members of society and the improvement of minority rights; it would, in time, lead Iran out of economic, social and political backwardness. Modern, enlightened society would make Iran more confident and tolerant of freedom of expression; intellectuals could use their pens freely as the instruments of justice

---

[18] For a discussion of these issues see Nahid Mozaffari, *Crafting Constitutionalism*.

and right—as the collective conscience of the community.[19] A modern, enlightened Iran would be less susceptible to the manipulations of the imperial powers.

Educating the people about the culture of servility and fighting against it, was an important goal not only for Dehkhoda and *Sur Esrafil*, but for many other newspapers such as *Tarbiyat, Majils, Mossavat,* and *Habl-ul Matin*. The secular intellectuals saw themselves as the facilitators of this process of transformation from a culture of servility (*farhang-e ta'abod*) to modern civilization (*tamadon-e jadid*). In order to accomplish this, they understood that they had to capitalize on the sentiments and the associations that had been mobilized during the constitutional revolution. They needed the active participation of the people (*mellat*) for this project to succeed. They utilized the power and influence of the constitutionalist ulama, though they knew that the *ulama* failed to grasp many of the contradictions between democratic institutions and the power of the clerical establishment. Their most formidable cultural rival was conservative, anti-constitutionalist religion. All the sustained argument and writing by Dehkhoda and others about the conservative *ulama* and the backwardness of their ideas was underscored by an implicit unspoken fear of the power that they wielded over the people or *mellat*.

The Clash of Meanings: The Discourse of Islam

Let us now consider for a moment what the conservative *ulama* or clerics understood of the constitutionalist project. The most vocal anti-constitutionalist cleric, Sheikh Fazlollah Nouri, agreed only with the setting of certain limitations on the power of the Shah and his ministers. He cautioned that changes should not be implemented too rapidly lest things get beyond control. But he fiercely objected to the desirability of 'freedom' and 'liberty' in society. Using the word *kufr* (heresy) to describe these concepts, Nouri called "unlimited freedom and absolute liberty" in society wrong and against Islam. In response to the laws envisaged by the constitutionalists, he stated:

> First, our law was written over one thousand three hundred years ago *Agha* (sir) and given to us. Even if they want to write a law today, it has to be in accord with the Quran, and the law of Mohammad and the *shari'a*. If you

---

[19] *Sur Esrafil*, issue 1, 4–5.

want my advice, remove the term 'freedom' because ultimately it is going to lead us into disaster. Also, you said that limits would be set on the *shari'a* as well. Know this: there are no limitations on the *shari'a*.[20]

As these discussions indicate, Nouri and his followers wanted certain limitations on the absolute power of the king and court, and more power for the ulama through the enhanced importance of the *shari'a* under the new order. Tabatabai, the constitutionalist cleric, was willing to pursue a version of constitutional government that was a codified and more just version of the status quo, with constraints on the power of the king, court and ministers. The position of Muslim law, or the *shari'a*, and the power of the *ulama* would basically be unchanged in his understanding, but in effect, the *ulama* would gain from the improvements in society through the prevalence of law and justice. The position of the constitutionalist *ulama* was well summarized by Ayatollah Molla Akhund Abdollah Mazandarani, whose letter from Najaf was published in the eleventh issue of *Sur Esrafil*. After acknowledging that the people had risen up against the excessive oppression and injustices of the rulers, he echoed Tabatabai's definition of constitutionalism or *mashrute* as the setting of limitations on and increasing the accountability of the rulers. He then stated that:

> ... it is evident that this matter [constitutionalism] has nothing to do with religion or faith. They have not suggested that constitutionalism or absolutism should apply to the religion or faith of the people... but due to the provocations of the absolutists and oppressors... some have attributed the respected Majlis, the establishment of which is meant to remove injustice and oppression, with heresy (*kufr*), the pretense of faith (*zandaqeh*) and the denial of God (*elhad*)....[21]

In short, the anti-constitutionalist clerics like Nouri *only* agreed to setting limits on the power of the absolute monarchy. Any new laws would have to conform to his interpretation of religious law. There was to be no separation of state from religion. The constitutionalist clerics like Tabatabai and Mazandarani saw the establishment of a parliament and the promulgation of new laws as *only* setting limits on the excesses of the absolute monarchy. This, in their opinion, would perpetuate justice and

---

[20] Nouri, *Kitab-e Tazakorat-ul ghafil wa Ershad ul-Jahel*, 56–57. Except for the Nouri quote, these are summaries of the comments of the two clerics as related by the witness Hashem Mohit-Mafi, *Moqadamat-e Mashrutiyat*, 107–108. According to the author Mohit-Mafi, this conversation took place very early in the constitutional struggle when Mozaffareddin Shah had sent Azod-ul Molk to negotiate with the ulama in Qom.

[21] *Sur Esrafil*, issue 11, 1–2 (Letters from Abdollah Mazandarani from Najaf).

strengthen religion, as the poor and oppressed depended on the clerics as their interlocutors against the injustices of the temporal rulers. There was to be a nominal separation in the affairs of state from the affairs of religion in this construct because the parliament and non-religious laws would act to limit the power of the temporal rulers. However, from their perspective, the moral power and influence of the clerics and religion on state and society would be strengthened.

The secular intellectuals seized upon this line of reasoning and articulated their preference for the complete separation of state and religion in terms of the differentiation between the affairs of this life from the next. Commenting on these letters, the *Sur Esrafil* suggested "it is obvious [from these two letters] that the purpose of the Majlis is the reduction of oppression and injustice; it redresses the affairs of *this life* (*omur-e mo'ashi*) and it has nothing to do with the affairs of the *next life* (*omur-e mo'ad*)."[22]

Having established and argued that this division between the realm of politics and the realm of religion was plausible, Dehkhoda and the secular intellectuals remained wary of the role that the *shari'a* and the *ulama* would play in a constitutional system. They were influenced by the anti-clerical trends of the European Enlightenment thinkers, and by the philosophy that put man not God at the center of attempts to reorganize society. They were furthermore wary of the influence—which they often considered detrimental—of the *ulama* on the masses. Therefore, they employed rational argument, polemic and satire to reach as many of the 'people' as they could in order to expose and undermine this influence.

Sheikh Fazlullah Nouri, the anti-constitutionalist cleric, understood the secular implications of the establishment of parliament and the rule of law better than the constitutionalist clerics. He knew that the separation of religion and politics would lead to a diminished role for religion in society. He wrote:

> It is obvious that our divine law is not intended for worship only; rather, it (also) contains the most complete and comprehensive commands for politics. Therefore, we have no need to devise laws, particularly since, based on our Islamic belief, we have to organize our worldly affairs (*nazm-e mo'ash*) in a manner that does not conflict with our dedication to the next world (*amr-e mo'ad*), and this is only possible with divine law because that is the only law that can combine these two directions.... If we consider *ourselves* capable of devising such a law, then we will have no rational justification for prophesy, *for if someone believes that the exigencies of the age can change*

---

[22] *Sur Esrafil*, issue 11, 2.

some elements of that divine law or can complete it, that person is outside the realm of Muslim belief, because our prophet (Peace be upon him) is the final prophet, and his law is the final law. Consequently, these beliefs contradict the belief in *khatamiyat*[23] and the perfection of the Prophet's religion. The denial of *khatamiyat* is heresy according to divine law.... Therefore, the fabrication of law whether in whole or in part is in contradiction with Islam....[24] If the benefit of constitutionalism was to protect the commands of Islam, why did they lay its foundations on equality (*mossavat*) and freedom (*horriyat*)? Each of these two devious principles destroys the steady foundation of divine law, because Islam is based on submission, not on freedom, and the structure of its commands is based on the calculation of differences, not on equality....[25]

In response, in the twelfth issue of *Sur Esrafil*, Dehkhoda wrote his essay on the limitless potential for human progress, which he insisted should not be hampered by any leader, spiritual or worldly. He provocatively defined freedom (*azadi*) thus:

The new word 'freedom'—which has been sought, directly or indirectly, by all prophets, men of wisdom, and men of knowledge all over the world; the word that we have just recently begun to utter with a thousand stutters on our tongues and doubt (on our minds), means precisely this— those who claim to be leaders of this graveyard which is Iran should not limit (the quest for) human perfection *to their definitions alone*, but grant permission for human beings to use their own innate powers to determine their path to progress and perfection, and to pursue it without fear.[26]

Dehkhoda went on to maintain that the only limitation on the pursuit and practice of this freedom was respect for the freedom of others.

Since there was no limit to human progress, then the sending of prophets in each age corresponded to the need for the renewal and adjustment of revealed laws to the changing demands of each period. But with Islam, and Mohammad, humanity achieved salvation, because of the perfection of this clear religion, humanity was able to do without the emergence of a new prophet and itself took hold of its eternal mission and the requirements of its will.[27]

---

[23] The principle of *khatamiyat* is the belief that Mohammad was the Seal of the Prophets, and that the validity of Islamic laws would remain until further notice from God (until the coming of the Mahdi or the Muslim version of the messiah).

[24] Nouri, *Kitab-e Tazakorat-ul ghafil and Ershad ul-Jahel*, 56 f.

[25] Nouri, *Kitab-e Tazakorat-ul ghafil and Ershad ul-Jahel*, 59.

[26] *Sur Esrafil*, issue 12, 2.

[27] *Sur Esrafil*, issue 13, 2. This is the only instance that I have used the translation of Soroudi, "Sur Esrafil, 1907–8," 238.

Implicit in this argument was that Islamic law was not eternally applicable; that human reason, will, and the knowledge afforded by modern science could in fact replace an all-encompassing divine law. The demands of modern times dictated the confinement of religious law to certain aspects of life.[28] This subordination of religious law to human reason is all the more clear in light of Dehkhoda's adherence to the philosophy of humanism or *adamparasti*.

One of Sheikh Fazlollah's recurring accusations against the constitutionalists was that they were "deniers of the *shari'a* and believers in nature"[29] What did this mean? Nouri had apparently become aware of and particularly sensitive to the problem that the embrace of constitutionalism meant a complete cultural transformation. He explained it thus in the proclamation which attempted to explain his change of heart about constitutionalism. "In the last year, a discourse (*sokhan*) from the land of the Franks [Europe] has spread amongst us...which has amounted to the adaptation of all laws to the needs of the times." To explain what this adaptation entailed, Nouri gave the following examples: "...such as the legitimization of intoxicants, the propagation of whorehouses, the founding of schools for the education of women and girls' primary schools, the use of income from prayer and pilgrimage to holy sites to build factories and roads...."

The worst of the effects of this constitutionalist worldview was yet to come for Nouri: "...that all the nations of the world should be equal in their rights, that the blood of dhimmi (non-Muslim) and Muslim could mix, that they could give wives and take wives from each other."

It is little wonder that the cleric remarked that the whole country was in turmoil from Azarbaijan to Kermanshah to Fars—because the rules and boundaries had broken down...and that this turmoil was visible in the private realm as well as in the political realm.

It is very significant that "impure" and "sinful" acts (in Islam) such as the promotion of intoxicants and the establishment of houses of prostitution were mentioned in the same breath as the establishment of schools and the education of women; for they presented the same calibre of challenge and threat to the predominance and hegemony of the reactionary (*kohne-parast*) outlook. In fact, both the question of women and the

---

[28] *Sur Esrafil*, issue 13, 1–3 and issue 14, 1–5.

[29] *"monker-e shari'at va mo'taqed be tabi'at"* see in Khandaniha-ye Qarn. Reprint of one of the proclamations of Sheikh Fazlullah during his refuge in the shrine of Shabdolazim in 1907, 90.

question of minorities were important elements in the "culture war" of the constitutionalist period, precisely because any proposed changes in the way these issues were traditionally dealt with, indicated the presence and the challenge of a different worldview and a different distribution of power. Nouri accurately observed that the advent of constitutionalism had come to mean a disruption in the hegemony of the *ulama* in the realm of culture.

He was also correct in noting that in the pages of *Sur Esrafil* and other constitutionalist newspapers, the features of the "other" worldview were promoted actively. The "discourse from the land of the Franks" clearly included the call to pursue modern knowledge and the endorsement of secular schools. Almost every issue of the *Sur Esrafil* weekly announced the opening of new schools and the publication of books.[30] As noted elsewhere in the discussions on politics and economics, Dehkhoda and his colleagues considered the study of the Western sciences and the propagation of such rational knowledge to be an essential pre-requisite to solving Iran's major problems, and to building a new, just society. Whereas 'modern' schools teaching the Western sciences, along with history, literature and military sciences had been set up since the previous century, they had not been considered such a threat to the conservative *ulama*, because they had only catered to the elite.

In the constitutional period, the question of modern education had been articulated as a "right" and a necessity, not only for the elite, but for the entire population. Articles arguing in favour of modern education abounded in newspapers. Furthermore, this right was advocated not only for the male half of the population, but also for women. Dehkhoda devoted many hours and pages in *Sur Esrafil* to lamenting the fact that the common people were ignorant, superstitious, and therefore susceptible to the control of the "malignant" *ulama*. As discussed above, he had spent much energy arguing with the *ulama* that the pursuit of knowledge was not contrary to the *shari'a* or any other aspect of "the pure religion of Islam." For him, modern education was the only practical solution to ignorance and backwardness.[31]

---

[30] See, for example, *Sur Esrafil*, issues 5, 16, 17, 18, 23, 25. In *Sur Esrafil* issues 17, 23 there were announcements regarding the activities or the Tarbiyat bookstore and educational center in Tehran. In issue 25, the readers were informed of the opening of the *Anjoman-e Farhang-e Olum-e Jadid* (Society of the Academy of Modern Sciences) offering free classes.

[31] This remained his most steady commitment throughout his life.

Another prominent example of Dehkhoda's secularizing discourse framed in Islamic language can be found in his economic discussions regarding land reform and the moral justifications for peasant land ownership. He superimposed the legal Islamic concepts of *mozare'e* (a good and just contract) and *mozarebeh* (a bad and exploitative contract) to address the current economic discussions spearheaded by the social democrats in parliament. According to the scholar Janet Afary, the "theoretical confusion that the humanistic attributes of Islam could be given a socialist interpretation by merging them with European socialist ideas" was a common tendency among Muslim socialists in the early twentieth century.[32]

I do not know if Dehkhoda was a Muslim believer in his heart, but his economic discussions demonstrate his belief that a version of Islam, as envisioned by educated, enlightened people, was a just and moral system, and that its tenets could help reformers towards their goal of a just redistribution of wealth in society. This belief may have been tempered by an awareness of the exigencies of the times: *that an ideology of reform could not reject religion altogether, considering the legal and cultural power of the ulama and the piety of the majority of the people.* Nevertheless, Dehkhoda made it abundantly clear that, above all, the economic, financial and organizational sciences had to be learned from the West and implemented in a manner that would increase productivity, distribute wealth more equitably, and benefit the majority of the population.

Conclusions

Informed by the work of Talal Asad and many contributions in this volume,[33] one can conclude that 'the secular', as opposed to 'secularism' as a political doctrine, comprises a variety of concepts, practices, and sensibilities that have come together and changed over time. Articulations of 'the secular' in constitutional Iran as exemplified by the writing of Ali Akbar Dehkhoda confirm Talal Asad's view that it is useful to look at the secular as an epistemic category. Dehkhoda's arguments in favor of the secular regarded it *not* as a colonial imposition or worldview that gives

---

[32] Afary, *The Iranian Constitutionalist Revolution*, 129. This is a long and involved discussion, which will hopefully appear in Crafting Constitutionalism in 2014.

[33] Reconfigurations of the Religious Field: Secularization, Re-Sacrilization and Related Processes in Historical and Intercultural Perspective. Dynamics in the History of Religions, Ruhr University Bochum: December 1–3, 2009.

precedence to the material over the spiritual and promotes alienation and consumerism—these views came later in twentieth century Iran with Al-Ahmad and Shariati. The secular, during its earliest articulations in Iran, was presented as a rational, humanist principle that would not deny the right to religious belief, but restrain "religious passion as a source of intolerance and delusion."[34]

Dehkhoda saw "the secular" as the relegation of religion to its role as the guide for personal conscience, as the guardian of morality in society. He focused his critique of religion not on religion per se, but on the agency of the conservative clerics in maintaining the power of the despot through the propagation of public ignorance. He systematically focused on the deconstruction of the culture of servility to raise awareness among the people in order to break the political alliance between despotism and the entrenched clerical establishment.

The shifting and relational meanings of 'religion' and 'the secular' can be observed through Dehkhoda's conscious use of religious language and symbols, at times as a concession to the constitutional clerics and at times to speak to a population well versed in religious belief, symbols and language. (Only five per cent of the population was literate in that period.) Thus, references to religious texts, such as the Quran and the hadiths, and religious terms such as *shirk, khatamiyat, mozare'e-e* and *mozarebeh* were imbued with different, more contemporary meanings to explain unfamiliar concepts to various audiences.

Dehkhoda's writing in the early constitutional period meant to communicate his "secular" social democratic vision to the public and to create shared critiques, shared symbols and shared solutions. The visibility of the small group of radical and secular intellectuals, of which Dehkhoda was a part during the constitutional period, and their presence on the political scene, did not accurately reflect their power base or their actual level of political organization. The failure of the constitutional revolution attested to that fact. However, throughout the rest of the twentieth century and at the beginning of the twenty-first century, Iranian intellectuals have continued to grapple with the different versions and interpretations of the secular as championed by Dehkhoda and his colleagues.[35]

---

[34] Assad, *Formations of the Secular*, 21.

[35] Parts of this paper were presented at the Centenary Conference on the Iranian Constitutional Revolution, 1906–1911, organized by the Iranian Heritage Foundation at the University of Oxford, 30 July–2 August 2006. A different version of this paper was published in Chehabi, *Iran's Constitutional Revolution*.

Fig. 1: The image on the first page of *Sur Esrafil.*

The image on the first page of *Sur Esrafil* (literally meaning the trumpet of Esrafil) depicts the angel Esrafil blowing his horn to awaken the dead on the Day of Judgment. In the case of the newspaper *Sur Esrafil*, the image symbolized the awakening of the people to assume their rights as represented by the words on Esrafil's scroll—*horriyat* (freedom), *mossavat* (equality), *okhovvat* (fraternity). This image exemplifies the discursive mélange between the European Enlightenment and indigenous concepts and meanings, including the discourse of Islam.

Bibliography

Abrahamian, Ervand. *Iran Between Two Revolutions.* Princeton: Princeton University Press, 1982.

Afary, Janet. *The Iranian Constitutionalist Revolution, 1906–1911.* New York: Columbia University Press, 1996.

Asad, Talal. *Formations of the Secular: Christianity, Islam, and Modernity.* Stanford: Stanford University Press, 2003.

Bayat, Mangol. *Iran's First Revolution: Shiism and the Constitutional Revolution of 1905–1909.* New York: Oxford University Press, 1991.

Chehabi, Houchang E., and Vanessa Martin, eds. *Iran's Constitutional Revolution: Popular Politics, Cultural Transformations and Transnational Connections.* London: IB Tauris, 2010.

Montesquieu, Charles. *The Spirit of the Laws*. Los Angeles: University of California Press, 1977.

Mohit-Mafi, Hashem. *Moqadamat-e Mashrutiyat*. Teheran: Elmi Publications, 1363.

Mozaffari, Nahid. *Crafting Constitutionalism: Dehkhoda and the Iranian Constitutional Revolution* (forthcoming).

Nabavi, Negin. "Readership, the Press, and the Public Sphere in the First Constitutional Era." In *Iran's Constitutional Revolution*, edited by H. Chehabi and V. Martin, pp. 213–223. London: IB Tauris, 2010.

Nouri, Sheikh Fazlollah. "Kitab-e Tazakorat-ul ghafil wa Ershad ul-Jahel." In Mohammad Torkman, ed. *Rasa'el, E'lamiye-ha, Maktubat va Roozname-ye Sheikh Fazlollah Nouri*, vol. 1. Tehran: Mahtab Publications, 1362.

Soroudi, Sorour. "*Sur Esrafil* 1907–8: Social and Political Ideology." *Middle Eastern Studies* 24 (April 1988).

Sur Esrafil (Tehran) in thirty-two issues, edited by Mirza Jahangir Khan Shirazi, and Mirza Ghassem Khan Tabrizi. Tehran: Nasseri Avenue, Tarbiyat Bookstore, 30 May 1907–20 June 1908.

Sur Esrafil (Yverdon and Paris) in three issues. Yverdon: Sur Esrafil Office, 23 January, 6 February, and 8 March 1908.

Soroush. Istanbul: July 1909–October 1909.

Tavakoli-Targhi, Mohamad. *Refashioning Iran: Orientalism, Occidentalism and Historiography*. New York: Palgrave, 2001.

EQUALITY IN HIERARCHY: SECULARISM AND THE PROTECTION OF RELIGIONS IN SRI LANKA

Sven Bretfeld

Introduction

Secularization can be understood in many ways. As an analytical concept it describes the general replacement of religion by means of a process of *Entzauberung* of the world (Weber). In a weaker form the secularization theory refers to a withdrawal of religious semantics from the public sphere in favor of individualized religiosity. In the latter sense, Sri Lanka can hardly be called a secularized society, though a tendency to relocate religiosity to the individual can clearly be detected since the emergence of the so-called Buddhist Modernism in the late nineteenth century and with the rise of meditation centers (*bhāvanā-madhyasthānaya*) in the 1950s.[1] In the sense of a reformulation of religious beliefs and practices in a non-religious, secularized language, David McMahan has dealt with the secularization of Buddhism as an important factor of the "Making of Modern Buddhism".[2] In my contribution I will approach secularism and secularization not as a sociological theory, but as modern words in the Sinhala language and their use in re-conceptualizing the relationship between religious institutions and the state.

The traditional concept of a Buddhist protector-king became obsolete in 1815 when the last Sinhalese king of Kandy abdicated and the whole country fell under the regency of the British crown. At this stage the traditional ideal of a functional symbiosis between Buddhist institutions and statecraft became crucial—not for the first time in history, but the social changes fostered during the British colonial phase soon made clear that the relationship between religion and the state had to be re-conceptualized. In the Kandyan Convention of 1815, the British colonial government had consented to respect and protect the Buddhist institutions and practices of the country. However, by the middle of the century the Sinhalese nobility

---

[1] Cf. Bretfeld, "Buddhistische Laien, buddhistische Profis."
[2] Cf. McMahan, *The Making of Buddhist Modernism.*

and the religious leaders of the Saṃgha[3] realized that the concept of what that could mean and imply were quite different on the two sides.[4] Towards the end of the nineteenth century the government formally subscribed to a politics of strict religious neutrality. This situation was interpreted by Buddhist intellectuals of independent Sri Lanka as a *lack* of protection which in reality intensified the Christian domination of society.

Before we deal with the problem of secularism in the political concepts of independent Sri Lanka, it is necessary to take a look at the religio-political ideal of Buddhist kingship as it was promoted by the historical Buddhist kings and in the literature of the Saṃgha. This imagination of an ideal 'state' serves as a 'utopian memory' against which the present structures and principles of statecraft are measured, especially by the powerful fundamentalist Buddhist forces of modern Sri Lanka.

The Idealized Buddhist Kingship

While Lankan Buddhists had developed and conceptualized a distinct local religious field not later than the emergence of historiographical literature—the so-called *vaṃsas*—in the fifth century C.E., overlappings and mutual permeations between the religious and the political field have been strong throughout history. Members of the Saṃgha served as advisors and court historians to the kings. As a religious institution, the monastic community served as a source of religious power and acted as 'tutelary deity' to the king, even providing protection for his armies during warfare.[5] The prosperity of the kingdom was closely associated to the measure of royal gratitude enjoyed by the Buddhist institutions. Thus, an important duty of the king was "to bring glory to Sāsana"[6] by protecting and increasing its personal and material installations. Especially the Saṃgha was perceived as a 'field of merit' which bears incomparable fruits for the after-life when 'tilled' with generous gifts (*dāna*). It seems that the kings' efforts of merit-making were recorded since ancient times in so-called merit books (*puñña-pota*) which, amongst other things, were

---

[3] The community of Buddhist monks, divided into several Nikāyas (sections).

[4] A good example for the disappointments with the execution of the Kandyan Convention is the fiduciary duty the British government was expected—but in the eyes of the Kandyan nobility completely failed—to assume for the Tooth Relic. Cf. Silva, "The Custody of the Sacred Tooth Relic."

[5] Cf. *Mahāvaṃsa* 25, 3–5.

[6] The Buddhist religion and its institutions.

ritually recited by monks to ensure a good rebirth for a dying king. The Buddhist *vaṃsa* literature, which largely draws on the merit books, judges a king as a good one depending on his merits in protecting and sponsoring the Sāsana. This includes not only the largesse of his material donations to the Saṃgha in the form of landholdings, monastic and ritual buildings, the regulation of the monks' sustentation etc., but also the military defence of the state against hostile invaders (who are generally presented as enemies of Buddhism). The king's merits also include his careful judgment to support the *correct* side in case of a dispute within the Saṃgha—many kings *failed* on this because they supported a different section (*nikāya*) of the Saṃgha from that favoured by the historiographer. Thus, as the prime patrons and protectors of the Sāsana, the kings also had the duty to control the inner affairs of the Saṃgha to a certain extent, so as to safeguard unity and order.[7]

Evidence that the legitimation of power was highly dependent on the kings' religious role as supporters and protectors of the Sāsana can not only be found in the (monk-authored) religious historiography of the island, but is also abundant in inscriptions. From the tenth century onward we even have inscriptional evidence that Sri Lankan kings were considered to be *bosats* (Bodhisattvas, i.e. future Buddhas). The role of the ideal Buddhist king is closely connected to the *dhamma-dīpa* ideology, in which Lanka is regarded as the chosen land appointed by the Buddha to house and preserve his pure teaching through the ages of decline.

The idealized traditional kingship and Buddhist institutions can thus aptly be described as a semantic symbiosis, with the king acting as a kind of mediator responsible for the welfare of both the political and the religious field. This role of combining the responsibility for the state and religion is conceptually symbolized by the double sphere of protection which converges in the royal office. In a rock inscription, king Niśśaṅka Malla (1187–1196), who is remembered for his generosity towards the Saṃgha and the public, presents himself as an ideal Buddhist savior-king for whom political and juridical power is nothing but a means to secure the happiness of his subjects in this and the other world:

---

[7] The monastic hierarchies regulated in the Theravāda Monastic Code (*vinaya*) mainly refer to local face-to-face communities living in the same location. Therefore, the Saṃgha's authority to act against deviating communities in a broader region is rather weak. A Saṃgharāja—a country-wide absolute leader of a whole Nikāya—was traditionally appointed by the king.

[King Niśśaṅka Malla] ensured the long stability of the state and the religion (*lokaśāsanaya*). Moreover, considering that the island of Lanka is a noble land because of the establishment of the *sāsana* there, that the living beings in it have lofty excellences (*guṇa*) and that, therefore, they should receive advice and protection, he out of compassion proclaimed the [following] maxims of good counsel:

Though kings appear in human form, they are human divinities (*naradēvatā*) and must, therefore, be regarded as gods. The appearance of an impartial king should be welcomed as the appearance of the Buddha. When kings inflict punishment commensurate with the offense, they do so with good intentions, just as a physician applies a remedy for a bodily ailment. They restrain [their subjects] from evil and thus save them from falling into hell. They lead them to do good, thereby securing for them the [bliss of] heaven and release from rebirth (*mōkṣa*). If the wishes of kings were respected, it would be like heaven.[8]

The copulative compound *loka-śāsanaya* or *lo-sasun* (state and religion) often occurs in historiography and in inscriptions. Both translation terms, *state* and *religion*, are tentative. *Loka* "the world" means the worldly matters of men and includes personal and societal welfare as well as the measures for regulating society: politics, economy and legislation. Already in ancient India the word *loka* was sometimes used in opposition to the religious sphere, in particular in the name of a decidedly anti-religious school of thought, the *lokāyata* "those directed towards the world". The *lokāyata* school was connected to the classical Indian science of politics and economy (*arthaśāstra*) and was further associated to an anti-religious attitude and consequent this-worldliness. *Sāsanaya* (Sanskrit: *śāsana*) is an abbreviation for *buddhaśāsanaya*, which literally means "instruction of the Buddha". In the Pāli using Buddhist cultures this term evolved into a collective term for the material and personal institutions representing and mediating the contents and powers of the Dhamma, especially a faultless Saṃgha of virtuous (and doctrinally correct) monks and nuns, the written or spoken word of the Buddha and the relics. *Sāsanaya* is not a comparative term for *religion*. If we can translate it as religion it means the Buddhist religion only. Neither in premodern nor modern times does *śāsanaya* denote any religion other than Buddhism. The use of *loka-śāsanaya* as denoting two fields of political responsibility thus implies a statement of Buddhist hegemony in the religious field. As we will see, this

---

[8] *Epigraphia Zeylanica* 2: 121, translation by Hallisey, "Works and Persons in Sinhala Literary Culture," 701.

circumstance is not without consequences in the language politics of the modern discourse on religion and secularization.

In modern times the memory of the old Buddhist protector-kings remained (or emerged) as a topos of the golden age of yore for those who see the influence of secularism and non-Buddhist religions as a danger for the country's cultural heritage. The last king remembered in many respects as an ideal Buddhist king is Kīrti Śrī Rājasiṃha (1747–1782) who held the kingdom of Kandy against the Dutch. While the British proved more tolerant to the indigenous religions than the Portuguese and the Dutch, Christian missionaries doubtlessly had a dominant position and constituted the major force within the religious field. Education was in the hands of Christian missionary schools, and access to the highly esteemed positions of the colonial administration was dependent on a modern education, including a good command of the English language. Probably most people in the south-western coastal area around Colombo at least paid lip-service to Christianity, even if they were still Buddhists or Hindus in their private lives.

In this situation, the concept of secularism started out as a politically highly charged and contested discursive formation in Sri Lanka.

Expressions for Secular in Sinhala

Expressions for *secular* in modern Sinhala are manifold and generally of recent making; some of them are historically loaded and derive from religious language. The most common expression is the negation of the likewise modern term for *religion: āgama sambandha no-vana* (not being connected to religion), or, the shorter *āgamika no-vū* (not religious). These adjectives can qualify any noun, whether signifying an animate being or an inanimate object or concept.[9] Also common is the word *ēhika* which is an adjectivized form of *ēhi* (here). This word refers to a distinction between immanence and transcendence, which in structural terms resembles traditional Pāli distinctions between 'this world' (*ayaṃ loka*) or 'here-world' (*iha-loka*) and 'the other world' (*para-loka*), where the latter represents the heavenly realms or other spheres of future rebirth. Similar

---

[9] The Sinhala language differentiates gender and sexus in a more congruent manner than modern European idioms. There is no neuter in the strict sense. Living beings are represented in the masculine or feminine, while things and concepts share an inanimate "gender."

associations are inherent in the term *laukika*. While this word, which literally means 'worldly,' is used in the sense of 'secular' today, its historical usages imply the difference between 'worldly' (Pāli *lokiya*) and 'world
transcending' (Pāli *lokuttara*), which are technical terms used in Buddhist
teaching to qualify persons or states of consciousness belonging to either
the sphere of rebirth (*saṃsāra*) or to the sphere of Nirvāṇa respectively.
The modern term *laukāyata* (secular) is likewise taken from the field of
traditional religious discourse. It is an adjective derived from *lokāyata*, the
'secular' or 'materialistic' world-view of ancient India which I mentioned
above.

The derivative nouns and verbal expressions *secularize, secularism*
and *secularization* are derived from these words by nominal composition
or periphrastical constructions: *ēhika-vādaya* (secularism, lit. the being-
here-view) *ēhi-karaṇaya* (secularization, lit. the here-making), *lokāyatta
karaṇava* (secularize, lit. to make attached to the world), *āgama dhar-
mayen tora karaṇavā* (secularize, lit. to put an end to [the influence of]
religion and religious teachings).

State and Religion

Although secularization, like religion (*āgama*), is a new entry in the
Sinhala dictionary, the distinction between the two goes back to an older
history. Especially the derivations of *loka* draw on the classical distinctions between *loka* and *śāsanaya*, the two spheres of responsibility of a
king. There are, however, two important differences:

1. Modern discourse on secularism does not only aim at a *conceptual distinction* between the religious and the non-religious fields, but rather
   goes one step further in *separating* the two. We will see that for proponents and opponents of secularization in Sri Lanka this separation is
   perceived as the chance or the threat of modernity, respectively.
2. The classical distinction only took the Buddhist religion, the *śāsanaya*,
   into consideration, while today several religions are meant when the
   term *āgama no-vū* (not religious, secular) is used, especially those most
   visible in Sinhala society (Buddhism, Hindu Religions, Christianity and
   Islam). The nineteenth and twentieth century witnessed the emergence
   of a chauvinist attitude toward non-Buddhist religions. As we will see,
   this is even reflected in language politics: Buddhism is an *āgama* like
   all the others, nevertheless the term Śāsanaya remains as a distinct

term for the Buddhist religion and is often used in subtle claims of superiority or incomparability of Buddhism vis-a-vis other religions.

In modern Sri Lanka, secularism has its advocates as well as its opponents. On the one hand, the on-going intermingling of religion and politics is regarded by many as a crucial problem of the modern Sri Lankan state. Since independence—at least since the legislature period following the elections of 1956—state politics has increasingly adopted Sinhala-Buddhist ideologies and has been manipulated by religious organizations and pressure groups often organized by Buddhist monastic networks. In this situation the call for secularization can be heard especially as a means to safeguard religious pluralism and to protect the rights of religious minorities as well as those of atheist/non-religious citizens. On the other hand, Sinhala-Buddhist nationalism is the extreme manifestation of a large part of the Sri Lankan population with attitudes towards secularization ranging from sceptical to strongly anti-secular. These attitudes were already found in the late nineteenth century, in the midst of the struggle for freedom from colonial power, when a negative image of the 'secular' West was created and associated with materialism, economic greed and moral decline.

The formulation and regulation of the relationship between the state and religious institutions is an on-going topic that is discussed, negotiated and manipulated—often through violent political action—by various pressure groups and lobbyists, including the Buddhist Saṃgha. As far as I can see, the call for a strong connection between the state and religion is only raised by actors belonging to the Buddhist community and is associated with the claim for political privileges for Buddhist institutions exclusively. This demand is justified by the predication that Buddhism had been made virtually extinct under colonial rule and had to be recompensed and restored by statecraft to its traditional role in the foremost position in society.

This argument emerged shortly after independence and was connected with the demand for a Sāsana reform.[10] In the early 1950s the question of the Sāsana reform became a major issue in the politics of the day. When in 1953 president D. S. Senanayake disapproved the appointment of a commission to execute the reform because of constitutional concerns, the so-called Buddhist Commission of Inquiry (Bauddha toraturu

---

[10] Cf. Bechert, *Buddhismus, Staat und Gesellschaft*, 267–293.

prarīkṣaka sabhāva) was formed without governmental support by the
All-Ceylon Buddhist Congress in December of that year. The assignment
of this committee, consisting of six Buddhist lay-people and six leaders of
the three monastic Nikāyas, was to evaluate the damage suffered by the
Śāsanaya under colonial rule and to recommend how to restore Buddhism
to its former place in society. Although the Buddhist Commission was not
appointed by the government but by a society of Buddhist lay-people, its
organization and mode of operation was oriented towards that of government committees.

That the final report of the Buddhist Commission would have an enormous political impact became increasingly clear as the next elections in
1956 came nearer. The report was published on schedule on 4 February
1956, only some weeks prior to the parliamentary elections in April, and
played a major role in the subsequent election campaigns. Indeed, the
elections were won by the MEP coalition headed by the Sri Lanka Freedom
Party (SLFP), with the help of a massive campaign supported by many
politicized monks who influenced the voting public through preaching and
public speeches, because the SLFP leader, S. W. R. D. Bandaranaike, had
promised to realize the recommendations of the Buddhist Commission.

The recommendations included the establishment of a Buddhist school
system, measures for a general improvement of the disastrous moral state
of society (alcohol prohibition, censorship of obscene literature etc.), the
establishment of the Buddhist Poya Days as national holidays (instead of
the Christian Sunday), the increase in numbers and registration of Buddhist
monks, real estate tax exemption for Buddhist monasteries, financial support for infrastructures for the education of monks, compensation for
the expropriation of monastic landholdings in the nineteenth century,
autonomous jurisdiction of the Saṃgha and administration of monastic property. Non-Buddhist religious communities should be allowed to
build places of worship only with government approval. Furthermore, a
Ministry for Religious Affairs should be created with the aim of rehabili-
tating those religious communities which had suffered under the colonial
government (i.e. all religions except Christianity). In its tone and argu-
mentation the report resonates the public notion of a cultural heritage of
the Sinhalese based on a certain reading of the *vaṃsa* literature, which is
interpreted as documents of a Sinhalese-Buddhist nation in the sense of
a moral community grounded on Buddhist principles and assigned with
the sacred mission of protecting the Sāsana.[11]

---

[11] Cf. Kemper, *Presence of the Past.*

The demands of the commission pretty much concur with what could be expected from a traditionally styled Buddhist king. Nevertheless, the report makes clear that the transfer of all traditional royal duties to a modern democratic government would be disadvantageous, because a parliament consisting of members of different religious affiliations would not be able to look after Buddhist affairs.[12] Instead, a Buddha Sāsana Council (Buddha Śāsana Maṇḍalaya) consisting of Buddhist clergy and lay-people should be appointed as a statutory body. This argument might also explain why the acknowledgment of Buddhism as state religion was not demanded in the report.

The suggestion to establish a Buddha Sāsana Council was emphasized by a further commission—the Buddha Sāsana Commission—appointed in the following year by the Governor-General. Its final report was published in 1959 and reconfirmed most of the issues raised by the Buddhist Commission of 1956. Nevertheless, the establishment of a Buddha Sāsana Council failed because the head-monks of the wealthy Syāma-Nikāya refused to hand over the administration of their considerable property to a central institution. In the following years opposition to the plans for a Sāsana-reform gathered momentum, propagating that the government was trying to destroy the Sāsana by attempting to bring the inner affairs of the Saṃgha under its control. By 1961 it was clear that the aim to establish a central Buddha Sāsana Council would ultimately fail.

In the meantime, the involvement of Buddhist monks in state politics grew to an unprecedented degree. Legitimized by a number of publications citing the important role the Saṃgha had played throughout history as spiritual and moral leader of society and advisor to the rulers—even claiming superiority of the Saṃgha to the king himself—,[13] monks, especially from the south-western lowlands around Colombo and in the southern rural areas, started to form political pressure groups to influence the voting public through preaching and to become involved in the politics of the day as lobbyists. This situation was the subject of fervent public debate right from the beginning. A law to prohibit the political activities of monks and their membership in political parties was planned after it was revealed that the assassination of president Bandaranaike in 1959 had been planned and arranged by his political opponent, the Buddhist monk

---

[12] Cf. Bechert, *Buddhismus, Staat und Gesellschaft*, 276.
[13] The most important books in this respect were doubtlessly Rāhula, Bhikṣuvagē urumaya, first published in 1946, and Vijayawardhana, *Dharmavijaya*; cf. Bretfeld, "Buddhistische Laien, buddhistische Profis," 119.

Māpiṭigama Buddharakkhita. This law was never introduced. In 2004 Buddhist monks were even elected into parliament for the party Jātika Heḷa Urumaya (JHU) which, since the elections of 2007, forms part of the government coalition. The political involvement of Buddhist monks and its impact on Buddhist fundamentalism and the civil war is the subject of several publications[14] and need not be repeated here. It must be mentioned, however, that Stanley Tambiah's critical book *Buddhism Betrayed?* on this subject was banned by the Sri Lankan government at the request of the leaders of the Saṃgha.[15]

Given this political involvement of religious actors, it is not surprising that the call for a secular state was inseparably connected to the question of dealing with religious pluralism. The institutions of Buddhism quickly learned to utilize the peculiarities of democratic processes to exert political pressure and to influence political decision making. And they had the necessary resources to do so—from organizational networks and an enormous amount of social (and financial) capital to the possibility of issuing threats to dissenting politicians to ban them and their families from religious services.[16] Of course, the attempt to achieve a dominating position or even monopoly among the religions of Sri Lanka is not uncontroversial, even among Buddhists, let alone non-Buddhist religious communities. The major thrust in this direction emanates from groups that Schalk addresses as the "ethnonationalist movements".[17] To a great extent the leadership of the Buddhist monastic Nikāyas can be subsumed under this heading. The far-reaching monopolization efforts of Buddhist representatives had an enormous impact on the religious neutrality of the state.

One indirect outcome of this pressure is obviously the fact that, in contrast to India, the word 'secular' was avoided in the Sri Lankan constitution together with all its amendments and draft bills. Sri Lanka is not a secular state by its own self-representation. Even if the much debated question of declaring Buddhism as the state religion was finally decided in the

---

[14] To name but a few: Deegalle, *Buddhism, Conflict and Violence in Modern Sri Lanka*; Bartholomeusz, *In Defence of Dharma*; Seneviratne, *The Work of Kings*; Seneviratne, "Buddhist Monks and Ethnic Politics"; Bartholomeusz and De Silva, *Buddhist Fundamentalism and Minority Identities in Sri Lanka*; Tambiah, *Buddhism Betrayed*.

[15] Cf. Schalk, "Present Concepts of Secularism among Ilvar and Lankans," 59f.

[16] This happened in 2000 when the Mahāsaṃgha threatened the MPs with refusing the bestowal of their funeral rites if they voted in favour of the Draft Constitution that guarantied autonomy to the northern and eastern provinces inhabited by a Tamil majority; cf. Schalk, "Present Concepts of Secularism among Ilvar and Lankans," 40.

[17] Schalk, "Present Concepts of Secularism among Ilvar and Lankans."

negative, Buddhism is officially assigned an elevated position in Article 9 of the 1978 version of the Sri Lankan constitution, though freedom of religion is granted by articles 10 and 14:

> 9. The Republic of Sri Lanka shall give to Buddhism the foremost place and accordingly it shall be the duty of the State to protect and foster the Buddha Sasana, while assuring to all religions the rights granted by Articles 10 and 14(1)(e).

In the Draft Bill (no. 372) to repeal and replace the constitution, presented to parliament by President Chandrika Bandaranaike Kumaratunga on 3 August 2000, this formulation is augmented by the appendage that guarantees "adequate protection to all [other] religions":

> 7.(1) The Republic of Sri Lanka shall give to Buddhism the foremost place and, accordingly, it shall be the duty of the State to protect and foster the Buddha Sasana while giving adequate protection to all religions and guaranteeing to every person the rights and freedoms granted by paragraphs (1) and (3) of Article 15.[18]

Paragraph (2) of this article reveals that Buddhist pressure was successful enough to establish a new institution of religious representatives with a direct interface to political decision making on religious concerns:

> 7.(2) The State shall, where necessary, consult the Supreme Council, recognized by the Minister of the Cabinet of Ministers in charge of the subject of Buddha Sasana, on measures taken for the protection and fostering of the Buddha Sasana.

This Supreme Council had already been recommended in 1990. It consists of the leaders (Mahānāyaka Theras) of the four main sections of the Buddhist Saṃgha (Malwatta, Asgiriya, Amarapura and Rāmañña Nikāya) and a varying number of other senior monks and Buddhist lay-people. This Supreme Council remained contested through the following years. On the one hand, conservative Buddhist forces demanded a reduction in lay influence within the council; on the other hand, some of its own members, including the Mahānayākas of the Malwatta and Asgiriya Nikaya, reneged on their commitment to the council and set up a competing institution, because the government had been reluctant to follow some of the council's radical suggestions.[19]

---

[18] The referred paragraphs 15 (1) and (3) are more or less identical to 10 and 14 (1)(e) of the constitution of 1978.

[19] Cf. Schalk, "Present Concepts of Secularism among Ilvar and Lankans," 63f.

It is not per se remarkable that a state like Sri Lanka, where religions play a considerable role in social life and order (as well as disturbances), has established a ministry for religious affairs. What is remarkable, however, is the attention given to Buddhism in this ministry. Under President Premadasa (1989–1993) it was introduced as Ministry of Buddha Sasana. The president himself presided over the ministry, which had no counterpart for other religions. Rathnasiri Wickramanayake held the position during the reign of Chandrika Bandaranaike-Kumaratunga (1994–2005). After his inauguration the currently incumbent President Mahinda Rajapaksha replaced this ministry by a Ministry of Religious Affairs with several secretaries for the different major religions. This situation appeared to be unbearable for part of the Buddhist public and soon rumours arose that the ministry was held under the sway of anti-Buddhist forces. At the beginning of his second term in 2010, Rajapaksha restructured and renamed it the Ministry of Buddha Sasana and Religious Affairs, in response to a formal request by the Mahānāyakas of the major monastic sections.

The duties and functions of the Ministry of Buddha Sasana and Religious Affairs include the "implementation of appropriate programs and projects to protect and foster the Buddha Sasana as provided for in Article 9 of the Constitution, while ensuring to all religions the rights granted by Article 10 and 14 (I) (e) of the Constitution", as well as "assisting the propagation of the Buddha Dhamma".[20] During the reign of Kumaratunga, the Minister of Buddha Sasana, Ratnasiri Wickramanayake, had launched a campaign to recruit 2000 children into Buddhist monastic orders to cope with the general shortage of monks. This met with harsh criticism from the celebrated Sinhalese scholar Gananath Obeyesekere which was published in two Colombo newspapers. In doing so, he broke the taboo of addressing the topic of child sexual abuse in Buddhist monasteries.[21]

The 'foremost place' of Buddhism is already reflected in the official and legal language in which Buddhism and other religions are represented. As we have seen above, the modern, but well established Sinhala term for *religion, āgama*, is right at the disposal of modern writers. In fact, *bauddha-āgama* (Buddhist religion), is in common use and linguistically equates Buddhism with other religions like *kristiyāni āgama* (Christianity)

---

[20] The Constitution of the Democratic Socialist Republic of Sri Lanka, Notification by President Mahinda Rajapaksa, November 22, 2010.

[21] The article can be found at http://www.infolanka.com/org/srilanka/cult/13.htm (accessed July 11, 2011). I have yet not been able to find out the exact issues of the original article in the *Daily News* and the *Sunday Island*.

or *mahammad āgama* (Islam) under a comparative term. Instead of using this term, the word Buddha Sāsana was preferred in the constitution and in the naming of the respective ministry as well as in other official and politically supported projects (e.g. the Buddha Sasana Fund Act of 1990), even in the English version. This linguistic practice—consciously or unconsciously—lifts Buddhism out of the assembly of religions spread among the Sri Lankan populace and, in a way, echoes the chronicle's notion of an ideal Buddhist society ruled by a king who takes responsibility for *lo-sasun*, the world and the religion of the Buddha. Buddhism is *not only* an *āgama* among *āgamas*, it is the one source of morality, guidance and spiritual liberation that has informed Lankan society and politics for more than 2000 years. Peter Schalk even goes one step further in correlating the use of the word *sāsana* by modern Sinhala-Buddhist ethno-nationalists to the use of the term in some classical Indian texts like the *Mahābhārata*, where it means "dominion, rule".[22] This meaning, according to Schalk, comes close to the 'dharmocracy' that ethno-nationalists envisage in their use of the word *sāsana* in the sense of a principle that governs every aspect of social life: law, economy, education etc.

The Sri Lankan state can hardly be called secular. This can be seen in the avoidance of the word *secular* in the constitution (where the term state religion is similarly avoided rather than negated) and the constitutionally warranted privileges of Buddhism (e.g. in the educational system), in political symbolism (e.g. the official act of paying worship to the tooth-relic by all presidents as part of their inauguration), and in the structures of political decision making which includes formalized religious (i.e. Buddhist) institutions as well as extra-parliamentary pressure. The necessary religious discrimination resulting from the 'Buddhism foremost' hierarchy is commonly masked in a rhetoric of compensation for the injustice suffered under colonial rule. The attempted domination or even monopolization of the religious field by individual and collective Buddhist actors is veiled with rhetorical strategies: all religions are equal in the Sri Lankan state system, but for historical reasons justice can only be established if Buddhism is granted "more equality" than the others.[23]

Controversy about how a secular Sri Lanka should be structured is still ongoing. Schalk distinguishes five models of the relationship between

---

[22] Schalk, "Present Concepts of Secularism among Ilvar and Lankans," 60.
[23] Cf. Schalk, "Present Concepts of Secularism among Ilvar and Lankans," 58.

religious institutions and the state.[24] He identifies these models among
different voices in the Indian and Sri Lankan discourse and policy measures. Four of them provide different solutions to how secularism must
be understood and implemented in political structures to cope with religious pluralism. The first model is the complete abandonment of state
support to any religion. This was the provision of the Illankai Tamil Arasu
Kachchi (ITAK, Lanka Tamil State Party) in 1951 when an autonomous
linguistic state of Tamils in the northern region was demanded. This
state was envisioned to be a democratic self-governing region ruled by a
mataccāraparra ōr aracu, a "government that is not related to religion".
We see here a similar expression of secular as the Sinhala term *āgama
no-vū.* This idea of a secular Tamil state was reinforced in a memorandum
by the ITAK in 1972. The second model is the one ultimately adopted by
the Tamil United Liberation Front (TULF) and the Liberation Tigers of
Tamil Eelam (LTTE). It promotes religious pluralism with state protection
for all religions. The ITAK switched to this model in about 1972, under
the impression of Sinhalese politics moving towards the 'Buddhism foremost' ideology. In a manifesto for the Tamil state of Īlam, the TULF, successor to the ITAK, in the independent secular state of Tamil Ealam no
religion was to be allowed to dominate another and each would receive
equal protection and aid. Models three and four are variants of promoting
religious pluralism with a fixed number of privileged religions. The Indian
constitution provides patronage only to Hinduism in the wider sense—
this is meant to include Jainism, Buddhism and Sikhism, but not Islam
and Christianity (Model 3). Model four is that of the Sri Lankan constitution, which reduces the number of privileged religions to only one. Model
five can be called 'anti-secularism.' In the Lankan discourse this position
is held by hard-core ethno-nationalists. It rejects religious pluralism and
attempts to give Buddhism monopoly status in society.

The first model, radical secularism, seems to enjoy growing support
in Sri Lankan society. It typically occurs in association with social criticism that attributes the grievances of the past decades to an outcome of
Sinhala-Buddhist nationalist influences in the political process. 'Sinhala-
only', 'Buddhism-foremost' and 'Sihaladīpa = Dhammadīpa'[25] have led to
an atmosphere of particularism, ethno-religious stereotypes and mutual
discrimination, resulting in a vicious circle of structural and physical

---

[24] Schalk, "Present Concepts of Secularism among Ilvar and Lankans," 42–52.
[25] "The island of the Sinhalese [!] is the island of the Buddhist teaching."

violence and counter-violence. A manifestation of this movement is the Secular Society of Sri Lanka (SSSL) which pleads for a national identity based on *Sri Lankan* values, not Sinhalese-Buddhist, Muslim-Islamist or Tamil-Hindu. The main activity of this "movement for constitutional separation of Sri Lankan state from religion" is web-based and consists of a comprehensive website,[26] Facebook and Twitter accounts as well as the so-called Sri Lankan Secularists' Blog of Reason. On these sites the society hosts critical essays, news, book and event recommendations, and provides a great number of links to thematically relevant sites. The topics range from contributions on Buddhist monks clamouring for state power[27] and reviews on Obeyesekere's debated article on child abuse in monasteries (see above) to discussions on the relationship of science and religion, including the promotion of Richard Dawkins' publications. As a typical Web 2.0 community the possibility to add user-comments is an important tool to express commitment to the society's ideals and to permit the exchange of opinions.

In its Mission Statement the SSSL declares:

> Secular Sri Lanka is a non-profit, non-partisan, educational association with the purposes/goals:
>
> To promote total and absolute separation of Temple (viharaya, kovil, church and mosque) and state of Sri Lanka through an amendment to the current Constitution.
>   To educate and inform the public about secularism and the required democratic process to achieve this goal.
>   To provide a forum for examination and discussion about secularism and the amendment to the Constitution for secularization of Sri Lanka.
>   To develop and engage in educational, cultural, charitable, and social activities that are beneficial to the members of Secular Sri Lanka, the secularist community of Sri Lanka, and the Sri Lankan community at large.[28]

Religion is discussed mainly from the perspective of the dangers posed by its connection with state power, though the SSSL understands itself not as explicitly anti-religious. Rather, 'secularism' is understood as the promotion of values based on religious freedom and science in the hope of creating an integral Sri Lankan national identity free from religious and

---

[26] http://www.secularsrilanka.com (accessed July 11, 2011).
[27] http://www.secularsrilanka.com/discussions/h-l-seneviratne/sinhala-buddhism-secularism-and-political-culture (accessed December 13, 2010).
[28] http://www.secularsrilanka.com/mission-statement-of-secular-sri-lanka (last accessed August 25, 2012).

ethnic particularism. This hope is expressed in the SSSL's *Declaration in Defense of Science and Secularism*:

siyalu śri lāṃkikayanṭa säkhā āgamika nidahasak—āgamikakaraṇaya novū āṇḍukrama vyavasthāvak...
āgamika balapämen tora rājya tantrayak! rājya balapämen tora āgamika parisarayak! vaḍā yahapat heṭa davasak...

A non-religious constitution, which every Sri Lankan—religious or free (from religion)—can accept...
A government without religious intervention! A religious environment without political intervention! A better tomorrow.[29]

Conclusion

In contrast to Europe, the colonized countries of Asia have not undergone a century-long process of separation between religion and politics. In Sri Lanka, a relaxation of the relationship between the two fields was triggered by the ambitions in the wake of independence. Especially after independence, social tensions shifted from confrontation with the British rulers as the 'common enemy' to struggles among disparate local groups distinguished by ethnicity, language and religion. The combination of these three distinction markers to construct patterns of social identity and alienation is a feature of the development of post-colonial nationalism which can similarly be found in India.

The concept of secularization entered the local Sri Lankan discourse within this context. The call for a secular state results from the identification of religion as one of, if not the single, most powerful sources of conflict and particularism within state politics. The expression "protection of religions" proves to be a crucial point in this discourse. Governmental protection of religion is widely perceived as being compatible with a secular state. However, 'protection' has an ambivalent meaning. It renders the notion of a secular state, its duties and its rights to regulate competition in the religious field a very flexible concept, thus accommodating the interests of particular actors. "Protection of religions" is not a binary question with a yes or no answer, but rather a question of range, scope and distribution. As we have seen, the TULF/LTTE manifesto has designed a secular state whose mission is to protect all religions in order to sustain religious

---

[29] http://www.secularsrilanka.com/home (last accessed August 25, 2012).

pluralism and to guarantee the rights of religious minorities. Even the Indian constitution calls itself secular, though it promotes protection as a privilege only for those religions that originated in India. Sinhalese-Buddhist nationalists, at the other end of the scale, extend the meaning of protection by analogy with the religious duties of the ideal Buddhist king who is idealized through a certain interpretation of the *vaṃsa* literature. Protection, here, is not an assurance of religious rights but the protection of a dominant position within the religious field. This concept of governmental protection is hardly compatible with a state that can be genuinely called secular. Even if this concept was not fully adopted in the Sri Lankan constitution, the influence of the religio-nationalist forces was powerful enough to prevent an explicit declaration of a secular state. Buddhism is state-protected against the loss of social importance and influence. It is guaranteed the foremost position in the state, a Sāsana among the *āgamas*—an equality in hierarchy.

Bibliography

Bartholomeusz, Tessa J., and Chandra R. De Silva, eds. *Buddhist Fundamentalism and Minority Identities in Sri Lanka*. Albany: State University of New York Press, 1998.

Bartholomeusz, Tessa. *In Defence of Dharma. Just-War Ideology in Buddhist Sri Lanka*. London. Routledge/Curzon, 2002.

Bechert, Heinz. *Buddhismus, Staat und Gesellschaft in den Ländern des Theravāda-Buddhismus. 1: Grundlagen, Ceylon (Sri Lanka)*. 2nd ed. Schriften des Instituts für Asienkunde in Hamburg, 5. Frankfurt: Alfred Metzner Verlag, 1966.

Bretfeld, Sven. "Buddhistische Laien, buddhistische Profis. Religiöse Individualisierung als Folge einer Neuverteilung religiösen Wissens in Sri Lanka." *Transformierte Buddhismen* 5 (2008): 108–135. http://www.ub.uni-heidelberg.de/archiv/8627 (accessed September 11, 2012).

——. "Dharmavijaya. The Revolt in the Temple." In *Kindler Literaturlexikon*, edited by Heinz Ludwig Arnold. 3rd ed. Göttingen: Metzler Verlag, 2009.

Deegalle, Mahinda, ed. *Buddhism, Conflict and Violence in Modern Sri Lanka*. Routledge Critical Studies in Buddhism. London: Routledge. 2006.

Frost, Mark. " 'Wider Opportunities'. Religious Revival, Nationalist Awakening and the Global Dimension in Colombo, 1870–1920." *Modern Asian Studies* 36, no. 4 (2002): 937–967.

Hallisey, Charles. "Works and Persons in Sinhala Literary Culture. Reconstructions from South Asia." In *Literary Cultures. Reconstructions from South Asia*, edited by Sheldon Pollock, pp. 689–746. Berkely: University of California Press, 2007.

Kemper, Steven. *Presence of the Past. Chronicles, Politics, and Culture in Sinhala Life*. Ithaca: Cornell UP, 1991.

McMahan, David L. *The Making of Buddhist Modernism*. Oxford: Oxford UP, 2008.

Rāhula, Valpaḷa. *Bhikṣuvagē urumaya*. Kolaṁba: Goḍagē saha Sahōdarayō, 1992.

Schalk, Peter. "Present Concepts of Secularism among Ilvar and Lankans." In *Zwischen Säkularismus und Hierokratie. Studien zum Verhältnis von Religion und Staat in Süd-und Ostasien*, edited by Peter Schalk, pp. 35–72. Uppsala, 2001.

Seneviratne, H.L. *The Work of Kings. The New Buddhism in Sri Lanka*. Chicago and London: The University of Chicago Press, 1999.

——. "Buddhist Monks and Ethnic Politics. A War Zone in an Island Paradise." *Anthropology Today* 17, no. 2 (2001): 15–21.

Silva, G. P. S. H. de. "The Custody of the Sacred Tooth Relic. From King to Committee." In *Saddhāmaṃgala Karuṇāratna abhistava granthaya. Saddhamangala Karunaratne Felicitation Volume*, edited by Malini Dias and K. B. A. Edmund, pp. 261–267. Colombo: Archaeological Survey Department, 2002.

Tambiah, Stanley J. *Buddhism Betrayed? Religion, Politics and Violence in Sri Lanka*. Chicago: The University of Chicago Press, 1992.

Vijayawardhana, D.C. *Dharmavijaya. The Revolt in the Temple*. Composed to Commemorate 2500 Years of the Land, the Race and the Faith. Colombo: The Daily News Press, 1953.

JAPANESE DISCOVERIES OF 'SECULARIZATION' ABROAD AND AT HOME, 1870–1945

Hans Martin Krämer

Introduction: Japanese Secularization as a 'Euro-American Project'?

Critical studies of secularization in modern Japan have usually focused on the specific mode in which Japanese political elites in the last quarter of the nineteenth century used Western models of state-church relationship to form a uniquely Japanese variant of such a relationship. After a period of trial and error, this unique relationship was found in State Shintō. Frequently misunderstood as a state religion,[1] State Shintō was rather a specific strategy to resolve a particular legal problem. This problem was that all the while the constitution had guaranteed freedom of belief ever since 1890,[2] the state at the same time forced its subjects to participate in certain rituals. These rituals, which were implemented by the state in schools (first only in the public sector, later also in private schools) with increasing pressure since the 1890s, included the worship of the (photographic) portraits of the emperor and his consort, of the Imperial Rescript on Education (promulgated in 1890), and visits to Shintō Shrines. The solution to this legal conundrum between freedom of belief and de facto forced participation in rituals was to define the national cult, later called State Shintō, as areligious, i.e. not even touching upon (constitutional) issues of faith.

The conventional critique of State Shintō holds that secularization before 1945 was incomplete (rather, State Shintō is held to represent

---

[1] Compare the definition in Betz, *Religion*: "State religion means the religious unity of the subjects ('un roi, une loi, une foi') regarded as indispensable for the state, in case of need to be implemented by force. It is the self-evident foundation of almost all older state formations. [...] State religion is regularly realized in the form of a state church." The goal of State Shintō, however, was neither to create religious unity among the populace by excluding other creeds, nor to establish a main religion against which the others would only have minority status. In contrast, private belief was free in pre-1945 Japan, as long as its practice did not run counter to the state cult.

[2] Article 28 of The Constitution of the Empire of Japan, which was promulgated in February 1889, reads: "Japanese subjects shall, within limits not prejudicial to peace and order, and not antagonistic to their duties as subjects, enjoy freedom of religious belief."

something like a re-sacralization of the public sphere) and really only fully achieved after the end of the Second World War.[3] Against this somewhat simple view, the post-secularist argument, which has recently been articulated, claims that the modern Japanese state, by emulating Western models, adopted a secularist posture in claiming religious neutrality for itself. In this way, the conventional critique of State Shintō as somehow deviating from rational modes of state-church relationships developed in the modern West can be overcome and instead Western secularist models subjected to criticism as well.[4]

In this paper, however, I want to focus less on actual policies than on the *conceptual* matrix of a non-European society and, by stressing the historical *semantics* of secularization, to analyze secularization as a concept *we* use to structure historical and actual experience, rather than as an objectified and quantifiable phenomenon. The way I intend to do this is by highlighting a specific twentieth century application of the trope of secularization to Japanese history and by attempting to establish a genealogy of discovering secularization abroad and at home in modern Japan.

In doing so, I will stress a different layer of the secularization paradigm than studies concentrating on the actual relationship of state and religion(s). Those studies mostly refer to what José Casanova has termed the differentiation thesis, or, in Charles Taylor's scheme, secularity in sense one, i.e. the shift from the premodern *connection* of political organization to some notion of ultimate reality towards the modern state, which is free from this connection.[5] In contrast, I will look at secularization in the sense of the 'decline-of-religion thesis' as formulated by Casanova.

An early Japanese verbalization of a secularization narrative in this sense can be found in an article series on the history of two thinkers of the Tokugawa period (1600–1868) penned in 1928 by one of the pioneers of the history of thought and religion in Japan, Muraoka Tsunetsugu (村岡典嗣 1884–1946). Muraoka wrote that:

> Two principal characteristics of Tokugawa culture distinguish it from medieval culture. First, Tokugawa culture was liberated from the special possessors of culture, the priests and nobles; and at the same time it was freed of

---

[3] This kind of argument has been espoused by leading social scientists both in and outside Japan for most of the postwar period. See e.g. Tominaga Ken'ichi, *Die Modernisierung Japans*, 61f, or Eisenstadt, "Japan," 88.

[4] For an exemplary version of this kind of argument, see the contribution by Isomae Jun'ichi to this volume.

[5] Taylor, *A Secular Age*, 1–3.

their traditionalism. Second, Tokugawa culture was secular—it had extricated itself from mystical and Buddhist other-worldly tendencies.[6]

Muraoka goes on to say that the means by which this trend "towards freedom and liberation," which "with the passage of time [...] became more pronounced and spread to the whole of culture,"[7] was fostered was through Neo-Confucianism, i.e. first the espousal of Zhu Xi Confucianism[8] in the early Tokugawa period and then its rebuttal by advocates of so-called Ancient Learning, i.e. the return to the early Confucian sources, from the second half of the seventeenth century onwards.[9] Although Muraoka nowhere explicitly calls this tendency 'modern' and does not speak of 'secularization' either, he clearly describes a process of the advancement of the 'secular,' a word he explicitly employs.

Such implicit ascriptions of modernity to non-Western cultures have come under increasing criticism ever since the 1970s. For a long time, religion has not been at the center of such criticism, but more recently it has become the subject of a particularly scathing indictment. This new view is best represented by US American anthropologist Talal Asad, who argues that modernity "is not a verifiable object" but rather "a project" of (some in) the West. This project is partly propelled by a political doctrine called secularism, which "arose in modern Euro-America,"[10] and which is "the attempt to construct categories of the secular and the religious in terms of which modern living is required to take place, and [in terms of which] nonmodern peoples are invited to assess their adequacy".[11] This is

---

[6] Muraoka Tsunetsugu, *Studies in Shinto Thought*, 97.

[7] Muraoka Tsunetsugu, *Studies in Shinto Thought*, 98.

[8] Zhuxi Confucianism refers to a branch of Confucianism developed in China during the Song Dynasty. The focus on ethics found in classical Confucianism was complemented during the Song Dynasty by an increased interest in metaphysics. This branch of Confucian thought and learning was taken up in Japan from the fifteenth century onwards, but rose to prominence only from the early seventeenth century on.

[9] In order to make sense of this argument, it is important to realize that Confucianism in premodern Japan (other than its variants in China or Korea) was never 'religious' in any meaningful sense: There were almost no Confucian temples or shrines and there were hardly any rituals surrounding Confucianism. Instead it was regarded as a philosophical teaching mostly concerned with individual or political ethics and questions of epistemology. The contrast to China is clearly visible in the fact that in sixteenth-century China, Christian missionaries quickly saw their counterparts in Confucian literati, while in Japan of the same period they identified Buddhist priests as their primary adversaries.

[10] Asad, *Formations of the Secular*, 1.

[11] Asad, *Formations of the Secular*, 14.

part of the way in which people committed to modernity "expect others (especially in the non-West) to do so too".[12]

Asad's position appears legitimate in regard to Japan if one considers the North American school of modernization theory of the 1950s and 1960s. For this line of inquiry, Japan was a favorite example as the sole non-Western success case perfectly suited to gauge its adequacy in a variety of respects.[13] The crucial importance of Japan resulted in a strategic alliance between the US government, private funds, and academics to support research into Japanese modernization. Since 1958, the US American government invested fifteen million US dollars per year in area studies under the National Defense Education Act,[14] and in the course of the 1960s the Ford Foundation not only invested several million US dollars in the build-up of several centers for Japanese Studies, but also sponsored a series of five conferences on "the problems of modernization in Japan" with 135,000 US dollars.[15]

In this sense, early postwar US style modernization theory was clearly a Euro-American project. This, however, has already been rather clearly acknowledged by the late 1960s both by social scientific observers[16] as well as erstwhile protagonists[17] of modernization theory.

What happens, however, if we confront Asad's critique with the historical argument of Muraoka? Do we have to conclude that Muraoka foolishly accepted the invitation to assess Japan's adequacy, in other words: that he fell victim to the Euro-American strategy of the project of projecting

---

[12] Asad, *Formations of the Secular*, 13.

[13] See Krämer, "Alte und Neue Modernisierungstheorie."

[14] Janssens, *Power and Academic Culture*, 53.

[15] Janssens, *Power and Academic Culture*, 49.

[16] As early as 1969, British sociologist of religion David Martin wrote: "A general theory [of secularization] can be stated for societies within a Christian ambit (or, if you prefer, societies with a Christian historical background) and subsequently be qualified for other societies, just as secularization itself was exported with modifications to other societies" (Martin, "Notes Towards a General Theory," 192f), i.e. to say it was clear to him that before this export there had been no such thing as secularization in these non-Christian societies.

[17] In 1968, John W. Hall, one of the organizers of the conferences on the problems of modernization in Japan, now president of the Association of Asian Studies, in his keynote lecture before the Association's annual meeting explained: "It was only as Japan came out of the war and began its rapid recovery that we began confidently to draw a line joining the prewar statistics of national development with those of the nineteen sixties to form an optimistic upward curve. [...] The result has been the current rash of essentially optimistic interpretations of Japan's modern history. Can we say that the 'success story' scenario is the natural, the objective, outcome of adopting a 'value free' method?" (Hall, "Reflections on a Centennial," 717f).

modernity as a normative umbrella over the whole world? While there may be some legitimacy to this view, the question is whether this kind of argument is not in itself again the product of a patronizing Euro-American gaze upon the 'subaltern.' At least we should take the Japanese seriously enough to grant them their own projects and agendas in employing the terminology of 'secularization' beyond merely falling prey to alleged Euro-American political strategies.

This independence or autonomy becomes clear, I will argue, by two lines of investigation that I plan to pursue in this paper. One is to look at further twentieth century articulations ascribing proto-modernizing tendencies of secularization to historical Japan. The other is to seek out the genealogies of such articulations by investigating both the history of the concepts involved from the premodern era onwards and the discourses making use of these concepts in the modern era. Accordingly, my first step will be to look at the leading representative of what has been called the modernist school of thought in postwar Japan, the thinker who has most fully elaborated on the problem of modernity, and—associated with it—of secularity, in early modern Japanese thought.

Two Twentieth Century Approaches to the History of Premodern Japan

Maruyama Masao, the Modernist

Maruyama Masao (丸山眞男 1914–1996) was not only probably the single most influential intellectual in postwar Japan, but also one of the most prominent Japanese abroad, certainly the most widely translated Japanese author of non-fictional texts. Part of Maruyama's appeal to a Western language readership was his vast background in European learning. Maruyama had received his early training in the intellectual history of *European* political thought, and although he was employed as a lecturer in the history of *Japanese* thought at Tokyo University in 1937, he never abandoned his early training.

It is thus typical of Maruyama how, in his *Studies in the Intellectual History of Tokugawa Japan*, written in the early 1940s and published as a book in 1952, he makes frequent reference to the European history of political ideas in order to elucidate his points about the history of early modern political thought in Japan. His central argument is that around 1700, Zhu Xi neo-Confucian orthodoxy broke up "under the external pressure of social and economic contradictions and the internal dissolution of the continuative mode of thought". By negating any natural, metaphysically guaranteed order, later neo-Confucian thinkers in Tokugawa Japan achieved a break-through towards universality and modern consciousness.[18]

Taking his cue from Ernst Troeltsch (1865–1923), Maruyama in a particularly noteworthy passage traces how early modern European political thinkers first had to stress God's absolute, transcendental nature before the supremacy of the divine will could be transferred to human individuals.[19] Historically, the first individuals where this transfer was realized were the absolute monarchs. The absolute monarch of early modern Europe, says Maruyama, was "a secularized version of the God of Duns Scotus and Descartes,"[20] but this was only a first step on the road to recognizing autonomy in every individual and, politically speaking, the acceptance of social contract theory:

> In order to give man, who had been contained within the social order and presupposed the social order, autonomy with respect to that order, the supremacy of all impersonal Ideas had to be eliminated and a personality free from all value judgments, whose existence itself is the ultimate source of all such values, making it unnecessary to trace them further back, had to be made the starting point for the mode of thought. [...] The image of a God who transcends the world in his absolute indifference was the precondition for the idea of a political personality possessing absolute autonomy with respect to the social system.[21]

The reason Maruyama elaborates on this somewhat intricate argument about Europe is because he sees a parallel in the Japanese history of thought. According to Maruyama, the seventeenth century neo-Confucian thinker Ogyū Sorai (荻生徂徠 1666–1728) developed a proto-modern 'concept of autonomous invention' of the social order. Just as the secularized version of God was at first not applied to every individual in early modern Europe, in Sorai "the personalities who invent the social order are above all the [mythical Confucian] sages, and then by analogy political rulers in general".[22]

---

[18] The wording of this summary partly relies on Barshay, "Imagining Democracy," 383.

[19] Maruyama Masao, *Studies in the Intellectual History*, 232–237 (this part was first published in 1941).

[20] Maruyama Masao, *Studies in the Intellectual History*, 237. Jap. original: Maruyama, *Nihon seiji*, 239.

[21] Maruyama Masao, *Studies in the Intellectual History*, 236.

[22] Maruyama Masao, *Studies in the Intellectual History*, 231. The 'rationalist' and 'positivist' attitude of Japanese neo-Confucians critical of Zhuxi had earlier prompted Itō Jinsai to argue for the "separation of the way of man from the Way of Heaven" (Maruyama 1974: 180; Jap. original: Maruyama 1952: 186) (this part was first published in 1940).

It is thus clear that Maruyama saw precursors to the autonomy of the modern individual in Tokugawa period thought and that one important element of this modernity for him was the secularization of a transcendent entity to an absolutely autonomous individual. Without making entirely clear what concepts precisely he is referring to, Maruyama also quotes Carl Schmitt's saying that "all the important concepts of the modern state are secularizations of theological concepts."[23]

In his introduction to the English translation of his early writings published in 1974, Maruyama explained the motives behind his reading 'modernity' into early modern Japanese history of thought. "[T]he extra-academic motive of combating the 'overcome modernity' theorists in my own professional field," dominant in the 1940 climate of fascism, ultra-nationalism and anti-Westernism, led him to stress, one, that even "contemporary Japan was still not so modernized that the 'overcoming of modernity' could conceivably be the greatest problem on the agenda" and, two, that "[e]ven Tokugawa ideas [...] could be seen as developing unceasingly toward modernity".[24]

For Maruyama in the early 1940s, arguing about secularization was obviously more a strategic means to achieving the goal of making plausible Japan's potential for modernity. Moreover, Maruyama refers to secularization here only in the genealogical meaning, i.e. in the sense of the "transformation of the meaning of a concept from a theological to a secular context".[25] An analysis of lecture manuscripts used by Maruyama after the war, however, reveals that he also interpreted the assumed process of secularization in early modern Japan quantitatively, i.e. in the sense of a "transformation of the meaning allotted to religion in societies".[26]

The 'Theory of Tokugawa-Period Buddhist Decline'

To wit, in 1948 Maruyama asserted that the ascendancy of neo-Confucianism was only possible after the decline of Buddhism:

> Regardless of the original ideology of Buddhism, the Buddhist sects actually developing in our country rather had a markedly secular hue. [...] The decline of the hegemony of Buddhism was due less to the otherworldliness

---

[23] Maruyama Masao, *Studies in the Intellectual History*, 234. Jap. original: Maruyama, *Nihon seiji*, 235. The German original reads: "Alle prägnanten Begriffe der modernen Staatslehre sind säkularisierte theologische Begriffe" (Schmitt, *Politische Theologie*, 49).

[24] Maruyama Masao, *Studies in the Intellectual History*, xxxii.

[25] Pollack, *Rückkehr des Religiösen?*, 21.

[26] Pollack, *Rückkehr des Religiösen?*, 22.

of the character of its thought, but it was to the contrary rather the decline of its secular power that rendered the power of its thought impotent.[27]

Maruyama's favorable view of the role neo-Confucianism played in the first half of the Tokugawa period was only possible because of his tacit acceptance of what has become famous as the 'Theory of Tokugawa-Period Buddhist Decline.' Usually associated with the ten-volume *History of Japanese Buddhism* by Tsuji Zennosuke (辻善之助 1944–1955), it was not only fully articulated by Tsuji as early as 1931, but had in fact been common sense among Buddhists, if not academic historians, since the Meiji period.[28] That is to say, Maruyama and even Muraoka were certainly aware of it.

The 'Theory of Tokugawa-Period Buddhist Decline' consists mainly of three crucial elements: 1) Buddhist priests adopted a decadent and amoral lifestyle; 2) Buddhism became formalized and politicized, losing its religious character,[29] 3) this stood in contrast to the preceding medieval period, in which Buddhism had flourished as an individual belief.

To elaborate, it was only in the twelfth and thirteenth centuries (i.e. the medieval period) that Buddhism, which had first spread to Japan from the Korean peninsula in the fifth or sixth century C.E., developed popular strands. Reformers appeared on the scene popularizing practices leading to individual salvation. During these years, four new schools of Buddhism were founded to which the majority of Japanese still claim adherence even today: the Pure Land School, the True Pure Land School, the Nichiren School, and the Zen School.[30] When these schools flourished, medieval Buddhism was at the height of its popularity and vitality; thereafter, however, a process of decline began with a fundamental change occurring in the early modern period. The sixteenth century wars of unification broke the worldly power of Buddhism. Powerful temples had previously acted like feudal lords, participating in the struggles for hegemony in politically fractured sixteenth century Japan. In the second half of the sixteenth century, the three unifiers did away with this worldly power for good. The last of these unifiers, the founder of the Tokugawa Shogunate, went even

---

[27] Maruyama Masao, *Maruyama Masai kōgiroku*, 59f. Scripts of lectures originally held in 1948.

[28] Klautau, "Against the Ghosts."

[29] In his summary of the 'Theory of Tokugawa-Period Buddhist Decline,' Paul B. Watt ("Jiun Sonja," 188–190) adds the element of sectarianism, which exacerbated the institutional fossilization and formalization.

[30] This is a simplified and even somewhat ahistorical summary of Japanese Buddhist sectarianism, but it is this understanding of medieval religious history that has informed the background of the 'Theory of Tokugawa-Period Buddhist Decline.'

further and co-opted all Buddhist sects into a system of population control. On the one hand, all sects had to establish a hierarchical system of main and branch temples. On the other hand, the whole population had to affiliate itself with temple parishes. No Japanese received permission for his funeral, a paramount concern for a populace in which ancestor veneration is of central importance, without being registered with a Buddhist temple. The Buddhist temples themselves received almost all of their revenues from this funerary system, for which reason they directed considerable energy towards the administration, maintenance and recruitment of parish members.[31]

In the way it plays down the (early modern) public aspect of institutional Buddhism and praises the (medieval) side of individual belief, one can immediately see that the fully articulated version of the 'Theory of Tokugawa-Period Buddhist Decline' presupposes an understanding of religion that is heavily tinged with Protestant understandings of individual belief (as the core of religion). That is, while this 'theory' drew on anti-Buddhist stereotypes widely spread even before the nineteenth century, it also integrated elements that were the result of Western impact on the Japanese cultural landscape in the second half of the nineteenth century.

Maruyama calls the result of the process of Buddhist decline in the early modern period secular. Using *secular* in this way is not unusual even in today's academic understanding of the secularization paradigm. Detlef Pollack, for instance, a recent advocate of the usefulness of the secularization thesis, lists the following central dimensions of secularization:[32]

- diminishing significance of religious ideational systems for the individual conduct of life
- decline of traditional religious institutions
- replacement of a religious by a technological-scientific interpretation of the world

If one accepts Confucianism as a more rational interpretation of the world, then all three of these dimensions are present in the 'Theory of Tokugawa-Period Buddhist Decline.' One reason for Maruyama's using the terms *secular*, *secular tendencies*, or *secularization* is surely to be found in

---

[31] For more information on the 'Theory of Tokugawa-Period Buddhist Decline' see Klautau, "Against the Ghosts," or Williams, "Religion." For the Tokugawa-period changes summarized here see Nosco "Keeping the Faith."

[32] Pollack, *Rückkehr des Religiösen?*, 10.

his reception of European social theory of the first half of the twentieth century, especially that of Max Weber. The words he used to express these concepts had also been coined as translation terms for European concepts towards the end of the nineteenth century. Yet a closer look reveals that Maruyama made use of a terminology with a much longer history than that of the European influence upon the Japanese language.

The Historical Semantics of 'Secular(isation)' in Japan Up to the Turn of the Twentieth Century

When Maruyama wrote about *secular tendencies* or *secularization*, he employed the term *sezoku* 世俗 (or *sezokuka* 世俗化 or *zokka* 俗化). The components of this compound have the following basic meanings: *se* means world, with the nuance of this-worldly or mundane, while *zoku* can mean base, vulgar, mundane, but also be a technical term for laity. Let us take just a quick glance at premodern usages of these words before turning to how this terminology was employed in Japan since the early Meiji Period.

Premodern and Early Modern Usages of sezoku

While to my knowledge there was no concept that denoted something like a process of diminishing religiosity, there was, in Buddhist Japanese terminology, a rather clear-cut vocabulary for expressing 'the secular.' This vocabulary operated as a term of opposition both

- on the institutional level (i.e. in opposition to monasticism or priesthood), often *zoku*
- on an abstract level (i.e. in opposition to religious substance, i.e. the Buddha Dharma), often *se*

We find an instance of meaning no. 1 in the oldest official chronicle of Japanese history, the *Nihon shoki* (日本書紀, completed in 720). Shortly after the first mention of Buddhism, it says there:

> This year Soga no Miumao no Sukune, having asked for these two Buddhist images, sent [three helpers] in all directions to search out persons who practiced Buddhism. Upon this he only found in the province of Harima [one man], who from a Buddhist priest had become a layman again.[33]

---

[33] Aston, *Nihongi*, 101.

The phrase "from a Buddhist priest [...] a layman again" reads *tokusō kan-zoku* 得僧還俗 in the original Sino-Japanese.[34]

Both terms, *se* and *zoku*, are employed in premodern Buddhist texts in the more narrow sense of lay life, such as in *shusse* 出世 (lit. leaving the world, i.e. entering monastic life). There are, however, also frequent discussions of the relationship of the Law of the Buddha to the more abstract realm of worldly affairs. There is in fact a plethora of examples from both older Chinese and from Japanese texts ever since the introduction of writing into Japan.[35] I present here two examples that show how sophisticated discussions of the secular were handled early on. They are found in the *Shōbōgenzō* (正法眼蔵), one of the best known works of Japanese Buddhism, the classic of Sōtō Zen written by Dōgen 道元, the founder of this lineage in Japan, and his disciples in mid-thirteenth century. In the chapter "Bendōwa" (弁道話), in a question-and-answer-format, a disciple asks Dōgen how "those of us involved in the daily pressures of lay life" could possibly attain salvation by practicing the strict method of seated meditation advocated by Dōgen. The master answers that the compassionate Buddhas have opened their gates to the truth for all sentient beings, concluding:

> Those who believe that worldly affairs are an impediment to the Law of the Buddha know only that there is no Law of the Buddha in the world; but they do not yet know that there is no Worldly Law within the Law of the Buddha.[36]

That is to say, once one has attained the Law of the Buddha, things such as worldly affairs no longer matter. The *Shōbōgenzō* here employs a clear dichotomy between *buppō* (佛法), the Law of the Buddha, and *se*, the secular world, or *sehō* (世法, *loka-dharma*), literally the Law of the World.[37]

---

[34] Sakamoto Tarō, *Nihon koten bungaku taikei*, vol. 68 (herafter NKBT 68), 149.

[35] Probably the oldest extant example from Japan is the statement "The world (*seken*) is false; the Buddha alone is true" contained in the *Tenju koku shūchō*, a seventh century embroidery. See Sonoda, "Secularity and Profanation."

[36] Nishio Minoru, *Nihon koten bungaku taikei*, vol. 81 (hereafter NKBT 81), 89.

[37] In older Buddhist texts, *loka-dharma* was used in the sense of a technical term for an inferior version of the *dharma*. Compare the following summary by Jamie Hubbard: "The Mahāparinirvāṇa-sūtra, too, makes a distinction between the conventional or worldly *dharma* (*sehō*) that can be destroyed and the ultimate *dharma* (*dai-ichi-gi hō*) that cannot (T no. 374, 12.472a)" (Hubbard, "Orthodoxy," 8). In the text introduced here and in most other instances in medieval and early modern Japan, however, the phrase seems to be employed in a more literal sense, referring to the fundamental (non-Buddhist) tenets of the worldly realm.

In another passage, the word *sezoku*, rarely used at this time, is employed to convey a similar distinction between the realm of Enlightenment and the secular realm:

> Zhaozhou[38] had another monk who asked him: 'Does Buddha Nature exist even in a dog, yes or no?' ... Zhaozhou said: 'Yes, It exists.' ...
> The monk then asked: 'If It already exists, why is It strongly impelled to enter into this body of flesh?' ...
> Zhaozhou replied: 'It is because a dog knowingly and intentionally breaks precepts.'
> Even though this statement had long been spread as a mundane saying, it was now Zhaozhou's way of expressing what he had realized.[39]

That is to say, as a mundane saying it meant that someone who breaks the precepts in this world will be reborn as a dog, a meaning which is here contrasted with the enlightened attitude of Zhaozhou.

Interestingly, *se* was not only used by Buddhists in a negative sense but also referred to by Confucians in a positive way; thus, *segai* (世外, lit. out of this world) can, in a *Buddhist* sense, mean "removed from the disturbances of this fleeting world,"[40] but was also used in Tokugawa-period Confucianists' criticism of Buddhists as "removed from the concerns of this-worldly society,"[41] i.e., in last consequence, unethical. While *se* thus can be said to have been established as a concept in its own right, there was, as I have already mentioned, no distinctive discourse on a process of inclination towards *se* up to the nineteenth century. The closest we get to a functional equivalent of a diagnosis of secularization is in Buddhist responses to the anti-Buddhist wave of the late Tokugawa period, when self-critical voices arose among Buddhist ranks, some of whom accused their own peers of having fallen into worldly patterns of behavior, such as the prominent reform Buddhist Shaku Unshō (釋雲照), a Shingon monk, who just after the Meiji Restoration in 1868 remarked upon his fellow brethren as follows:

---

[38] Zhaozhou Zhenji, also known as Congshen Zhaozhou, Chan master of the Tang Dynasty.
[39] NKBT 81, 140.
[40] Morohashi Tetsuji, *Dai kanwa jiten*, 269.
[41] Ketelaar, *Of Heretics and Martyrs*, 19.

Buddhist priests forgot the meaning of their beliefs, and having deranged themselves in polluted world affairs, brought upon themselves the disciplinary actions of the politicians.[42]

Here, *zoku* can be seen to be used almost synonymously with *se*.

With this linguistic and conceptual background of a well-established dichotomy between a secular realm and a transcendental one, it is not surprising that we find the same terminology in the first translations from Western books on contemporary politics and in Japanese descriptions of things Western from the 1870s onwards.

The Meiji Period

One of the earliest examples of this is the translation of the Swiss legal scholar Johann Caspar Bluntschli's (1808–1881) *Allgemeines Statsrecht* [sic!]. Originally published in German in 1852, it was translated into Japanese by Katō Hiroyuki (加藤弘之), who went on to become one of the most influential conservative statesmen and educators in the latter half of the Meiji period. Katō's 1872 translation was one of the most important texts for early legal studies in modern Japan and was quoted widely. Bluntschli discussed legal issues in the relationship between church and state in a separate chapter of his book, starting with a historical overview of this relationship, in which he frequently referred to the distinction between secular (*weltlich*) and religious spheres. Thus, in describing the situation in the medieval age, Bluntschli writes:

> While the Church fought for its supremacy and set itself as a divine institution high above the merely human state, the state contented itself with the modest demand for liberty in secular matters.[43]

Katō translates "secular matters" (*weltliche Dinge*) with *seji* (世事), employing the same *se* we have just discussed in premodern Buddhist terminology.[44]

Another example is the highly influential translation of Thomas Henry Buckle's (1821–1862) *History of Civilization in England* (vol. 1: 1857, vol. 2:

---

[42] Quoted in: Klautau, "Kinsei bukkyō," 585; translation from Klautau, "Against the Ghosts," 276.

[43] German original: "Während die Kirche für ihre Ueberordnung kämpfte, und sich als eine göttliche Institution hoch über den nur menschlichen Stat setzte, begnügte sich der Stat mit der bescheidenen Forderung der Freiheit in weltlichen Dingen" (Bluntschli, *Allgemeines Statsrecht*, 304f).

[44] Katō Hiroyuki, *Kokuhō hanron*, 17f.

1861). Buckle, one of the founding fathers of modern historiography, offered a teleological view of the history of human progress that was eagerly taken up by the early Meiji elite. Secularization had its firm place in Buckle's view of history, visible for instance in his sketch of the end of the Middle Ages:

> How the prospects of the church were subsequently darkened, and how the human reason began to rebel, will be related in another part of this Introduction, where I shall endeavour to trace the rise of that secular and sceptical spirit to which European civilization owes its origin.[45]

A few pages later, Buckle describes how since the "end of the sixteenth century [...] the theological fervour began to subside in England and France, and the way was prepared for that purely secular philosophy, of which Bacon and Descartes were the exponents, but by no means the creators".[46] The Japanese translation, published in 1879,[47] again employs *seji* both times, speaking literally of "the secularity and the doubting mind that are the sources of European progress".[48]

The trope of the secularity of modern Europe was not just found in translations but also in original works. It is clearly visible in the works of the most prominent Meiji-period educator and proponent of Western ideas, Fukuzawa Yukichi (福澤諭吉 1835–1901).[49] Fukuzawa, who was well known to have drawn heavily on Buckle[50] (and also the French historian François Guizot (1787–1874), among others), was generally suspicious of religion, which he regarded as creating a climate favorable to superstitions and irrationality, his declared main enemies. It is thus small wonder that he was keen on detecting in the West so revered by him a history of getting rid of religious thinking. Usually employing a rather simple, journalistic style, the most elaborate exposition of his ideas can be found in his 1875 *An Outline of a Theory of Civilization*.[51] He characterized the European Middle Ages as opposed to the spirit of inquiry:

---

[45] Buckle, *History of Civilization*, 318.

[46] Buckle, *History of Civilization*, 329.

[47] This translation (Bakkuru, *Eikoku bunmei shi*) only covered the first volume of the original.

[48] Bakkuru Tōmasu, *Eikoku bunmei shi*, vol. 4, 88.

[49] Later, Maruyama was to be influenced decisively by Fukuzawa. See Hiraishi Nao'aki, "The Formation of Maruyama."

[50] Fukuzawa was, however, sensitive to Buckle's intimations that Asian civilizations could not progress because of external impediments and preferred to argue for a spirit of civilization as the main driving force of progress (Aydin, *The Politics of Anti-Westernism*, 29f).

[51] Jap. *Bunmeiron no gairyaku*.

In Europe, too, from the Dark Ages down to the end of the feudal period
the power of learning was completely monopolized by the monasteries. It
was only from the seventeenth century on that learning finally was opened
to society as a whole.[52]

Instead of stressing the pervasiveness of religion in all spheres, however,
Fukuzawa emphasized the opposition of secular and religious already in
medieval times:

> In general, to regulate the body belonged to secular physical power, and to
> regulate the spirit pertained to the Church's authority, so that secular and
> religious powers were opposed to each other.[53]

Progress is discerned by Fukuzawa with the onset of Reformation:

> In secular society, however, human intelligence was making daily progress.
> Now the gullibility of the past did not suffice; knowledge of letters was no
> longer the exclusive preserve of the monks, and laymen also learned to
> read.[54]

Terminologically, Fukuzawa, like his contemporaries, made use of com-
binations containing *se* and *zoku* (secular power: *zokuken* 俗権; secular
society: *sejō* 世上; society as a whole: *seken* 世間), also employing the
compound *sezoku*, the later lexical standard for *secular*. Fukuzawa does
not speak explicitly of 'secular*ization*.' It is clear, however, that he is
describing a process of, in the words of Casanova, "progressive shrinkage
and decline of religion".[55]

The establishment of *sezoku* as a term identifying that domain of social
life which is distinct from religion or which is not (or no longer) determined by religious considerations was paralleled by the terminological
clarification of the word for *religion*. In fact, we find this opposite pair as
early as in 1882 when a Japanese translation of James Fitzjames Stephen's
(1829–1894) 1873 *Liberty, Equality, Fraternity* appeared.[56] The Japanese
translation has a chapter entitled "Sezoku Shūkyō Niken no Kubetsu,"
the original of which reads "The Distinction Between the Temporal and
Spiritual Power." In this chapter, Stephen argues that "[t]he spiritual and
temporal power differ not in the province which they rule, but in the

[52] Fukuzawa Yukichi, *An Outline*, 149.
[53] Fukuzawa Yukichi, *An Outline*, 126.
[54] Fukuzawa Yukichi, *An Outline*, 132.
[55] Casanova, *Public Religions*, 20.
[56] Suchīben, *Jiyū byōdō ron*, translated by Kobayashi Eichi. Japanese library catalog
entries to this translation routinely but erroneously name the brother of James Fitzjames,
Leslie Stephen, as the author of the original.

sanctions by which they rule it," with the spiritual power referring to the
"power in heaven, purgatory, and hell," and the temporal power referring to "power to deal with life and limb, goods, liberty, and reputation".[57]
Thus, we find here the same usage of *sezoku*, albeit not as a literal translation of *secular* (Stephen uses *temporal* throughout the chapter).

We find a clearer example of translating this dichotomy with the said
terms in the translation of Thomas Raleigh's 1886 *Elementary Politics*.[58]
Raleigh's book starts with a brief historical outline of politics in Europe,
featuring a section on Secular Politics in a chapter entitled "Modern
Society," which begins:

> In the 16th and 17th centuries, all political questions were more or less con-
> nected with religion; but it was precisely during this period that the secular
> notion of politics developed itself in the minds of thinkers and statesmen.
> [...] This secularizing tendency may be observed in the two powers, which
> had most to do with the guidance of the Reformation in England and
> elsewhere.[59]

The two powers Raleigh refers to are the rising power of royalty ("Kings
are usually compelled to regard religion from a secular point of view") and
the "secularizing tendency in the middle classes". The Japanese translation from 1902, penned by Akasaka Kamejirō (赤坂亀次郎),[60] rendered
religious vs. *secular* by *shūkyō* (宗教) vs. *sezoku*, which was apparently
already well-established by this time.

Inoue Tetsujirō and the Idea of the Secular Tokugawa Period

Thus, in the early Meiji period, secularization was discovered in Europe
but not applied to Japan. Yet, it did not take until the late 1920s (Muraoka)
or 1940s (Maruyama) until secularizing elements *were* identified in early
modern Japanese history. In fact, one of the earliest instances of using
both the term *secularization* (*sezokuka*) itself (i.e. with the suffix indicating '-ization') *and* its application to Japanese history can be found as
early as 1905.[61] In that year, the final volume of a trilogy on early modern
Confucian philosophy, Inoue Tetsujirō's (井上哲次郎) monumental *The
Philosophy of the Japanese Zhu Xi School* appeared. Like Maruyama, albeit

---

[57] Stephen, *Liberty, Equality, Fraternity*, 106.
[58] Sir Thomas Raleigh (1850–1920), reader in English Law at Oxford University.
[59] Raleigh, *Elementary Politics*, 20f.
[60] Rarē Tōmasu, *Seigaku genron*, 35–37. Akasaka was head of a publishing company and
translator of works on politics and economy in the 1880s.
[61] Paramore, *Ideology and Christianity*, 154.

two generations earlier, Inoue Tetsujirō (1856–1944) had studied Western philosophy (in Germany from 1884 to 1890), but was then appointed to the chair of Eastern philosophy at the University of Tokyo and was, by the turn of the century, one of the leading conservative intellectuals of the country. In his large-scale attempt at reconstructing Tokugawa period Neo-Confucianism, Inoue took care to clarify what was religious about it and what was not. In his conclusion to volume 2, he highlights several points as "of particular note to scholars," the first of which reads as follows:

> *The Japanese Zhu Xi teaching is the result of what Buddhist monks advocated after they had shed Buddhism and thus taken the initiative.* Fujiwara Seika, doyen of the Kyōto School, despite having been in Sōkokuji as a monk of the Zen School, began to subscribe to the Zhu Xi School after returning to secular life himself; Tani Tokitaka, founder of the Southern School, also began to subscribe to the Zhu Xi School after returning to secular life himself, after he had lived in Shinjōji in Kōchi as a man with shaved head and sacred robes; even someone like Yamazaki Ansai converted to Confucianism and contributed greatly to the advance of the Zhu Xi School, after he had one morning awoken to the falsity of Buddhism, although he had once been in Myōshinji, having worn a tonsure. *In this way Buddhist monks themselves converted to the Zhu Xi School after discarding Buddhism and, by closing their eyes to queer old legends concerning matters of life and death, they expounded only everyday ethics indispensable to social intercourse among us humans. By doing so, they came to contribute to popular education. That is to say, by destroying the distance between monk and lay and changing their attitude, they drew nearer to the secular and one can see this as a sign that they came to a compromise with common sense.* In other words: *Traces of secularization are conspicuous and impossible to deny. By the time especially the Zhu Xi School that was advocated by Buddhists monks in this way was slowly gaining power, Kogaku and the Wang Yangming School were also advocated, so that Confucianism, finally replacing Buddhism, exhibited the power to dominate the realm.*[62]

Inoue here speaks of secularization—and he gives both the Japanese term *sezokuka* and the corresponding *secularization* in English—first in a limited sense, meaning only that former Buddhist monks returned to lay life and turned to (or, in Inoue's words, "converted to") Confucianism. Yet, in a second step, he employs a more abstract usage of the term *secularization*, using it to refer to the process during which Confucianism allegedly replaced Buddhism as the main ideological power of the Tokugawa period. While Inoue's somewhat crude line of reasoning appears to be a far cry from Maruyama's discovery of the budding idea of the autonomous

---

[62] Inoue Tetsujirō, *Nihon shushi gakuha*, 595f. Original author's emphasis.

individual in Tokugawa Japan, the conceptions of the two are actually more closely related than might appear at first sight.

Concluding Remarks

Before returning to the question of autochthonous independence of thought, an observation concerning the explanatory function of secularization has to be made. Contrary to the interests of contemporary sociologists of religion such as Hans Joas or José Casanova,[63] who set out from changes in religion that they seek to explain, the central question for the leading Japanese political theorists of the nineteenth and twentieth centuries—just as their counterparts, as exemplified by Weber—was never what effects modernization would have on religion; rather, the explanandum was always modernization, and religion was drawn upon as one possible explanans. Viewed from the vantage point of the nation, the Japanese elite regarded the ability to modernize as a question of life or death—certainly in the age of semi-colonial status of the 1870s and 1880s, but even up to the period of precarious international status of the 1930s and 1940s, after Japan had withdrawn from the League of Nations. In this sense, religion was clearly an issue of secondary importance for the political and intellectual elite and often made reference to only when its usefulness for the advancement of the modern nation was questioned.[64]

Why religion still figures relatively prominently in the discourses analyzed here becomes clearer when we look at the genealogy of conceptualizations of secularization from Fukuzawa to Maruyama. When Fukuzawa Yukichi introduced early modern European history to his Japanese readership in 1875, one of the themes he could not ignore in his sources like Buckle or Guizot was the relationship of religion and politics. Fukuzawa lauded the secular spirit of Europe emerging with the Reformation; indeed, he presented the Reformation as an opportunity for bringing "to the surface the spirit of freedom in the people" and Protestantism as the bearer of "the progress of civilization".[65] Within Casanova's scheme, Fukuzawa

---

[63] See Casanova, *Public Religions*, 11, or Joas, "Gesellschaft, Staat und Religion," 15.

[64] The Japanese religious studies scholar Hoshino Seiji has analyzed this attitude for the early Meiji period: "It was a generally observable stance among the enlightenment intellectuals to discuss 'religion' entirely from the point of view of 'enlightenment,' focusing on its potential use." (Hoshino Seiji, "'Shūkyō' no ichi-zuke," 233).

[65] Fukuzawa Yikuchi, *An Outline*, 170.

in identifying a process of secularization in Europe followed the 'decline-of-religion thesis'.[66]

When Fukuzawa turned to Japan, he was unable to find an equivalent there, because there was no religious authority that the secular spirit could have revolted against, a finding which he lamented.[67] Inoue Tetsujirō and Maruyama Masao can be said to have followed in Fukuzawa's footsteps in their evaluation of the merits of secularization, but in contrast to Fukuzawa they discovered a functional equivalent in Japanese history that Fukuzawa had overlooked. While Inoue had a very limited understanding of what secularization could mean, in Maruyama it became an integrated element of his approach to what made early modern Japan modern in the first place.

What enabled him to do this was the 'Theory of Tokugawa-Period Buddhist Decline.' This theory implied a) that Buddhism itself was secularized and b) that Confucianism, as a secular force, could rise to prominence against a now degenerated Buddhism. It was only through mediation of this discourse, itself brought about by a reading of Japanese religious history through the eyes of the newly formed and Western-influenced modern concept of 'religion,' that Muraoka and Maruyama were able to discover secularization in Japanese history.

At the same time, when Maruyama declares early modern Japanese Buddhism to have been "secular," he not only makes use of a modern westernized category, but he is also part of a semantic tradition allowing similar ascriptions which goes back to the Tokugawa period. Another factor of change between Fukuzawa and Maruyama which made Maruyama's discovery possible was the reevaluation of Confucianism already visible in Inoue Tetsujirō:[68] As John W. Hall has put it, from being considered part of the problem Confucianism became part of the solution.[69] That is to say, for Fukuzawa, Confucianism was clearly an obstacle to modernization, while for Maruyama it was a factor in Japanese history offering potential

---

[66] Casanova, *Public Religions*, 20.

[67] Fukuzawa Yukichi, *An Outline*, 146–148.

[68] Contemporaneously to Fukuzawa, the prominent Enlightenment thinker Nishimura Shigeki had already called for a more positive evaluation of the Confucian heritage in his influential 1887 *Nihon dōtoku ron* (*On Japanese Morality*). Interestingly, he employs here a dichotomy between *sekyō* (worldly teachings, among which he counts Chinese Confucianism and European philosophy) and *segaikyō* (otherworldly teachings, such as Christianity and Buddhism), offering another bridge between the premodern terminology and the modern translation words for *secular* (see Shimizu Masayuki, "Sezokuka to shūkyō kyōiku").

[69] Hall, "Changing conceptions," 41.

for modern elements (although one fraught with problems, as he was quick to point out). For both of them, Confucianism was beyond doubt a non-religious entity, which is unsurprising given the Japanese tradition of a Confucianism with almost no rituals or institutionalization.

Protestantism played a rather ambivalent role in this development. On the one hand, for Fukuzawa, due certainly in part to his reading of Buckle, Protestantism was a major force in bringing about that change towards secularization in European history that he also wished for Japan. Especially when viewed against the role Buddhism played in Japan, Fukuzawa valued European Protestantism rather highly. On the other hand, Fukuzawa, like the other protagonists of the story as laid out so far, never considered converting to Christianity, unlike so many other progressive intellectuals of modern Japan before 1945.[70] In the Japanese context, Christianity, even in its North American Protestant variant so prevalent in modern Japan, was seen as a religion ultimately very similar to Buddhism by Fukuzawa, Inoue, and Maruyama.[71] Indeed, the latter hardly even considered Christianity in his summary of the history of early modern political thought in Europe. In Maruyama's mind, the important shifts towards the liberation of the individual had been achieved in Europe by secular thinkers regardless of their religious persuasion.

Finally, when describing Maruyama's stance above, I claimed that his approach could be explained by his Weberian background. Yet, what one would expect from a Weberian argument is not a quantitative transformation of religion but rather a qualitative one, i.e. an argument about how a religion could have served through its particular ethic as a motor of modernity. Maruyama was perhaps too disinterested in religion proper to follow such a line of reasoning.[72] This is not to say that it has never

---

[70] For the early Meiji period, this phenomenon has been studied by Scheiner, *Christian Converts*.

[71] This is unsurprising given the fact that by the 1880s the neologism *shūkyō* had firmly taken root with Protestant Christianity as its prototype. By the end of the nineteenth century it had been well established that Buddhism was the closest peer of Christianity as a 'religion,' while Confucianism, equally clearly, did not belong to this category. See Isomae Jun'ichi, "State Shinto."

[72] In fact, as Wolfgang Schwentker has pointed out, in his early work Maruyama's reliance on Weber was rather shallow: "Man sollte jedoch den Einfluß Webers auf Maruyamas Ideengeschichte der Tokugawa-Zeit nicht überschätzen. Die Rezeption bei Maruyama beschränkte sich doch vorwiegend auf die pragmatische Anwendung weberianischer Kategorien; die systematischere Fragestellung nach dem Verhältnis von Religion und Wirtschaftsethik wurde von ihm nicht aufgegriffen" (Schwentker, *Max Weber in Japan*, 245). Yagyū Kunichika, in contrast, has argued that Maruyama did consider this Weberian perspective but simply failed to find evidence for a development of something

been attempted. In fact, we find a heavily Weberian approach taken by Robert N. Bellah in his maiden work *Tokugawa Religion*, his dissertation thesis produced under the supervision of Talcott Parsons in 1957.[73] In his thesis, Bellah, who was ignorant of Maruyama's work (which had only been published as a book in 1952),[74] argues against secularization and in favor of the existence of a school of thought in early modern Japan that developed an inner-worldly asceticism and a concurrent work ethic functionally equivalent to what Weber had identified in Calvinism. For Bellah this tendency was an important factor towards explaining Japan's success in modernization, as he saw it.

Bellah, of course, and with him the whole North American modernization school wanted to explain modern Japan's *success* (i.e. economic development), while Maruyama[75] and indeed other Japanese observers[76] wanted to explain modern Japan's *failure* (i.e. its political defects, the lack of democracy at least until 1945)—a failure of modernity that is, despite the existence of important prerequisites in the early modern era, a distortion of "genuine modernization, that is, one that would embody universalistic principles".[77] Next to the conceptual legacy, it is in this difference of goals that we can perhaps most clearly discern the autonomy of Japanese arguments about secularization and modernity in the twentieth century.

Bibliography

Asad, Talal. *Formations of the Secular: Christianity, Islam, Modernity.* Stanford: Stanford UP, 2003.

Aston, William George. *Nihongi: Chronicles of Japan from the Earliest Times to A.D. 697.* London: K. Paul, Trench, Trübner, 1896.

Aydin, Cemil. *The Politics of Anti-Westernism in Asia: Visions of World Order in Pan-Islamic and Pan-Asian Thought.* New York: Columbia UP, 2007.

---

like a religiously motivated ascetic work ethic in Tokugawa Japan (Yagyū Kunichika, "Max Weber," 487, 491–493).

[73] Bellah, *Tokugawa Religion.*

[74] Bellah himself later acknowledged that he first learned of Maruyama through a review of *Tokugawa Religion* by Maruyama published in 1958 (Bellah, *Imagining Japan*, 146).

[75] Partly because of his adherence to a standard of modernization success informed by Western ideals, Maruyama has been accused of Eurocentrism in Japanese debates. See Barshay, "Imagining Democracy," 384, and Conrad, *Auf der Suche*, 373–377.

[76] Most prominently the Kōza group, dominant within Japanese Marxism from the 1920s to the 1950s, refused to acknowledge the Meiji Revolution as a modern bourgeois revolution and saw Japan as still stuck in a feudal phase of political development. Gayle, "Marxistische Geschichtstheorie," 88–93.

[77] Bellah, *Imagining Japan*, 147.

Bakkuru, Tōmasu. *Eikoku bunmei shi 1–6 hen.* Tōkyō: Hōbunkaku, 1879.
Barshay, Andrew E. "Imagining Democracy in Postwar Japan: Reflections on Maruyama Masao and Modernism." *Journal of Japanese Studies* 18, no. 2 (1992): 365–406.
Bellah, Robert N. *Tokugawa Religion: The Values of Pre-Industrial Japan.* New York: The Free Press, 1957.
———. *Imagining Japan: The Japanese Tradition and its Modern Interpretation.* Berkeley: University of California Press, 2003.
Betz, Hans-Dieter, ed. *Religion in Geschichte und Gegenwart. Handwörterbuch für Theologie und Religionswissenschaft.* Fourth edition. Tübingen: Mohr Siebeck, 2007.
Bluntschli, Johann Caspar. *Allgemeines Statsrecht.* München: J. G. Cotta, 1852.
Buckle, Henry Thomas. *History of Civilization in England.* vol. 1. London: John W. Parker and Son, 1857.
Casanova, José. *Public Religions in the Modern World.* Chicago: University of Chicago Press, 1994.
Conrad, Sebastian. *Auf der Suche nach der verlorenen Nation. Geschichtsschreibung in Westdeutschland und Japan 1945–1960.* Göttingen: Vandenhoeck & Ruprecht, 1999.
Eisenstadt, Shmuel N. "Japan: Paradoxien einer nicht-axialen Modernisierung aus weberianischer Sicht." In *Max Weber und das Moderne Japan,* edited by Wolfgang J. Mommsen, and Wolfgang Schwentker, pp. 67–107. Göttingen: Vandenhoeck & Ruprecht, 1999.
Fukuzawa, Yukichi. *An Outline of a Theory of Civilization.* Tokyo: Sophia UP, 1973.
Gayle, Curtis Anderson. "Marxistische Geschichtstheorie im modernen Japan." In *Geschichtswissenschaft in Japan. Themen, Ansätze, Theorien,* edited by Hans Martin Krämer, Tino Schölz, and Sebastian Conrad, pp. 87–105. Göttingen: Vandenhoeck & Ruprecht, 2006.
Hall, John W. "Changing Conceptions of the Modernization of Japan." In *Changing Japanese Attitudes Toward Modernization,* edited by Marius B. Jansen, pp. 7–41. Princeton: Princeton UP, 1965.
———. "Reflections on a Centennial." *Journal of Asian Studies* 27, no. 4 (1968): 711–720.
Hiraishi, Nao'aki. "The Formation of Maruyama Masao's Image of Japanese Intellectual History during the War Period." *Social Science Japan Journal* 6, no. 2 (2003): 241–254.
Hoshino, Seiji. " 'Shūkyō' no ichi-zuke o megutte. Meiji zenki ni okeru kirisuto kyōto-tachi ni miru." In *'Shūkyō' saikō,* edited by Shimazono Susumu, and Tsuruoka Yoshio, pp. 228–253. Tōkyō: Perikansha, 2004.
Hubbard, Jamie. "Orthodoxy, Canon, and Other Buddhist Heresies." Online Publication Smith College, 2007. http://sophia.smith.edu/~jhubbard/publications/papers/Orthodoxy EtCanon.pdf (accessed Feburary 22, 2013)
Inoue, Tetsujirō. *Nihon shushi gakuha no tetsugaku.* Tōkyō: Fuzanbō, 1905.
Isomae, Jun'ichi. "State Shinto, Westernization, and the Concept of Religion in Japan." In *Religion and the Secular: Historical and Colonial Formation,* edited by Timothy Fitzgerald, pp. 93–101. London: Equinox Publishing, 2007.
Janssens, Rudolf V.A. *Power and Academic Culture: The Founding and Funding of Japanese Studies in the United States.* Program on U.S.-Japan Relations Occasional Paper Series. Cambridge/Mass.: Harvard UP, 1996.
Joas, Hans. "Gesellschaft, Staat und Religion. Ihr Verhältnis in der Sicht der Weltreligionen." In *Säkularisierung und die Weltreligionen,* edited by Hans Joas, and Klaus Wiegandt, pp. 9–43. Frankfurt/Main: Fischer, 2007.
Katō, Hiroyuki. *Kokuhō hanron.* Tōkyō: Monbushō, 1872.
Ketelaar, James. *Of Heretics and Martyrs in Meiji Japan: Buddhism and Its Persecution.* Princeton: Princeton UP, 1990.
Klautau, Orion. "Kinsei bukkyō darakuron no kindaiteki keisei. Kioku to bōkyaku no Meiji bukkyō o meguru ichi kōsatsu." *Shūkyō kenkyū* 81 (2007): 51–71.
———. "Against the Ghosts of Recent Past: Meiji Scholarship and the Discourse on Edo-Period Buddhist Decadence." *Japanese Journal of Religious Studies* 35, no. 2 (2008): 263–303.

Krämer, Hans Martin. "Alte und neue Modernisierungstheorie in Japan." In *Geschichtswissenschaft in Japan. Themen, Ansätze, Theorien*, edited by Hans Martin Krämer, Tino Schölz, and Sebastian Conrad, pp. 135–160. Göttingen: Vandenhoeck & Ruprecht, 2006.

Martin, David. "Notes Towards a General Theory of Secularisation." *European Journal of Sociology* 10, no. 2 (1969): 192–201.

Maruyama, Masao. *Nihon seiji shisō shi kenkyū*. Tōkyō: Tōkyō daigaku shuppankai, 1952.

——. *Studies in the Intellectual History of Tokugawa Japan*. Princeton: Princeton UP, 1974.

——. *Maruyama Masao kōgiroku, vol. 1: Nihon seiji shisō shi 1948*. Tōkyō: Tōkyō daigaku shuppankai, 1998.

Morohashi, Tetsuji. *Dai kanwa jiten*, vol. 1. Tōkyō: Taishūkan. 1955.

Muraoka, Tsunetsugu. *Studies in Shinto Thought*. Tokyo: Japanese National Commission for UNESCO, 1964.

Nishio Minoru, ed. *Nihon koten bungaku taikei*, vol. 81: *Shōbō genzō, Shōbō genzō zuimonki*. Tōkyō: Iwanami.

Nosco, Peter. "Keeping the Faith: *Bakuhan* Policy Towards Religions in Seventeenth-Century Japan." In *Religion in Japan: Arrows to Heaven and Earth*, edited by Peter F. Kornicki, and Ian J. McMullen, pp. 135–155. Cambridge: Cambridge UP, 1995.

Paramore, Kiri N. *Ideology and Christianity in Japan*. London: Routledge, 2009.

Pollack, Detlef. *Rückkehr des Religiösen?* Tübingen: Mohr Siebeck, 2009.

Raleigh, Thomas. *Elementary Politics*. London: Henry Frowde, 1886.

Rarē, Tōmasu. *Seigaku genron*. Tōkyō: Maruzen, 1902.

Sakamoto Tarō, ed. *Nihon koten bungaku taikei*, vol. 68: *Nihon shoki*, vol. 2. Tōkyō: Iwanami.

Scheiner, Irwin. *Christian Converts and Social Protest in Meiji Japan*. Berkeley: University of California Press, 1970.

Schmitt, Carl. *Politische Theologie. Vier Kapitel zur Lehre von der Souveränität*. München: Duncker & Humblot, 1922.

Schwentker, Wolfgang. *Max Weber in Japan. Eine Untersuchung zur Wirkungsgeschichte 1905–1995*. Tübingen: Mohr Siebeck, 1998.

Shimizu Masayuki. "Sezokuka to shūkyō kyōiku." *Chikyū shisutemu, rinri gakkai gakkai kaihō* 2 (2008). http://www.jasgse.com/publish/kaiho/2008/c_6-3 (accessed February 22, 2013).

Sonoda Minoru. "Secularity and Profanation in Japanese Religion." *Cultural Identity and Modernization in Asian Countries: Proceedings of Kokugakuin University Centennial Symposium*, 1983. Tokyo: Institute for Japanese Culture and Classics, Kokugakuin University. http://www2.kokugakuin.ac.jp/ijcc/wp/cimac/sonoda.html (accessed February 22, 2013).

Stephen, James Fitzjames. *Liberty, Equality, Fraternity*. New York: Holt & Williams, 1873.

Suchīben. *Jiyū byōdō ron*. Tōkyō: Jiyū shuppansha, 1882.

Taylor, Charles. *A Secular Age*. Cambridge/Mass.: Harvard UP, 2007.

Tominaga Ken'ichi. "Die Modernisierung Japans und die soziologische Theorie Max Webers." In *Max Weber und das Moderne Japan*, edited by Wolfgang J. Mommsen, and Wolfgang Schwentker, pp. 41–66. Göttingen: Vandenhoeck & Ruprecht, 1999.

Watt, Paul B. "Jiun Sonja (1718–1804): A Response to Confucianism within the Context of Buddhist Reform." In *Confucianism and Tokugawa Culture*, edited by Peter Nosco, pp. 188–214. Honolulu: University of Hawai'i Press, 1997.

Williams, Duncan Ryūken. "Religion in Early Modern Japan." In *Nanzan Guide to Japanese Religions*, edited by Paul L. Swanson, and Clark Chilson, pp. 184–193. Honolulu: University of Hawai'i Press 2006.

Yagyū Kunichika. "Max Weber und Ernst Troeltsch in Japan. Die Rezeption ihrer Werke bei Maruyama Masao." In *Max Weber und das Moderne Japan*, edited by Wolfgang J. Mommsen, and Wolfgang Schwentker, pp. 481–498. Göttingen: Vandenhoeck & Ruprecht, 1999.

DISCURSIVE FORMATIONS SURROUNDING 'RELIGIOUS FREEDOM' IN MODERN JAPAN: RELIGION, SHINTŌ, THE EMPEROR INSTITUTION

Jun'ichi Isomae

For a long time, right up to the present, it has often been stated that "Japanese people are not religious". As a result today even Japanese consider themselves "not a religious people". Certainly it is the case that many Japanese do not follow a specific religion and are not members of any specific religious institution. However, various practices can be offered as instances of religion, such as going to a shrine before a school examination in order to pray for a passing grade or visiting one's traditional family Buddhist temple at the *higan* (彼岸 equinox season) in order to pray to one's ancestors. In this sense, even though a belief in the existence of specific anthropomorphic deities or gods is absent, and even though the person herself or himself may not be conscious of it, a widespread belief exists in the operation of something which can be called an invisible, overriding power. Or perhaps, more strictly speaking, it is a wanting to believe in such a power.

The word *shūkyō* (宗教), the term used for 'religion' in the modern Japanese language, has acquired a particular meaning because of how the word came into existence. *Shūkyō* is the translation for the English word *religion*, which was transmitted to Japan after the opening of Japan by the West at the end of Japan's early modern or Tokugawa period. Many Japanese are hesitant to express themselves by using a phrase such as "I believe in religion (*shūkyō*)," for this term *religion* was formed with its core in Christianity, causing a mismatch of meaning with the Japanese practices of going to temples or shrines. The Western word *religion* also included connotations of belonging to a church, that is a community of followers held together by individual convictions, or having belief in a sacred text with a written doctrine forming the nucleus of a teaching.

Thus a discrepancy is apparent between the concept of 'religion' imported from the West and Japan's indigenous forms of religious life.[1] From the standpoint of Christian religious conceptualization, to even call Japanese religiosity by the term *religion* may be accompanied by a sense

---

[1] Isomae Junichi, "Deconstructing 'Japanese Religion'."

of discomfort. Nevertheless, feelings of belief in the operation of some invisible entities are present in Japanese people. If such feelings are called *religion*, then a way of being religious which differs from the Western way exists in Japanese society. The sense of discomfort for Japanese using the word *religion* arises because the term makes people feel how its meaning was formed in the womb of Christianity.[2] So, in instances where Japanese assert they do not believe in Western 'religion,' the difference has to be expressed at least as "Japanese people are not religious". By thus referring to 'religion' in a negative mode a Japanese person can insist on his or her non-Western type of religiosity.

Even though Japanese people thus may be non-religious, the term *religion* is still included intrinsically as a necessary reference concept in the linguistic structure which comprises their world interpretation. On the basis of that linguistic structure can emerge a feeling that the particularistic Japanese way of religiosity, which cannot be reduced to a Christian concept of religion, is a kind of marginal space. Yet this does not mean it is to be fixed as an ahistorical entity representing some Japanese indigenous uniqueness. Indeed, for Japanese the concept of religion is something dual, with layered implications, including both Western meanings and non-Western connotations. Like the Western concept of religion too, Japanese religion is a metaphor, empty of any essential contents, which becomes articulated only in the contingent, discursive formations which will come to surround the concept.

In what time period did this Japanese word *shūkyō*, standing for 'religion' and becoming a part of the everyday modern Japanese language, acquire the meanings so familiar in this way? And why is it that even though they use the word so frequently, Japanese people came to be thought of as the possessors of a worldview which was in the Western sense non-religious? For the discussion I want first to clarify the relationship between Japanese people and the word *shūkyō*.

The Modern West and the Concept of Religion

Shūkyō (宗教) as a term as such can be found since early times in Chinese-character Buddhist dictionaries. However, for example in the early modern period, it conveyed the meaning 'the true teaching which is Buddhism.'

---

[2] Isomae Junichi, "Religious Studies in Japan."

In the society of that time Buddhism was the only tradition recognized within that era's temple membership and registration system, and other religions did not have any co-ownership of the word, especially in the word's modern sense of referring to a larger truth which transcends any specific religious tradition. However, at the end of the Tokugawa period in 1858, beginning with the Harris Treaty (Treaty of Amity and Commerce) with the United States, Japanese society was opened up by the Western world. Christianity flowed in at the same time and a situation arose in which three different religions now existed side by side: Buddhism (仏教 *bukkyō*), Christianity (基督教 *kirisutokyō*), and finally Shintō (神道), which had separated from Buddhism in the modern period.[3]

At first, the Harris Treaty did not concern individual religious freedom. The old Tokugawa prohibitions on Christianity among Japanese people were not dissolved; according to the agreement, at the same time that the Tokugawa shogunate would not interfere in the practice of Christianity among Americans, the American government would not meddle in the shogunate's old Christian prohibition policy. Religious freedom would be recognized separately nation by nation. However, tacit approval of Christian faith among the Japanese was marked by the removal in 1873 of the official government notice boards which since the seventeenth century in Japan had posted the official prohibition. When that moment came, for the first time a site of comparison of the multiple religions of Buddhism, Christianity and Shintō became necessary for Japanese. Such a site of coexistent commensurability and homogeneity was now given the name *shūkyō*. However, the meaning of the term was not the one found in the old Buddhist dictionaries but rather something new, as a translation for the Western word *religion*.

Now 'religion' (宗教 *shūkyō*) expanded its meaning from that of a teaching related to the truth of Buddhism in the Tokugawa period to "a teaching about a common truth which exists beyond the frameworks of the specific religions," which had become available after the contact with the modern Western world. This was not a situation where change in the human conceptual dimension occurred autonomously. The Buddhism of the early modern period, which had possessed a monopoly over the religious system (this in reality referring to the membership system consisting of funerals and population registration), was transformed. Now, a change occurred which was brought about by the shift to modern conditions in

---

[3] Isomae Junichi, *Kindai Nihon niokeru Shūkyō-gensetsu to sono Keifu*, chap. 1.

the social system and by the new religious competition among several religions which accompanied the opening of the country.

With Christianity as the axis and with Buddhism and Shintō intertwined, a language treating Shintō and Buddhism as 'religion' was newly born.[4] In the sense that it took as a premise an individualism making personal interiority supreme—the universal concept of the modern West of "freedom of individual belief"— it was something extremely Protestant, having absorbed especially the influence of the United States which was the vanguard of Christian missionizing in Japan. Differing from Catholicism which was deeply tied to supernatural effects and folk religion of the masses, Protestantism as it came to Japan took as its aim the construction of communities of faith with individual interiority as their keynote. Faith belonged to the private realm of personal interiority and was not to be brought into the public space of politics. Since it consisted of people from differing religious institutions and religious traditions, that public social space ought to be a neutral, secular arena not biased towards any religious special interest.

In contrast, the Catholic tradition did not separate the private and the public in the same way as the Protestant one, but instead—rather in the fashion of Islam or premodern Buddhism—religion permeated the public space. Because at the same time a turn towards indigenous religion took place, in spreading into the public space Catholic tradition also became rooted in every nook and cranny of the general population's everyday life.

From the standpoint of comparative religious studies, such confinement of religion to private space and an understanding of it as separated from a secularized public space are rather rare in world history and constituted a special feature of Protestantism. However, as Japanese society became westernized, it came under the influence of the United States which happened to be a centre of such Protestantism. Thus an understanding of religion was established which had as its premise a dichotomy with the secular sphere.

However, that level of understanding was mainly a trend among intellectuals who could come into contact with the West. Among the ordinary people who had no connection with that Western world, the new term *shūkyō* remained unfamiliar up through the end of the Second World War. Instead, for this population, an older term for religiosity which had persisted from the Tokugawa period—a character compound pronounced

---

[4] Ketelaar, *Of Heretics and Martyrs*, chaps. 4 and 5.

shinkō (信仰) in current Japanese but at that earlier time pronounced *shingyō* (信仰)—was the ordinary household term. Notwithstanding, the settling of *shūkyō* as a word which indicated a kind of individual interior realm was not limited only to being an intellectual tendency among the intellectuals. In 1889, as was apparent in the phrase 'freedom of religion' (信教 *shinkyō*) in the twenty-eighth article of the new Meiji Constitution, *shūkyō* was set up in the legal system as an object of free choice founded on the will of the individual.

Although the ordinary masses of people did not have a clear idea of such a concept of religion, their speech and behaviour regarding the term *shinkyō* in the constitution was enclosed within the new legal system which took such an idea of religion as its premise and was strictly controlled by the authority of the state. And just as the new word for 'religion' did not come directly into the ordinary conversation of everyday life, ordinary people's existence was still embedded as a kind of 'primitivism' in the hegemonic intellectual and legal structure in which the intellectuals and the state authority were only the top dimension. The idea of religious freedom involved was a sort of sign of civilization, which was demanded in implementing treaty revisions by the Western great powers for the Japanese state which had been coerced into the unequal treaties. In reality, more than being a matter of protecting the human rights of Japanese people, it was a device used by the Western world to implant into Japanese society the Christian tradition which saw itself as the religion of universal civilization.[5]

In short, the word *religion* was not familiar in Japanese society before the modern period and was not established spontaneously out of the world of the ordinary Japanese population. It arose from the contact with the West and the external pressure of demands from the Western great powers for freedom on behalf of Christianity and was brought to Japanese society from the outside. For that reason it was natural to feel a discrepancy between the hitherto existing world of Japanese religiosity and a concept of religion which had Christianity at its centre.[6]

Except for individuals who converted to Christianity, this kind of discomfort about the proper fit of the word *religion* was felt in the same way by many Japanese intellectuals since they were living within Japanese society. The intellectuals showed two responses. One was to modify their

---

[5] Paramore, *Ideology and Christianity*, chap. 6.
[6] Asad, *Genealogies of Religion*.

own religious beliefs in the direction of the Western concept of religion. The model here was Buddhism which tried to reform itself, distancing itself from its former beginnings as a phenomenon founded on the temple registration system of the early modern period and engaged mainly in the ritual business of funerals. It moved towards doctrines which taught relief from individual suffering and equipped itself with churches, texts and founders, thus trying to match Christianity as a modern 'religion.' The same was true for the popular religions of Konkōkyō (金光教) and Tenrikyō (天理教).[7] These religions sent their own children and institutional officers to the Western-style religious studies departments at the imperial universities, and their spiritual practices shifted from being matters of physical healing towards being instead matters of doctrine which emphasized the inward conversion experiences of individuals.

In the case of Buddhism, an additional point was that on the basis of the doctrines of Herbert Spencer concerning evolution, which started to enter Japan in the 1880s, intellectuals began to adopt an emphasis that their religion was a philosophy which had matured into rationalism. As a result, it could frequently be observed that Buddhism positioned itself by developing a polemic according to which Buddhism was a rational philosophical tradition not excelled by any other religion and evolved even beyond the level of Christianity. Here Buddhism was not being modelled after a concept of religion based on traditional Christianity; instead the most up-to-date Western intellectual framework was brought in and a distinct effort budded to overturn the existing hegemony of the Western concept of religion. Yet what really accomplished that radically was instead the path of modernization followed by the Shintō religion which formed the second phase of this response.

Shintō, at the time when the concept of religion was first coming into Japan, was called *shinkyō* (神教 *kami*-teaching) among other terms, and tried to liken itself to the Western concept of religion. However, because it became embroiled in the competition for membership with Christianity and Buddhism which were also considered religions, the Meiji government, out of fear of Shintō's defeat in this competition in the 1880s, again stipulated the use of a distinctive name *shintō* (神道 *kami*-way). Now it was emphasized in the public declarations by the government and the

---

[7] Shimazono, *From Salvation to Spirituality*, part 3.

Shintō institutions that Shintō would not be considered to be in the category of religion.[8]

The Chinese character compound term *shinkyō* (神教) which had been applied instead of *shintō* (神道) at the beginning of modern period had happened to include in its elements one of the same Chinese characters (教 *kyō*) as used in the new Western-oriented word *shūkyō* (宗教) for *religion*. In contrast, both characters of the word *shintō* (神道) were different, so that there was no connection at all with the word *shūkyō*. Also, another term which came to be used contrastingly as an antonym to religion, *dōtoku* (道徳 morality), contained one of the Chinese characters in the word *shintō* (神道) but again no character from the new word *shūkyō* (宗教). Through this terminology a completely separate semantic field from the concept of religion was established for the term *shintō*.

By the 1880s, the word *shūkyō* (宗教) had become established for purposes of the individual, private realm and for reference to the legal-rights question of religious freedom, whereas the word *dōtoku* (道徳 morality) expressed the public realm of the Japanese people or citizenry and came to be understood as relating to the public duty of the subjects of the state. Hence the two Japanese terms *religion* and *morality* became paired as a dichotomous, contrasting set dividing human activity into the private and the public realms. Yet the terms *kyō* (教, teaching) or *taikyō* (大教, great teaching), which had been inherited from the Tokugawa period and previously had not marked any distinction between public and private, also remained commonly used in the early years of Meiji. Therefore it can be understood that this dichotomy between public and private, which went together with the word *shūkyō* from the West which was tied to the inner realm and a dichotomous conception of religious and secular, was established in the process of colonization. Religion in the private realm was established versus a public non-religious secularity.[9]

Under such a dichotomy of religion and the secular, the premise was the establishment of a secular public realm distinguishable from the private realm of religion. According to this idea of separation of state and religion, particularly represented by Protestantism, it was precisely because a non-religious character had been accomplished in the public sphere that an intent to protect freedom was so clearly evident towards religious activity in the individual private sphere, at least to the extent that the latter did

---

[8] Isomae Junichi, "Tanaka Yoshito."
[9] Isomae Junichi, *Kindai Nihon niokeru Shūkyō-gensetsu to sono Keifu*, chap. 2.

not contravene the public good. In this context, modern Shintō did not occupy the private realm called religion but instead overlapped with the public realm of the secular. This being the case Shintō succeeded in making its acts of religiosity prescribed as public duty for all the people of the state regardless of their religious lives as private individuals. Even though Shintō belonged in the category of religion in the sense that it held festivals for *kami* (神), it was more basically stipulated as nonreligious public moral behaviour and could be demanded as a duty of any subject of the state. Under these circumstances Shintō was also redefined as rational morality more than as religion, giving it a position of precedence. This was the path of modernization taken by Shintō.

Shintō and the Emperor Institution

Since it originally had avoided competition for followers with Christianity and Buddhism in the area of religion, Shintō did not have any doctrine about personal salvation, nor did it have clear founders or sacred texts. It conspicuously lacked the character of a religion which resolved the individual's private problems. Furthermore, its traditional ritual events were rooted in the everyday life of regional local communities and were intimately tied to the people's activity in public arenas. Even today, when carrying *mikoshi* (神輿) portable shrines at summer festivals comes to mind, one recognizes a dynamic, physical, bodily experience tied to a local community. For that reason it was quite reasonable that Meiji-period government politicians and bureaucrats thought that linking Shintō to moral behaviour in the public sphere and regulating its social character were appropriate. However, above and beyond the fact that Shintō was originally the ritual celebration of *kami*, one also could not say that it was completely disconnected from religion. In stipulating Shintō as public moral behaviour the public realm itself could become capable of a religious character. Here arose the problem of what exactly would be the nature of the *kami* to be celebrated by Shintō.

Among the *kami* celebrated in Shintō festivals a majority can be traced back to the household lineage of the Japanese emperor. Today Shintō is composed of a diversity of elements including shrines, imperial rituals, popular religions related to Shintō, or generic folk beliefs. Among the shrines there are some like Yasukuni Shrine which have a thick coloration of modern national state ritual, and others which are local tutelary shrines rooted in regional communities. Imperial rituals generally

referred to ancient rituals for worshipping imperial gods, involving especially rituals of the emperor's worship of heavenly deities. Shintō-derived
popular religions like Tenrikyō or Konkōkyō have doctrinal and ritual
structures which incorporate veneration of the imperial house along with
mythology from the ancient imperial texts *Kojiki* (古事記) and *Nihonshoki*
(日本書紀). Until the Second World War, these groups were called "sect
Shintō" but unlike the rest of Shintō—while similar to Christianity in
the sense of being formed out of a community of belief based on their
own doctrines—these groups alone were treated as belonging to religion. Finally, generic popular beliefs were enmeshed in everyday life,
such as kitchen gods or 'celebrity gods' which fell rapidly in and out
of popular attention; unlike in Christianity these had a largely magical
character.

Already in the ancient period, when Buddhism came over from China
and penetrated Japanese society, Shintō became thought of as a native
religiosity different from Buddhism. However, from the start Shintō was
different from a faith congregation with a clearly existing doctrinal structure or founder, as in the cases of Buddhism and Christianity; Shintō
had no clear religious tradition at all. The miscellaneous indigenous religious practices of the people were mixed up in it, the imperial mythology overlapped with it, and from the beginning a syncretic character was
its keynote. Thus, despite the awareness that Buddhism had a different
character, as native religiosity became the effective receiving vessel for
Buddhist teaching, Shintō became treated as another part of the discourse
which supported Buddhism.

The self-conscious designation of this kind of native religiosity by the
term *shintō* only began in the medieval period. In that era the imperial
house lost its political authority and the mythologies of the *Kojiki* and
Nihonshoki were liberated from earlier political constraints and infiltrated
into the general culture in a popularized form as cultural symbols which,
in the phrase of Benedict Anderson, offered "homogenous empty time," in
other words, an abstract notion of cultural co-existence and communality.
In the process, at the same time that Shintō increased its syncretism with
Buddhism, the *Kojiki* and *Nihonshoki* myths were expanded into Shintō's
own special doctrine by fusions with Buddhist doctrine. The new understandings of the myths extensively included material which deviated
from the original written texts of *Kojiki* and *Nihonshoki*—a great deal of
Buddhist *setsuwa* (説話) tale material was included—but due to this new
interpretation in terms of Buddhism the number of people who thought

of the imperial household lineage as part of their own historical origins dramatically increased compared to ancient times.[10]

However, in the early modern period appeared intellectual movements like National Learning (国学 *kokugaku*) which searched for an authentic, pure Japaneseness, and by cutting Shintō away from Buddhism they strengthened the move to connect it solely with the imperial house. Subsequently entering the modern period this nativist movement assumed a decisive form through the Buddhism-Shintō separation campaign of the early Meiji years and Shintō became oriented towards its own independent doctrinal and ritual structures. Its connection to the emperor institution, which had restored the imperial house to the summit of the political structure, was deepened by the mediation of imperial rituals and shrines. At this point the Buddhist elements of the medieval *Kojiki-Nihonshoki* mythology were completely eliminated. As marked in the *Daijōsai* (大嘗祭) or *Niinamesai* (新嘗祭) rituals or in formal pilgrimages to the Ise Shrine by means of the Meiji government, Shintō increasingly advanced a return to the shrine practices of ancient times.

However, what the Meiji government revived as ancient Shintō was not actually ancient tradition itself, but something demanded by the politics of a modern, extremely Western national state. Ever since the Tokugawa regime had been opened up by the Western world, Japanese politicians and intellectuals constantly felt a strong danger of becoming subject to colonization by the Western great powers. This sensation of crisis directed against the outside aroused the movement known as *sonnōjōi* (尊王攘夷 Revere the Emperor, Expel the Barbarian Foreigners) and a new self-consciousness regarding the Japanese nation as sacred was generated with the eternal imperial lineage situated as the axis. The emperor institution, restored in the modern period as a cultural and political symbol, could not play its role by simply extolling a return to the ancient past; at the core of the institution was also a motivation to form a modern national state which could achieve equal rank with the Western great powers. In this sense the modern emperor institution was no more than an 'invented tradition.'

In such a national state each individual subject person composing it constitutes the national consciousness; the structure of support of the nation is achieved by the individual life commitment of each such person. In that sense the subjects are not just guests of the state; rather, with

---

[10] Isomae Junichi, *Japanese Mythology*, chap. 1.

the state constituting the kernel of the subjective existence which gives each person a reason for living, each person's interiority has to be directly linked to the state. If we consider how a modern state aims at imperialistic expansion by means of warfare, to carry out such warfare efficaciously some device is necessary to promote a transition to a subjectivity in which subjects will offer their lives on behalf of the state. In Japan the Yasukuni Shrine where the state commemorated the war dead played this role. Of course in the background, as a symbol of the nation state, the emperor existed as the physical manifestation of the 'National Body.'[11]

Sites were provided for the inner conversion of the subjects, i.e. for the transformation process which tied the emperor institution to the subjects. As two of these, shrines presented deities which incorporated *kami* possessing affinities to the imperial house, and schools presented the Emperor Meiji's portrait (御真影 *goshin'ei*) and the Imperial Rescript on Education (教育勅語 *kyōiku chokugo*). The Meiji government made the head priests of such shrines into officials of the national state and tried to control their education via centralized government-recognized specialty schools and universities. All this was intended to implant the ideology of the emperor institution in the interior consciousnesses of the subjects efficiently through the shrines. Control of the subjects was sought not only by organization into regional and local administrative units: the state also had to individually and directly control the private realm of the individual's interiority which was intimately connected to religion. Actually, government policy concerning control of the private realm of religion differed according to time period. However, after around 1905, in the wake of the Russo-Japanese War, the Meiji government realized that the moral education conducted in the school system was insufficient by itself to cultivate a passion for loyalty to the state among the people. Thereafter the policy of indoctrination of the subjects was substantially shifted towards shrines. Its extreme form was the establishment of the institution called the Jingiin (神祇院 Institute of Divinities) in the middle of the Second World War. It is easy to understand how pre-war Shintō tried to nurture through war a sense of the 'communality of death' tightly focused around the national government.

Modern Shintō organized the subjects on a regional geographical basis, but in its further aim to control each individual's interiority—along with the effort to shape an external perspective via public morality—it is clear

---

[11] Isomae Junichi, *Soushitsuo to Nostalgia*, 228–274.

that an extremely Western, modern concept of religion was adopted for the logic of their modernist reconstruction. However, two problems arose.

One of these was that Shintō, as already mentioned, was originally just the ritual practice of local communities. It could not completely transform into a logic supporting a national state which took as its foundation a Western, modern idea of individualism. Therefore the national state which had selected Shintō as the starting point for its indoctrination converted its strategy into one of taking local communities as units rather than individuals. Moreover, since in order to avoid competition with religious Christianity Shintō was regulated instead as public morality, the modern Western side of religion grounded in individual interiority was ceded over solely to the sect Shintō groups. Thus any chances to nurture a religiosity of some individualistic character were completely lost from the shrines which were the footings for national indoctrination.

A second problem was changes in the nature of the public realm. Shintō, being a public realm which was regulated in public moral terms, could be said to have somehow changed the public space itself into a kind of religious realm. The interiority of the individual was not the keynote; people were not swearing loyalty to the *kami* affiliated with the emperor. Further, as far as modern Japanese society also maintained its public position on the new dichotomy of religion and the secular,[12] it had become a society which recognized freedom of religion. However, because of how the 'living *kami*' emperor had been placed at the pinnacle of the state, the secular realm nevertheless became covered by the shadow of something religious. The religiosity in this context is actually something that cannot really be captured within the frame of modern Western Protestantism. Yet even though the thing called *shūkyō* for Japanese retained a certain Christian meaning with a non-Japanese flavor, on the other hand it can be detected that some concept of religion still permeated into Japanese society albeit with a non-Western connotation.

To put it more precisely, Shintō and the emperor institution refused to accept the full modern Western concept of religion. They made themselves into a public morality which was required as the foundation supporting the modern nation state, but the only thing they tried to learn from the Western concept of religion was a logic of individual interiorization applied narrowly for imperial indoctrination. As the concept of religion underwent a process of becoming a public morality and incised into

---

[12] Asad, *Formations of the Secular*, chap. 1.

the public realm, the word religion conspicuously backed away from any emphasis on a Protestant-like private realm and instead shifted towards the public religion and its connotations. Here Shintō and the emperor institution relativized the modern dichotomy of religion and the secular and deviated from that framework.

By making Shintō the channel for grounding the authority of the emperor institution, in the modern period subjective consciousness among the Japanese people was doubtless advanced, and through the specific, historically manifested human personality of the emperor, the people sought a foundation for their own identity. Yet for other purposes, especially for nurturing in individuals concepts of freedom and legal rights backed up by a sense of responsibility, that Japanese mode of subjectification clearly became a fatal obstacle. As a historical fact this kind of citizen subjectification—which formed the basis of the emperor institution for the Japanese, lacking an idea of any Christian, absolutist monotheism—certainly dissolved the existential anxiety of the people, condensed power around the nation state, and drove modernization forward. It is also an undeniable fact that this subjectification brought a great deal of suffering to other people in Asia who were entangled in the rule of the Japanese empire.

Thus, the reception of the concept of religion in modern Japan is not only a matter of religion as a private realm observed in the interiority of individuals. Other problems now also come into range: how did the emperor institution, which took Shintō as its support, manage such a dislocation of the Protestant concept of religion? As a result what kind of changes did Japanese society make? This is perhaps the key to understanding Japanese modern society, which has arrived at a concept of religion which both diverges from and appropriates that of the modern West.

Bibliography

Asad, Talal. *Formations of the Secular: Christianity, Islam, Modernity.* Stanford: Stanford UP, 2003.

Isomae, Junichi. "Deconstructing 'Japanese Religion'." *Japanese Journal of Religious Studies* 32, no.2 (2005): 235–248.

——. *Japanese Mythology: Hermeneutics on Scripture.* London: Equinox Publishing, 2010.

——. *Kindai Nihon ni okeru shūkyō-gensetsu to sono keifu: Shūkyō, kokka, shintō.* Tokyo: Iwanami-shoten, 2003.

——. "Religious Studies in Japan, with Reference to Christianity and State Shinto." *The Council of the Societies for the Study of Religion Bulletin* 34, no. 4 (2006): 64–69.

——. *Sōshitsu to Nostalgia: Kindai Nippon no yohaku e.* Tokyo: Misuzu-shobo, 2007.

———. "Tanaka Yoshito and the Beginnings of Shinto-gaku." In *Shinto in History: Ways of the Kami*, edited by J. Breen, and M. Teeuwen, pp. 318–339. Richmond: Curzon Press, 2000.

Ketelaar, James. *Of Heretics and Martyrs in Meiji Japan: Buddhism and its Persecution*. Princeton: Princeton UP, 1990.

Paramore, Kiri. *Ideology and Christianity in Japan*. London: Routledge, 2009.

Shimazono, Susumu. *From Salvation to Spirituality: Popular Religious Movements in Modern Japan*. Melbourne: Trans Pacific Press, 2004.

RELIGIONIZING CONFUCIANISM AND THE RE-ORIENTATION OF CONFUCIAN TRADITION IN MODERN CHINA

Chen Hsi-yüan

Around a century ago, the first republic in Asia was established in China and allegedly ushered in a new anti-monarchist political order. As the main ideological pillar of the imperial system for centuries, the fate of Confucianism was inextricably intertwined with that of the fallen Empire. Accordingly, Confucianism inevitably faced a struggle for survival in Republican China.

In reaction to the unprecedented crisis, the Association for Confucian Religion (孔教會 Kongjiaohui) was established in the year Republican China was founded. Its inaugural meeting was deliberately held on the 2463rd anniversary of Confucius' birthday (the twenty-seventh day of the eighth month in the traditional lunar calendar) on 7 October 1912 and soon became the bastion of Confucian Religion.[1]

The Association for Confucian Religion was neither the only nor the first society established in the name of defending Confucianism. Numerous societies in the name of Confucius were formed in the year the Republic of China was established. These were notably the Association for Worshipping the Sage (宗聖會 Zongshenghui) in February; the Association for the Confucian Way (孔道會 Kongdaohui) in July; and the Association for Sustaining the Confucian Way (孔道維持會 Kongdao weichihui) in October, among many other small and locally oriented societies.[2]

---

[1] In their own publications, the name of this association is simply translated as the Confucian Association. Yet in order to avoid any confusion with other similar societies at that time, I hereby employ the term Association for Confucian Religion to designate *Kongjiaohui*. The first serious study on this association was conducted by Hajime Abumiya, "Kokyōkai to kokyō no gokyōka: mingoku shoki no seijitōgō to rinrimondai."

[2] *Kongjiao shinian dashiji* (hereafter *KJSN*), vol. 7, 65. There might have been clandestine competition among these groups to win over one another's supporters, but at least on the surface they maintained friendly relationships. After all they were sharing the same aspirations in the name of Confucius. There were cases where some members had joined more than one of these societies. To name a few, Yan Fu (1854–1921), a well-known translator of Western scholarship, and Liang Qichao (1873–1929), a multi-talented man and political activist, became members of the Association for the Confucian Way, and later they also joined the Association for Confucian Religion.

However, after the Association for Confucian Religion was established, it immediately won the support of many prominent literati and became the most illustrious and influential of all the organizations. For example, the Worshipping the Sage Association established sixty-four branches in its Shanxi base, but had only ten branches in the other seven provinces. In sharp contrast, the Association for Confucian Religion, though established a few months later than the other Confucian societies, developed so rapidly in size that in less than two years it had set up 130 nationwide and overseas branches. Some lawless elements even tried to solicit contributions by assuming its name or a similar one to confuse its supporters. Consequently, the Association for Confucian Religion issued a special notice that they had no relationship with societies by the name of Chinese Association of Confucianism (中國儒教會 Zhongguo rujiaohui) or Global Association of Worshipping Confucius (寰球尊孔會 Huanqiu zunkonghui).[3]

What made the Association for Confucian Religion the most influential of all the Confucian societies? In terms of their professed purposes, theoretically there was only one notable difference between the Association for Confucian Religion and other Confucian groups: it firmly and fiercely claimed to uphold Confucianism as a religion. As they claimed, Confucianism had long been enshrined as the state religion of the old dynasties and should continue to be worshipped as the national religion of the new Republic.

Confucianism's Early Association with 'Religion'

Linguistically, the modern Chinese equivalent of *religion* (宗教 *zongjiao*) did not exist until the end of the nineteenth century. The Chinese cognate *jiao* had been widely used for centuries to designate Buddhism (佛教 Fojiao), Taoism (道教 Daojiao), and Islam (天方教 Tianfangjiao *or* 回教 Huijiao). When Christianity was first introduced into China through Nestorius's followers during the seventh and eighth centuries, it was termed *jingjiao* (景教) in Chinese, presumably denoting a teaching that embraced the "bright and vast Way".[4] Later Christianity was reintroduced

---

[3] *Kongjiaohui zazhi* (hereafter *KJHZZ*), vol. 1, no. 9.
[4] A Nestorian tablet with abstruse inscriptions was first found in an excavation of 1625. Emmanuel Diaz (1574–1659), a Portuguese Jesuit, and his Chinese contemporary Yang Tingyun, one of the earliest Christian converts, had endeavored to decipher this tablet

into China and was rendered with various names, all with the suffix *jiao*. Nonetheless, the meanings of *jiao* did not necessarily correspond to those associated with *religion*. This untranslatable term *jiao* might be interpreted as "a teaching of value system". More significantly, the traditional discourse on *jiao* was defined mainly by Confucianism instead of other religious traditions. Among the majority of the Chinese literati, Confucianism was not only viewed as the archetypal *jiao* but also the orthodox *jiao*. The status of Confucianism as a *jiao* had never before been questioned. In contrast, most of the other *jiao* in the past had strived to secure their legitimate status in the realm of *jiao*, or they might have been adjudged to be heterodox or evil teaching (邪教 *xiejiao*).

Notably when the modern Chinese equivalent of *religion* was denominated through the Japanese loanword *shūkyō*, it took time for it to be acknowledged as a new conceptual category signifying 'religion' and differentiated from the traditional usage of *jiao*. At first, this Chinese usage of *zongjiao* was not regarded as an alien concept, but instead as a fashionable binomial term for the traditional cognate *jiao*. Thus, this compound was even adopted in the official documents to promote Confucianism.

Like most of their predecessors in other dynasties throughout Chinese history, the Manchu rulers of the Qing dynasty also assumed the role of patronizing Confucianism. As their political authority was weakened by continuing domestic troubles and foreign invasions, manipulating the symbolic power of Confucianism became an expedient means for consolidating their regime. During the last seventy years of the Qing dynasty, from 1840 to 1911, about twenty Confucian scholars were canonized with imperial approval to join the Subordinate Worship (從祀 *congsi*) in the Confucian temple, which was instituted from central to local level on each and every administrative tier. This number was unusually large, given that, beside Confucius' alleged seventy-two renowned disciples, only about one hundred Confucian scholars had been canonized since the Subordinate Worship system was initiated in the Late Han dynasty.[5] Even when the traditional Civil Examination system was gradually replaced in the beginning of the twentieth century by the modern educational system, Confucianism

---

and determined its relationship to Christianity. They interpreted the connotation of *jing* as "vast, illustrious, and bright." See Emanuel Diaz [Manuel Dias; Yang Manuo], *Jingjiao beiquan*. See also Xu Zongze, 85.1.

[5] For the significance of the Confucian Temple and its political implication, see Huang Chin-shing, *Youru shengyu*. Huang also has a concise discussion on Confucian Canonization in English: see Huang Chin-shing, "The Confucian Temple as a Ritual System."

still maintained its predominant position as the official ideology. In 1903, the official Guiding Principles on Education (學務綱要 Xuewu gangyao) was formulated for the newly installed school system, which was intended as the eventual replacement of the Civil Service Examination. It clearly stipulated that "foreign teachers are forbidden to preach their religions (*zongjiao*) in class," but it also required that the study of Confucian classics should be emphasized in both elementary and high schools in order to preserve "the Sage's teaching" (聖教 *shengjiao*). To stress the significance of studying Confucian classics, they even adopted the neologism *religion* (*zongjiao*) and stressed that

> In foreign countries schools all have a curriculum concerning 'religion.' In China the [Confucian] Classics are our Chinese 'religion.'[6]

Furthermore, Venerating Confucius/Confucianism (尊孔 *zunkong*) was clearly stipulated as one of five Educational Objectives (教育宗旨 *jiaoyu zongzhi*) in 1906. In the official memorandum on the Educational Objectives, the emphasis on the significance of Venerating Confucius was made by drawing an analogy with the Western educational system:

> In the education systems of the [Western] nations, their own languages, history, customs and religions (*zongjiao*) are all honored and preserved. Therefore, in their schools they all have concrete measures to worship their 'national religion' (國教 *guojiao*).[7]

In this regard, it was suggested that the study of the Confucian classics should be compulsory, and, furthermore, the ceremony of worshipping Confucius should be held in schools on the birthday of Confucius and at the beginning of each spring and autumn term.[8] It concluded that

> The more the 'national religion' is revered, the more popular support is secured. This is exactly what we intend by Venerating Confucius.

Among the five Educational Objectives, Venerating Confucius was placed second after Pledging Loyalty to the Sovereign (忠君 *zhongjun*). It evidently suggested that the throne was still by all means superior to

---

[6] Shu Xincheng, *Jindai zhongguo jiaoyu shiliao*, vol. 2, 12.

[7] *Daqing fagui daquan xubian*, 1:1a–3a. There were five objectives stipulated in the imperial policy of education: Pledging loyalty to the Sovereign (*zhongjun*), Venerating Confucius (*zunkong*), Cultivating Militancy (*shangwu*), Cultivating Public Spirit (*shanggong*), and Cultivating Practicality (*shangshi*).

[8] Traditionally it was called the Sacrificial Rites of Spring and Autumn (*chunqiu shicai*) where certain vegetables served as sacrificial offerings, according to the *Book of Rites*.

Confucianism. However, at a time when the regime was in danger of collapse and Confucianism was needed to win the support of the literati, the relationship between the throne and Confucianism became more fragile and complicated. Shortly after the official Educational Objectives were promulgated, it was proposed at court that the worship of Confucius be promoted from a Secondary Sacrificial Rite to a Grand Sacrificial Rite. Now, Confucius could symbolically enjoy the highest status parallel to Heaven and Earth which was even above the throne, given that in the Grand Sacrificial Rites the emperor should lead all of his subjects and perform prostrations.[9] Yao Darong (姚大榮 1860–1939), the initial petitioner, formulated his arguments exactly upon the Five Educational Objectives:

> We traced the origins of these five Educational Objectives: the significance of Pledging Loyalty to the Sovereign, Cultivating Public Spirit (尚公 *shang-gong*), Cultivating Militancy (尚武 *shangwu*), and Cultivating Practicality (尚實 *shangshi*) is in all cases derived from Confucian doctrines, which are implied here and there in the Confucian classics. The more we studied these classics, the more these notions were revealed. Hence to observe these principles is to observe Confucianism.

Yao also used Western religion as his supporting evidence by arguing:

> In the West, people of the entire country worship religion as if placing it in the 'host seat.' Once the 'host seat' is settled, it would never be altered no matter how many various kinds of arrangements [surrounding it] would be adopted. In China, Confucius was treated as if being situated in the 'guest seat.' Even though he was honoured as 'the Greatest Sage' or respected as the 'Grand Master,' yet in terms of the state cults, [the worship in] the Confucian temple was merely placed among the 'Middle Sacrifices.'[10]

Yao's petition was immediately granted by the throne. It was proclaimed in an imperial edict that "Confucius is the Greatest Sage, His virtue parallel to Heaven and Earth and He is the paragon for all generations. The Worship of Confucius certainly should be promoted to a Grand Sacrifice".[11]

Ostensibly it seemed that Yao's reasoning was well-founded and the Qing government readily accepted this sound proposal and hence was

---

[9] For the system of sacrificial rites in the Qing, see *Qing huidian shili, juan* 415, pp. 634–647.

[10] *Lidai zunkong ji*, 24–25.

[11] This imperial edict was issued by the Empress Dowager Cixi who assumed real power then. See *Qing Shilu: Dezong, juan* 566, p. 496. For the detailed changes concerning the ceremony of Confucian Worship after it was elevated to a Grand Sacrifice, see the memorial by the Board of Rites on the deliberation of ceremony, *Daqing fagui daquan, juan* 1, 1a–2b.

willing to accept Confucianism as the national religion and even place it symbolically above the throne. However, the truth was that Confucianism was patronized by the throne and in return the throne utilized Confucian ideology to justify its continuation in power. In the past, assigning the worship of Confucius merely as a Secondary Sacrifice had been a deliberate decision which implied the superiority of the throne over Confucianism. The Qing court's consent to elevate the worship of Confucius to a Grand Sacrifice indicated that the weakened sovereign was in desperate need of Confucianism to reconfirm its legitimacy and win the support of the masses, or at least the majority of the Confucian literati. It is safe to assume, however, that Venerating Confucius and Pledging Loyalty to the Sovereign became more closely intertwined, a direction the tottering Qing regime pursued.

By the late Qing, the status of Confucianism was promoted to its highest level in Chinese history, but at the same time the highest price ever would be paid in the future. The parallel drawn between Christianity in the West and Confucianism as the national religion in Qing China gave official affirmation to the affinity between the traditional Confucian teaching and the foreign neologism *religion*. In a way Confucianism enjoyed an unprecedented peak of glory just before it fell into an unprecedented abyss of misery.

A Marriage on Trial: Confucian Religion versus Republican Education

This interdependence between Confucianism and the Qing regime reached its peak as the last dynasty in China came to an end. The parallel drawn between Christianity and Confucianism and the neologism *zongjiao* adopted in official proposals strongly suggested that Confucianism had been elevated to the extent that Christianity appeared to be worshipped in the West.

Yet after Republican China was established, most of the imperial rituals were believed to go the way of the doomed emperorship, except for the official ceremonies for worshipping the Heaven and Confucius. In regard to the educational system, which was supposed to be the cradle for the nation's new generation, it also became problematic whether schools should keep the study of the Confucian classics as part of the compulsory curriculum and whether students should continue to perform the ceremony of worshipping Confucius in schools.

The first Minister of Education Cai Yuanpei (蔡元培 1868–1940), who had passed the Metropolitan Examination in the Qing dynasty and who later converted and joined the revolutionary force, published an article in 1912 entitled "Opinions Regarding Modern Education,"[12] in which he proposed a new set of Educational Objectives. Cai Yuanpei claimed that modern education should comprise (1) military training, (2) technical training, (3) moral education, (4) aesthetic education, and (5) cultivation of a *Weltanschauung* (世界觀 *shijieguan*), an idea he had presumably acquired during his scholarly sojourn in Germany (1907–1911). In contrast to the previous set of five Educational Objectives issued by the late Qing court, the Minister of Education of the new Republican China argued that Pledging Loyalty to the Sovereign contradicted the principle of the Republican regime; and Venerating Confucius violated the principle of 'religious freedom' (信教自由 *xinjiao ziyou*). Accordingly, these two objectives were no longer applicable to the new educational system.

In his argument regarding the conflict between Venerating Confucius and 'religious freedom,' Cai Yuanpei evidently assumed that Confucianism was, or had become, a religion. In fact, just two years previously, when he was working on the *History of Ethics in China*, Cai had argued that since the Han dynasty Confucianism had manifested certain characteristics of a *national* religion in terms of rituals. He also noted that it was the efforts of scholars in the Song and Ming dynasties who had endeavoured to disseminate Confucianism among the populace that made this state Confucianism become a real 'popularized religion.'[13] What worried Cai Yuanpei was that once Confucius was worshipped as a 'religious founder' and his teachings were regarded as sacred and inviolable 'religious tenets,' then all later intellectual endeavours were strictly measured and censored by Confucius' doctrines. Consequently, hardly any new ideas were initiated.[14]

Although Cai assumed that Confucianism was, or had become, a religion, at the same time he also tried to draw a distinct line between Confucius' doctrines and Confucian Religion. In his 1912 article Cai Yuanpei emphasized that "Confucius' scholarship" should be distinguished and thus treated

[12] Cai Yuanpei, *Duiyu xinjiaoyu zhi yijian*, (hereafter *CYPQJ*) Vol. II, 130. This influential article has been published in several newspapers and journals, such as *Minli Bao* (February 8–9, 1912), Jiaoyu Zazhi 3:11(February 10, 1912), Dongfang Zazhii 8:10 (April 1912).

[13] *CYPQJ*, Vol. II, 1–107. This work was originally published in 1910 by Shangwu Press. It was translated into Japanese by Nakajima Tarō as *Shina rinri gakushi* (Tokyo UP, 1941).

[14] *CYPQJ*, Vol. II, 75.

differently from either the so-called *rujiao* (儒教) or *kongjiao* (孔教), which both might signify Confucian Religion.[15] This point was later elaborated in his 1916 lecture at the Association for Religious Freedom. Here, Cai argued that Confucius had pondered upon the issues concerning education, politics and morality, but not religion. Cai affirmed that

> Confucius is Confucius, religion is religion; Confucius and 'religion' are irrelevant to each other.[16]

In short, if Confucianism was Confucian Religion, then Confucius himself was not a Confucian at all.

In this regard, Cai Yuanpei suggested in his article of 1912 that "educational circles should have a special deliberation on the treatment of Confucius and Confucian Religion respectively". This deliberation took place in July 1912 when the Provisional National Conference on Education was convened in Beijing at the invitation of the Ministry of Education. In his opening remarks to this conference, Cai Yuanpei argued that "education was to be solely for the purpose of the future" and that modern education should serve as the pivotal instrument to cultivate the new generation of Chinese intellectuals. Evidently, according to his Educational Objectives, Cai Yuanpei envisioned that in the future the 'religious' concern about the other world should be completely replaced by the 'aesthetic' appreciation of the mundane world.

Before this 1912 conference on education, the fourteen-article Provisional Regulations of General Education had already been issued, in which the study of Confucian classics was to be abolished in primary schools.[17] This order was reaffirmed and formally stipulated in May when the Ministry of Education published an open telegram to all provinces.[18] Evidently, Cai Yuanpei had already determined to carry out the abolition of the study of the Confucian classics in curricula.

It would be incorrect to infer that Cai Yuanpei intended to negate the value of the Confucian classics. As a holder of the Metropolitan Graduate degree in the late Qing (1892), Cai's familiarity with the Confucian classics was beyond question. Besides, it is easy to find various citations from the Confucian classics in his writings to support his arguments. Even his essay "Opinion Regarding Modern Education" contains several quotations

---

[15] *CYPQJ*, Vol. II, 130.
[16] Cai Yuanpei, "Zai xinjiao ziyouhui zhi yanshuo," *CYPQJ*, Vol. II., 491.
[17] "Putong jiaoyu zhanxing banfa" (January 19, 1912), *Jiaoyu Zazhi*, vol. 10.
[18] Wu Yanyin and Weng Zhida, 15.

from Confucius and Mencius which were adopted to argue for the significance of ethics as one of his new Educational Objectives. What Cai really opposed was to regard Confucian classics as well as Confucianism as the only sacrosanct authority. For him, it was the monopoly of the Confucian classics, rather than the classics *per se*, in the former educational system that should be held responsible for Chinese cultural megalomania.

Along with the abrogation of the study of the Confucian classics, the abolition of the worship of Confucius was regarded as another major way to get rid of the monopoly of Confucianism in the educational system or, as it were, to 'secularize' Confucianism in the educational system. Reportedly, this was initiated by Xiao Youmei (蕭友梅 1884–1940) who represented Zhong Rongguang (鍾榮光 1866–1942), the Director of the Department of Education in Guangdong Province, at the 1912 conference. Zhong Rongguang suggested in a motion that all kinds of religious idols and deities' tablets should not be worshipped in public schools. Since 'religious freedom' had been granted by the Provisional Constitution in March, Confucian Religion should cease to be practiced in public schools. He explained that for those students who were believers of other religions, "Confucian followers could pray in Confucius' temples. Likewise, Buddhists, Christians and Muslims could do so in their own temples respectively".[19]

During the conference, the retention or abolition of the worship of Confucius in schools became a topic of heated debate. Although the conference was almost evenly divided, it ultimately reached consensus that Confucian worship should no longer be stipulated in the regulations for school administration. It concluded that

> Confucius is not a religionist and there shall be a proper way [other than worship] to honour him. 'Education' and 'religion' should not be lumped together. Moreover, 'religious freedom' is generally stipulated in the [Provisional] Constitution, hence it is inappropriate to set up an absolute authority.[20]

Evidently, for the majority of delegates, the ceremony of worshipping Confucius could misleadingly suggest that Confucianism was a religion. Thus, under the principle of 'religious freedom,' they had to root out all activities suggesting that Confucian Religion was preached and worshipped in schools.

---

[19] KJHZZ Vol. 1, no 1. "News concerning Confucianism," 1f.
[20] Shu Xincheng, *Jindai zhongguo jiaoyu shiliao*, vol. 3, 220f.

As previously discussed, Confucianism was closely associated with the neologism *religion* in the late Qing period; it was not merely bias on the part of Cai Yuanpei and others to treat Confucianism as Confucian Religion. In contrast to the official assertion by the late Qing government that "the Confucian classics are the religion of China" and thus the study of the Confucian classics should be compulsory in school, Cai Yuanpei followed its assumptions to a certain extent but argued that any educational regulations suggesting that Confucianism was a religion should be avoided in the new school curriculum. By the same token, once the Qing court drew analogies between Western religion and Confucianism and promoted the worship of Confucius in the name of 'national religion,' it was almost inevitable for those at the conference to associate the worship of Confucius with religious significance.

Consequently, a verdict on Confucianism was reached: the charisma of Confucius as a religious founder was negated and he should from then on be regarded as a philosophical thinker, an educational advocate or a political theorist. As for the Confucian classics, they were no longer treated as a holistic set of sacred and inviolable 'bibles' but as separable ancient texts with certain philosophical ideas, literary value, and historical references. The marriage of Confucianism and 'religion,' if it existed, was condemned.

Chen Huanzhang: the Man behind the Association

Ostensibly there were thirteen initiators responsible for the establishment of the Association for Confucian Religion, but it was the youngest one, Chen Huanzhang (陳煥章 1880–1933), who really took charge of matters.[21]

Chen Huanzhang, a native of Guangdong, had studied in Kang Youwei's (康有為 1858–1927) Wangmu academy in Guangzhou at the

---

[21] According to its official mouthpiece, the *Confucian Association Monthly* (*Kongjiaohui zazhi*), the idea of organizing the Association for Confucian Religion was initially raised in spring by Shen Zengzhi (1850–1922) at a gathering in his house in Shanghai. These thirteen initiators were, in the order of signature, Shen Zengzhi, Zhu Zumou (1857–1931), Wang Renwen (1863–1941), Liang Dingfen (1859–1919), Chen Sanli (1852–1937), Zhang Zhenxun (1841–1916), Mai Menghua (1875–1915), Chen Zuolin (1837–1920), Yao Wendong (1853–1929), Shen Shoulian, Yao Bingran, Shen Engui, and Chen Huanzhang. Most of them had degree of either Metropolitan Graduate (*jingshi*) or Provincial Graduate (*juren*) of the past dynasty. Zhang Zhenxun was an influential figure in the overseas Chinese society in Nanyang; he was appointed by the Qing government to serve as first consul in Penang, Malaysia and later as consul general in Singapore.

age of fifteen. Arguably enlightened and inspired by Kang Youwei, the earliest Confucian thinker who endeavored to promote the religiosity of Confucianism to strengthen China, Chen had organized the Society for Advocating Confucian Religion (昌教會 Changjiaohui) in his home village at the age of nineteen. The memorial tablet of Confucius was placed alongside with those of Chen's ancestors in his clan hall and worshipped by his clansmen, both male and female.[22] Encouraging female public participation was a significant part of Chen Huanzhang's lifelong advocacy of spreading Confucian Religion. At the beginning of 1900 Chen taught at the Shimin school, where he and others initiated not only the worship of Confucius at the beginning of each semester and every first day of the lunar month, but also a grand ceremony which included special lectures on Confucianism to celebrate Confucius' birthday.[23] In 1904 Chen received the Metropolitan Graduate degree and the following year went abroad to study political economy at Columbia University.

During his stay in New York City, Chen Huanzhang did not confine his life to the campus of Columbia University. Note that he had already obtained the most competitive Metropolitan Graduate degree before he came to the States. This academic achievement gave him a privileged social status in the Chinese immigrant communities in New York. He was treated more like a quasi-mandarin than merely a PhD hopeful. Chen also organized the Society for Advocating Confucian Religion in Chinatown, which became one of the overseas branches of the Association for Confucian Religion after 1912. Many means of spreading Confucianism were first experimented with there and later put into practice in republican China. For example, Chen designed a special religious (Confucian) banner for Chinese stores to fly on Confucius' birthday.

On Sundays he gave lectures to overseas Chinese students and guest scholars on the teachings of Confucius. Arguably Chen Huanzhang was imitating Western methods in his promotion of Confucianism, since Sunday was usually observed by Christians as a day of rest and worship in commemoration of Christ's resurrection. The cycle of seven days, recognized in the Jewish calendar and then adopted in the calendars of Christians and Muslims, was never officially adopted in China until Republican China was established. However, many late Qing scholars had

[22] See Chen Huanzhang, *Gaoyao xianzhi.*
[23] Wu Qingshi, *Dongzhai Zazhi*, (1928) 1:7a. For a general history of the Shimin school, see Huang Yanpei, "Qingji gesheng xingxue shi," *Renwen yuekan* 1:8.

already argued that the 'week' system was not foreign to China but in fact of Chinese origin, since a cycle of seven days (七日來復 *qiri laifu*) was already mentioned in the *Book of Changes*. *Sunday* was intentionally introduced into Chinese as the Day of Coming Return (來復日 *laifuri*). Therefore to worship Confucius and to study Confucian classics on every seventh day was believed to revive the original Confucian way of regulating days.

In 1911 Chen Huanzhang finished his dissertation, *The Economic Principles of Confucius and His School*, which was later published in the series of *Studies in History, Economics, and Public Law* (no. 112–113) by Columbia University. Although his dissertation dealt mainly with Confucius' doctrines on various economic issues, Chen took pains to argue against the resounding thesis by the noted Scottish classicist and Sinologist James Legge (1815–1897) that Confucianism was the ancient state religion of China and that Confucius was merely a transmitter. In both his lengthy introduction and conclusion, Chen repeatedly argued that Confucianism was the new religion founded by Confucius to replace the old worship of polytheism. Chen wrote,

> Confucius frees all mankind from supernatural power, and lays stress on the independent cultivation of one's own personality. Any individual, who has reached the highest standard of the means and harmony, can fix the Heaven and Earth and can nourish all things. In fact, such a religion not only was new to China in ancient times, but is also new in the Western World today.[24]

Accordingly, Chen believed "Confucianism is a religion of the highest development, so we must not think Confucius unreligious". Evidently, the religious nature of Confucianism had already concerned him before he went back to China.

When Chen returned to China, Kang Youwei's connections and support would help him set up the Association for Confucian Religion, and the news of Cai Yuanpei's proposal to abolish Confucian Religion might also prompt the literati to support the Association for Confucian Religion. However, considering Chen's enthusiasm and devotion to the Confucian Religion movement before 1912, it was likely that he would continue to promote Confucian Religion as his vocation.

---

[24] Chen Huanzhang, *The Economic Principles*, 39–51, 717–730.

Undoubtedly Chen Huanzheng's aspiration to promote Confucian Religion was mostly inspired by Kang Youwei. Unlike Kang Youwei, however, who was ambivalent about defining his role whether in the political arena (政 *zheng*) or in religious enterprise (*jiao*), Chen Huanzhang openly demonstrated his promotion of Confucian Religion. For Kang Youwei, *zheng* and *jiao* were two crucial means of equal significance through which to exert his influence and to realize his ideal. Thus, he wrote to Chen Huanzhang asking him to devote himself to the enterprise of 'religion,' while his other disciple, Liang Qichao cultivated his influence through the channel of 'politics.' Kang expressly hoped that Chen and Liang would eventually become two key players in the arenas of 'religion' and 'politics' respectively. He recognized that these two arenas were not separate at all and, in fact, Kang was always inclined to make use of one to influence the other. Thus, for example, he suggested that Chen Huanzhang should take advantage of the situation that many literati were offended by Cai Yuanpei's decision to abolish Confucianism, because, he believed, it would be "very easy to agitate people and would not be offensive to any political parties". Kang envisioned further that

> If our members prevail in Parliament and nine-tenths of members in Parliament are our allies, then we can control both the political Parties and the Cabinet. Thereupon we will have plenary power to save China. Who else then could compete with us? It is a so-called short cut to a long-term end.[25]

It appeared that Confucian Religion was not the ultimate concern *per se* but rather a political agenda for Kang Youwei to realize his goal, no matter how lofty and just it might be. After all Kang Youwei never gave up exerting his influence through political channels and he was eventually involved in the scandalous attempt to restore the Qing regime in 1916.

It might be true that no organization, religious or otherwise, in Republican China or elsewhere, has ever been able to avoid entanglement with politics, and the Association for Confucian Religion was no exception. It would be fair, however, to conclude in the case of Chen Huanzhang that the enterprise of Confucian Religion was his ultimate concern. Throughout his life, he consistently and exclusively devoted himself to promoting Confucian Religion. It was his lifelong calling.

---

[25] This letter is included in *Kang Youwei yu Baohuanghui*, 369f.

The Manifesto of the Association for Confucian Religion

Chen Huanzhang was arguably the only Chinese student ever to receive both the Metropolitan Graduate degree from the traditional civil examination system in China and a doctoral degree from the modern school system in the West. After he returned to China, his new foreign PhD degree along with his old *jinshi* title enabled him not only to mobilize support from the old generation of the Chinese literati, but also to attract attention from the new generation of intellectuals.

A month before the Association for Confucian Religion was officially established, Chen Huanzhang was invited by Gilbert Reid (1857–1927) to deliver two lectures at the International Institute of China in Shanghai in September of 1912. These two lectures, which comprise his main arguments concerning Confucian Religion, were later incorporated into his *Instruction to the Association for Confucian Religion* and released under the title *On Confucian Religion* (孔教論 *Kongjiaolun*). It was published and immediately reprinted six times in the following three years and more than ten thousand copies were sold. In fact, most of the major points he made in this book could be traced back to his PhD dissertation, which should be carefully examined not only as Chen Huanzhang's personal interpretation of the religiosity of Confucianism but also as the manifesto of the Association for Confucian Religion and its official stand on Confucian Religion.

The 'Religiosity' of Confucianism

Chen Huanzhang was certainly aware of the controversy initiated by his fellow disciple Liang Qichao, who published an influential essay in 1902 to renounce his previous position and now insisted on the distinction of Confucius' teachings from religion. It might be part of the reason why Chen took pains to affirm the religiosity of Confucianism in his Columbia dissertation, although Confucian economic principles were his proclaimed topic. Thus, at the very beginning of his two lectures at the International Institute of China, he noted that "in the past ten years there have been certain arguments refuting the idea that Confucius is a religionist". His first lecture was therefore intended to prove Confucianism as a religion and Confucius as the founder of a religion. In this regard, he aimed to solve three major issues: first to clarify the definition of the putative term *zongjiao* corresponding to the Western term of *religion*; second, to firmly establish the relationship between Confucius and Confucianism, namely, Confucius as the very founder of the Confucian Religion; third, to prove that Confucianism fits perfectly into the definition of 'religion.'

Chen recognized that the two-character Chinese *zongjiao* was originally a Japanese translation of the Western term *religion*. However, he insisted that "in Chinese, the one-character *jiao* was enough [to denote the idea of religion]". Chen quoted several passages from the Confucian classics to argue that there were generally two kinds of *jiao*. One was based upon the 'Human Way' (人道 *rendao*) and focused on human relationships; the other was based upon the 'Divine Way' (神道 *shendao*) and centered on the world beyond. Although Confucianism, he argued, laid particular emphasis on the 'Human Way,' it bore elements concerning both the 'Divine Way' and the 'Human Way.'

Chen admitted that in Western literature most definitions concerning 'religion' "lay particular stress on the Divine Way". He even pointed out that in its narrow sense, the closest correspondence to the Western concept 'religion' should be *li* (禮) in Chinese, because, according to the classical definition, *li* was originally associated with sacrificial rituals to pray for blessings from the gods. However, he also reminded his audience that even the ritualistic dimension of *li* was incorporated in the connotation of *jiao*. As the compound term *lijiao* was widely used in reference to Confucian norms on human relationships, *li* was equivalent to a kind of *jiao*. What Chen Huanzhang was trying to achieve here was to redefine the Western concept of 'religion' by the traditional Chinese meaning of *jiao*. To be more specific, Chen Huanzhang insisted that the Chinese neologism *zongjiao* should be interpreted exactly like conventional *jiao; jiao* was thus perfectly interchangeable with *zongjiao/religion*. He even stated that

> It is not necessary to inquire what the Westerners meant by *religion/jiao*, we should only ask ourselves what we Chinese meant by *religion/jiao*. It is not necessary to inquire what other religious believers meant by *religion/jiao*, we should only ask ourselves what the Confucian followers meant by *religion/jiao*.

Once Chen adopted the connotation of traditional *jiao* to define, or redefine the neologism *zongjiao*, there was no need for him to prove Confucius to be a religious founder or Confucianism to be a religion. If the modern terminology *zongjiao* could correspond perfectly with the conventional *jiao*, then Confucianism as *rujiao* or *kongjiao* could be perfectly interpreted as Confucian Religion or Confucius' Religion.

Chen Huanzhang, however, still felt the need to address the speculation, notably proposed by Cai Yuanpei and others, that in the course of
history Confucianism might have become a religion, but that Confucius
himself had nothing to do with it. Chen went on in detail to draw evidence to argue that not only Confucius himself, but his disciples, his contemporaries, people of later generations, including foreigners, all regarded
him as a religious founder. Obviously, as the classical term *jiao* could be
interchanged with modern *religion* in its broad sense, as Chen had already
defined, his arguments for Confucius as a founder of Confucian Religion
were little more than tautological.

Intriguingly, even though Chen clearly defined 'religion' in terms of
jiao and explained that Confucian Religion was a "religion centring on
the *Human Way*" rather than a "religion based upon the *Divine Way*," he
was still inclined to demonstrate the religiosity of Confucianism by fitting
Confucianism into the Western definition in terms of the 'Divine Way.'
In the third part of his lecture, Chen Huanzhang listed twelve attributes
pertaining to the religiosity of Confucianism and discussed each of them
accordingly. These twelve attributes can be summarized as following:

1) The Confucian Religion had a specific designated name: *ru*
2) There was a specific "Confucian robe and cap" (儒服 *rufu*) designed
   by Confucius for his followers to wear
3) The Confucian classics, which Chen Huanzhang insisted were authored
   by Confucius, served as the 'bibles' of Confucian Religion
4) The Confucian creed, also stipulated by Confucius, was stated in the
   "Code of Confucian Conduct" (儒行 "Ruxing"), a chapter originally
   included in the *Book of Rites*
5) Confucianism had systematic rituals and ceremonies for serving both
   humans and deities
6) Confucius asserted the existence of ghosts and deities
7) The Confucian theory of the immortality of the soul
8) The Confucian idea of retribution (報應 *baoying*; one inevitably reaps
   what he sows)
9) The spread of Confucianism: 'proselytizing'
10) The ramification and lineage of Confucian schools
11) Confucian Temples served as places for both study and worship
12) Holy Land: The tomb of Confucius in Qufu, Shandong Province.

The attributes listed above in fact reflected Chen's understanding of the
common characteristics of 'other' religions in general. Hence, when he

argued that Confucianism has its own attire, sacred scripts, rituals, temples, and even its own Holy Land, he was trying to draw certain analogies between Confucianism and 'other' religions, notably Christianity, Buddhism, Islam and even Taoism.

Of these twelve attributes, Chen spent most of his time elaborating on the Confucian concept concerning 'ghosts and deities.' Chen first clarified that Confucius was not an agnostic, but that on the contrary, Confucius asserted the existence of spirits and even embraced the idea of God (上帝 Shang Di). Chen stressed that:

> In the religion of Confucius, there is not only one god. There is, however, God (Shang Di) above all those hundreds of gods. The idea of 'God' is surely not an exclusive possession of certain religions.

Several passages from the orthodox Confucian *Classic of Odes* were thus quoted by Chen to demonstrate that the worship of Shang Di was practiced very early in the Confucian tradition. Note that Chen did not distinguish the Chinese term *shangdi* from the Christian *god*, which had already been adopted by James Legge, the first Oxford professor of Sinology, in his innovative translation of the Confucian classics.[26] In order to prove a similar perception of *god* in both Confucianism and Christianity, Chen Huanzhang even cited a quotation of Confucius from the work by Wang Chong (王充 27–ca. 96), a versatile Confucian thinker in the Han dynasty: "the relation between Heaven (天 *tian*) and man is like that between father and son." Chen Huanzhang thus inferred that the way Confucius

---

[26] It was in fact a heated debate among Western missionaries in China whether *di* or *shangdi* in Chinese should be translated by *god* and vice versa. When James Legge made the translation of the Confucian classics as part of the project of *The Sacred Books* and *Early Literature of the East* organized by Max Müller, the leading scholar of comparative religions, he decided to render *shangdi* by *god*. In 1880 many bishops and missionaries in China wrote a letter of protest to Max Müller concerning James Legge's translation. They suggested that the name Shang Di should either have been left untranslated, or that it should have been rendered by *supreme ruler*. In his reply, Max Müller argued that from an historical point of view *god* could be called "of many names the one person." He also suggested to these missionaries that they might slowly cut down the rank growth of mythology that has choked so many names of *god*. However, they should also be advised that "in tearing up the roots, they kill the stem on which alone their new grafts can live and thrive." For the letter and Max Müller's response, see Max Müller, "On the Chinese name for God" in his *Introduction to the Science of Religion: Four Lectures Delivered at the Royal Institution in February and May, 1870.* Indian Reprint (1970): 260–272. For James Legge's explanation, see Legge, *An Argument for* 上帝 (*Shang Te*). For a vivid and captivating biography of James Legge as a pioneering translator of Chinese culture, see Girardot, *The Victorian Translation of China.*

venerated God as Father "tallied perfectly with the idea of the Heavenly Father in Christianity".

It seems that Chen was trying to make a precarious interpretation or drawing farfetched analogies of the Confucian classics in order to fit Confucianism into the category of 'religion.' Of course, he still paid some attention to the differences between similar notions employed in Confucianism and in other religions. When he explicated Confucian theory on the immortality of the soul, he noted that the Confucian classics mention no concept of 'hell' but only 'heaven.' It is fair to say, however, that Chen was trying to argue that Confucian Religion has whatever 'religious elements' other religions might have in order to be confirmed as a religion. Even if all the evidence Chen drew from the Confucian classics or other works served to demonstrate that the notions of 'soul,' 'Heaven' or even 'God' were mentioned in the Confucian classics, these notions never constituted a systematic Confucian theology in the development of Confucianism through history. In fact, Confucian theology, if any, never became the centre of Confucianism.

On the one hand, Chen insisted on the uniqueness of Confucianism in contrast to other religions. He stressed that Confucianism was a religion of the 'Human Way,' the most advanced form of religion. However, on the other hand, in order to prove that Confucianism was in the same category as other 'religions,' he argued that Confucianism also encompassed the attributes of the religion of the 'Divine Way.'

'Human Way' versus 'Divine Way'

A week after his first lecture Chen delivered his second one titled "Confucian Religion should be promoted in present China." He started out by defending why Confucianism should not be held responsible for China's stagnancy. Chen claimed that the reason for the weakness of China in the past hundred years was that Confucian ideas had not really been realized. He contended that the rise of the Western powers was precisely because the European countries and America had actually put into practice the fundamental tenets of Confucianism, such as "to nourish people," "to protect people," and "to educate people".

Note that when he tried to defend Confucianism in the light of its applicability to the past, to the present or even to the future, Chen seemed to shift his focus from Confucianism as a "religion of the Divine Way" to Confucianism as a "religion of the Human Way". All of his arguments on the applicability of Confucianism were made to prove that Confucianism was equipped with the best political, social and economic doctrines. For example, in regard to the applicability of Confucianism in the present Republican era, Chen argued that Confucianism provided specific doctrines concerning each of the five concentric realms of inter-human relationships, namely, individual, family, nation, society and, ultimately, the world. Thus, his discussion was divided into five parts:

1) Confucian Religion is applicable to the individual: self-cultivation
2) Confucian Religion is applicable to the family
    i) The ethical relationship between husband and wife
    ii) The ethical relationship between father and son
    iii) The ethical relationship among brothers
3) Confucian Religion is applicable to the nation
    i) The ethical relationship between ruler and subject
    ii) The principle of valuing people
    iii) Patriotism
4) Confucian Religion is applicable to society
    i) The ethical relationship among friends
    ii) The way of universal love (博愛 boai)
    iii) Social policy
    iv) Philanthropic undertakings
5) Confucian Religion is applicable to the world

It would be too hasty to conclude that Chen Huanzhang tried to defend conventional Confucian values when he relocated the traditional Confucian norms of the five human relationships in respective realms. In fact, his defence was more like a reinterpretation. For example, Confucian ethical doctrines on the five human relationships were interpreted in a new light. In contradiction to Cai Yuanpei's criticism that the Confucian notion of 'loyalty' violated the principle of republicanism, Chen argued that Confucian ethics concerning the relationship between ruler and subject should not be treated in its narrow sense and thus regarded as Confucian apology for monarchy. Instead, Chen believed, although the system of government had evolved from monarchy to democracy, which was also anticipated by Confucius in his *Doctrine of Three Ages*, the relationship between ruler and subject did not cease to exist. It should be interpreted in a new light as in the context of collaboration between superior and subordinate, in which mutual reciprocity was underlined. He believed it was what Confucius meant by "the superior treats his subordinate with propriety, and the subordinate serves his superior with loyalty"

(*Analects* 3: 19). In fact some of his explications were too 'extreme' for some Confucian conservatives to accept. When Zhong Rongguang was censured by the Guangdong Provincial Assembly, besides the main charge against his resolve to abolish worship of Confucius in schools, some assembly members were also offended by his advocating the stipulation of monogamy in civil law. In contrast, Chen Huanzhang admitted that Confucius had consented to the practice of polygamy in his times, for the sake of the continuity of the family line by producing male heirs. However, based upon his interpretation of various passages in the *Book of Changes*, Chen affirmed that Confucius had actually endorsed the idea of monogamy and equality between male and female. In regard to the Confucian vision for the future, Chen even anticipated that "women's rights will be full-fledged" and male and female will become more independent from each other.[27]

It might well be questioned whether Chen Huanzhang imposed personal concerns and contentions upon his interpretations of Confucianism. One thing is evident: when he tried to prove the applicability of Confucianism to the present or even the future situation, he shifted his focus, whether unconsciously or not, to the 'Human Way' side of Confucian Religion. That is, assuming his hermeneutics of the Confucian classics were grounded and Confucius did have appropriate political doctrines, ethical principles or economic theories to deal with each realm of the present and even the future world, these all concerned the mundane affairs and were neither derived from nor based upon any Confucian theology. Most of the features he revealed in his earlier lecture to prove the religiosity of Confucianism, such as the notions of gods and God, heaven, or anything concerning the 'Divine Way,' seemed to be either irrelevant or insignificant to the worldly applicability of Confucianism.

Interestingly enough, when he concluded his lecture by proposing various methods to promote Confucian Religion, he seemed again to emulate other "religions of the Divine Way". These methods included:

1) Establishing the Association for Confucian Religion nationwide and internationally
2) Setting up membership of Confucianism

---

[27] Arguably many of his 'hermeneutics' of Confucian Religion were elaborated upon or at least bore resemblance to Kang Youwei's. For example, most of his statements on the applicability of Confucius in the future can be traced to Kang Youwei's utopian *Datong shu.*

3) Adopting a special 'religious banner' to fly along with the national flag
4) Adopting the 'Confucian Calendar'
5) Practicing worshipping God, Confucius, and one's ancestors together
6) Worshipping Confucius in schools
7) Holding daily gatherings to study Confucian classics in school
8) Preaching Confucian Religion on every Day of Coming Return (*laifu ri*; Sundays)
9) Celebrating Confucius' birthday
10) All ceremonies should be taken care of by the Confucian church
11) All followers should exert themselves to disseminate Confucian Religion.

Many of these had been put into practice by Chen Huanzhang before. No doubt these measures would enhance the development of Confucian Religion in various ways. However, they all seemed to focus on promoting Confucianism as a "religion of the Divine Way" and had nothing to do with the realization of Confucian secular doctrines in the mundane world.

'Religion' as the Salvation for Confucianism

A question might be raised in this regard: if the applicability of Confucianism related mostly to the 'Human Way,' why then was it necessary for Chen Huanzheng to promote Confucianism in the way of other "religions of the Divine Way?" Moreover, since the term *religion* was already tainted by the understanding of other religions, notably Christianity, and was widely employed in its narrow sense, why not simply exclude Confucianism from the category of 'religion?' Instead, Confucianism could be regarded as a school of philosophy, a system of political and ethical theories concerning the 'Human Way,' or it could simply be called the Confucian Way (孔道 *kongdao*) or Confucian Learning (孔學 *kongxue*).

Chen Huanzhang's answer was clearly revealed in his *Instruction to the Association for Confucian Religion (Kongjiaohui xu)*, which was also included in his *On Confucian Religion*. On behalf of the Association for Confucian Religion, Chen strongly condemned the Ministry of Education for abolishing Confucian worship in schools and the Ministry of the Interior for identifying Confucianism as the Confucian Way instead of Confucian Religion. However, what concerned him most was that even the supporters of Confucianism were afraid to defend Confucianism as a religion. Chen was certainly aware that some Confucian societies had already been established before the Association for Confucian Religion. They were either named as Society of the Confucian Way or Society of Venerating Confucius. Although he admitted that classically the connotations of *dao* (way) and *jiao* (religion) were interchangeable, especially in Confucian thought, he resolutely refused to employ terms like *Confucian Way* or *Confucian Learning* as a substitute for *Confucian Religion*. To him, even the phrase Venerating Confucius (尊孔 *zunkong*) was too ambiguous and nebulous as the objective of Confucian societies because it failed to manifest in what specific way Confucius should be venerated.

Chen Huanzhang expressed sympathy for those who defended Confucianism by adopting the terms *Confucian Learning* or *Confucian Way*, because they were trying to place Confucianism above all other religions. However, he also warned them:

> Although originally it was intended to revere Confucius in the way that Confucius was superior to Buddha, Jesus and Mohammed, yet as a result Confucius descended into one of the hundred thinkers in the pre-Qin period.

Chen believed that once the religiosity of Confucianism was refuted, then it would became nothing but a school of philosophy and Confucius would become merely a secular scholar, no matter how great he was. Consequently, even the appeal to Venerate Confucius would become at best "nothing but hero-worship". He asserted that if even the Confucian followers failed to treat Confucianism as a religion, then the Confucian Religion *per se* would ultimately cease to exist. In addition, he claimed,

> If we do not identify Confucianism as a religion, then even if the Confucian Way still exists, it is but an empty theory; even if Confucian Learning still survives, it is but the doctrines of a private school; even if the Six Classics are not abolished, readers of the world will only treat them as the works of the Hundred Schools [in the pre-Qin].

To Chen, the lethal threat to Confucian Religion did not come from those who were trying to abolish Confucian worship or abrogate the study of Confucian classics by associating them with 'religion.' Instead, it was from those who regarded themselves as followers of Confucianism but hesitated to advocate Confucian Religion. Confucianism would eventually be de-religionized by them. In this regard, the emphasis of the 'Divine Way' aspect of Confucianism is, for Chen Huanzhang, vital to assuring the inviolability of Confucianism. Confucianism merely as a secular school of worldly doctrines would not survive the inevitable attacks from the modernizing, Westernizing world.

Chen Huanzhang was at least right about one pivotal point pertaining to the nature of 'religion': most, if not all, religions would require their believers to take a Kierkegaardian 'leap of faith' without questioning absolute authority. Or in Chen Huanzhang's own wording, if the followers "do not have the sincere heart of believing, there will be no concrete conduct in observing their worship". In short, faith precedes knowledge as well as action. Chen Huanzhang clearly recognized that, "only if Confucianism is worshipped as a religion that 'in it are included the forms and the scope of everything in the Heaven and on earth, so that nothing escapes it; in it all things everywhere are completed, so that nothing is missing'".[28] Indeed, only if Confucianism was worshipped as a religion by its followers would the Confucian classics be canonized as the Confucian bibles and all its secular doctrines become sacred dogmas.

Conclusion

Just before Imperial China drew its last breath, the prestige of Confucianism had ironically reached its climax. The interdependence of Confucianism and the past dynasty allowed Confucianism to reach the peak of its power, but Confucianism also paid the price when the monarchy was overthrown. The abolition of the ceremony for worshipping Confucius and the obligatory course for studying Confucian classics in schools were regarded by many intellectuals of the old generation as a potential threat to the survival of Confucianism, which had long been identified as the one and only legitimate cultural tradition in China.

The Association for Confucian Religion was established just in time to strive for the survival of Confucianism. Through a nationwide network, it aimed to gain the support of the majority. Indeed, within a short period of time, the Association had developed into one of the most influential societies in the early Republican period in terms of members and branches all over China.

---

[28] Although it was not expressed in a form of quotation, Chen Huanzhang here actually made an allusion to the *Book of Changes*. My translation here was based upon Wilhelm, *The I Ching*, 296.

The emergence of various societies in the name of Confucius right after the establishment of Republican China could be interpreted as an indication of a sense of crisis among the majority of Confucian intellectuals who used to enjoy social and political privileges. On the other hand, however, once the predominance of Confucianism over other cultural and religious traditions in China was no longer endorsed by the imperial authority, it also became a valuable symbolic asset over which unofficial circles could exercise patronage. From that time on, Confucianism had to attract its followers through channels other than the former official examination and education system. Moreover, without any official support, Confucianism now had to learn to compete with other traditions, and, most importantly of all, other religious organizations which had already been evolving on their own for centuries.

In contrast to Cai Yuanpei's emphasis that Confucianism might have developed into a form of religion but that the original Confucius was not a religious founder, Chen Huanzhang argued that from the very beginning the Confucianism founded by Confucius was already a religion by nature, although this Confucian Religion paid particular attention to the 'Human Way,' while other religions centred mostly on the 'Divine Way.' However, Chen's clear-cut stand of advocating Confucian Religion did not resolve the problematic predicament of Confucianism raised by Cai Yuanpei at all. On the contrary, the rationale behind Cai Yuanpei's proposals might have been perfectly justified by Chen Huanzhang's interpretation. If Confucianism was identified as a religion among others, then it should certainly be treated equally to other religions. Accordingly, under the Constitutional principle of religious freedom, any activities suggesting the promotion of the Confucian Religion, such as the worship of Confucius and the study of the Confucian 'bibles,' should be avoided in the education system.

There was only one way left for the Association for Confucian Religion to advocate Confucianism as a religion on the one hand and to insist on the necessity of worship of Confucius and the study of Confucian classics in the education system on the other: Confucianism should be treated as not only a religion but as the national religion of the Republic of China. Immediately after the Association for Confucian Religion was established, its urgent and ultimate goal was defined as to promote or, in their logic, to restore, Confucianism as the national religion.

In retrospect, the 'national religion' campaign initiated by the Association for the Confucian Religion eventually failed. The attempt to enshrine Confucianism as the national religion in the Republican

Constitution did not win the majority vote during the deliberation in the bicameral National Assembly. Consequently the frustrated supporters of the Association for Confucian Religion gradually lost their enthusiastic confidence in the marriage of Confucianism and 'religion.' Many came to believe that the label of 'religion' was a dead end for the future of Confucianism.

In fact, after the establishment of Republican China, not only the old tradition of Confucianism was on trial, but the new discourse on religion was also being questioned. The neologism *religion* was inevitably imprinted onto the Chinese discourse at the turn of the century as the 'Western *jiao*,' with all the biased associations of the West's colonialist and proselytizing encounter with China. The Chinese perception of 'religion,' then, was evidently affected and deflected by their understanding of Christianity. This bias was consequently embodied in the partial convergence of the Anti-Religious Campaign and Anti-Christian Campaign in the 1920s. Any form of 'religion' was believed to be nothing but 'superstition' in various disguises that could only delude the populace. For many Chinese intellectuals, the modern mission of 'enlightening the populace' entailed the emancipation of all people from any form of 'superstition,' namely, 'religion.' Consequently, the advocacy of Confucian Religion was engulfed by a counter-current to de-religionize Confucianism, a movement which basically set the tone for many decades to come.

Bibliography

Abumiya, Hajime. "Kokyōkai to kokyō no gokyōka: mingoku shoki no seijitōgō to rinri-mondai". *Shihō* (March, 1990): 20–55.

Cai, Yuanpei. "Duiyu xinjiaoyu zhi yijian". In *Cai Yuanpei quanji*, vol. 2, edited by Gao Pingshu, pp. 135–137. Beijing: Zhonghua shuju, 1984.

———. *Cai Yuanpei Quanji*. Beijing, Zhonghua Press, 1984.

Chen, Huanzhang. *The Economic Principles of Confucius and His School*. New York: Gordon Press, 1974 (1911).

Girardot, Norman J. *The Victorian Translation of China: James Legge's Oriental Pilgrimage*. Berkeley: University of California Press, 2002.

Huang, Chin-shing. *Youru shengyu: quanli xinyang yu zhengdangxin*. Taipei: Yuncheng, 1994.

———. "The Confucian Temple as a Ritual System: Manifestations of Power, Belief and Legitimacy in Traditional China." *Tsing Hua Journal of Chinese Studies* XXV: no. 2 (1995), pp. 115–136.

Kang, Youwei. *Datong shu*. Beijing: Guji chubanshe, 1956.

Kang Youwei yu Baohuang hui. Shanghai: Renmin, 1982.

Legge, James. *An Argument for* 上帝 *(Shang Te) as the Proper Rendering of the words Elohim and Theos in the Chinese language: with Strictures on the essay of Bishop Boone in favour of the term* 神 *(Shin)*, Hongkong: 1850.

Müller, Max. "On the Chinese name for God." In *Introduction to the Science of Religion: Four Lectures Delivered at the Royal Institution in February and May, 1870*, pp. 260–272. London: Longmans, Green, and Co. 1893.

Shu, Xincheng, ed. *Jindai zhongguo jiaoyu shiliao*, vols. 1–3. Shanghai: Zhonghua, 1928.

Wilhelm, Richard. *The I Ching: or. Book of Changes*. Translated by Cary F. Baynes, Princeton: Princeton UP, 1977. English translation of *I Ging*.

Wu, Yanyin and Weng Zhida. "Sanshiwu nian lai zhongguo zhi xiaoxue," In *Zuijin sanshiwu nian zhi zhongguo jiaoyu*, Shanghai: Shangwu, 1931, reprint Hongkong: Longmen, 1969.

Xu, Zongze. *Zhongguo tianzhujiao chuanjiaoshi gailun*. Shanghai: Shengjiao zazhishe, 1938.

THE HISTORICAL FORMATION OF THE 'RELIGIOUS-SECULAR' DICHOTOMY IN MODERN KOREA

Jang Sukman

Introduction: Pre-Modern Uses of the Term sesok (世俗)

In contemporary South Korea, the term *chonggyo* (宗敎 religion) is an extremely common idea which is used in everyday life and academic settings. However, the opposite term *sesok* (worldly) has not been frequently used in the past or in the present. The oldest document in which we can find the term *sesok* is the *History of the Three Kingdoms* (三國 史記 *Samguk sagi*) which was completed in 1145. It is a historical record of the ancient three kingdoms of Korea, written in Classical Chinese by Kim Pusik (金富軾 1075–1151).

Inter alia, this work contains a story of a Silla Buddhist monk, Wŏn'gwang (圓光). When two youths asked him for instruction around 600 CE, he composed the *Sesok ogye* (世俗五戒 *Five Commandments for 'Secular' Life*) as a guide for instruction. Later, this was considered to be the moral norm for an aristocratic group of male youth (*hwarang*). The five commandments are as follows: to serve the king with loyalty (事君 以忠 *sagun ich'ung*); to respect one's parents with filial piety (事親以孝 *sach'in ihyo*); trust among friends (交友以信 *kyou isin*); not to retreat in battle (臨戰無退 *imjŏn mut'oe*); and not to take life indiscriminately (殺生有擇 *salsaeng yut'aek*).[1]

Wŏn'gwang's teaching presupposes other commandments of the Buddhist monasteries. Furthermore, there was a division between the Buddhist priesthood and the political powers—even though in 527, Buddhism had been officially recognized as a state ideology in the Silla dynasty. However, in his teachings, the domain of *sesok* indicates the space of social and military activities of an aristocratic group. Initially, this term makes no reference to the worldly affairs of the common people.

---

[1] *Samguk Sagi*, Vol. 45, Biographies Book 5, *Kwisan*. http://www.khaan.net/history/samkooksagi/sagi4150.htm (accessed June 20, 2011).

The term *sesok* appears 164 times in the *Annals of the Chosŏn Dynasty* (朝鮮王朝實 • *Chosŏn wangjo sillok*), the annalistic records of the Chosŏn dynasty of Korea, which were maintained from 1413 to 1865. We can classify the uses of the term in three ways. First, the term *sesok* has a negative connotation. It means the domain of vulgarity and stupidity. This interpretation of *sesok* reflects the common views of ordinary people, not the (allegedly) noble and respectable perspective of the bureaucratic officials and Confucian scholars.[2]

Second, it sheds light on the lifestyle of the common people, in other words, it refers to folk customs. In this sense, it seems to have an objective connotation, although sometimes it can be used negatively.[3]

Third, in comparison with other unworldly areas such as remote Buddhist temples or Buddhist paradises and mysteriously secret Daoist places, it indicates this world as a whole that consists in the secular relationships of human beings.[4]

To sum up, the traditional term *sesok* had a negative meaning when it was used to signify 'common' in the context of status differences. However, it had a positive implication when used to compare the mundane world with the spiritual sphere.

However, when the new concept of *chonggyo* became dominant in the late nineteenth century in Korea, the conceptual meaning of *sesok* changed accordingly. It came to denote the non-religious area, which includes the wide range of human relationships. As an umbrella term, it embraced the space of society, economics, politics, culture, art, etc. To make the situation even more complicated for Westerners with the Cartesian tendency to carefully define concepts, the power of inclusiveness of this term is wide enough to incorporate religion as its domain. Therefore, it has a double identity character, signifying both a strictly non-religious area and a holistically human area, including religion.

The more comprehensive the term *sesok* is, the more unwieldy it becomes. In modern Korea, religious concerns have revealed themselves mostly through their relationships with political and social problems. While the territory claimed by religion is quite visible, the *sesok* space

---

[2] *T'aejong sillok*, Vol. 1, 22 March, the first year of King T'aejong's reign (1401). *Chŏngjo sillok*, Vol. 10, 12 November, fourth year of King Chŏngjo's reign (1780). This can perhaps best be translated as 'profane.'

[3] *Chŏngjo sillok*, Vol. 1, 13 June, the first year of King Chŏngjo's reign (1776). An approximate translation might be 'mundane.'

[4] *T'aejong sillok*, Vol. 3, 22 April, second year of King T'aejong's reign (1402).

remains obscure. This is one of the reasons why the present article tries to explain the process by which the idea of *sesok* developed through the combination of the effects of various policies in colonial Korea. As *sesok* is part of the 'religious-secular' dichotomy, these two conceptual areas cannot be separated. Thus, the emergence of the term *chonggyo* in Korea will be explained in section one of this paper.

The period between 1890 and 1940 is very important in Korean conceptual history, particularly to understand the dichotomy of religion and secularity. The period can be divided into two parts: first, the period from 1890 to 1919; second, the period between 1920 and 1940. The turning point was the March First Movement, which took place in 1919. This was a large-scale revolt against Japanese rule. In the second section of this paper, I will deal with the first period, when the dichotomy was formed, and in section three, I will describe its establishment in the second period.

The Emergence of the Term chonggyo

The first newspaper/official gazette in Korea, the *Hansŏng sunbo* (漢城 旬報) began publication in 1883, and used only Chinese script. Its contents included foreign news, which was cited from various Japanese and Chinese newspapers. It was in the second issue of this newspaper, published in November 1883, that the term *chonggyo* was first used. It has the same Chinese characters (宗教) as the Japanese word pronounced *shūkyō* and Chinese *zongjiao*. Current scholarship suggests that the term was first coined in Japan and soon transferred to China and Korea. However, even before the acceptance of the term, there was the awareness in Korea of numerous 'teachings' (教 *kyo*) such as Christianity, Buddhism, Daoism, Confucianism, Judaism and Islam.

Due to the literal meaning of *chong* (宗) in *chonggyo*, the term could be interpreted as 'prime or superior teaching'. However, the framework of the term *chonggyo* (宗教) is very different from that of the term *kyo* (教).

Using Kuhn's terminology, we can call this conceptual change a kind of "paradigm shift". First, the *chonggyo* paradigm does not possess the value neutrality of the *kyo* paradigm. In the *kyo* paradigm, as we can see in the example of *sagyo* (邪教 deviant teaching or improper teaching), even an abominable *kyo* was possible. However, in the *chonggyo* paradigm, a nefarious religion could not be possible, because it would be included under the concept of pseudo-religion or superstition. Once we accept the *chonggyo* paradigm, we can recognize either the implicitly positive value of *chonggyo* or totally criticize it (as the Korean communists have done).

Second, even though the division between orthodoxy and heterodoxy existed in the *kyo* framework, its dividing line was more ambiguous than that of *chonggyo*. It was a moral duty of the orthodox group to bring the heterodox group under its influence and to make it rejoin the orthodoxy. Furthermore in the chonggyo framework, it was an obligation of the state to try to suppress the criminal and potentially subversive activities of pseudo-religious groups.

Third, while the *kyo* paradigm focused on moral reform and personal cultivation, the *chonggyo* paradigm considered the achievement of 'civilization' to be of prime importance. Since 1920, the element of 'culture' has been added.

Fourth, the division between religion and non-religion has functioned not only in the sphere of religion but also in the wider context. The space of non-religion came to be called the secular world. It became apparent when the 'religious' domain was formed. The so-called principle of separation of religion and politics represents the demarcation of the duality of religion and non-religion. However, in the *kyo* framework, there was no need to separate the non-*kyo* sphere because it would ultimately be reintegrated into the *kyo* sphere.

The conceptual shift was partly the outcome of a collective identity crisis in East Asian countries in the late nineteenth century. To overcome this crisis, it was necessary to replace the old conceptual framework and to create a new *Weltanschauung*.

Therefore, adopting the new term *chonggyo* was not just the result of one-sided pressure from Western and Japanese powers, but also part of efforts to transform the epistemological framework in order to overcome the impending disaster in Korea. One of the most urgent things for Korean intellectuals to do was to find the secrets of the military strength of the West and Japan and to imitate their ways as quickly as possible. The slogan of Wealthy State, Strong Army (富國强兵 *puguk kangbyŏng*) for this achievement of Western civilization expressed the attitude well. Furthermore, it was emphasized that 'civilization' should be attained to maintain *our* collective identity. Therefore, the historical task for Korean intellectuals in the late nineteenth century and early twentieth century can be summarized as follows: the achievement of 'civilization' and the maintenance of a collective identity. These tasks made up the two axes of Korean modern thought, and several interpretations of the term *chonggyo* emerged according to differing attitudes towards religion.

Since the adaptation of the term to Korea, there have been four types of views on *chonggyo* based on the two criteria *the achievements of civilization*

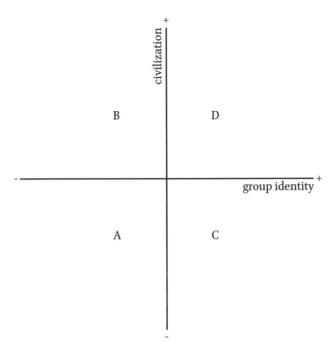

Fig 1: Relevance of religion in terms of 'civilization' and 'group identity'.

and *the maintenance of a collective identity.* In the first view (A) religion is irrelevant in terms of both criteria; in the second (B) religion meets the criterion of civilization but is irrelevant to the criterion of collective identity; in the third (C) religion is irrelevant to the criterion of civilization but is relevant to the criterion of collective identity; and in the fourth (D) religion fulfills both criteria.

The first view (A) is manifested in the anti-religious discourse and the argument for religious extinction; while the second (B) is evident in the Great Revival (a Pentecostal religious movement between 1907 and 1910) and the principle of the separation of religion and politics, which tried to limit the religious domain solely to the inner spiritual life of an individual. The third view (C) is apparent in the attempt to make Confucianism a state religion, and the fourth (D) is demonstrated in the argument to make Christianity a state religion as well as in the advocacy of national revival through Ch'ŏndogyo (天道教), the Religion of the Heavenly Way.

The first and second views (A & B), clearly distinguish between religion and the secular world, while the third and fourth views (C & D) need not necessarily distinguish between the two domains. The third view, in particular, did not have much real influence. The fourth view implied the obstruction of the process of (dichotomously) separating religion and the secular world and creating a nation-state and achieving a national revival through religion(s).

The Formation of the 'Secular Domain' in Modern Korea

The secular world was considered to be a non-religious space when the 'religious' domain was formed. The same can be said of the opposite (the religious world as a non-secular space) because both concepts belong to the 'religious-secular' duality. However, the concept of the *secular* itself is less visible than the religious as it is comprehensive enough to include even the religious, and thus becomes very vague. In Korea, secularism came to be established as a result of the combined effects of several discourses such as freedom of religious belief, the separation of religion and politics, and the separation of religion and education.

Freedom of Religious Belief

While the *kwagŏ* system (a civil service exam to recruit governmental officials, which was founded on Confucian scriptures), played a pivotal role in the reproduction of administrative elites during the Chosŏn dynasty, ancestral worship was considered to be indispensable in sustaining regime stability by securing a sense of generational continuity.

Thus, when in the latter part of the eighteenth century, the Catholics refused to participate in ancestral rites, claiming that ancestor worship was against the Catholic doctrine (which prohibited idol worship), the Chosŏn government was of the opinion that it had no choice but to brutally persecute these Catholics. For in the state's viewpoint, this religious group was undermining the very fabric of the regime.

This persecution ended in 1866 after countless martyrdoms, when the strength of the dynasty withered, making it too feeble to continue its suppression of the Catholics. Nevertheless, the Chosŏn rulers had not forgotten the threat of foreign religions, which were perceived to be closely associated with the Western military powers.

Upon concluding a treaty with Japan in 1876, the Chosŏn government also signed trade treaties with Western powers and established modern diplomatic relations. Throughout this process, it remained on the alert in order to prevent the occidental religions, construed as conduits for Western powers, from intruding into the country's internal affairs.

The government attitude was revealed by the insertion into the draft trade treaty with the USA in 1882 of the clause "A Protestant Church shall not be established,"[5] and also in the fact that during the treaty negotiations with France, Kim Yun-sik (金允植 1835–1922), the head of the Chosŏn delegation, mentioned that the people of Chosŏn reacted very sensitively to the word *kyo*.[6]

With regard to the latter, these negotiations encountered rough waters when the French insisted on a provision in the treaty for religious freedom to allow missionary activity, while the Chosŏn counterpart adamantly objected to this proposal. The treaty was eventually signed in 1886 after the two governments agreed to insert a clause that would allow the French people to freely travel to and from Chosŏn and provide 'teachings' (敎誨 *kyohoe*). Here the word 'teachings' was the general term meaning education, but the French interpreted it as religious teaching—permission to engage in missionary work—causing an unrelenting tension between the Chosŏn government and the Catholic Church. This conflict lasted for some fifteen years until a series of treaties between the church and the government clearly stipulated mutual noninterference.

The first thing that Western powers demanded upon entering a non-European territory was freedom of religious belief (or more precisely the right to propagate *their* religions). This freedom, together with the separation of Church and State, was advocated by Westerners as if it were a universal element of civilization. Hence, Western people thought it their mission to secure this freedom in non-occidental regions. The claim for freedom of religion, which was reborn in the course of Western history, took on a universal 'missionary' character as Western influence spread across the globe.

Paradoxically, to those non-Western intellectuals studying the roots of the Wealthy State, Strong Army of the West, freedom of religious belief was one of the secrets to achieving such national strength. Gradually, the idea of freedom of religion came to be not something coercively imposed upon the non-Western world, but rather something that was called for voluntarily. As a result, from the viewpoint of Korean intellectuals at the time, freedom of religion became a prerequisite for each country to

---

[5] Kim Yun-shik, "Non myŏngnip choyak," Vol. 1, March, nineteenth year of Kojong's reign (1882), 112.

[6] Kim Yun-shik, "Non myŏngnip choyak," cited in Yi Wŏn-sun, "Hanbul choyak-kwa 'chonggyo' chayu-ŭi munje," 209.

function effectively in the international community led by the Western states.

Yet, in Korea, the domain of religion had to be defined before the argument advocating religious freedom could be accepted. As I mentioned in the previous section, the term *chonggyo* was first introduced in Korea in the late nineteenth century in the midst of a strong sense of crisis that urged society to transform the traditional frames of perception.

Discovering the secrets to Western supremacy and quickly imitating them was perceived to be the best way to deal with Occidental threats and build up what was considered at the time to be 'civilization'. To do this, a new perceptual frame was required. The agent of this sense of crisis was not individuals but the existing political body that was compelled to react to threats from the West. It is for this reason that in modern Korean history, the religious domain occupied greater space on the level of collective identity, (as, for example, the nation-state), than in the individual's inner self.

Accordingly, it is not surprising that this new notion of religious freedom emphasized collective characteristics rather than individual beliefs. In other words, the idea of freedom of religion embraced the rights of religious organizations to engage in missionary activities and to influence an individual's spiritual ideals, which were subordinate to the maintenance of a collective identity.

The colonial period demonstrated that an individual's religious freedom could be constrained and manipulated at any time to serve the needs of colonial rule. This attitude of colonial government derived from the constitution of the empire of Japan, promulgated on 11 February 1889. Article 28 of this constitution states that "Japanese subjects shall, within limits not prejudicial to peace and order, and not antagonistic to their duties as subjects, enjoy freedom of religious belief".[7]

According to this view, religious freedom could be permitted only if a believer or a religious group was obedient to the state power. Considering that the modern state currently represents the secular world, one could say that the religious domain was subordinated to the secular, not daring to compete with worldly powers.

---

[7] Itō Hirobumi, *Commentaries on the Constitution.* http://history.hanover.edu/texts/1889con.html (accessed September 10, 2010).

Separation of Religion and Politics

Protestantism came to Korea in the late nineteenth century, but unlike Catholicism, which was involved in an on-going conflict with the Chosŏn government, it did not intervene directly in politics but rather opted for indirect missionary work: becoming involved in medical and educational activities.

By deliberately propagandizing the view that Western achievements of Wealthy State, Strong Army were closely associated with Protestantism, the missionaries stressed that Protestantism was the religion of 'civilization.' The juxtaposed images of Catholicism and Protestantism demonstrated an attempt to make a clear contrast between the "French religion versus the American religion" and a "politically intervening religion versus a hands-off religion".[8]

As the number of followers of Protestantism grew, the Western concept of religion became more firmly established in Korea. The basic principles adopted at the Presbyterian Council in 1901 were essentially about the church not interfering in state or government affairs. Here, a definite line was drawn between worldly matters and unworldly affairs.

In 1905, the tide finally turned in favour of Protestantism, as its followers began to outnumber those of Catholicism and the gap steadily widened. Along with this trend, the view of the Protestant Church that religion and politics should be separated gradually acquired greater influence. The fact that the Korean Protestant Church's Great Revival Movement occurred almost at the same time as the signing of the 1905 treaty portending the annexation of Korea by Japan is not unrelated to this phenomenon.

The Great Revival Movement in Korea was a movement where participants confessed their sins and conducted intense prayers out loud to internalize their sense of guilt. This was related to the decline of the Chosŏn dynasty. The effect that this produced was that political problems ended up as personal issues of the individual.

In October 1906, the Catholic Church also declared that it would adhere to the principle of separation of religion and politics, as interpreted by Protestant missionaries in Korea. This Protestant strategy was pursued even under Japanese colonial rule in order to expand the respective power bases of these religions. For example, the Protestant Church felt it urgent to safeguard its vested interests as quickly as possible by consolidating its position without running into conflict with the new regime in power.

---

[8] Jang Sukman, "Protestantism in the Name of Modern Civilization."

The Japanese rulers strongly supported this view and made it clearly known that the Church's non-intervention in politics would be rewarded with special treatment. In February of 1906, the first Resident-General Itō Hirobumi (伊藤博文 1841–1909) gathered together Protestant missionaries and emphasized that "the Resident-General will take care of politics, and religion will take care of spiritual salvation".[9] Indeed, the Japanese Governor-General always reacted sensitively to the potential threats that religious forces in Korea could pose. These officials felt more threatened by the religious groups functioning as strong bonds in the hearts and souls of the Korean people than by the government-in-exile operating beyond their jurisdiction. The inflexible policy on separation of religion and politics enforced by the Japanese colonial rulers was intended to prevent these religious forces from challenging the authority of the Governor-General. It particularly stressed that the Protestant and Catholic Churches, which had ties with foreign powers, should not interfere in politics.

The separation of religion and politics was propagandistically considered the path to 'civilization'. The 'reasoning' was that the religions of civilization, i.e. Protestantism and Catholicism, would strongly underpin 'civilized' society's principle of separation of church and state, and be committed to 'civilizing' Chosŏn.

The principle of separation of religion and politics, however, applied only to those religions recognized by the Governor-General. Although it was argued that the Rules for the Mission announced in August of 1915 were created to protect freedom of religion, recognize missionary work, and provide for the equal treatment of religions, it included the clause: "Here, religion refers to Shintoism, Buddhism, and Christianity."[10]

In fact, this law was designed to exercise control over religion while claiming to respect religious freedom. According to the Rules, the data (concerning the converts) of the missionaries and the manner in which they engaged in missionary activities had to be reported to the Governor-General. In the case that activities with objectives other than purely missionary ones were carried out, the religious facilities risked being shut down. All other religions besides the three recognized by the Governor-General fell into the category of 'pseudo-religions' and were not included in the Rules. Such pseudo-religions were seen as mixtures of politics and religion and hence dangerous. Given that Buddhism had already been

---

[9] Chōsen sōtokufu, *Chosen no tōchi to kirisutogyō*, 6.
[10] Kim Sŭng-t'ae, *Ilche kangjŏmgi 'chonggyo' chŏngch'aeksa charyojip*, 91.

put under the control of the Governor-General with the Buddhist Temple Ordinance of 1911, the Rules for the Mission of 1915 were formulated to put the reins on Christianity and to 'confirm' that Ch'ŏndogyo (天道教) was a pseudo-religion. The Rules were revised upon two occasions, first in April 1920 and secondly in December 1933, to the effect that a shorter leash was put on the religions in question.

These developments show that the separation of religion and politics during Japanese colonial rule was certainly not characterized by mutual non-intervention but rather by a one-way rule of non-interference of religion in politics. It was clear that politics had clout over religion and could instrumentalize it. In this situation, the inner self or private realm of religion as preached in the West was relegated to an unimportant role. The policy on separation of religion and politics during this era aimed to prevent religious forces from challenging the authority of the Governor-General and to control religion through the rhetoric of 'civilization'.

However, there were those on the other side of the debate who argued that religion and politics should be one. This contention received greater support as nationalist emotions ran high among Koreans after 1905 when the Japanese stripped the country of its diplomatic rights. For example, the Methodist pastor Ch'oe Pyŏng-hŏn (崔炳憲 1858–1927) stated that religion was the very foundation of politics, pointing out the close relationship between the two domains. He asserted that religion has to do with "the areas which man's knowledge is unable to reach and matters which human power can do nothing about," while politics is mainly about exercising national sovereignty and government. He identified politics as a means to achieving national sovereignty, and claimed that religion is the thread of a nation's existence and the foundation of politics since politics would become difficult if religion waned.[11]

To Ch'oe, religion was not a trivial side effect of civilization (as the socialists believed) but rather its root. Moreover, he never doubted that Protestantism was the model for all religions.

Furthermore, Confucian scholars at the time were at the centre of this argument for the fusion of religion and politics. Pak Ŭn-sik (朴殷植 1859–1925) tried to reform Confucianism in order to initiate a movement to re-establish the power of the state; and Yi Pyŏng-hŏn (李炳憲 1870–1940) organized the Movement for Confucian Religion, claiming

---

[11] *Taehan maeil sinbo*, " 'Chonggyo'-wa chŏngch'i-ŭi munje," 5 October, 9 October 1906, 2343 and 2355.

that Confucianism should be recognized as a religion. This trend of religion playing a political role is also found in the efforts of Protestantism and Catholicism to seek independence from Japan by actively joining the March First Movement of 1919 (a massive resistance effort by the Koreans), and also in the activities of the Taejonggyo (大倧敎), which was founded in 1909, and emphasized the unity of the Korean nation and the worship of Tan'gun (the legendary founder of the first Korean kingdom) and led the Korean independence movement in Manchuria.

The March First Movement in particular alerted the Japanese Governor-General to the threats that religions could potentially pose. The Governor-General's policies thereafter focused on placing tighter reins on religion so that it would not cross over into politics, but alienated religious groups it did not recognize by categorizing them as pseudo-religions.

In some cases such policies backfired, as some people used them to protest against the Governor-General. An advocate of the principle of separation of religion and politics, Han Yong-un (韓龍雲 1879–1944) criticized the Buddhist Temple Ordinance of 1911 as being unreasonable and called for its abolition, maintaining that it encouraged overly tight ties between Buddhism and politics.[12] Moreover, one of the main justifications for rejecting the coerced worship at Japanese Shintō shrines during the latter years of colonial rule was the principle of separation of religion and politics. This is an example of how this ideological tool employed by the Japanese to control religion under the paradigm of 'civilization' was used against them.

Separation of Religion and Education

The strict separation of education and religion was called for in the *Revised Private School Rules*, which were modified in 1915. Sekiya, Director of Academic Affairs under the Governor-General, summarized the gist of the Rules as follows:

> The basic policy of the Empire is to put education completely outside of religion...The revision only serves to reiterate this basic stance. In general, if education and religion do not each hold their own without becoming mixed up, then we cannot expect perfection. Only when the boundaries between the two are distinct can the real aims of education be achieved and the freedom of religion secured.[13]

---

[12] Jang Sukman, "Manhae Han Yong-un-kwa chŏnggyo pulli wŏnch'ik."
[13] Kim Sŭngt'ae, "Sarip hakkyo kyuch'ik kaejŏng-ŭi yoji," 95.

Komatsu, the Foreign Affairs Director for the Governor-General, was also quick to point out that separating education and religion was essential in Chosŏn (the Japanese name for their colony), countering the argument for a Protestant style education raised by a US missionary and principal of a private missionary school in P'yŏngyang. He explained that there were two different types of civilized countries in the world: one that completely separates politics and religion, such as the US and France, and the other that designates a national religion and educates its people in it. Here, he included countries such as Great Britain and Germany. He went on to emphasize that neither Japan nor Chosŏn had a national religion. Thus, if education and religion were combined in Chosŏn, its educational system would become a victim of missionary competition and religious disputes could ensue. The following is a statement made by Komatsu:

> The roles of the government and mission of the Churches are distinct and clear, committing each to remain faithful to its entrusted functions and not to intrude into the other's domain. In other words, religious propaganda falls under the jurisdiction of the Churches, while the educational system is the responsibility of the government. The Church is free to engage in the propagation and preaching of the gospel as long as it does not harm public order or popular morals; and the government should be free of any intervention in the process of implementing its educational system necessary for national sustainability and security. The government must not intervene in the affairs of religion, and at the same time, the Churches are not to intervene in administration, which includes education. This is not simply my personal view. It is public opinion in many civilized countries such as the U.S. and France, and the unwavering truth.[14]

Article 6, Clause 2 of the Revised Private School Rules stipulates that the "Educational curriculum shall not include courses on the Bible, geography, and history". The Governor-General prohibited education in geography and history with the intention of preventing a form of instruction that could foster nationalism. It also banned bible courses, citing the separation of education and religion as its justification. The notion of separation of education and religion caught on as the principle of separation of politics and religion became established as the norm. The aforementioned laws were enforced immediately upon promulgation, but a ten year grace period was granted to the private schools that had previously offered religious education.

---

[14] Kim Sŭngt'ae, "Kyoyuk, 'chonggyo' pullijuŭi-rŭl nonhayŏ Chosŏn-ŭi kyoyukchedo-e mich'im," 99.

After their crackdown on the March First Movement of 1919, the Japanese shifted their policy direction from suppressive iron rule to 'cultural governance'. The missionary arm of the Protestant Church sensed this change in mood and asked the Governor-General to approve religious education for private schools. In 1922 and the following year, the Governor-General revised the law to allow bible education and worship services in private schools. This easing of regulations was predicated upon the assurance that religious groups would not interfere with Japanese rule in any way, carry out their duties as subjects, and actively cooperate in the maintenance of the social order. However, in the 1930s, worship at Shintō shrines became a burning theological issue, and the private Protestant schools that refused this ritual, dubbing it idolatry, were shut down and their foreign missionaries deported.

After these three colonial policies had been carried out, the distinction between secularity and religion could be established in Korea. Religion was prohibited from interfering in worldly areas such as politics and education, and was required to stay within its permitted sphere of influence. Only then could a limited form of religious freedom be permitted.

The Deepening Dichotomy between Religion and the Secular Domain

The March First Movement was a large-scale independence movement in which the leadership and followers of Ch'ŏndogyo and Protestantism took part with such fervour that it is sometimes called the "Independence Movement of Ch'ŏndogyo and Protestantism". Ch'ŏndogyo was the new name given by Son Pyŏng-hŭi (孫秉熙 1861–1922) in 1905 to the original Tonghak (東學) movement, which had been launched in reaction to Western influences in 1860.

The March First Movement, which was steered by religious groups, sent huge shock waves towards the Governor-General. It was not only a direct challenge to his authority but also a breach of the laws promoting separation of religion and politics, which the Governor-General had propagated as the *principle* of civilized society. The fact that participation in the movement ran counter to the 'separation principle' of state and church was also a theological problem for the leaders of the movement.

The Great Revival Movement of 1905–1907 and the March First Movement of 1919 demonstrate opposing characteristics in terms of the relationship between politics and religion or the secular and the spiritual worlds. While the Great Revival Movement, which focused on the individual's spiritual salvation, later evolved into mysticism in the 1930s, the March First Movement for national salvation sowed the seeds for the fusion of religion and politics to fight against the Japanese power. A similar situation had occurred later with the Taejonggyo (The Religion of the Divine Progenitor), which was one of the main forces of the militant Korean independence movement in Manchuria. However, most religious activities inside the Korean peninsula were apparently non-political and tried to focus upon the spiritual salvation of the individual. For it was clear that the Japanese would oppress a religious group at the slightest hint of involvement in politics. As a result, merging politics and religion or sensitive parts of the secular world and religion came to be considered abnormal, and the dichotomy of the religious and secular was firmly established. This tendency was strengthened by the conflictual debate between religion and science, religious critiques of materialism and the resistance movement against Shintō shrine worship.

Anti-Religious Movements and the Conflict between Religion and Science

The Bolshevik Revolution of 1917 and the end of the First World War in 1918 were historical milestones that fundamentally transformed the way that Western civilization was viewed in Korea. The then prevailing idea that the civilization of the West was something to be unconditionally imitated for the sake of survival was on the verge of being shattered. The dreadful nature of the First World War fuelled scepticism about Western civilization, while the Bolshevik Revolution bred the idea that an approach different from that of the capitalist West could be adopted to outperform its progress.

When the March First Movement failed, the need for a better organized and more systematic movement for national independence became much more compelling. Furthermore, the promises of self-determination by President Wilson for all nations were not honoured during the March First Movement, and only resulted in instilling a feeling of betrayal in Korean intellectuals.

Against this historical backdrop, socialism and communism generated great interest among the Korean population, and expectations placed on the Russian Communist Party were high. In April 1919, a government-in-exile was established in Shanghai, China, and in 1921, the Koreans created the first communist organization outside of the country. The formula that linked Protestantism with civilization stood on shaky ground. For example, Yi Tong-hŭi (李東輝 1873–1935) had called on the people to believe in Protestantism to achieve Western civilization:

> If you desire to resuscitate a crumbling country, believe in Jesus, build
> churches, educate your children, and change your traditional hair style.
> Only then can we live in prosperity like those in civilized Western coun-
> tries. Build a church and a school at every corner of the country, and the
> day a church or school is found in every neighbourhood will be the day of
> independence.[15]

However, as he was disappointed with Protestantism, he became a socialist.

As the influence of socialist ideology grew, anti-religious movements
also spread very quickly. The news of the anti-Christian movement that
had been in full swing in China since 1922 also played a part in incit-
ing the anti-religious movement in Korea. This movement in Korea
began in March 1923 and quickly gathered momentum when the Korean
Communist Party was created in April 1925. Criticism of religion took on
two dimensions: an attack upon institutionalized religion and another
where religion itself was criticized.

Institutionalized religion was called the anaesthesia that legitimizes and
sustains the capitalist system, which in turn exploits the people. Religion
itself was thought to be a fantasy created by man, and was alleged to inevitably conflict with science, and thus would eventually cease to exist.

It was in 1926 that the anti-religious movement underwent a change.
The June Tenth Independence Movement against Japanese imperialism
was staged around the time of the funeral of the last Korean Emperor
Sunjong. Widespread support for this demonstration indicated that there
was a strong public opinion that backed the idea that the nationalists
and socialists should collaborate in order to encourage independence
movements. The two groups heeded this popular opinion to establish the
Shinganhoe (新幹會) organization.

However, in 1928, the sixth meeting of the Comintern passed a resolu-
tion banning all compromises with the nationalists, and reignited anti-
religious sentiment in Korea. In 1931, the internal strife between the
nationalists and socialists further escalated and the Shinganhoe was dissolved. From then on, the anti-religious advocates launched fierce attacks
on targets such as Protestantism and Ch'ŏndogyo, giving rise to a rhetoric
that went beyond merely criticizing religion, to the extent that they even
called for the complete destruction of religious beliefs. The confrontation
between the nationalists and socialists had turned violent.

---

[15] Sŏ Chŏng-min, *Yi Tong-hŭi wa kidokkyo*, 40.

Now, the strength of Western civilization was no longer seen to rest upon religion but upon science and technology. At this time, religion was considered to clash with science and hinder its advancement. Religion was seen to be an unrealistic domain that was dependent on gods, devils and other supernatural beings and believed in irrational phenomena such as miracles. It was alleged to be a world of falsity and fallacy. The attack on the make-believe and fantastical dimension of religion by the anti-religious socialists in fact overlapped with the religion versus science conflict and the arguments for the abolition of religion supported by modernists. This further deepened the division between secular and religious ideologies.

Religious Criticism of Materialism

The religious community did not only react with indignation towards the critical socialists. Some Protestants and Ch'ŏndoists reflected on and regretted their passive attitude towards social issues and began to show an interest in labour and rural problems. The necessity for social evangelism was raised and a group of Christian socialists also emerged. Nevertheless, as the anti-religious movement turned more and more aggressive, the argument for social evangelism dwindled, making way for calls for the return to religion for purely spiritual purposes. It was now believed that taking an interest in social issues adversely affected the purity of religious faith and contaminated it.

In the case of Protestantism, this view was best epitomized by the theologian Pak Hyŏng-ryong (朴亨龍 1897–1978). He was famous for his influence in the Presbyterian Church since the 1930s.

The theological language of Pak is characterized by simplicity and repetition. His theology distinguished between two branches of theology: theocentrism and anthropocentrism. Everything fell into one of these two categories. Theocentrism was orthodox and anthropocentrism was perceived to be heretical. The former was truth and the latter was falsehood and fallacy. Theocentrism did not make comprises with the world and followed the commandments of God, and anthropocentrism pursued the pleasures of the body and curried favour with worldly trends.[16]

The secular world and religion are in sharp contrast in Pak's mind. Preserving the purity of religion required the blockage of worldly

---

[16] Pak Hyŏng-ryong, *Pak Hyŏng-ryong paksa chŏjak chŏnjip*, 178.

contamination. In order to do this, the text of the Bible must be interpreted faithfully and religion should focus solely on the spiritual salvation of the individual. Secular materialism must be strongly condemned
and kept at a distance. Pak felt that all religions aside from Protestantism
merged with the secular domain and he therefore took on a conqueror's
attitude toward other beliefs. That is why Pak's dismissive attitude natu-
rally invited confrontation with other religions. This view on "the others
outside" was also directly applied to "the others inside" and 'produced'
many 'heretics' within Protestantism as a result. The rationale behind this
was that in order to claim the purity of his specific brand of religion, he
needed to produce people allegedly contaminated by the secular world—
the more the better...

The critical attitude of the so-called orthodox platform toward secular
materialism drove Protestantism to remain aloof from social issues and
only concentrate on the individual's faith. The mainstream Protestants like
Pak considered it wise to follow the religious path of the missionaries.

However, the various mystical religions that began to emerge after the
March First Movement forced the orthodox Protestants to react not only
to materialism but also to the threats from these somewhat enigmatic
doctrines. Pastor Yi Yong-do (李龍道 1901–1933), a leader of the mysticism wave during this period, had actively participated in the independence movement of 1919 and spent nearly three years in prison. He also
took part in the Korean revival meetings while suffering from lung disease,
and burst into tears as he experienced the amazing grace of healing and
rebirth. The revival was similar to that of 1905–1907 in that participants
unleashed suppressed emotions and experienced repentance. However,
the mystical religions were unique in that they had close affinity with the
traditional religions of Korea, departing from the approach of simply following the path of the missionaries.

From the perspective of mainstream Protestants such as Pak Hyŏng-
ryong, materialism (as in socialism) leaned too close to the secular world
and mysticism inclined too much toward religion. This critique, however,
was based on arbitrary standards and thus was always at the root of power
struggles among religious groups.

The Effect of Worship at Shintō Shrines

Following the Manchurian Incident (instigated by the Japanese in
September 1931 with the motive of invading China), the Governor-
General operated according to wartime policies. The mandatory worship

at Shintō shrines first imposed upon the schools in P'yŏngan Province (平安道) in November 1935 was intended to consolidate the spirit of the public in time of war. However, the private Protestant schools refused this order, maintaining that Shintō worship was a religious ceremony. The Governor-General warned that the worship at Shintō shrines was a requirement of national education and therefore continued refusal would mandate closure of the schools.[17] The Sino-Japanese War broke out in July 1937 and the Governor-General demanded even more strongly that the schools should take part in the worship. Schools that refused were shut down. In 1938, this worship duty was imposed on religious groups as well.

As the Governor-General continued to enforce Shintō worship, the Presbyterian Church, the largest Protestant denomination, capitulated in September of 1938. It was resolved at the twenty-seventh General Assembly of the Presbyterian Church that "Shintō worship is not a religion but a state ceremony, and therefore, let us all take part and pledge allegiance as subjects of the Emperor". The Catholics for their part carried out this worship without any particular resistance, as the Vatican had already approved of it in May 1936. The Methodist Church, more centralized than the Presbyterian denomination and adaptive to indigenous religions and ideologies, also consented to the worship.

However, since early 1939, a resistance movement against Shintō worship evolved nationwide and foreign missionaries also started to become actively involved. The Governor-General imprisoned anyone rejecting the worship and imposed cruel punishments. As a result, about fifty people died and many missionaries were deported.

After the defeat of Japan in 1945, the issue surrounding the condemnation of pro-Japanese acts of the Protestant leadership was subject to much controversy. The most serious of the pro-Japanese acts was worship at Shintō shrines. For the Protestants who placed extreme emphasis upon monotheism, Shintō worship could be considered a sin of idolatry. Although the worship was carried out after agreeing to conform to Japanese policies, the Protestant Church members had strong resentments against their leadership. The leading hierarchy of the church correspondingly fought back and the tension between the two parties became more and more obvious.

The refusal to participate in Shintō worship did not arise out of the independence movement. Rather, it was aimed at maintaining a stronghold

---

[17] Kang Wi Jo, "Church and State Relations in the Japanese Colonial Period." 107f.

of monotheist convictions. Thus, it only *appeared* to be a form of anti-Japanese resistance. Yet, those who objected were treated as heroes by the Protestant Church. The bad memories of Shintō worship under Japanese rule produced a stronger obsession with pure monotheism, and this purism came to be highly regarded by the Korean Protestant Church. The far-right Protestant faction, which had existed since the pre-liberation years, became empowered to an unprecedented degree. Consequently, the effort to reduce the distance between the secular world and religion, such as in social evangelism, hardly got the limelight in the Korean Protestant community. Spiritual salvation of the individual was considered to be the true mission of religion.

Epilogue: the 'Religious-Secular' Dichotomy in the Aftermath of the Nation's Founding

After the surrender of Japan, a US military government was installed in South Korea and the Republic of Korea was founded in 1948. The constitution stipulated, that "all people are endowed with the freedom of religion. No state religion shall be recognized, and religion and politics shall be separated." This all reaffirmed the dichotomy between religion and the secular world. With the Korean War of 1950 and the ensuing Cold War, South Korean society became increasingly pro-American and anti-communist, and any negative criticism of the US became a virtual taboo. Moreover, the belief that Protestantism, introduced in the late nineteenth century, "is an American religion" acquired greater support, and the Protestant Church received special treatment from the political world. As strong US influence took root in South Korea, the Protestant Church gained strength, which extended beyond religion to encompass diverse areas of society. The followers of Protestantism and the Protestant Church were like symbols of modernity and representatives of Western sophistication. Furthermore, as communism spread in North Korea, the Protestants defecting to the South were incorporated into the mainstream of the South Korean Protestant community, which fostered stronger anti-communist orientations in this religious movement. The church became a political supporter of the pro-American administrations. Yet, the mainstream Protestant Church has stressed that it strictly abides by the principle of separation of religion and politics and that it does not in any event intervene in politics, claiming a strict dichotomy between the religious and secular world.

Following 1945, the Protestant Church underwent an internal power struggle over the issue of Shintō worship. The faction that prevailed was the conservative faction, which advocated a clear separation principle. The Shintō worship by Protestants was viewed as a serious mistake and a product of collusion with politics. Since then, the conservative faction has dominated Protestantism in South Korea, and matters of politics and social justice have been excluded from church affairs.

Throughout the 1970s and 1980s, the mainstream Protestants did not participate in the on-going struggles for democracy. Instead, they were busy criticizing their followers who joined the pro-democracy movements for not adhering to the separation policy.

Although the principle of separation of religion and politics evolved into a normative institution that had to be obeyed, one could not deny that religion and politics were closely associated with each other. Those who 'openly' proclaimed that they complied with this principle actually engaged in political deals in an indirect and discreet manner. The religious groups with cosier collusive ties with political power tended to more fervently emphasize this principle. While serving as covert public relations puppets of the authoritarian administrations, they argued that street demonstrations accusing the government of injustice were all violations of the rule that religion should not intervene in politics.

In the post-1998 period when a more progressive administration held power and inter-Korean relations started to become more cooperative, the far-right religious groups that had been so insistent on the principle of separation of religion and politics paradoxically began to actively organize political rallies and stage anti-government demonstrations under a pro-American and anti-communist banner. The pro-American, anti-communist platform that had been such a natural part of society in the past has now become something that even has to be expressed through political demonstrations by the conservatives.

Nowadays, those who criticize President Lee Myung Bak and his administration (which was established in February 2008) claim that his administration does not adhere to the constitutional principle of the separation of religion and politics. Particularly the Buddhist community strongly expressed resentment against it in 2011 because of Lee's pro-Protestantism. Korean politicians today regularly attend all important religious functions and gatherings. As the election season approaches, they visit major religious organizations even more frequently. On the occasion of state funerals, the Protestants, Catholics, Buddhists, and Wŏn-Buddhists (圓佛教信者 Wŏnbulgyo *sinja*) all take turns in performing religious rituals.

Politicians hope to maintain friendly ties with major religious groups because of their organizational and financial power, combined with their influence over their followers. On the other hand, religious organizations themselves want to sustain close relations with those in political power, if only not to relinquish their vested rights. Thus in Korea, although the separation of religion and politics is often violated, it is respected in the form of mutual recognition or even through compromises.

The so-called principle of the separation of religion and politics is part and parcel of the 'religious-secular' dichotomy. Since the late nineteenth century, the dichotomy of the religious and secular worlds seems to have worked as a norm and such a rule is still valid today. Nevertheless, this dichotomy, construed as the alleged standard of civilization, was introduced in Korea just over a hundred years ago and still remains somewhat elusive in its relevance to this society. Is this because such a dichotomy did not exist in the Chosŏn dynasty and the some one hundred years of its history in modern Korea is not long enough for it to take root? My opinion is that it is not so much an issue of time. There seems to be a more intrinsic problem inherent in the very act of defining the scope and making of distinctions. In a dichotomous relationship, religion and the secular are each given separate conceptual definitions upon being distinguished as different domains. The two domains are distinguished but interdependent. In order to clearly identify themselves, one domain needs the other. However, the alleged dichotomy of religion and the secular world in Korea veils its interdependency and only stresses the oppositional aspect in theory. The fact that the separation of religion and politics had to be clearly stated in the constitution of Korea is testimony to the difficulty in separating the two in reality. This declared wish for separation always implies the danger of intermingling.

Bibliography

"Chŏngjo sillok." In *Chosŏn wangjo sillok.* http://sillok.history.go.kr/inspection/inspection.jsp?mTree=0&id=kca (accessed September 15, 2010).

Chōsen sōtokufu (朝鮮總督府). *Chosen no tōchi to kirisutogyō* (朝鮮の統治と基督敎). Tokyo, 1921.

Itō, Hirobumi. "Commentaries on the Constitution of the Empire of Japan." Hanover Historical Texts Project. http://history.hanover.edu/texts/1889con.html (accessed September 15, 2010).

Jang, Sukman. "Manhae Han Yong-un-kwa chŏng-gyo pulli wŏnch'ik." *Pulgyo p'yŏngron* 8 (2001).

———. "Protestantism in the Name of Modern Civilization." *Korea Journal* 39, no. 4 (1999): 187–204.

Kang, Wi Jo. "Church and State Relations in the Japanese Colonial Period." In *Christianity in Korea*, edited by Robert E. Buswell Jr., and Timothy S. Lee. Honolulu: University of Hawai'i Press, 2006.

Kim, Sŭng-t'ae. *Ilche kangjŏmgi 'chonggyo' chŏngch'aeksa charyojip, 1910–1945*. Seoul: Korean Christian History Institute, 1996.

Kim, Yun-sik. *Ŭmch'ŏngsa*. http://db.history.go.kr/url.jsp?ID=sa_006b (accessed October 5, 2010).

Pak, Hyŏng-ryong. *Pak Hyŏng-ryong paksa chŏjak chŏnjip* Vol. 14, 1935. Seoul: The Association for Reformed Faith, 1983.

Samguk sagi (三國史記). http://www.khaan.net/history/samkooksagi/sagi4150.htm (accessed September 19, 2010).

Sŏ, Chŏng-min. *Yi Tong-hŭi wa kidokkyo: Hanguk sahoejŭ (sahoejuŭi) i-wa kidokkyo kwan'gye yŏn'gu*. Seoul: Yonsei UP, 2007.

T'aejong sillok. In *Chosŏn wangjo sillok*. http://sillok.history.go.kr/inspection/inspection .jsp?mTree=0&id=kca.

Taehan Maeil Sinbo. Seoul, 1906.

Yi, Wŏn-sun. *Chosŏn sidaesa nonmunjip*. Seoul: Nŭt'inamu Press, 1993.

——. "Hanbul choyak-kwa 'chonggyo' chayu-ŭi munje," in *Chosŏn sidaesa nonmunjip*, edited by Yi Wŏnsun. Seoul: Nŭt'inamu Press, 1993.

INDEX OF OBJECTS AND TERMS

(Objects are registered in recte, terms in italics)

INDEX OF PERSONAL NAMES